MU
SHI
SHI
6

Yuki Urushibara

Translated and adapted by
William Flanagan

Lettered by
North Market Street Graphics

Ballantine Books ∗ New York

Mushishi volume 6 is a work of fiction. Names, characters, places, and incidents are the products of the author's imagination or are used fictitiously. Any resemblance to actual events, locales, or persons, living or dead, is entirely coincidental.

A Del Rey Manga/Kodansha Trade Paperback Original

Published in the United States by Del Rey, an imprint of The Random House Publishing Group, a division of Random House, Inc., New York.

Publication rights arranged through Kodansha Ltd.

First published in Japan in 2005 by Kodansha Ltd., Tokyo.

ISBN 978-0-345-50166-0

Printed in the United States of America

www.delreymanga.com

9 8 7 6 5 4 3 2 1

Translator/adapter: William Flanagan
Lettering: North Market Street Graphics

Contents

Honorifics Explained

Throughout the Del Rey Manga books, you will find Japanese honorifics left intact in the translations. For those not familiar with how the Japanese use honorifics and, more important, how they differ from American honorifics, we present this brief overview.

Politeness has always been a critical facet of Japanese culture. Ever since the feudal era, when Japan was a highly stratified society, use of honorifics—which can be defined as polite speech that indicates relationship or status—has played an essential role in the Japanese language. When addressing someone in Japanese, an honorific usually takes the form of a suffix attached to one's name (example: "Asuna-san"), is used as a title at the end of one's name, or appears in place of the name itself (example: "Negi-sensei," or simply "Sensei!").

Honorifics can be expressions of respect or endearment. In the context of manga and anime, honorifics give insight into the nature of the relationship between characters. Many English translations leave out these important honorifics and therefore distort the feel of the original Japanese. Because Japanese honorifics contain nuances that English honorifics lack, it is our policy at Del Rey not to translate them. Here, instead, is a guide to some of the honorifics you may encounter in Del Rey Manga.

-san: This is the most common honorific and is equivalent to Mr., Miss, Ms., or Mrs. It is the all-purpose honorific and can be used in any situation where politeness is required.

-sama: This is one level higher than "-san" and is used to confer great respect.

-dono: This comes from the word "tono," which means "lord." It is an even higher level than "-sama" and confers utmost respect.

-kun: This suffix is used at the end of boys' names to express familiarity or endearment. It is also sometimes used by men among friends, or when addressing someone younger or of a lower station.

-chan: This is used to express endearment, mostly toward girls. It is also used for little boys, pets, and even among lovers. It gives a sense of childish cuteness.

Bozu: This is an informal way to refer to a boy, similar to the English terms "kid" and "squirt."

**Sempai/
Senpai:** This title suggests that the addressee is one's senior in a group or organization. It is most often used in a school setting, where underclassmen refer to their upperclassmen as "sempai." It can also be used in the workplace, such as when a newer employee addresses an employee who has seniority in the company.

Kohai: This is the opposite of "sempai" and is used toward underclassmen in school or newcomers in the workplace. It connotes that the addressee is of a lower station.

Sensei: Literally meaning "one who has come before," this title is used for teachers, doctors, or masters of any profession or art.

**Onee-san/
Onii-san:** Normally older siblings are not called by name but rather by the title of older sister (*Onee-san*) or older brother (*Onii-san*). Depending on the relationship, *-chan* or *-sama* can also be used instead of *-san*. However, this honorific can also be used with someone unrelated when the relationship resembles that of siblings.

**Obaa-san/
Ojii-san:** Japanese grandparents are called by their titles rather than by name. Grandmothers are called Obaa-san (or Obaa-sama to imply added respect and distance, or Obaa-chan for more intimacy). Likewise grandfathers are called Ojii-san, Ojii-sama, or Ojii-chan.

-[blank]: This is usually forgotten in these lists, but it is perhaps the most significant difference between Japanese and English. The lack of honorific means that the speaker has permission to address the person in a very intimate way. Usually, only family, spouses, or very close friends have this kind of permission. Known as *yobisute*, it can be gratifying when someone who has earned the intimacy starts to call one by one's name without an honorific. But when that intimacy hasn't been earned, it can be very insulting.

蟲師

むしし

Mushishi

6

Yuki Urushibara

Contents

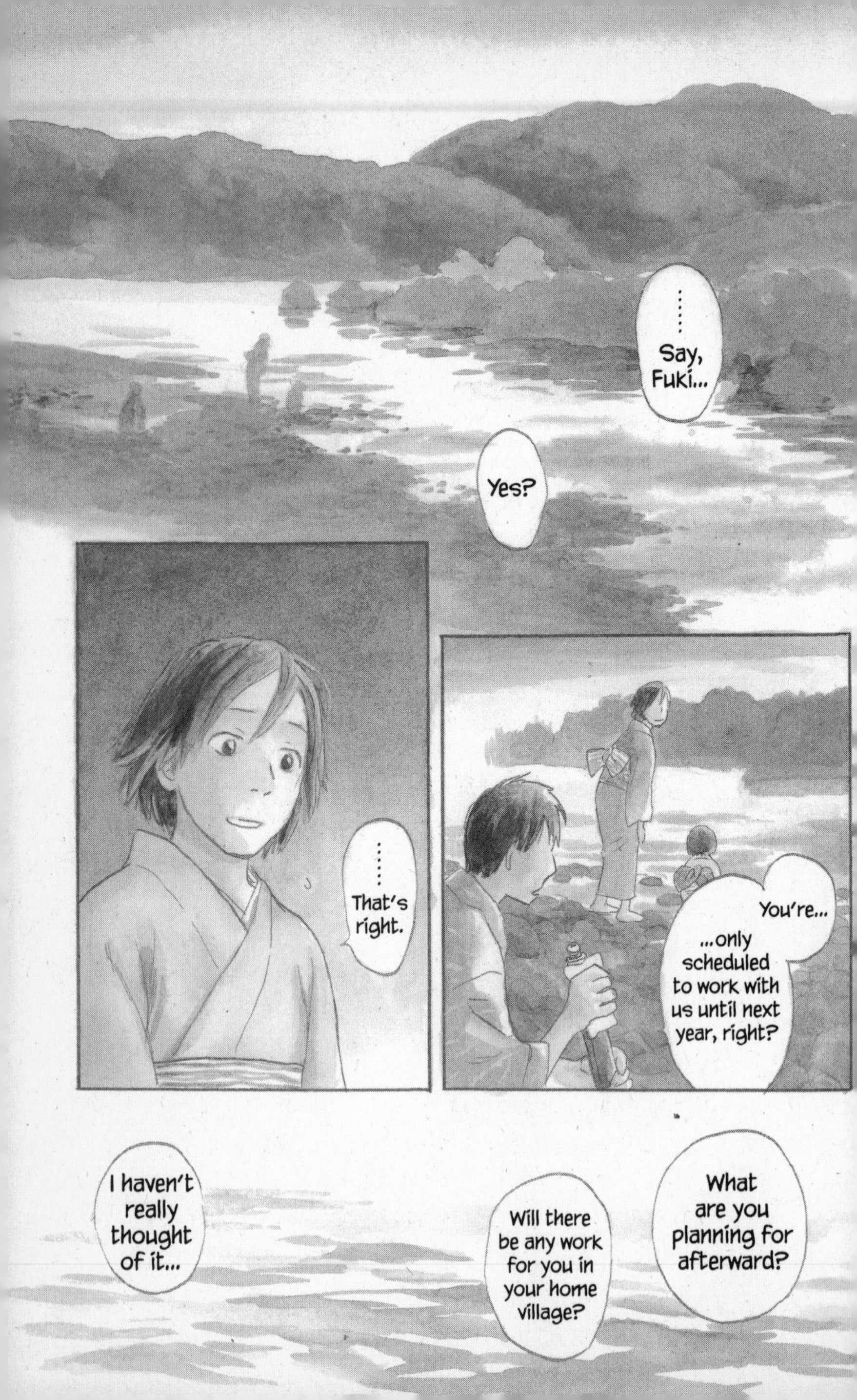
......
Say, Fuki...
Yes?
You're...
...only scheduled to work with us until next year, right?
......
That's right.
What are you planning for afterward?
Will there be any work for you in your home village?
I haven't really thought of it...

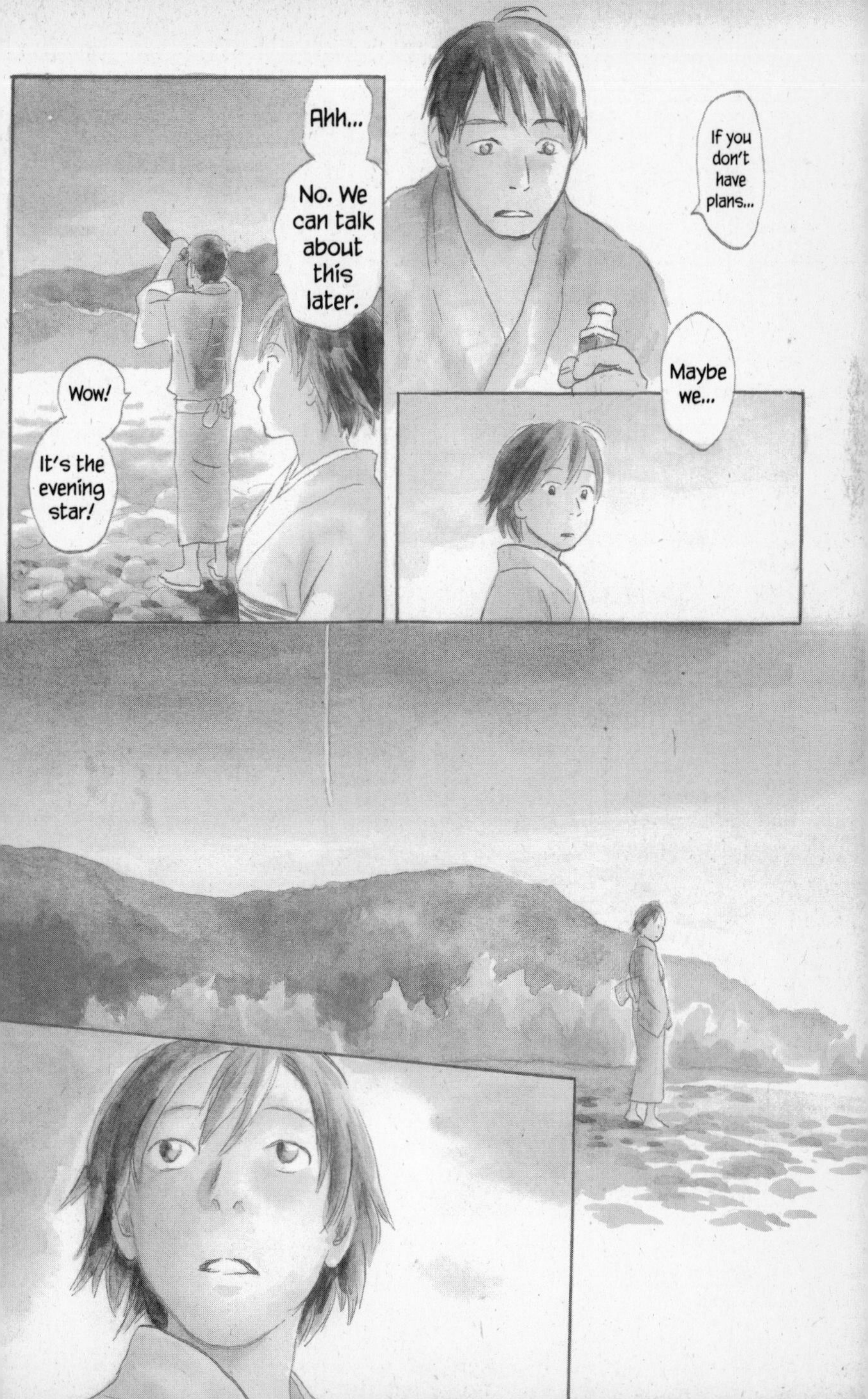
If you don't have plans...
Maybe we...
Ahh...
No. We can talk about this later.
Wow!
It's the evening star!

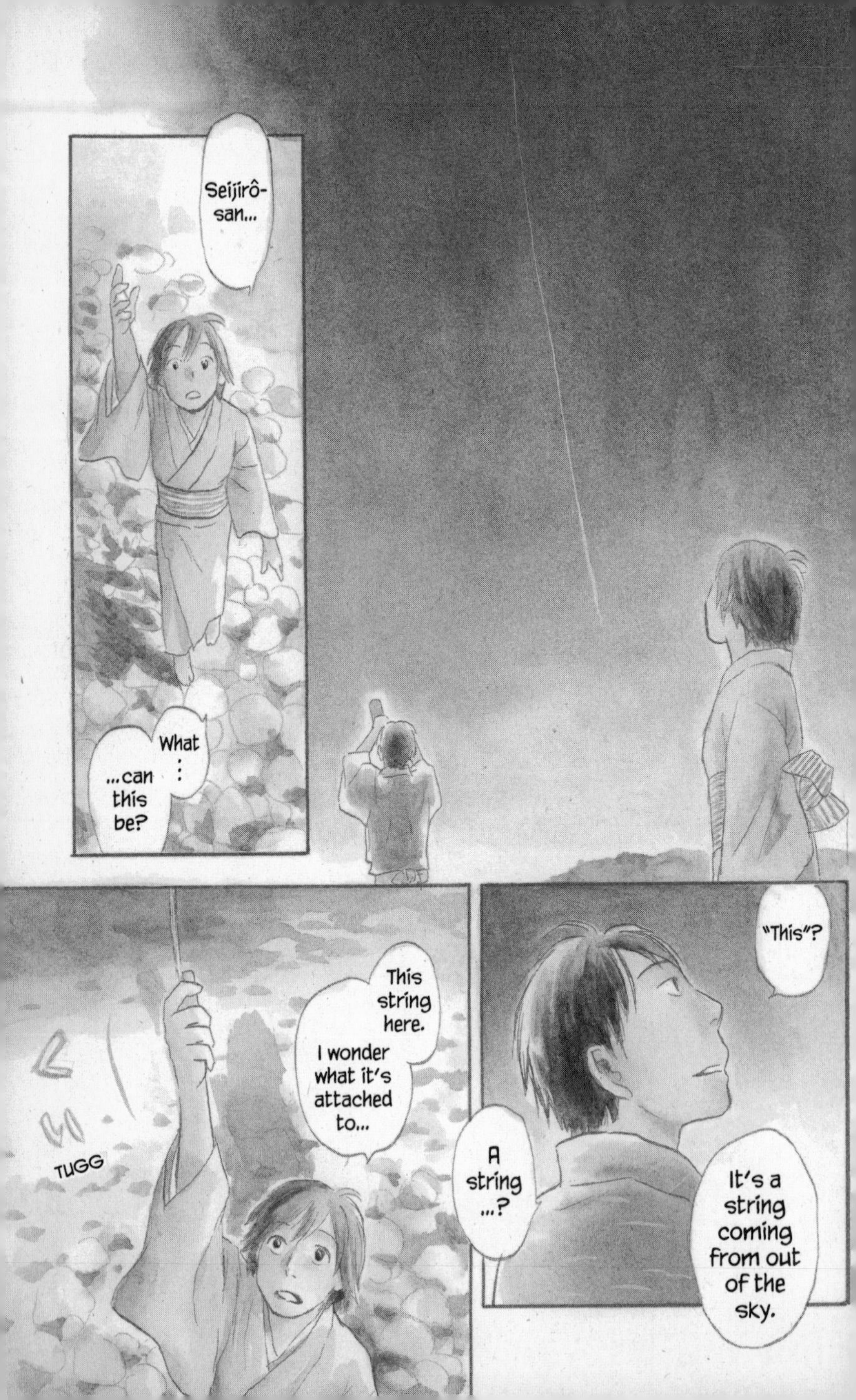
Seijirô-san...
What ... ...can this be?
"This"?
It's a string coming from out of the sky.
A string ...?
This string here.
I wonder what it's attached to...
TUGG

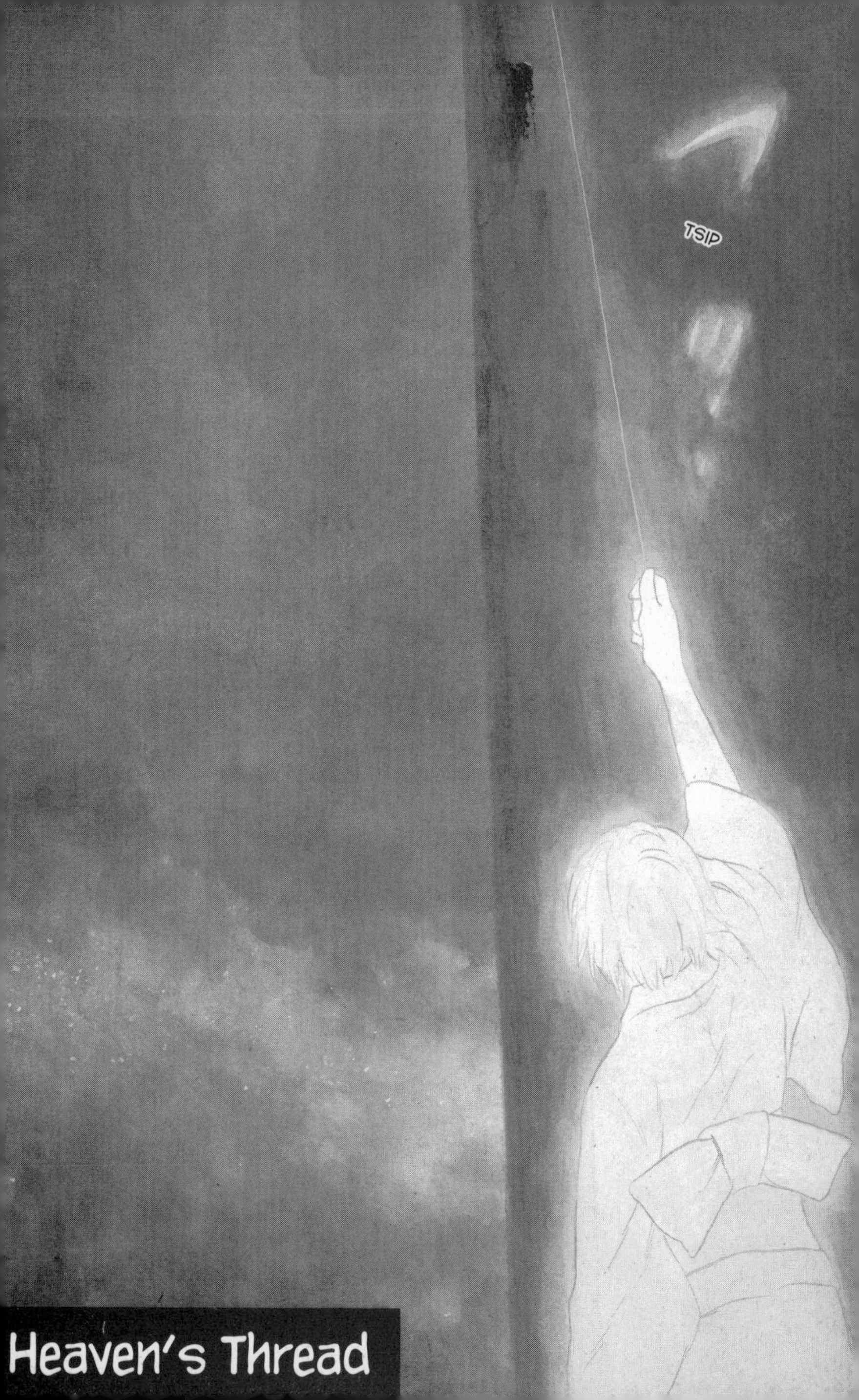
TSIP

Heaven's Thread

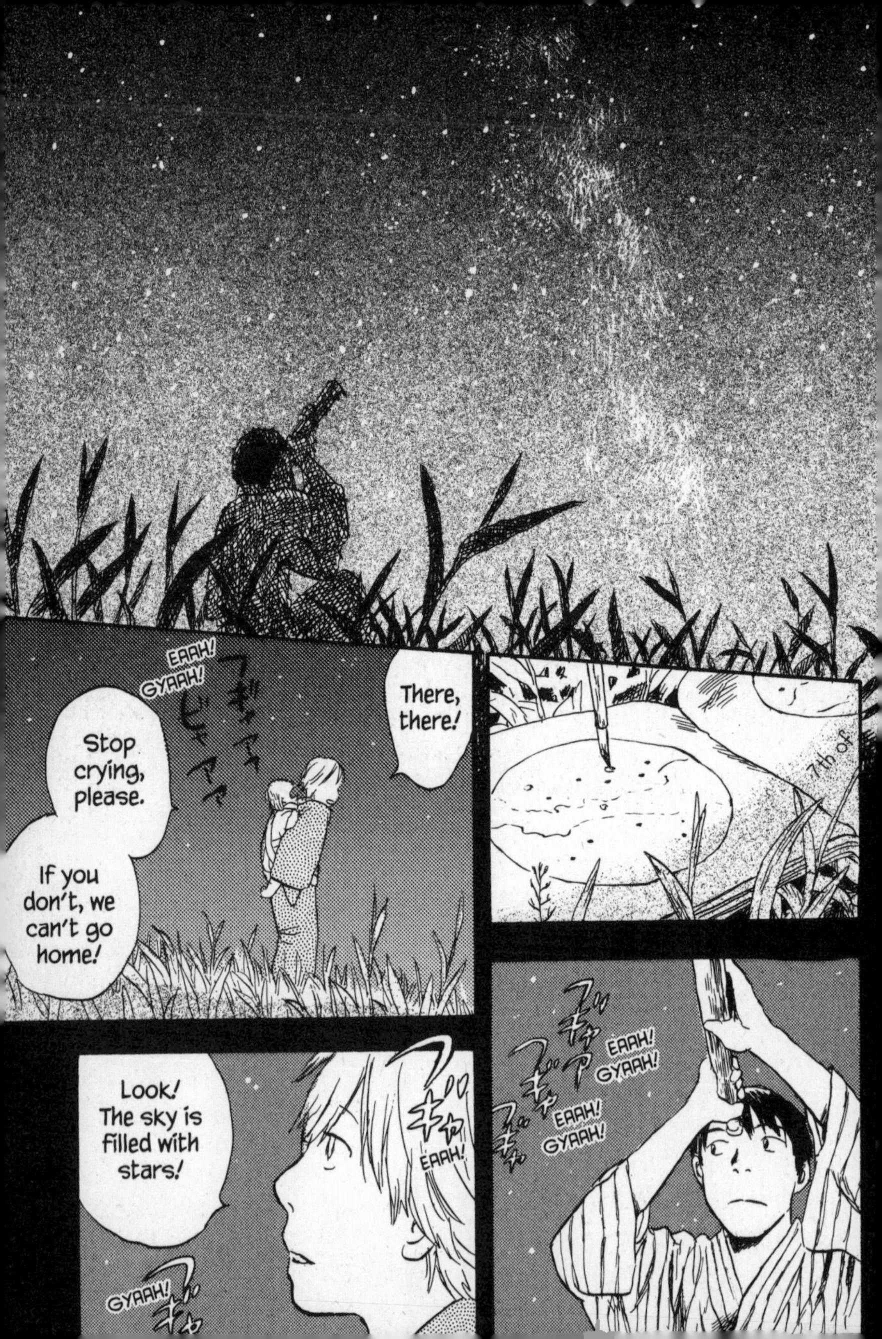
7th of
There, there!
EAAH! GYAAH!
Stop crying, please.
If you don't, we can't go home!
EAAH! GYAAH!
EAAH! GYAAH!
Look! The sky is filled with stars!
EAAH!
GYAAH!

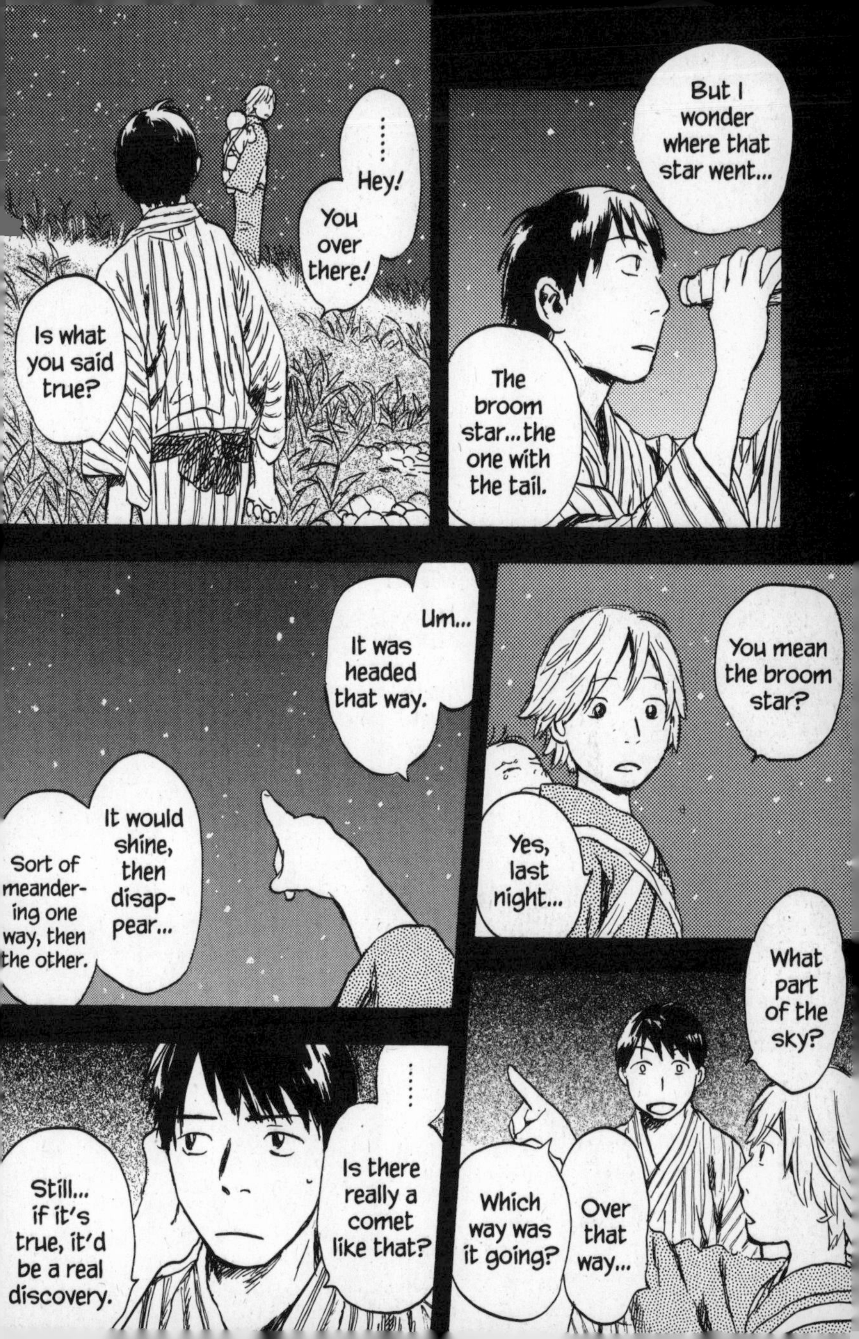
But I wonder where that star went...
The broom star...the one with the tail.
...... Hey!
You over there!
Is what you said true?
You mean the broom star?
Yes, last night...
Um... It was headed that way.
It would shine, then disappear...
Sort of meander-ing one way, then the other.
What part of the sky?
Over that way...
Which way was it going?
......
Is there really a comet like that?
Still... if it's true, it'd be a real discovery.

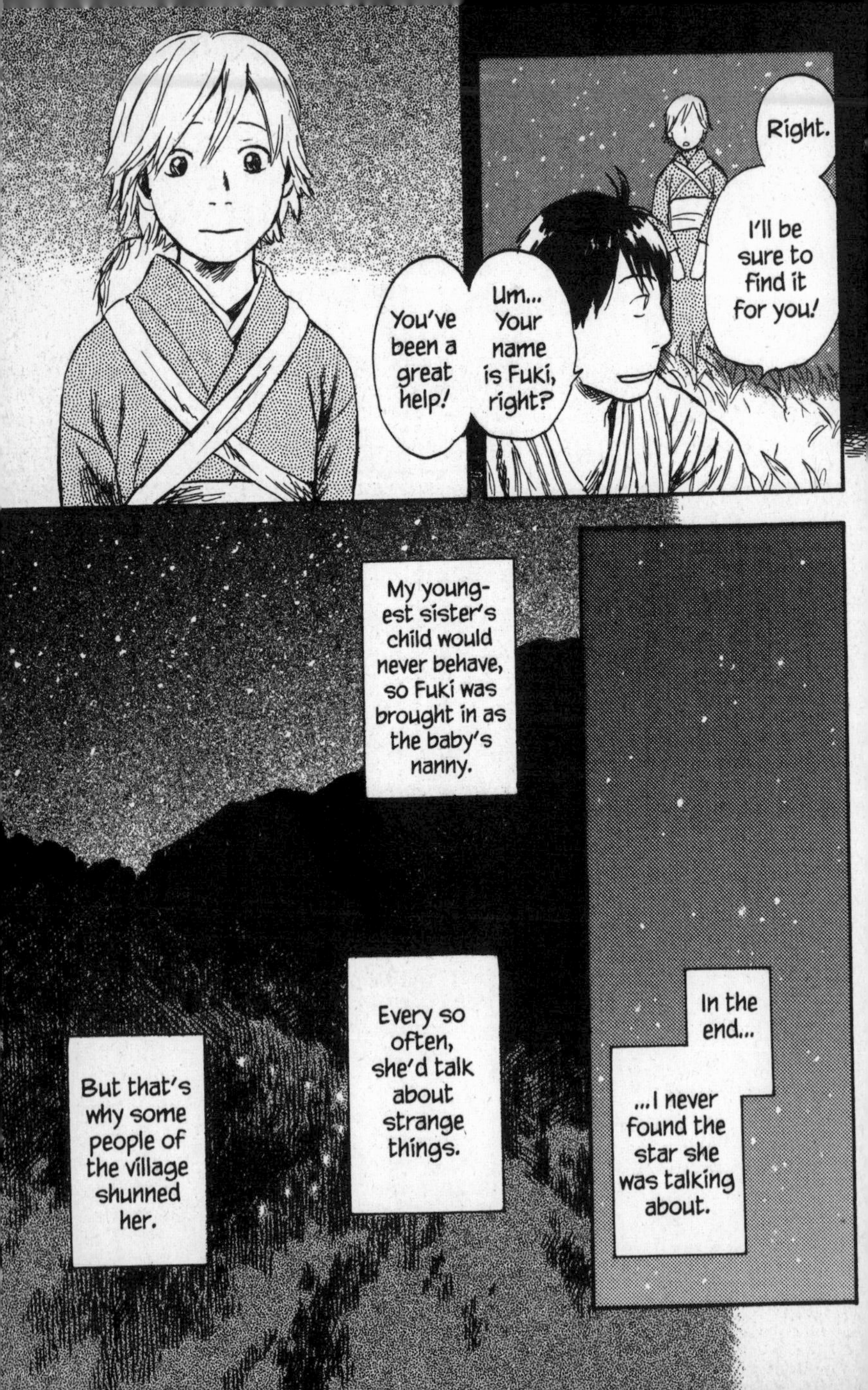
Right.
I'll be sure to find it for you!
Um... Your name is Fuki, right?
You've been a great help!
In the end...
...I never found the star she was talking about.
My young-est sister's child would never behave, so Fuki was brought in as the baby's nanny.
Every so often, she'd talk about strange things.
But that's why some people of the village shunned her.

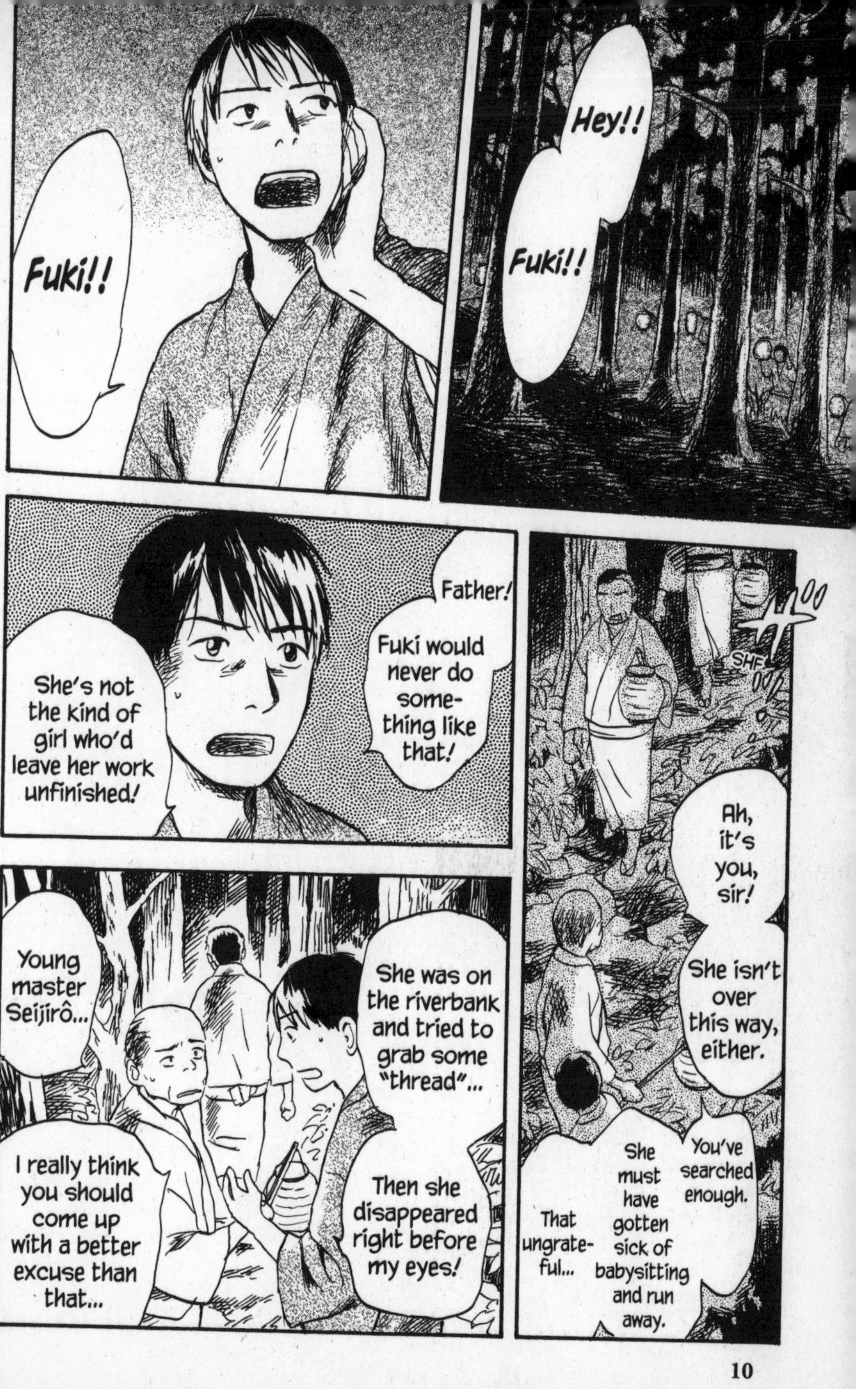
Hey!!
Fuki!!
Fuki!!
SHF
Ah, it's you, sir!
She isn't over this way, either.
You've searched enough.
She must have gotten sick of babysitting and run away.
That ungrate-ful...
Father!
Fuki would never do some-thing like that!
She's not the kind of girl who'd leave her work unfinished!
She was on the riverbank and tried to grab some "thread"...
Young master Seijirô...
Then she disappeared right before my eyes!
I really think you should come up with a better excuse than that...

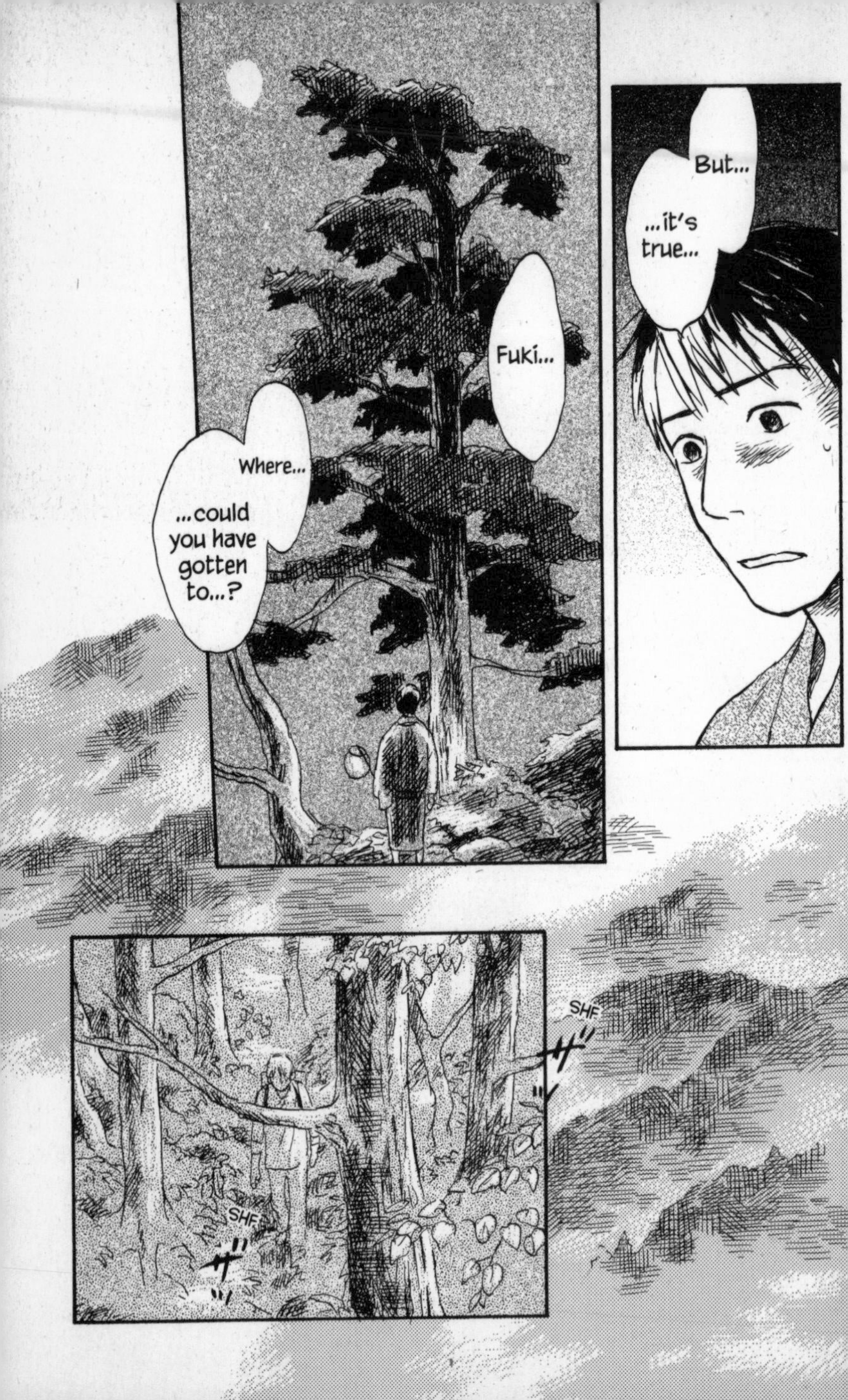
But...
...it's true...
Fuki...
Where...
...could you have gotten to...?
SHF
SHF

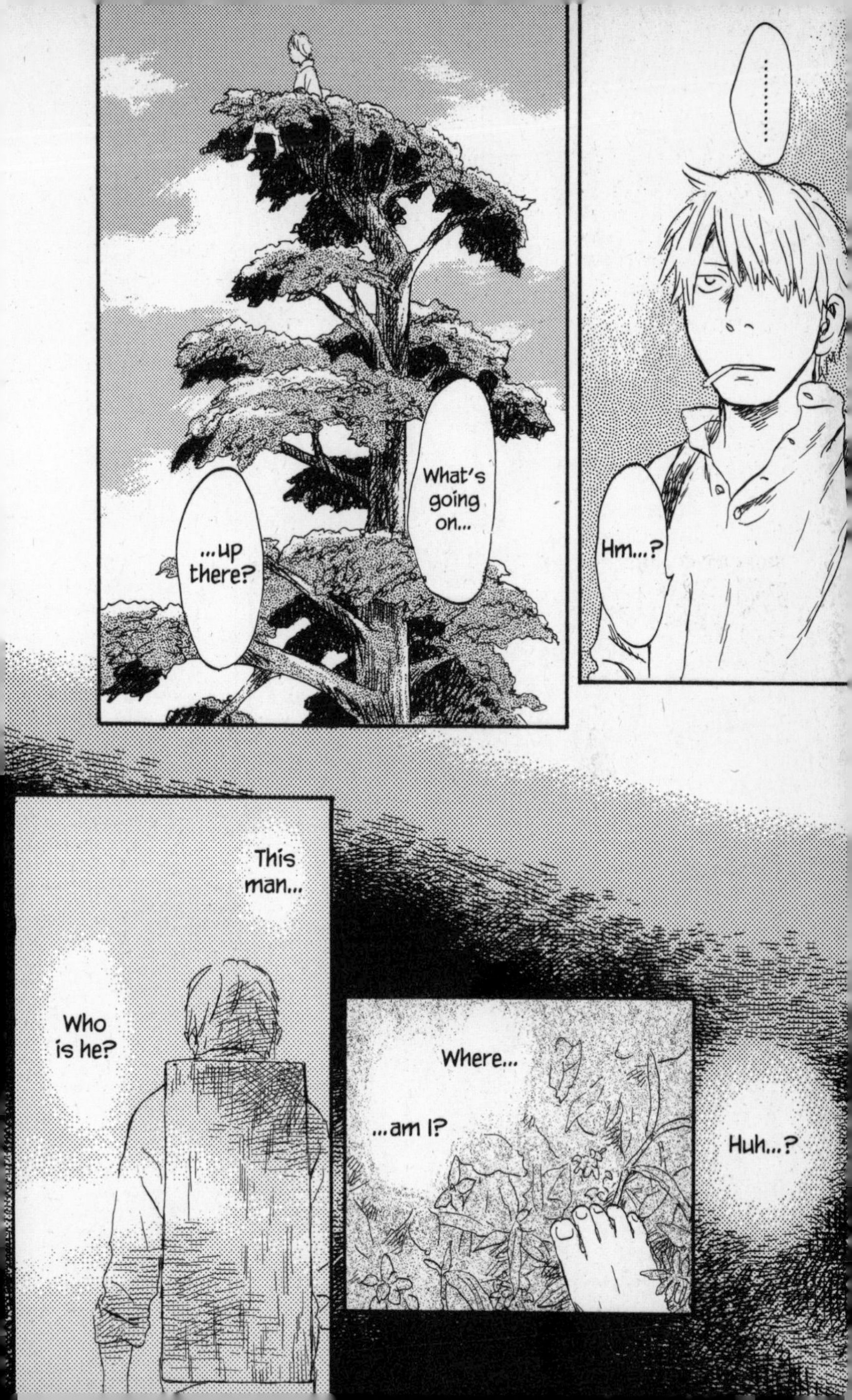
......
Hm...?
What's going on...
...up there?
Huh...?
Where...
...am I?
This man...
Who is he?

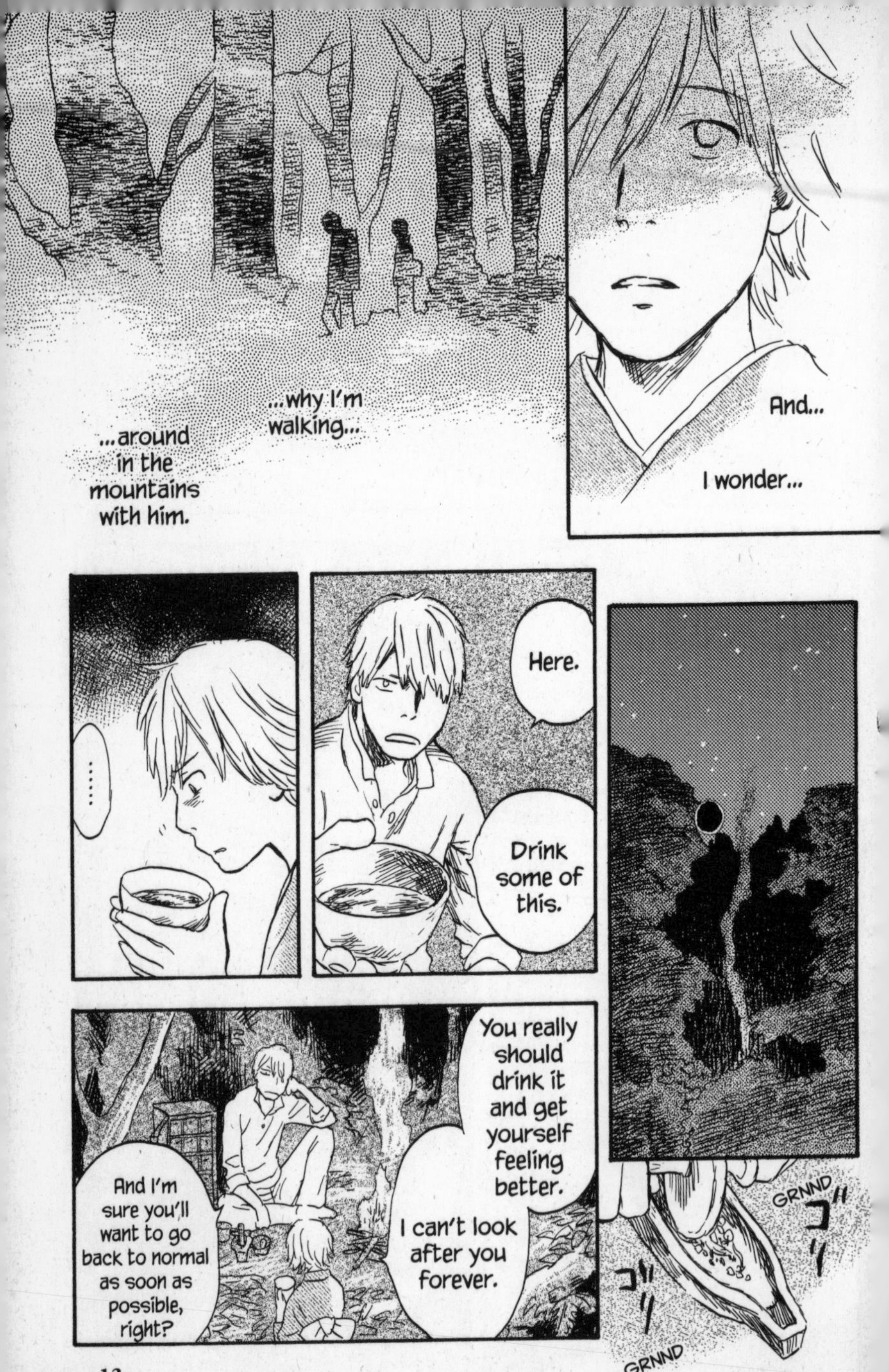
And...
I wonder...
...why I'm walking...
...around in the mountains with him.
GRNND
ゴリ
ゴリ
GRNND
Here.
Drink some of this.
......
You really should drink it and get yourself feeling better.
I can't look after you forever.
And I'm sure you'll want to go back to normal as soon as possible, right?

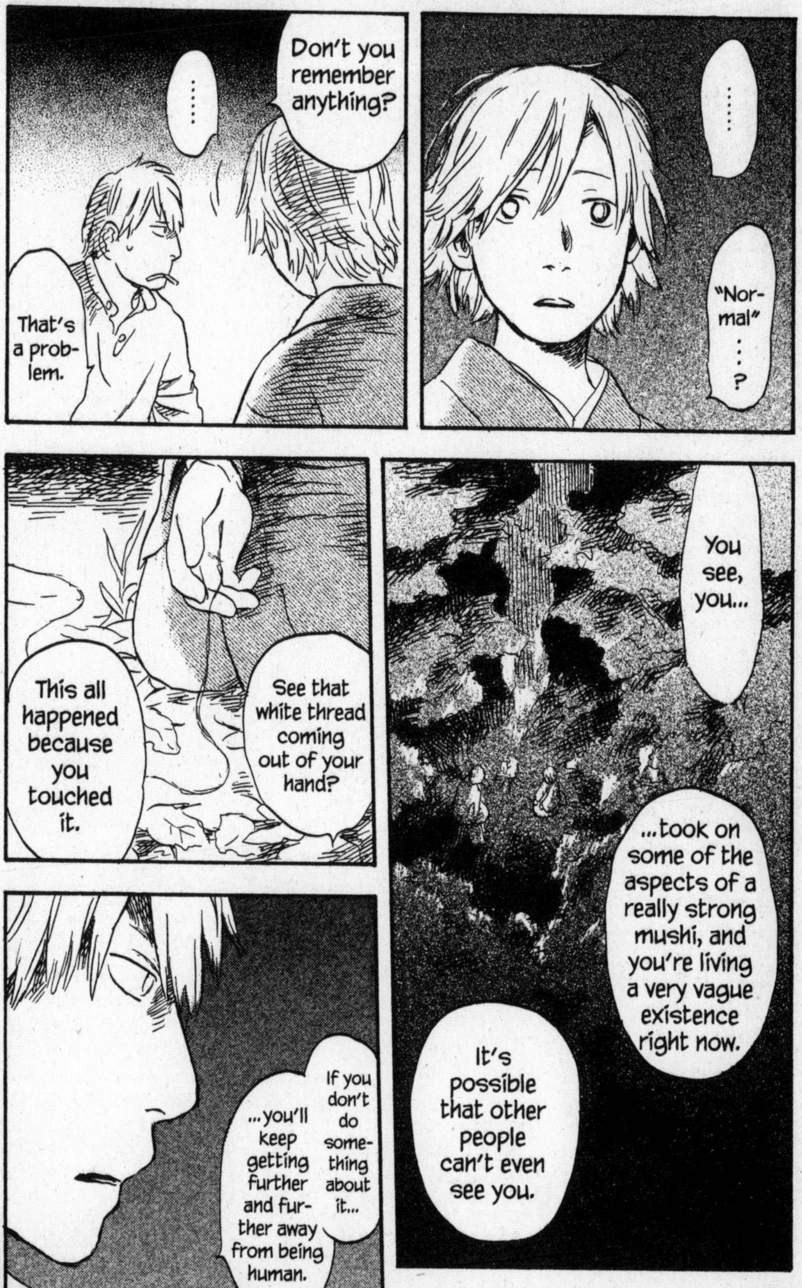
……
"Nor-mal" …?
Don't you remember anything?
……
That's a prob-lem.
You see, you...
...took on some of the aspects of a really strong mushi, and you're living a very vague existence right now.
It's possible that other people can't even see you.
See that white thread coming out of your hand?
This all happened because you touched it.
If you don't do some-thing about it...
...you'll keep getting further and fur-ther away from being human.

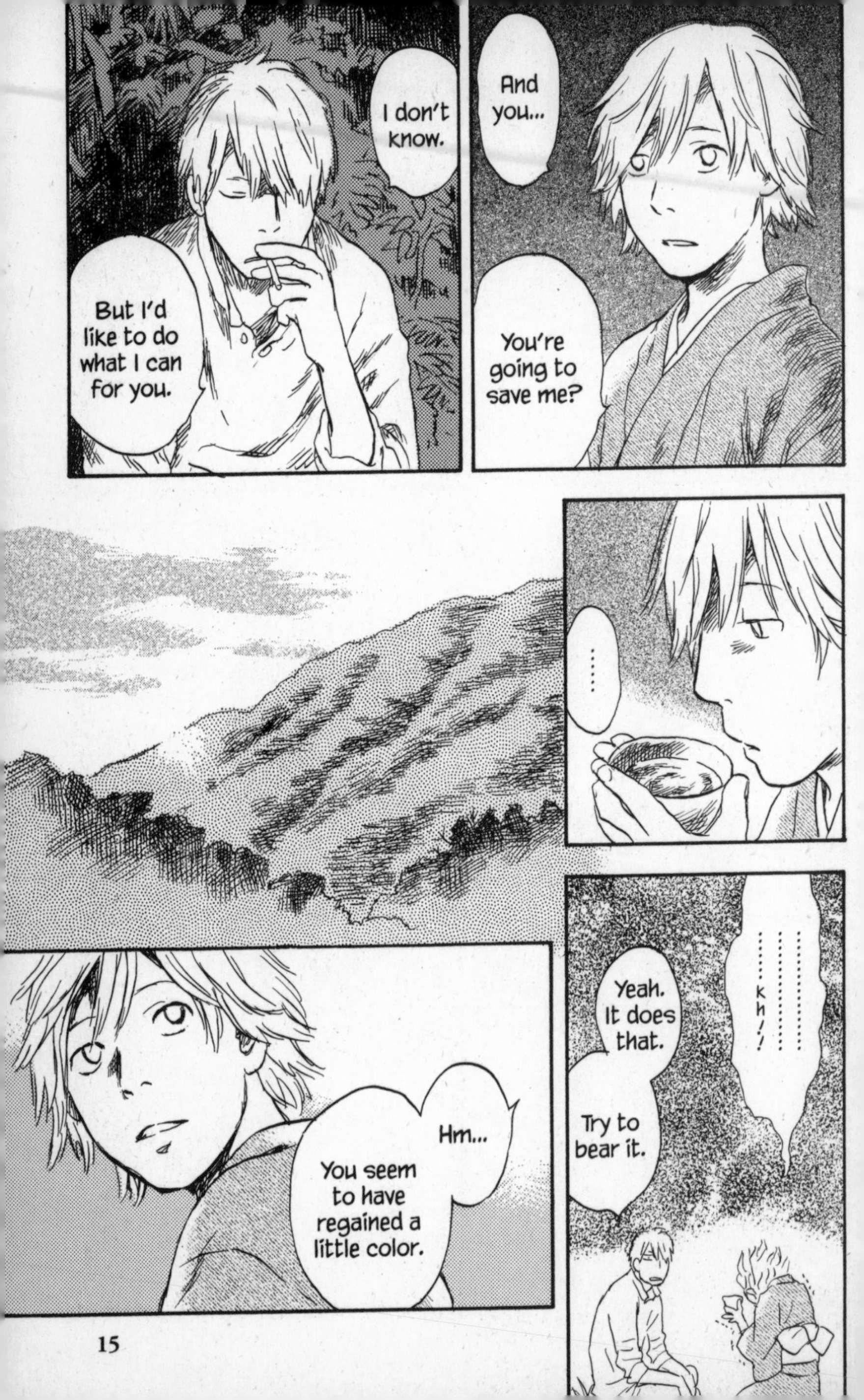

And you...
You're going to save me?
I don't know.
But I'd like to do what I can for you.
......
....
......kh!!
Yeah. It does that.
Try to bear it.
Hm...
You seem to have regained a little color.

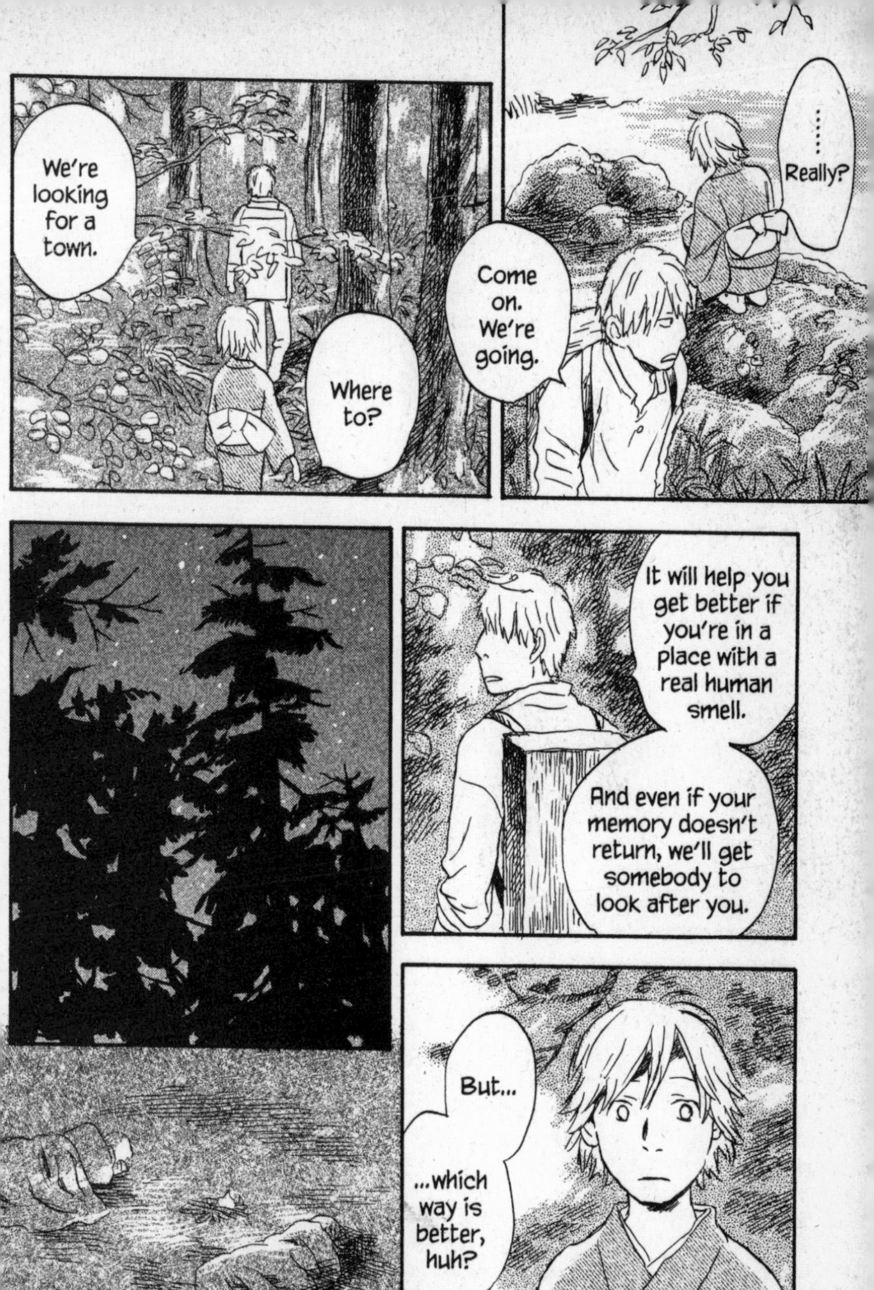
......Really?
Come on. We're going.
Where to?
We're looking for a town.
It will help you get better if you're in a place with a real human smell.
And even if your memory doesn't return, we'll get somebody to look after you.
But...
...which way is better, huh?

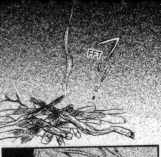

FFT
FOOH
......?
There's something...
...some light coming from beneath the ground...
......
Yeah.
I guess you can see it pretty well the way you are now.

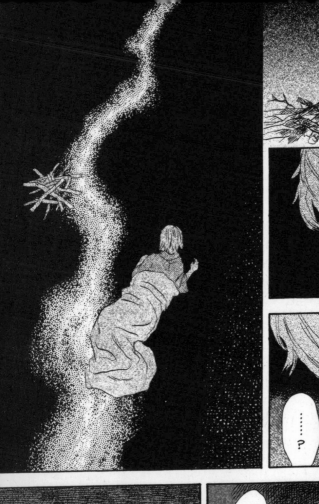

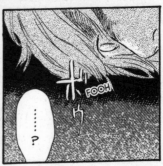

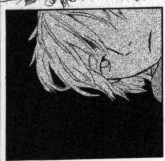

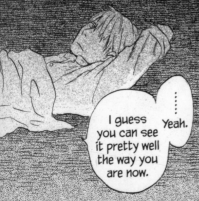

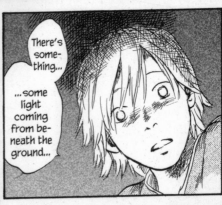

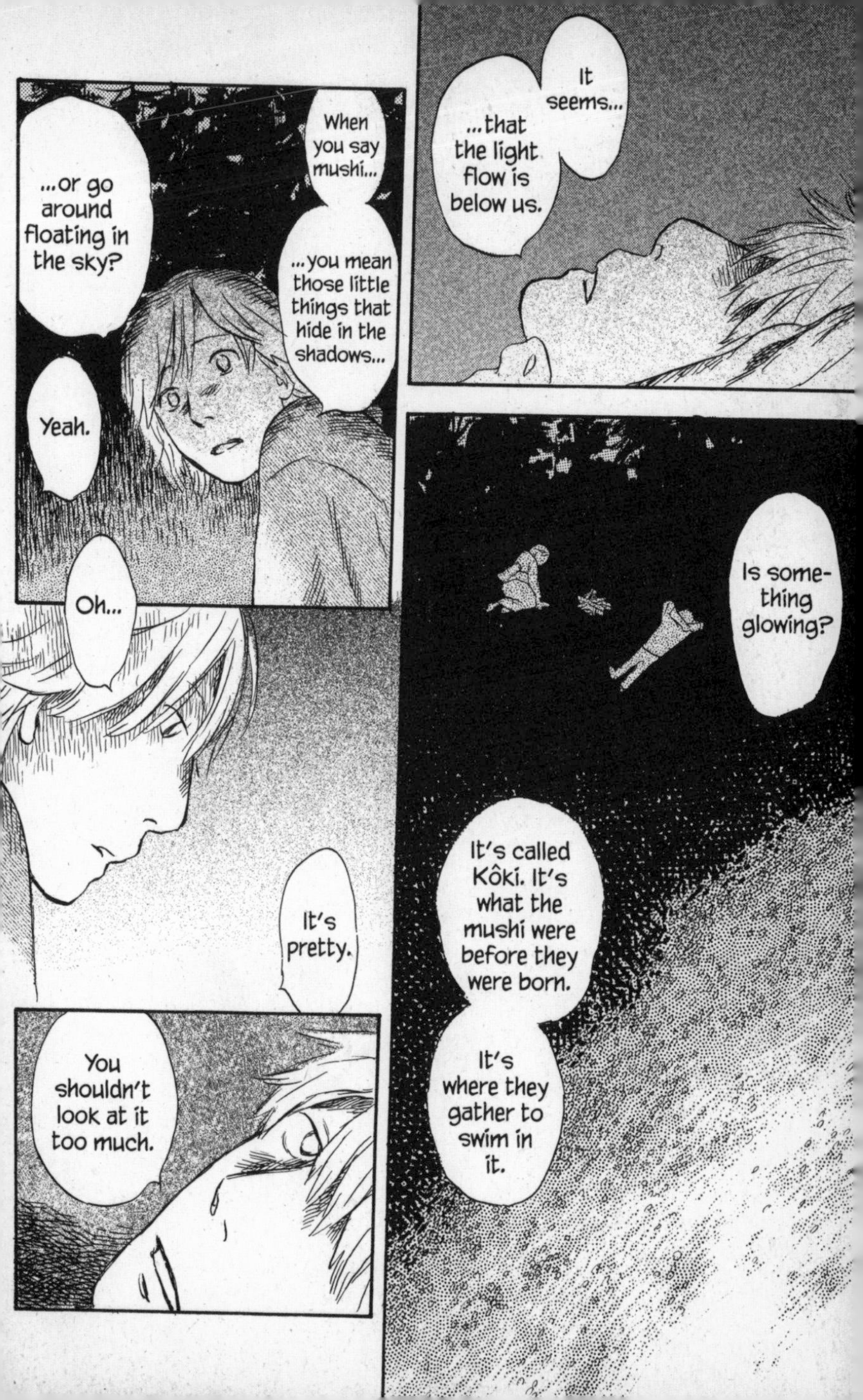
It seems...
...that the light flow is below us.
Is something glowing?
It's called Kôki. It's what the mushi were before they were born.
It's where they gather to swim in it.
When you say mushi...
...you mean those little things that hide in the shadows...
...or go around floating in the sky?
Yeah.
Oh...
It's pretty.
You shouldn't look at it too much.

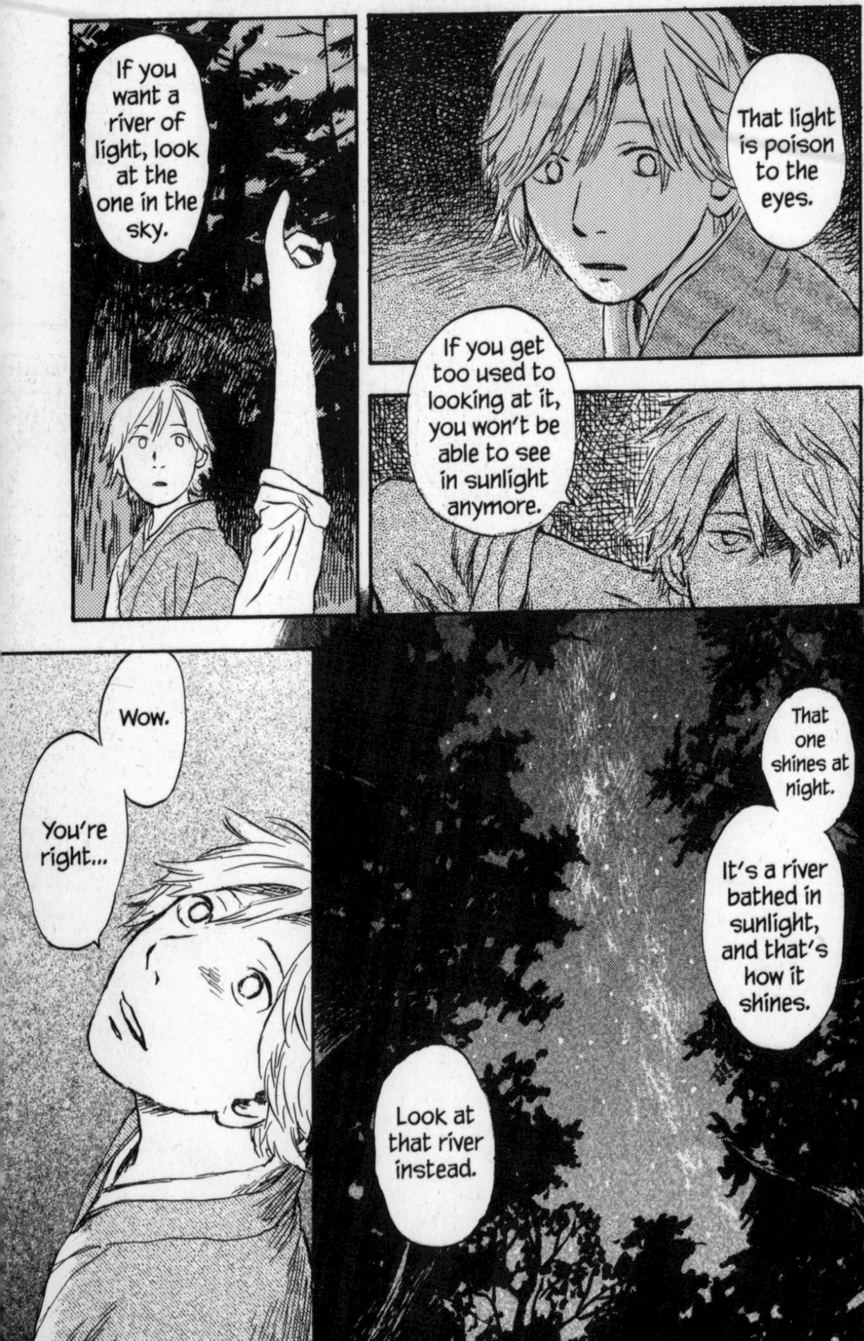
That light is poison to the eyes.
If you get too used to looking at it, you won't be able to see in sunlight anymore.
If you want a river of light, look at the one in the sky.
That one shines at night.
It's a river bathed in sunlight, and that's how it shines.
Look at that river instead.
Wow.
You're right...

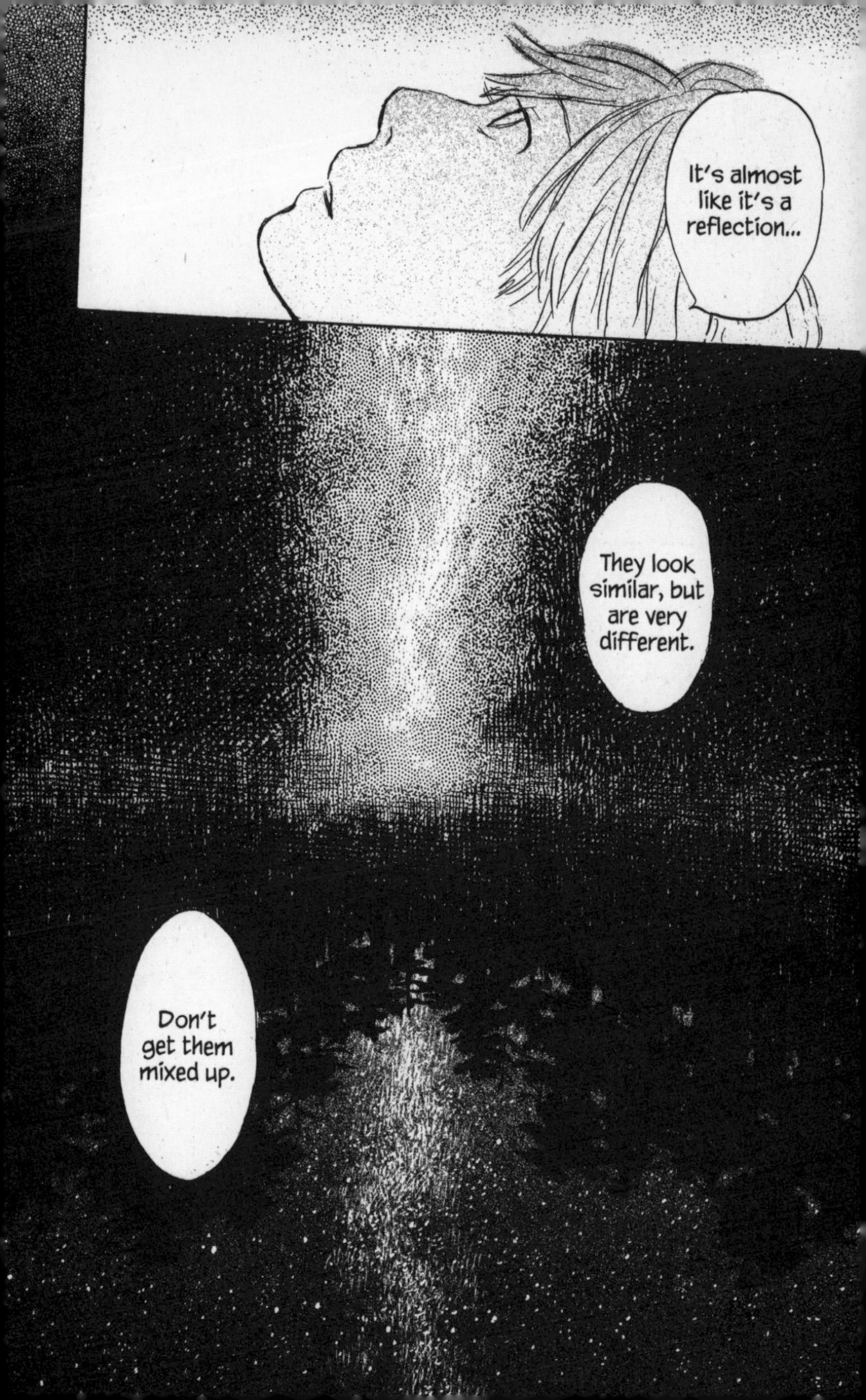
It's almost like it's a reflection...
They look similar, but are very different.
Don't get them mixed up.

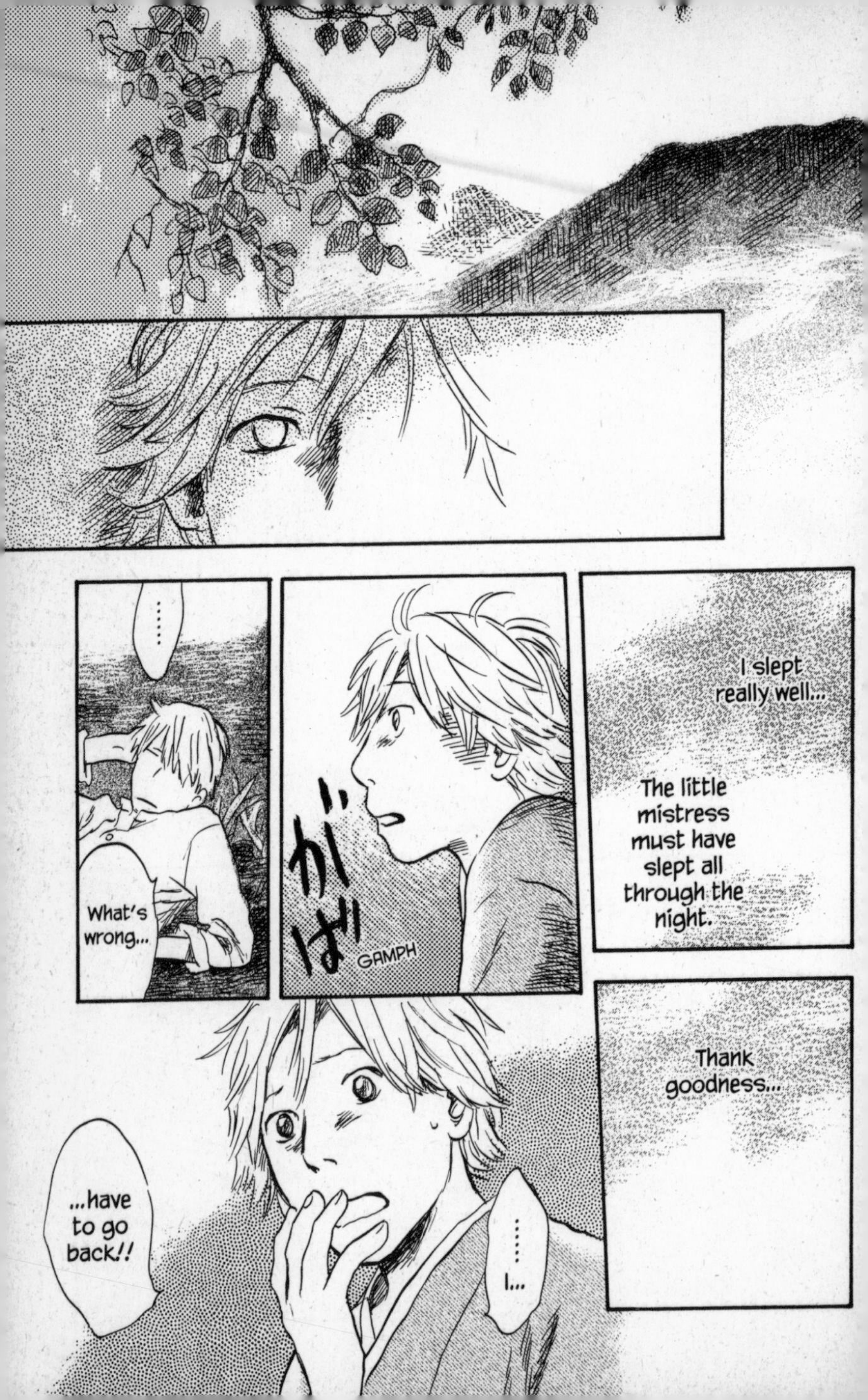
I slept really well...
The little mistress must have slept all through the night.
がば
GAMPH
......
What's wrong...
Thank goodness...
......
I...
...have to go back!!

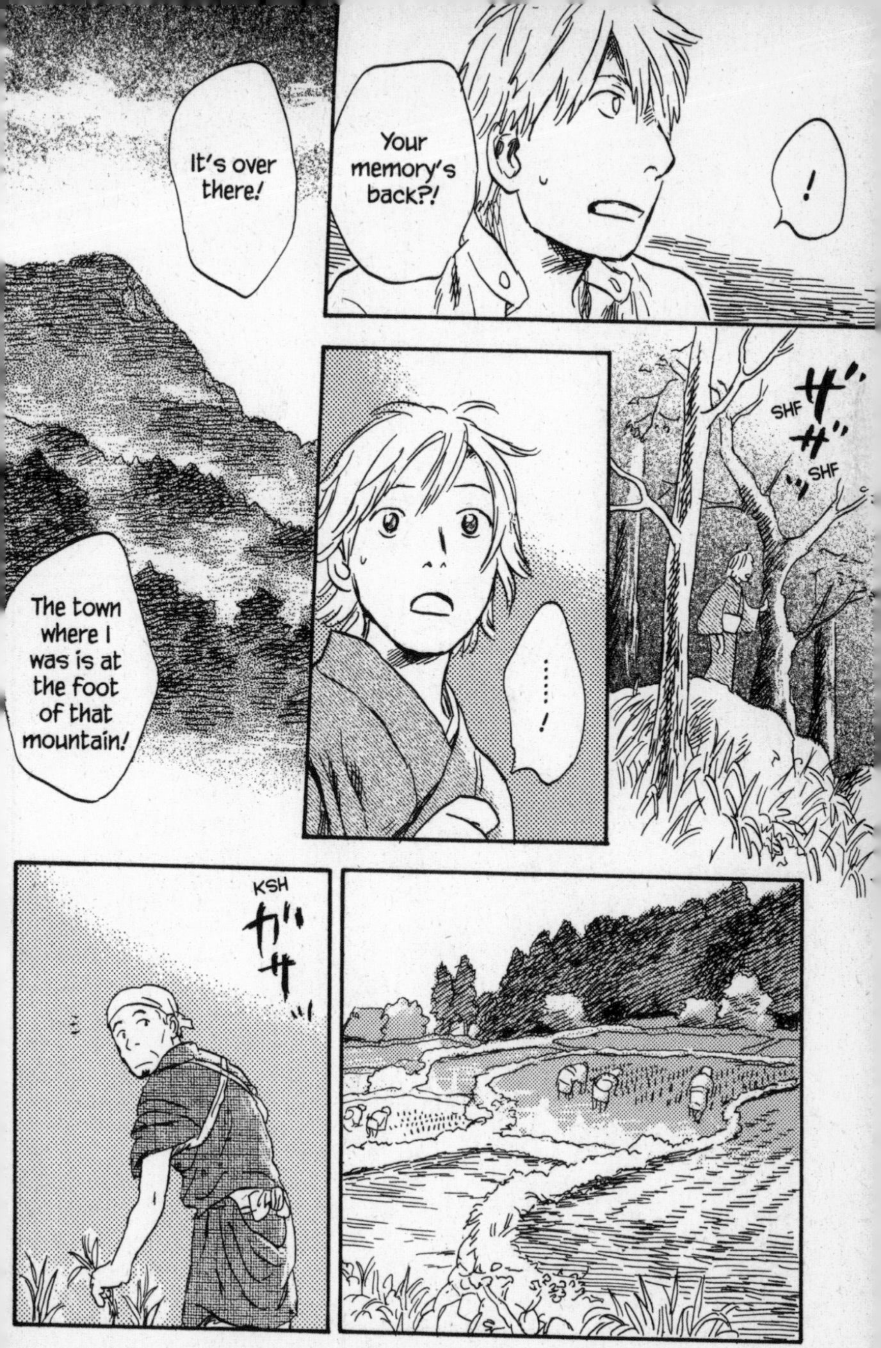
!
Your memory's back?!
SHF
ザッ
ザッ
SHF
......!
It's over there!
The town where I was is at the foot of that mountain!
KSH
ガサッ

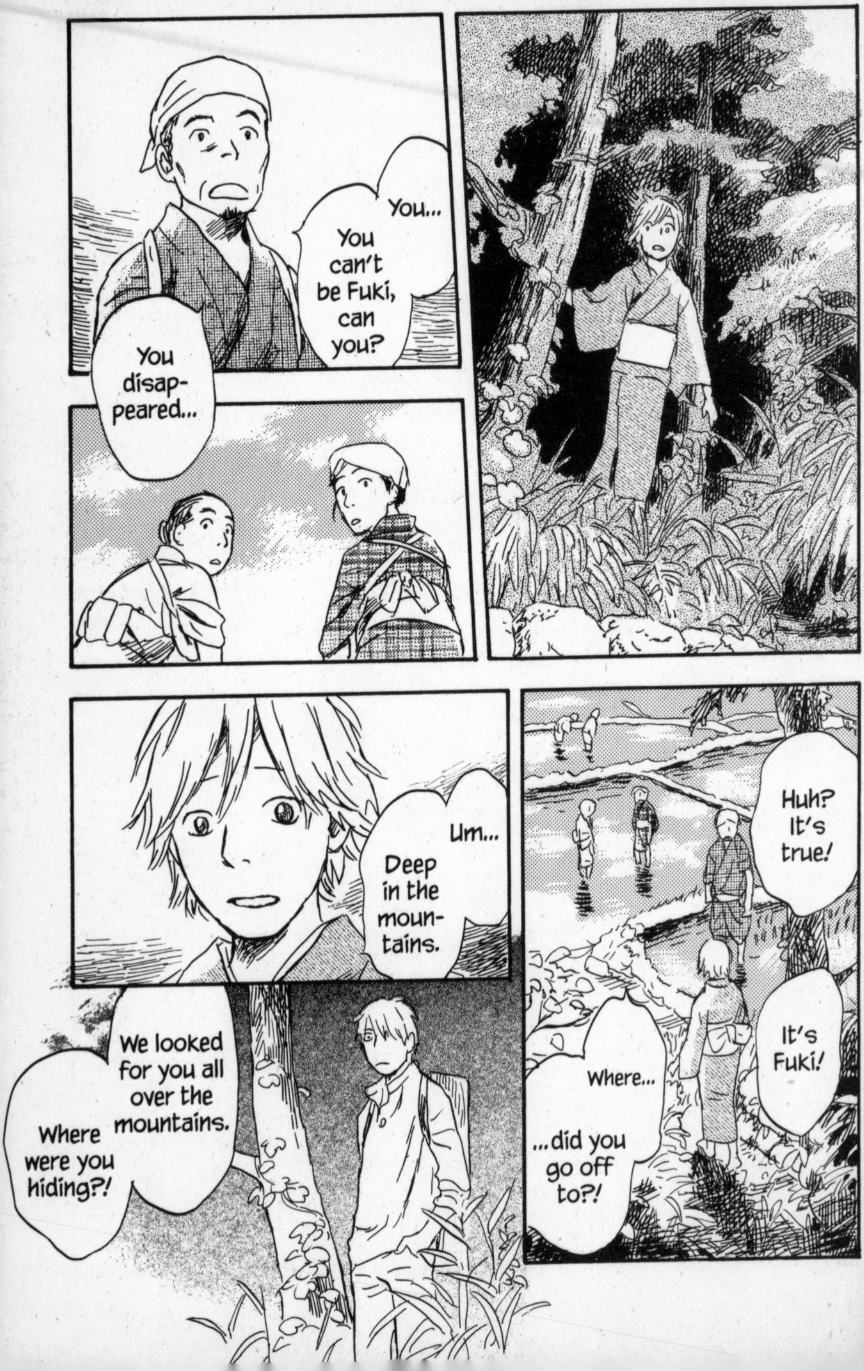
You...
You can't be Fuki, can you?
You disap-peared...
Huh? It's true!
It's Fuki!
Where...
...did you go off to?!
Um...
Deep in the moun-tains.
We looked for you all over the mountains.
Where were you hiding?!

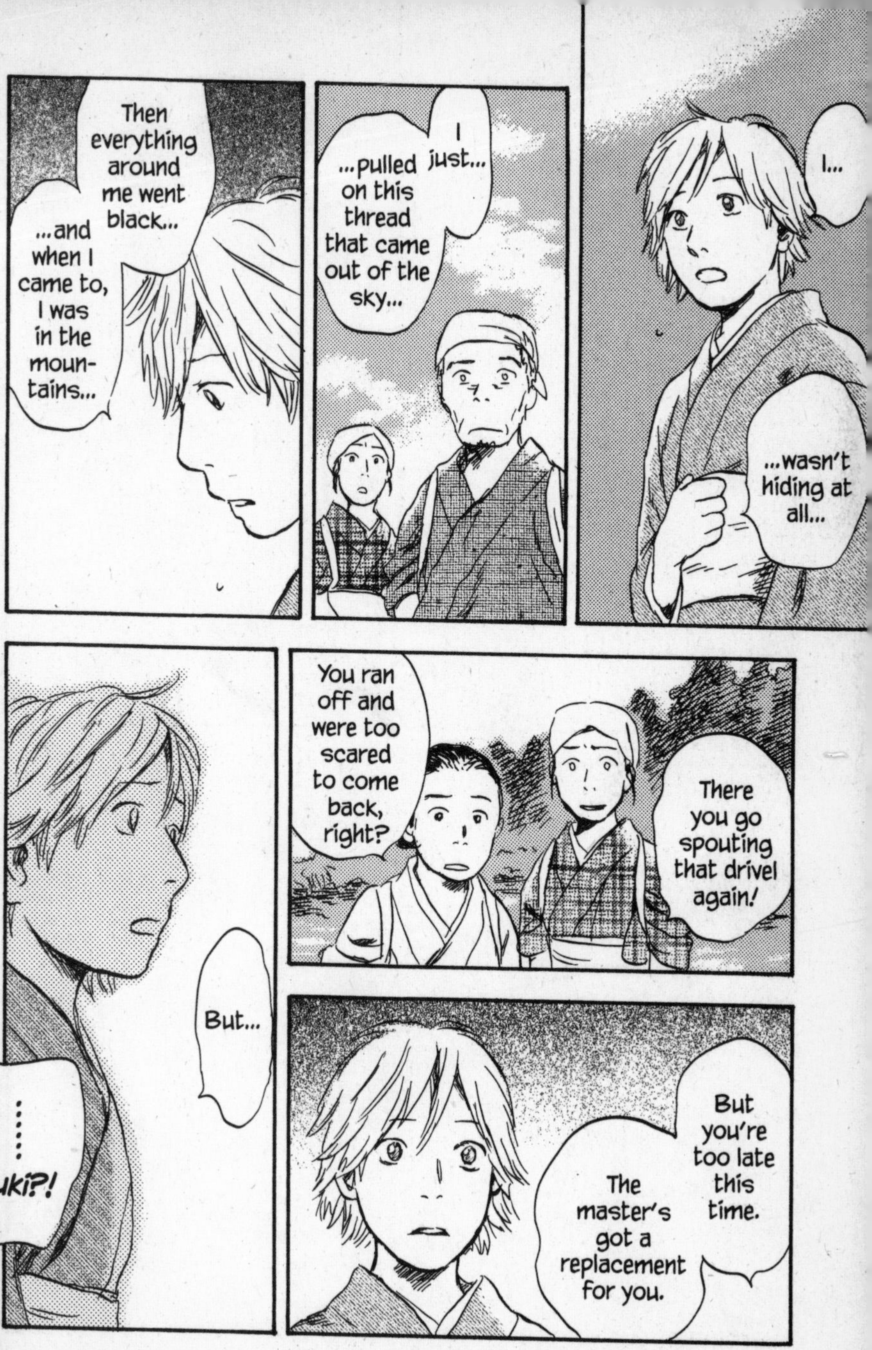
I...
...wasn't hiding at all...
I just...
...pulled on this thread that came out of the sky...
Then everything around me went black...
...and when I came to, I was in the mountains...
There you go spouting that drivel again!
You ran off and were too scared to come back, right?
But you're too late this time.
The master's got a replacement for you.
But...
......
uki?!

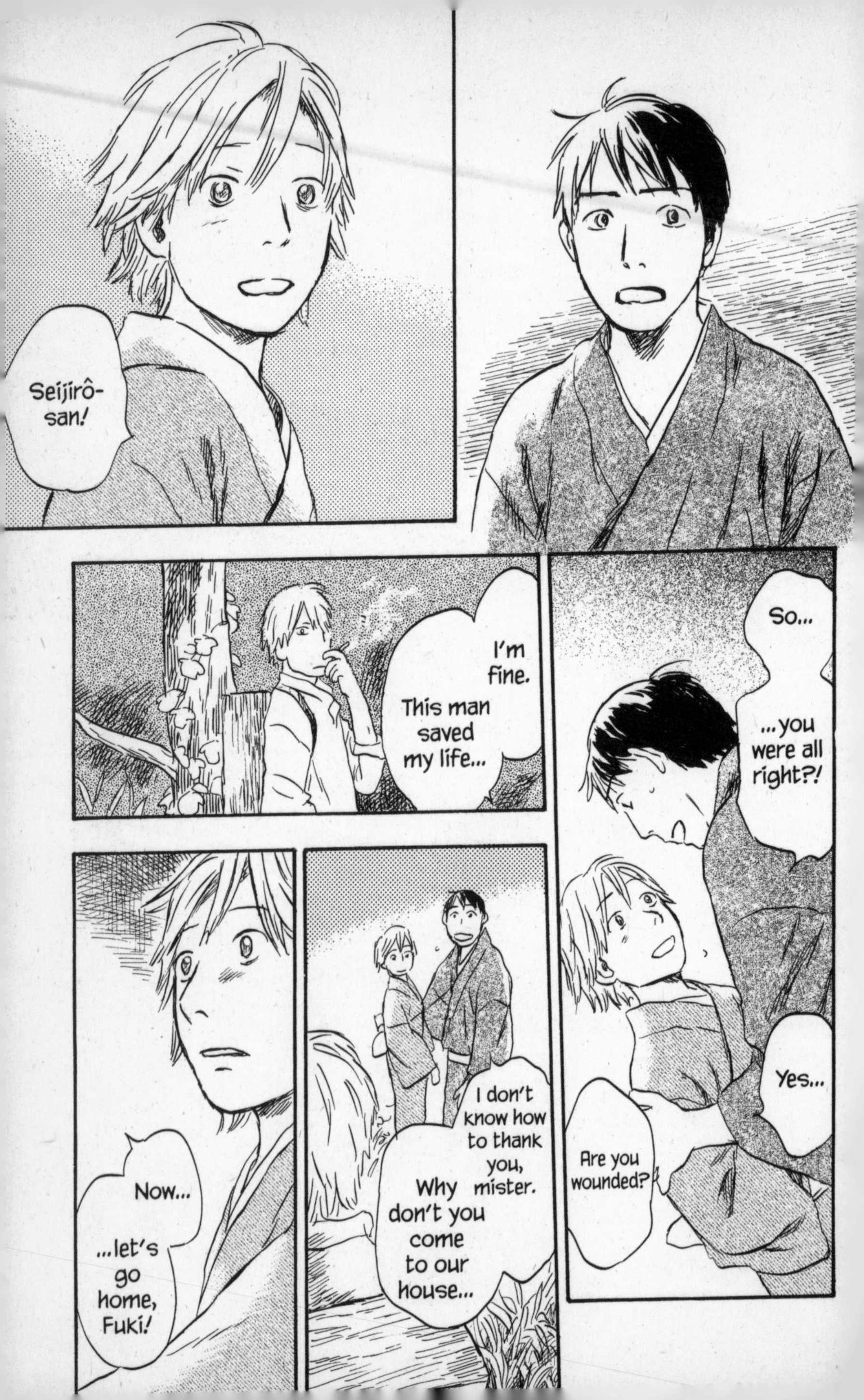
Seijirô-san!
So...
...you were all right?!
Yes...
Are you wounded?
I'm fine.
This man saved my life...
I don't know how to thank you, mister.
Why don't you come to our house...
Now...
...let's go home, Fuki!

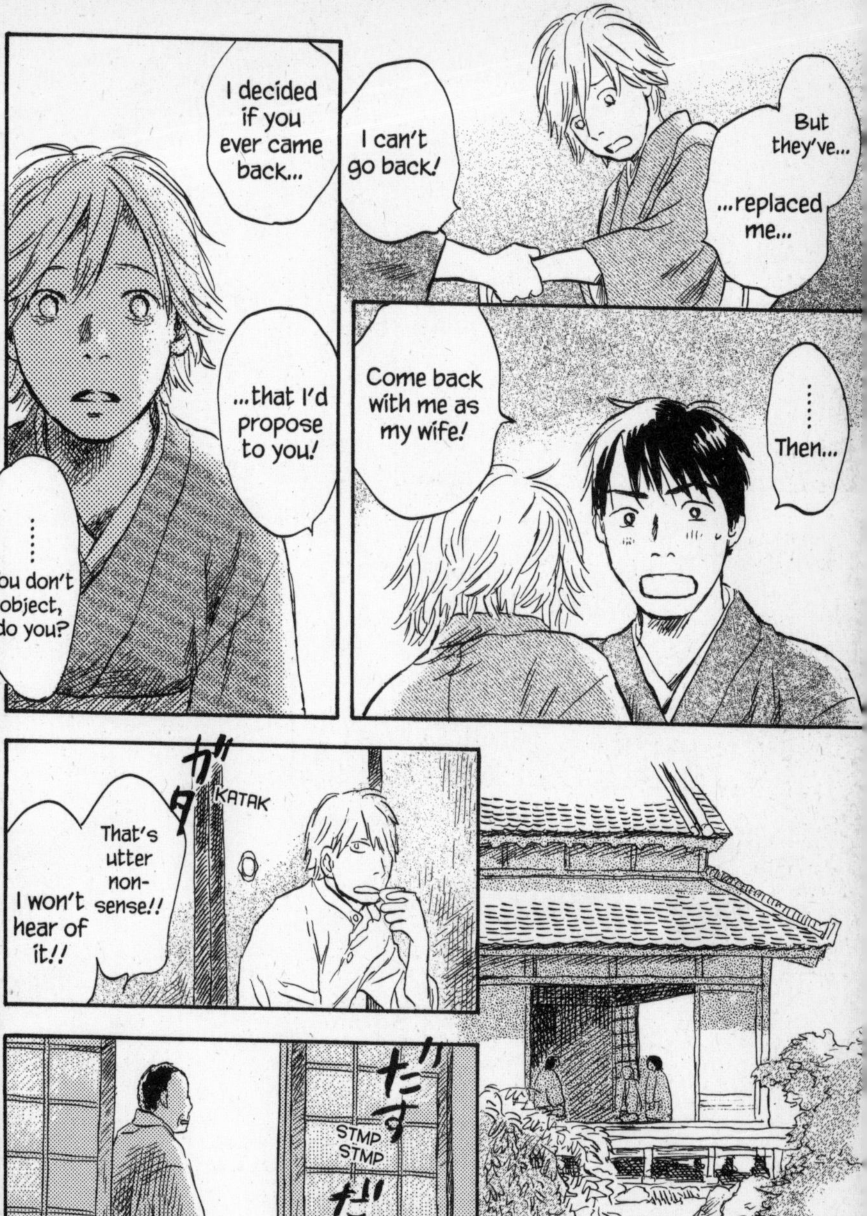
But they've...
...replaced me...
I can't go back!
...... Then...
Come back with me as my wife!
I decided if you ever came back...
...that I'd propose to you!
...... You don't object, do you?
ガタ
KATAK
That's utter non-sense!!
I won't hear of it!!
だす
STMP STMP
だす

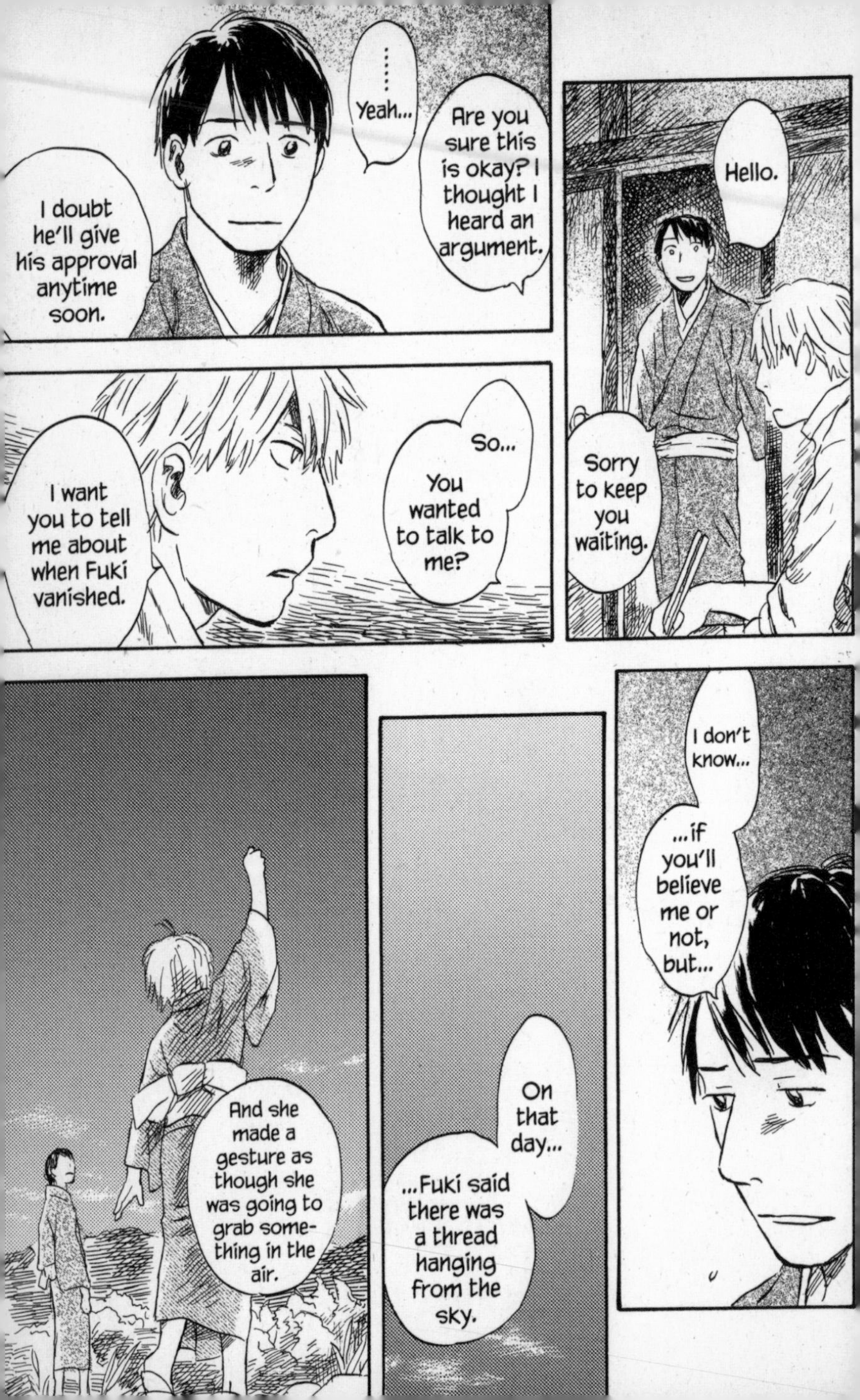
Hello.
Sorry to keep you waiting.
Are you sure this is okay? I thought I heard an argument.
...... Yeah...
I doubt he'll give his approval anytime soon.
So... You wanted to talk to me?
I want you to tell me about when Fuki vanished.
I don't know...
...if you'll believe me or not, but...
On that day...
...Fuki said there was a thread hanging from the sky.
And she made a gesture as though she was going to grab some-thing in the air.

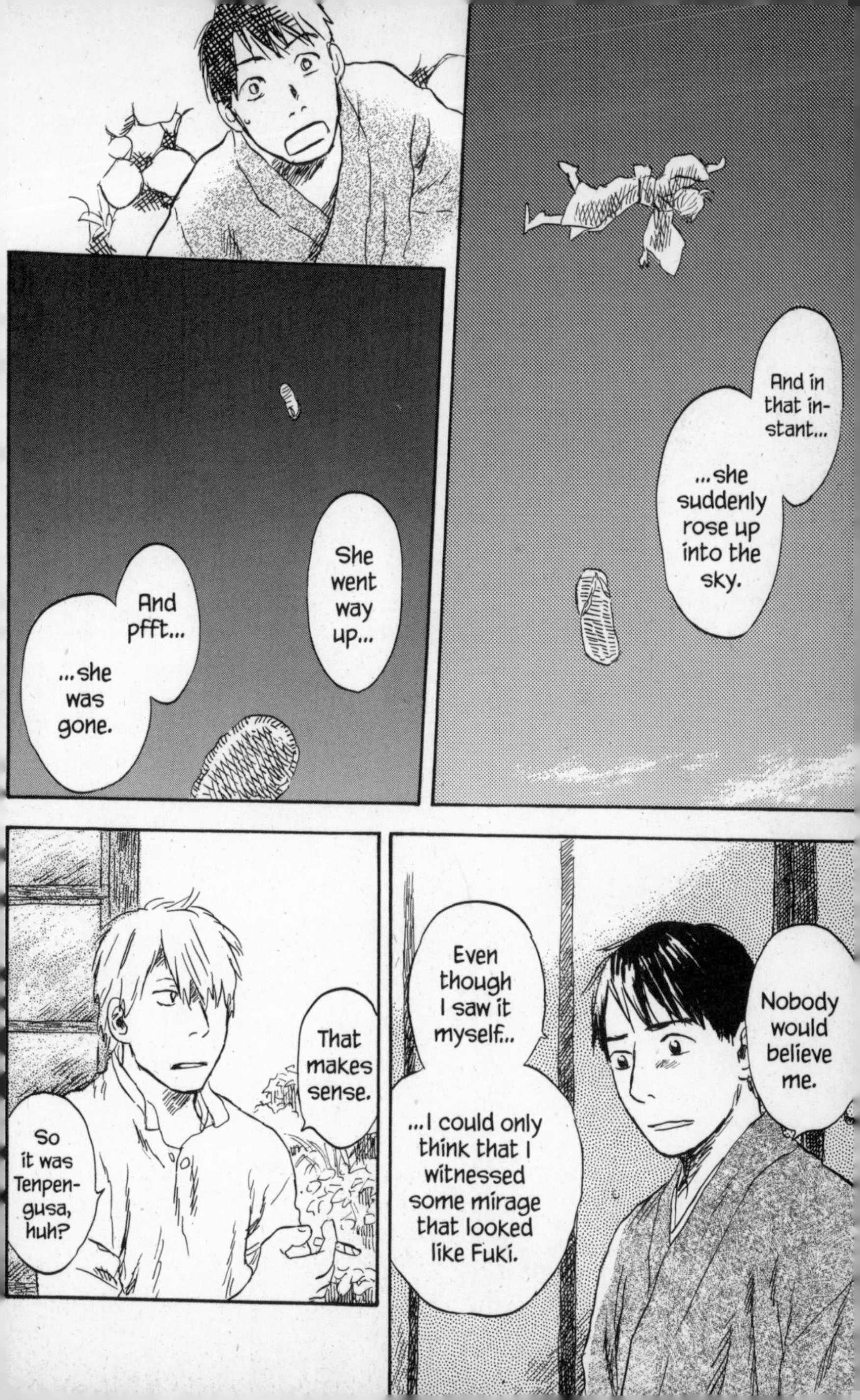

And in that instant...
...she suddenly rose up into the sky.
She went way up...
And pfft...
...she was gone.
Nobody would believe me.
Even though I saw it myself...
...I could only think that I witnessed some mirage that looked like Fuki.
That makes sense.
So it was Tenpengusa, huh?

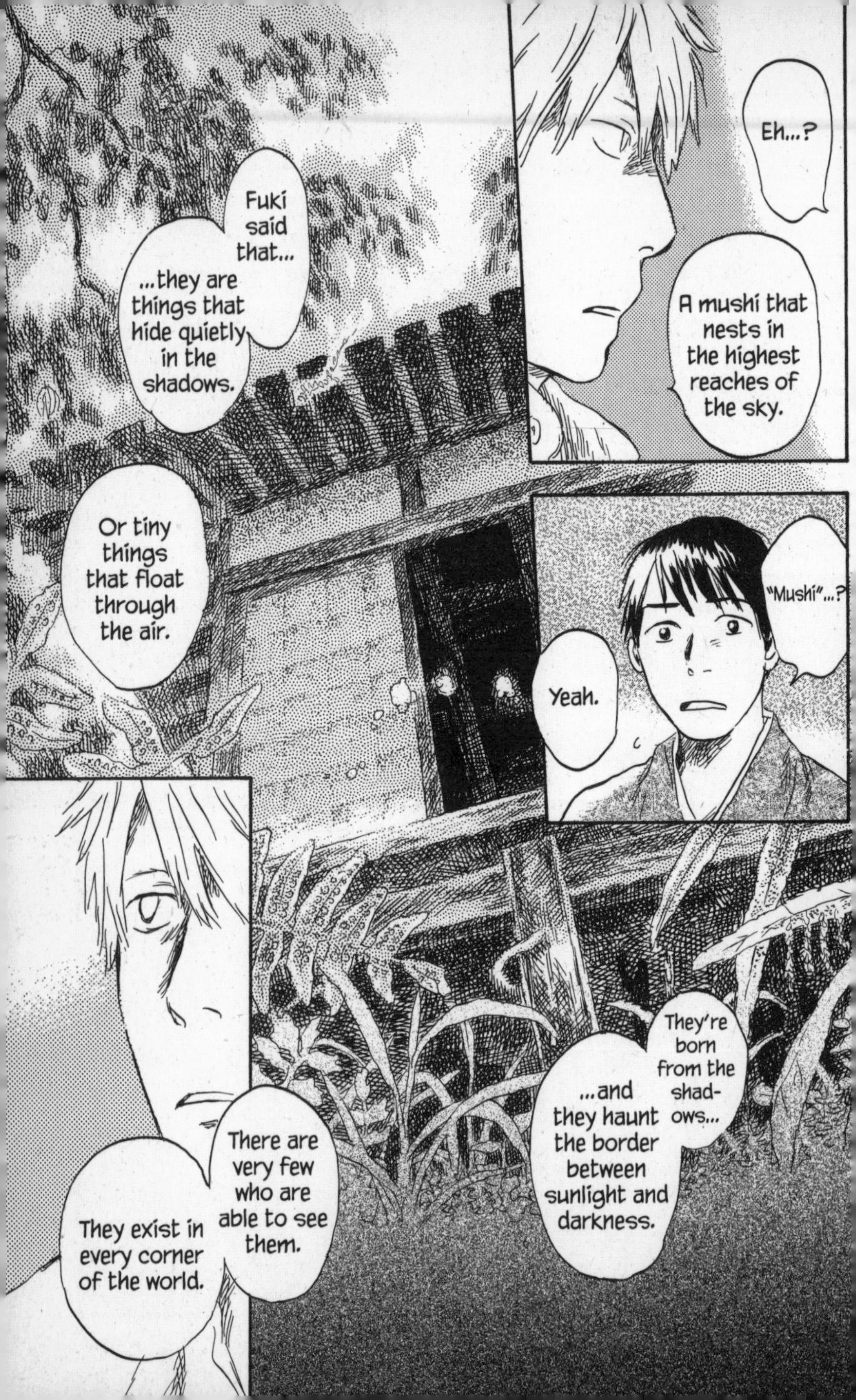
Eh...?
A mushi that nests in the highest reaches of the sky.
Fuki said that...
...they are things that hide quietly in the shadows.
Or tiny things that float through the air.
"Mushi"...?
Yeah.
They're born from the shadows...
...and they haunt the border between sunlight and darkness.
There are very few who are able to see them.
They exist in every corner of the world.

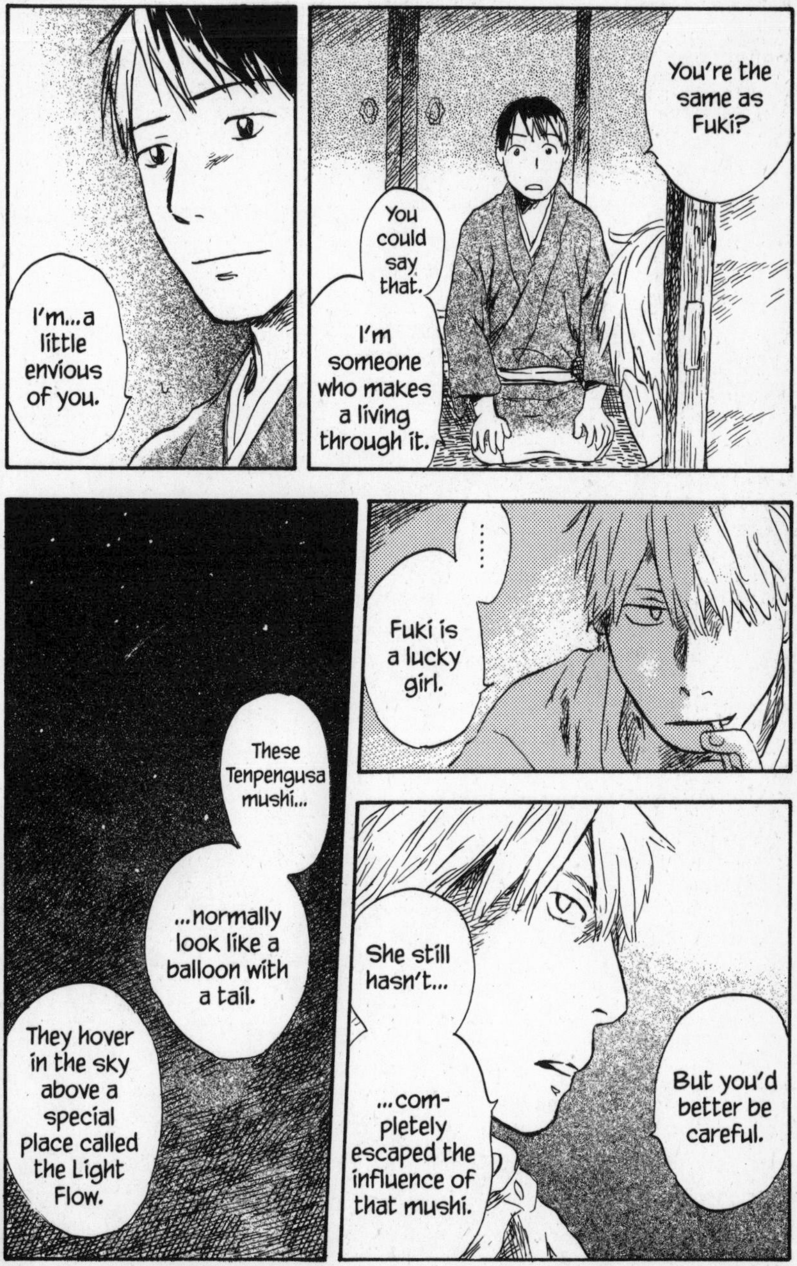
You're the same as Fuki?
You could say that.
I'm someone who makes a living through it.
I'm...a little envious of you.
......
Fuki is a lucky girl.
She still hasn't...
...com-pletely escaped the influence of that mushi.
But you'd better be careful.
These Tenpengusa mushi...
...normally look like a balloon with a tail.
They hover in the sky above a special place called the Light Flow.

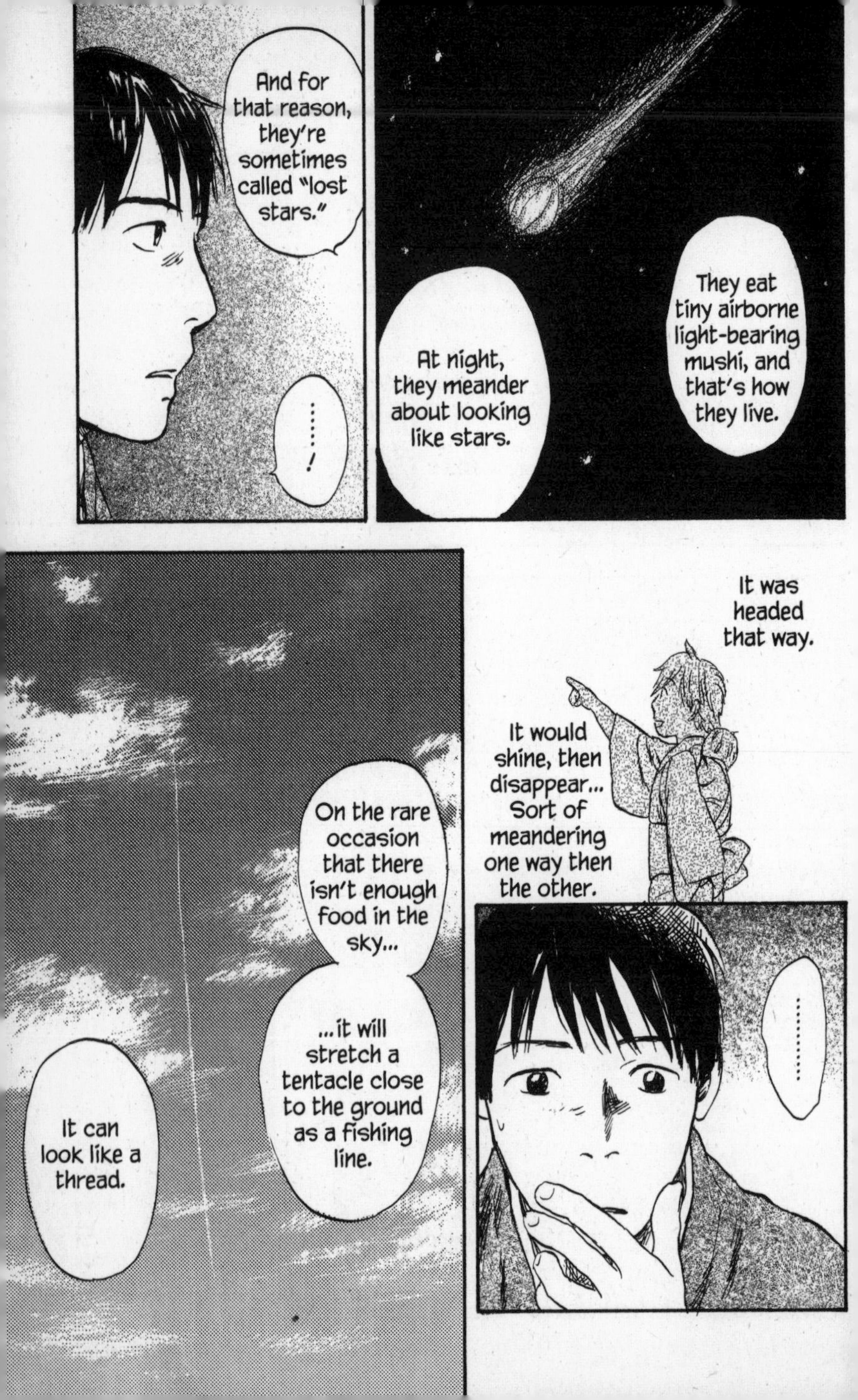
They eat tiny airborne light-bearing mushi, and that's how they live.
At night, they meander about looking like stars.
And for that reason, they're sometimes called "lost stars."
......!
It was headed that way.
It would shine, then disappear... Sort of meandering one way then the other.
....
On the rare occasion that there isn't enough food in the sky...
...it will stretch a tentacle close to the ground as a fishing line.
It can look like a thread.

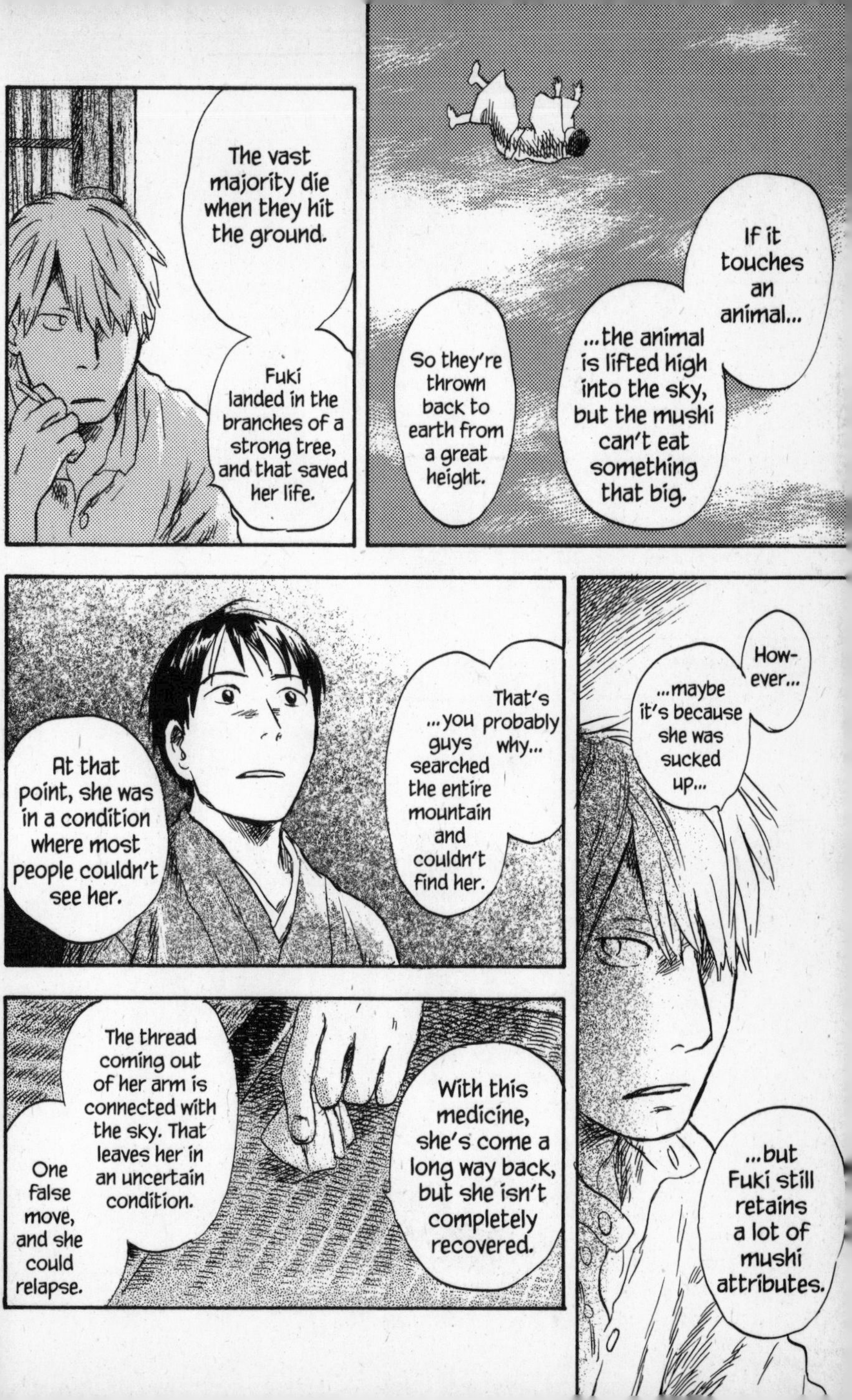
If it touches an animal...
...the animal is lifted high into the sky, but the mushi can't eat something that big.
So they're thrown back to earth from a great height.
The vast majority die when they hit the ground.
Fuki landed in the branches of a strong tree, and that saved her life.
However...
...maybe it's because she was sucked up...
...but Fuki still retains a lot of mushi attributes.
That's probably why...
...you guys searched the entire mountain and couldn't find her.
At that point, she was in a condition where most people couldn't see her.
With this medicine, she's come a long way back, but she isn't completely recovered.
The thread coming out of her arm is connected with the sky. That leaves her in an uncertain condition.
One false move, and she could relapse.

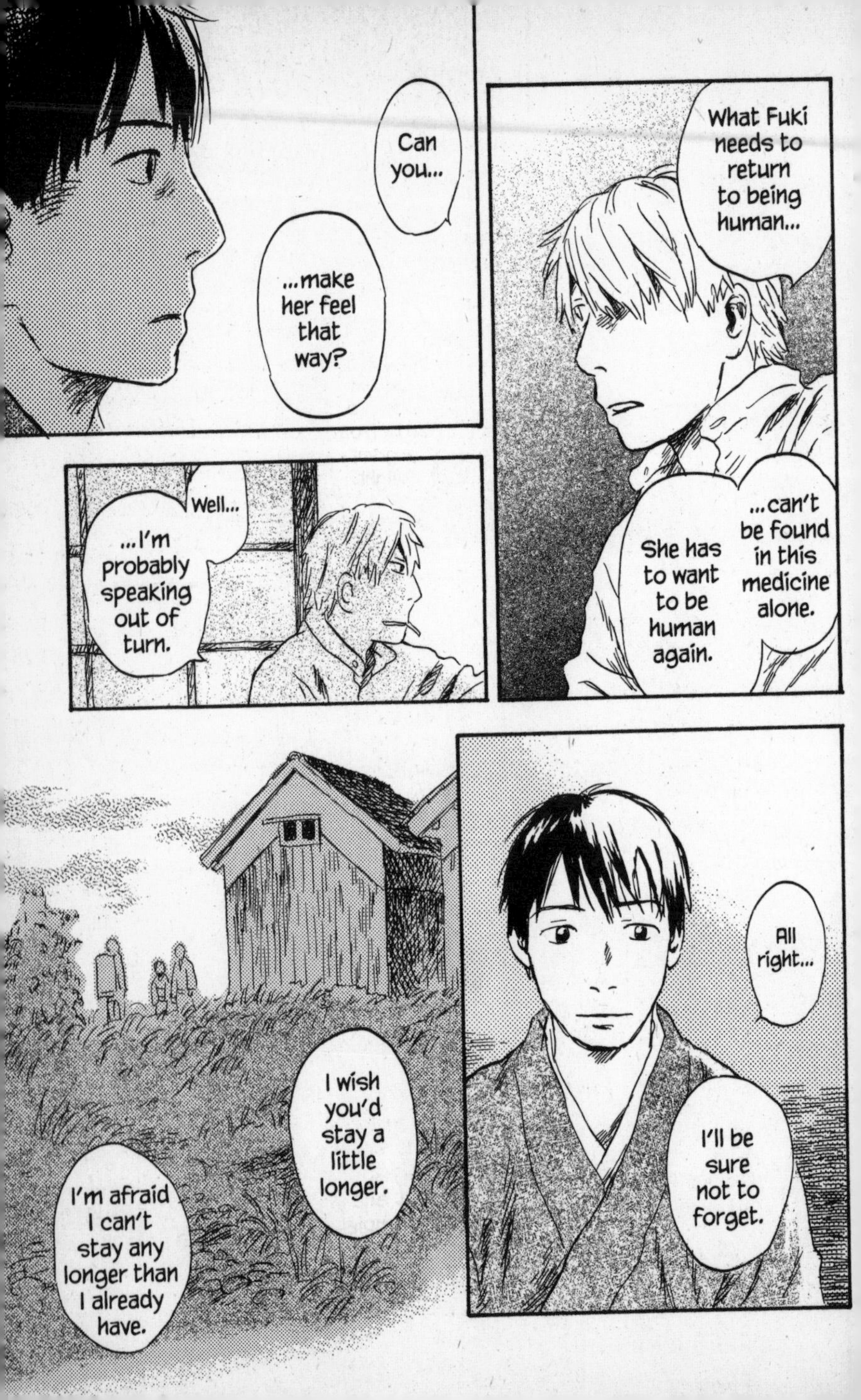
What Fuki needs to return to being human...
...can't be found in this medicine alone.
She has to want to be human again.
Can you...
...make her feel that way?
Well...
...I'm probably speaking out of turn.
All right...
I'll be sure not to forget.
I wish you'd stay a little longer.
I'm afraid I can't stay any longer than I already have.

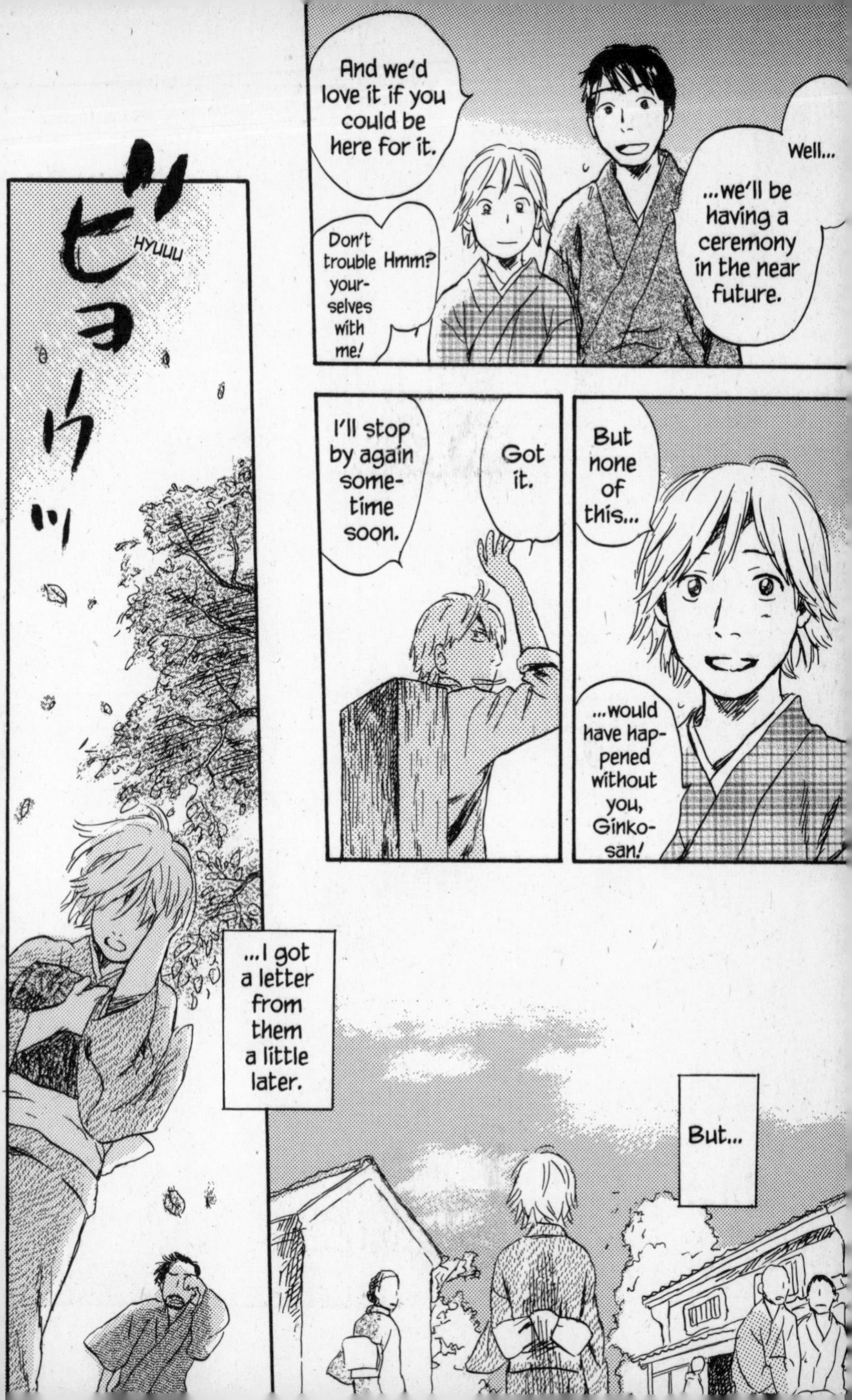
Well...
...we'll be having a ceremony in the near future.
And we'd love it if you could be here for it.
Hmm?
Don't trouble yourselves with me!
But none of this...
...would have happened without you, Ginko-san!
Got it.
I'll stop by again sometime soon.
But...
...I got a letter from them a little later.
HYUUU

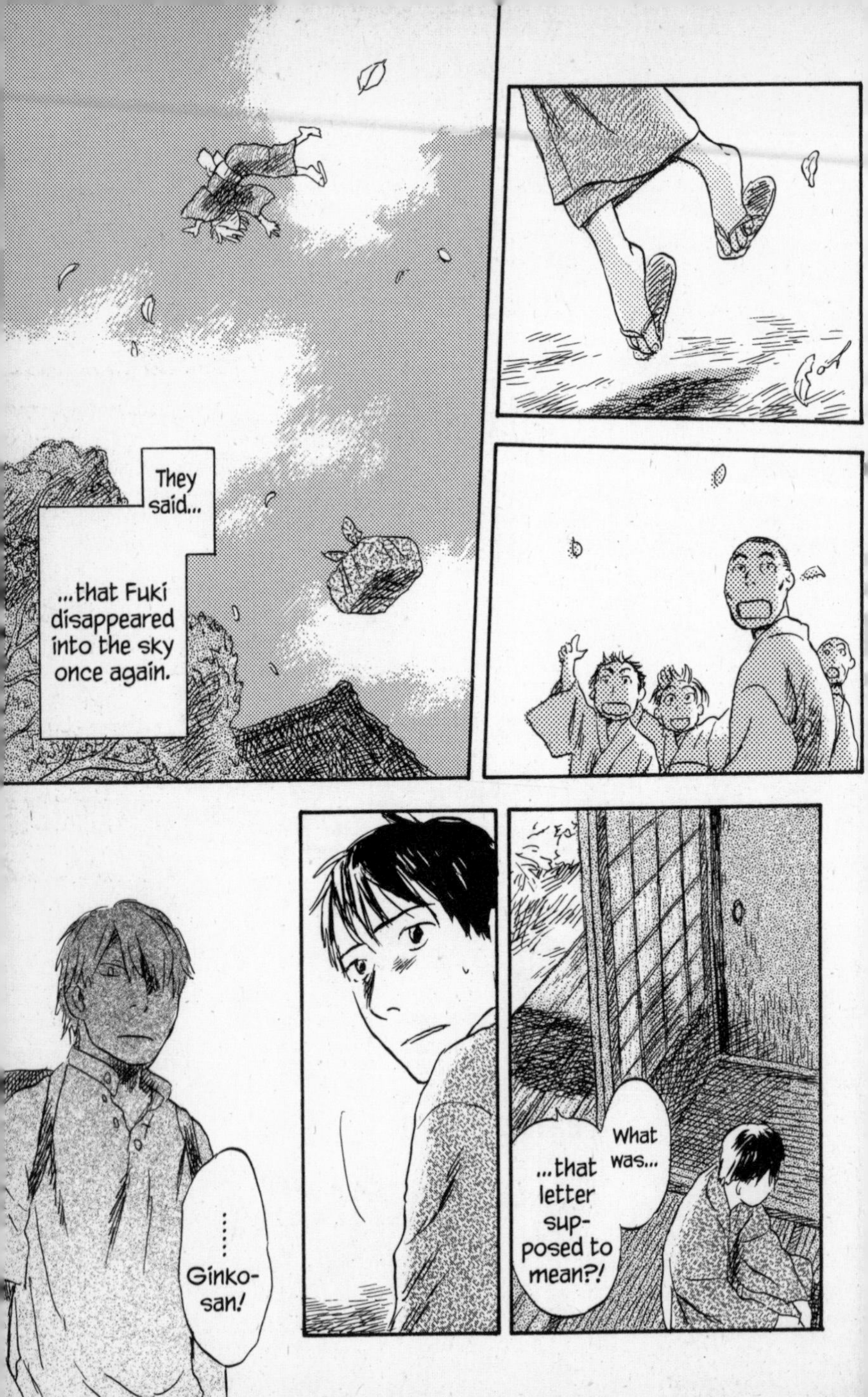
They said...
...that Fuki disappeared into the sky once again.
What was...
...that letter sup-posed to mean?!
...... Ginko-san!

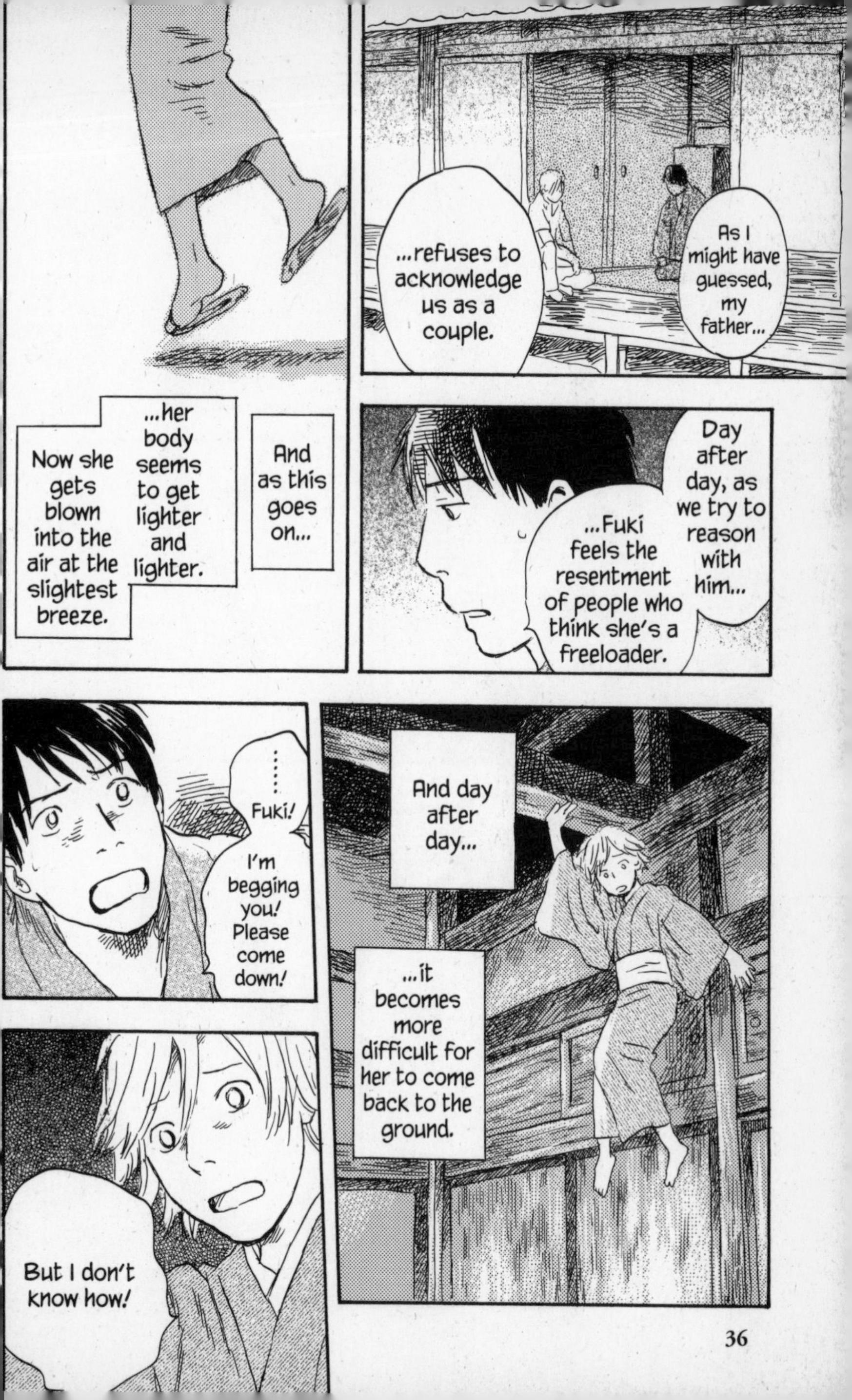
As I might have guessed, my father...
...refuses to acknowledge us as a couple.
Day after day, as we try to reason with him...
...Fuki feels the resentment of people who think she's a freeloader.
And as this goes on...
...her body seems to get lighter and lighter.
Now she gets blown into the air at the slightest breeze.
And day after day...
...it becomes more difficult for her to come back to the ground.
......
Fuki!
I'm begging you! Please come down!
But I don't know how!

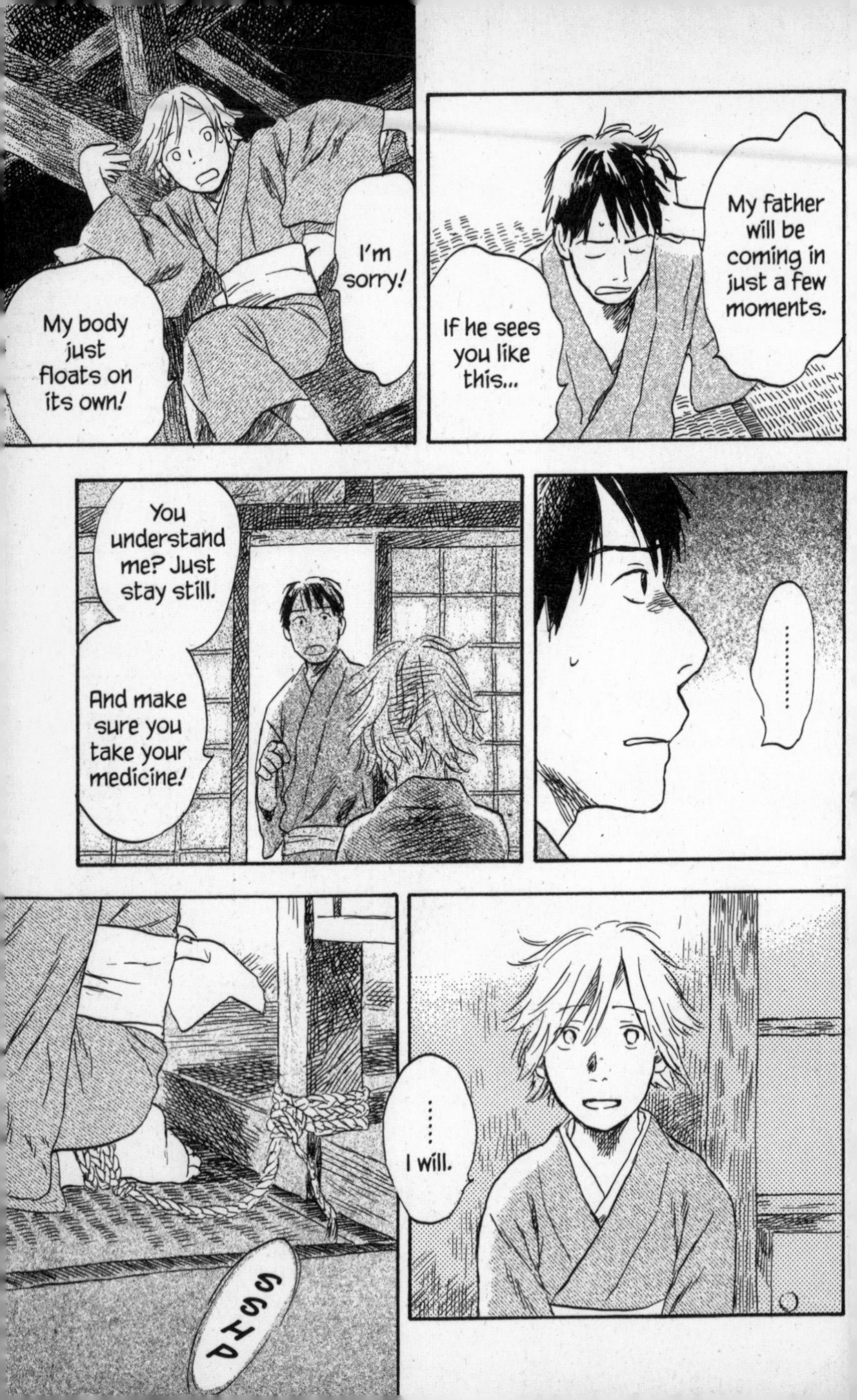
My father will be coming in just a few moments.
If he sees you like this...
I'm sorry!
My body just floats on its own!
......
You understand me? Just stay still.
And make sure you take your medicine!
...... I will.
SSHP

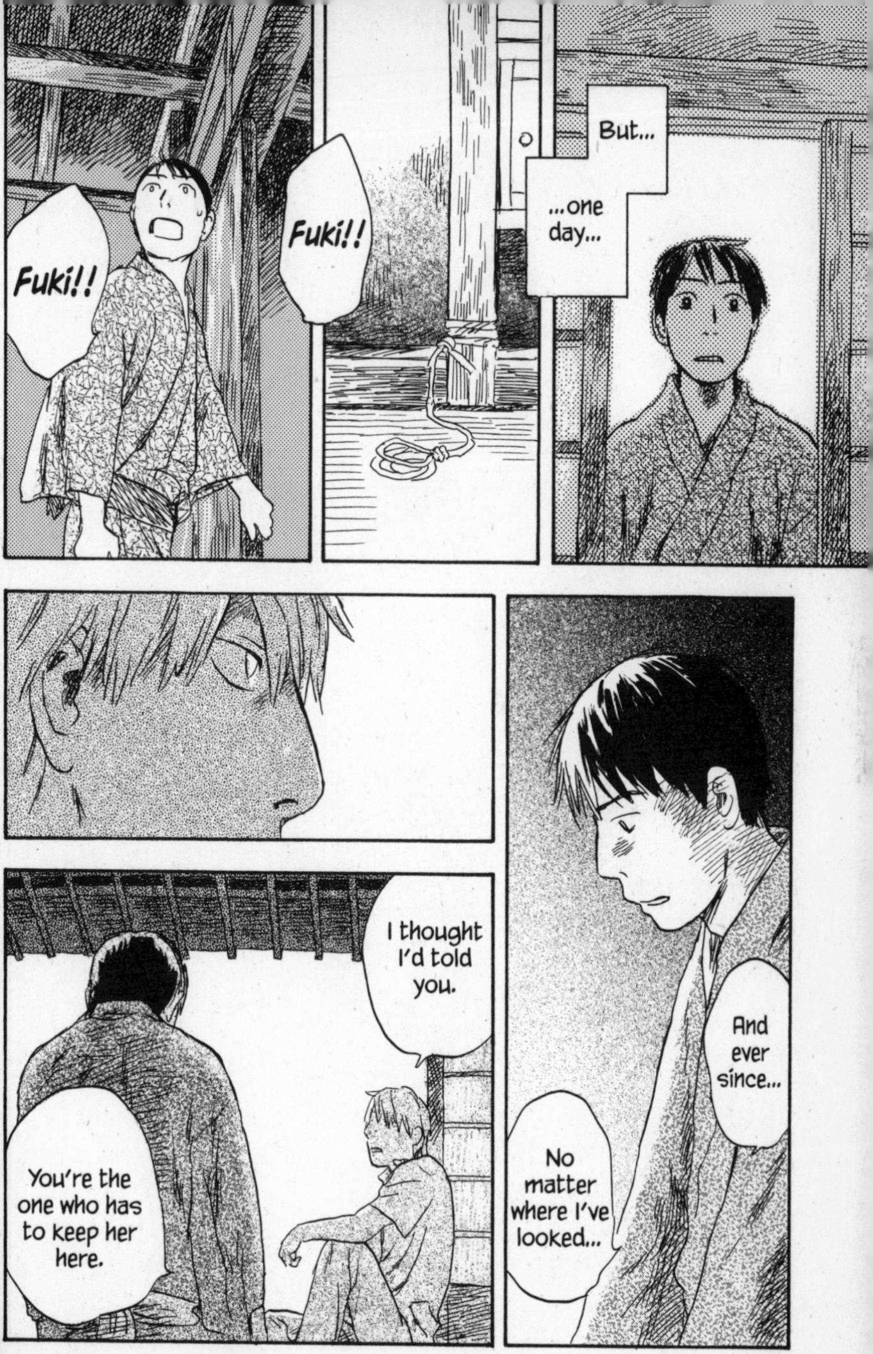

But...
...one day...
Fuki!!
Fuki!!
And ever since...
No matter where I've looked...
I thought I'd told you.
You're the one who has to keep her here.

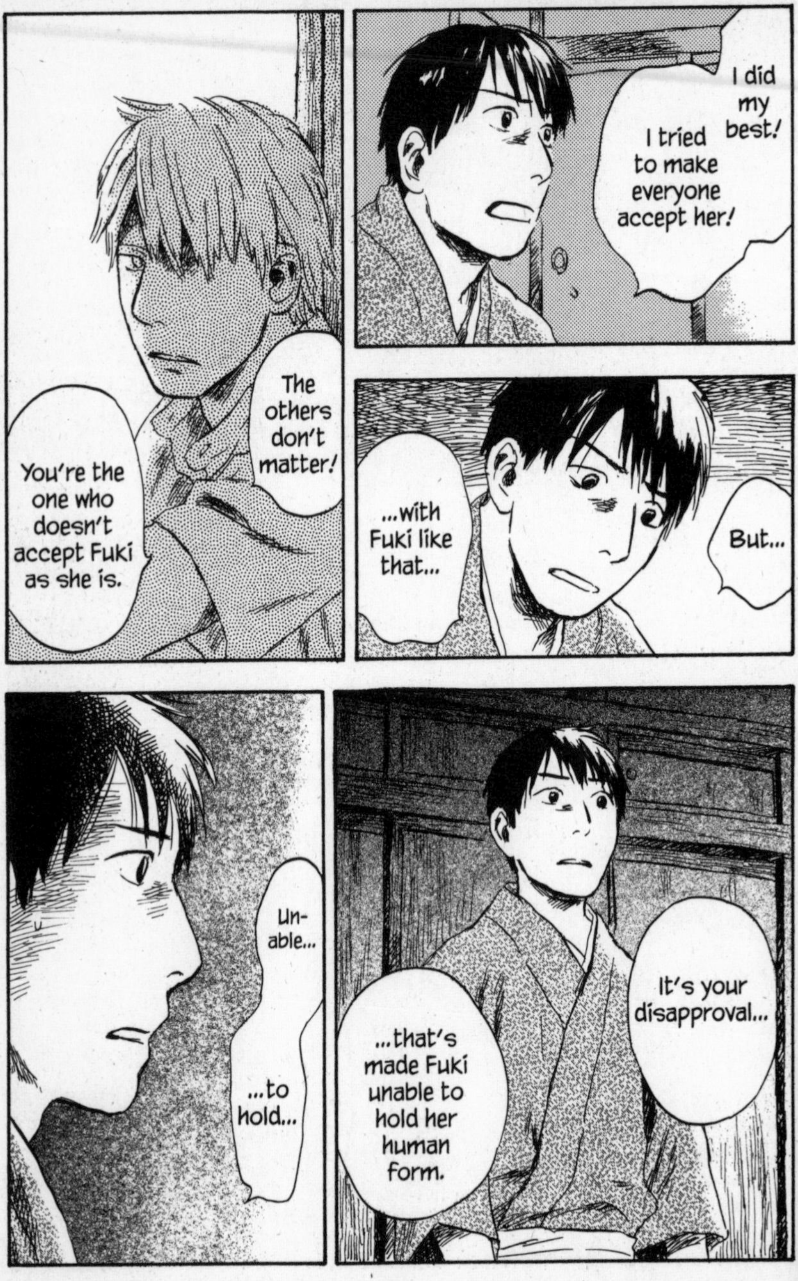

I did my best!
I tried to make everyone accept her!
But...
...with Fuki like that...
The others don't matter!
You're the one who doesn't accept Fuki as she is.
It's your disapproval...
...that's made Fuki unable to hold her human form.
Un-able...
...to hold...

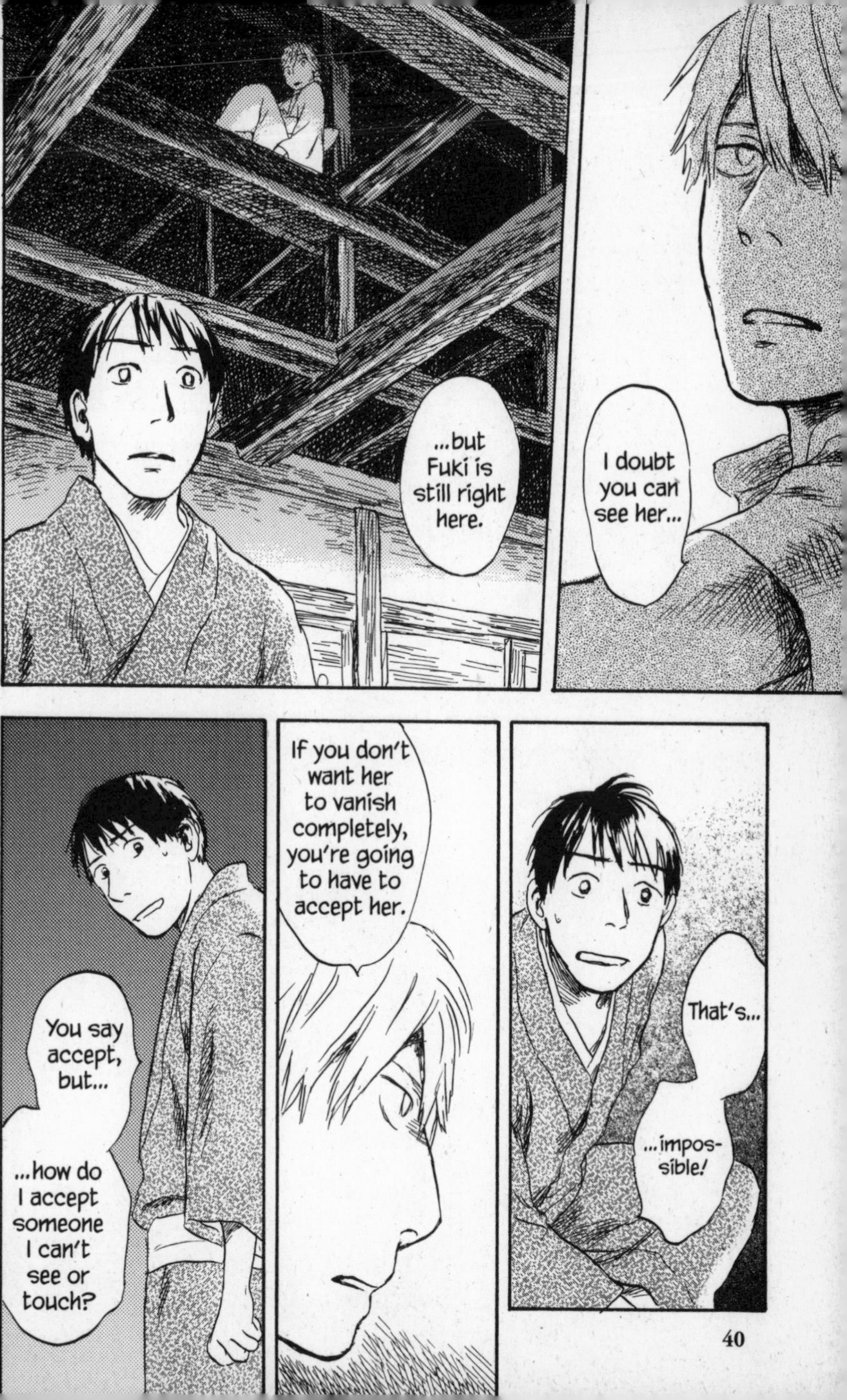
I doubt you can see her...
...but Fuki is still right here.
That's...
...impos-sible!
If you don't want her to vanish completely, you're going to have to accept her.
You say accept, but...
...how do I accept someone I can't see or touch?

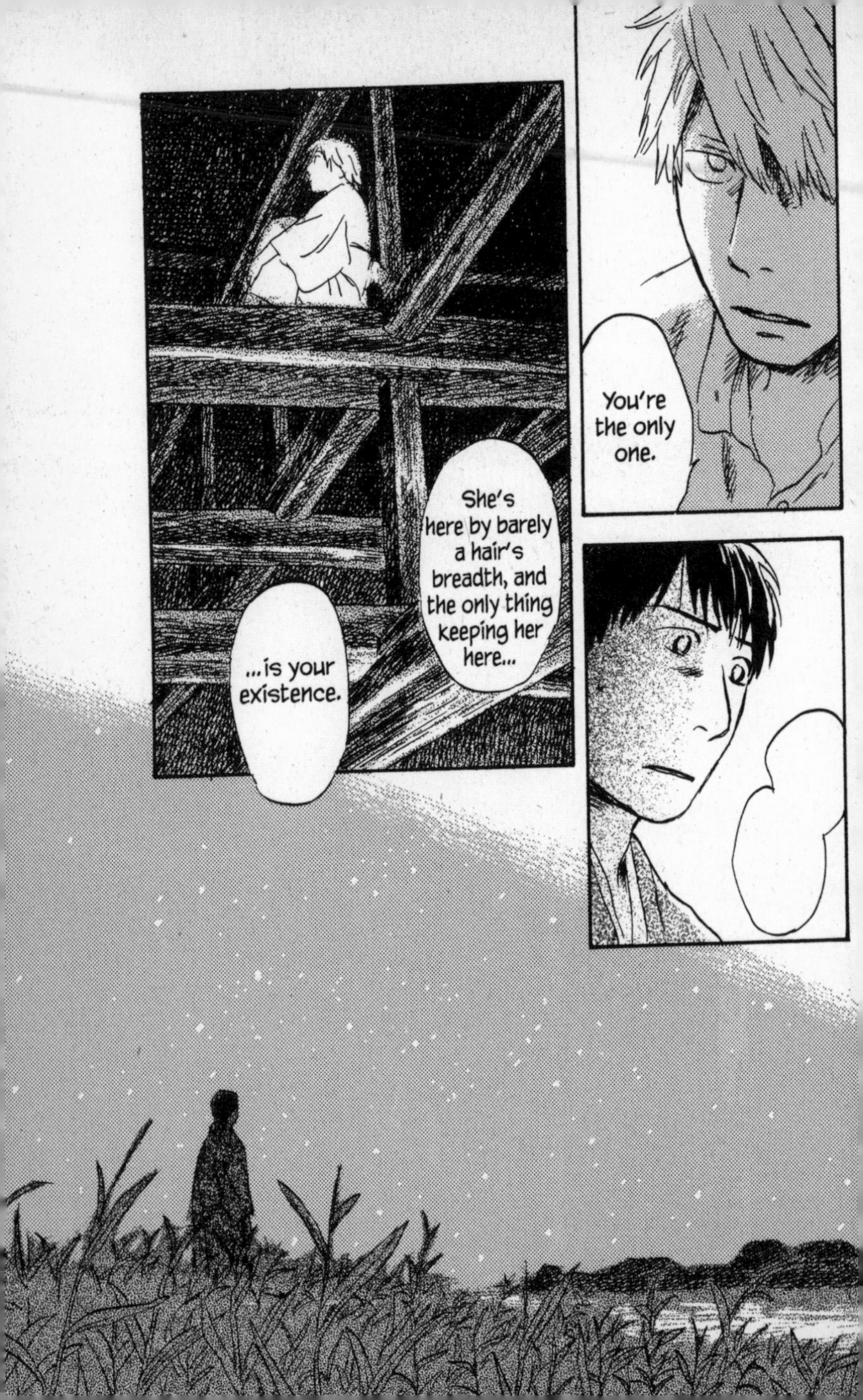
You're the only one.
She's here by barely a hair's breadth, and the only thing keeping her here...
...is your existence.

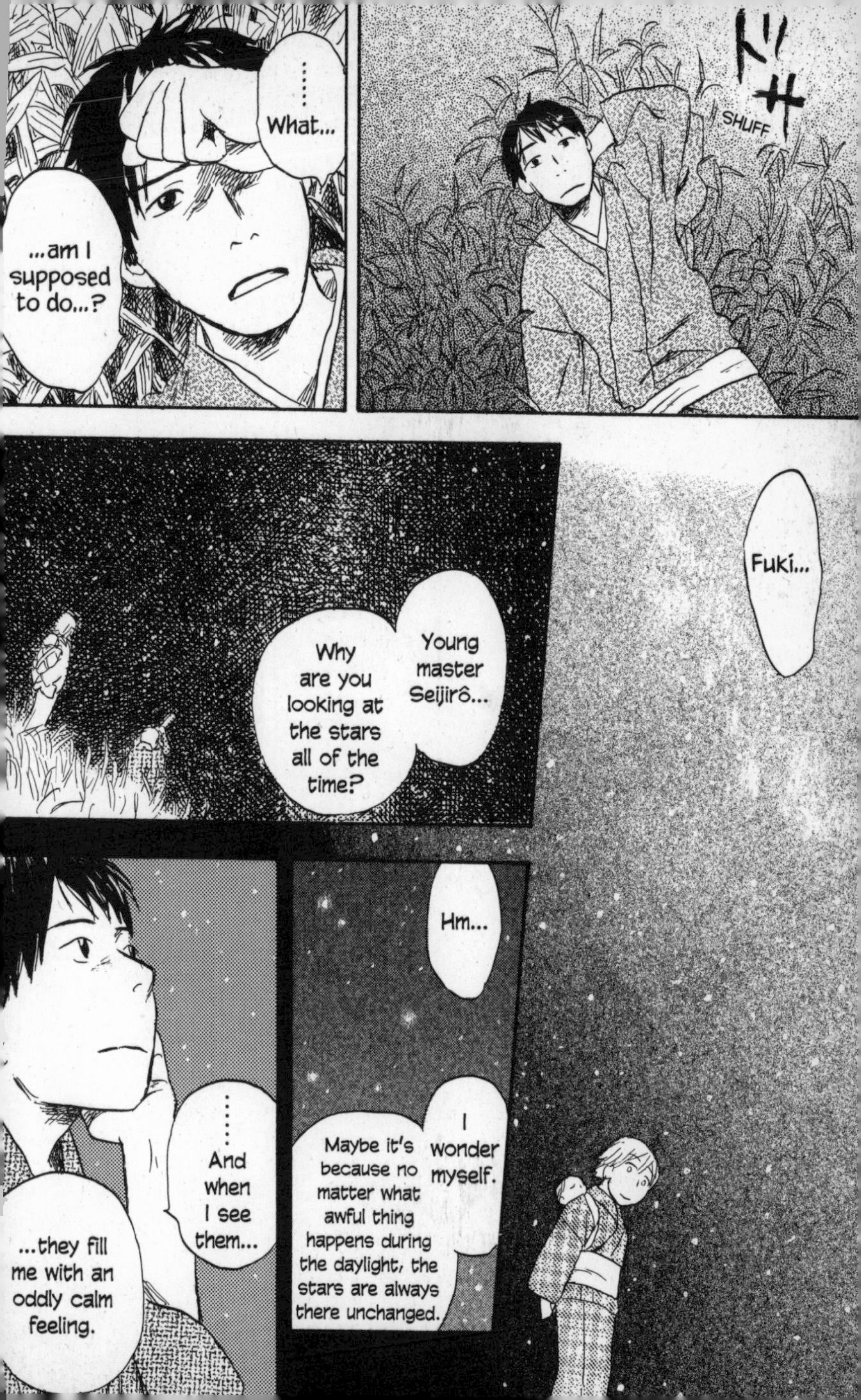

ドサ
SHUFF
......What...
...am I supposed to do...?
Fuki...
Young master Seijirô...
Why are you looking at the stars all of the time?
Hm...
I wonder myself.
Maybe it's because no matter what awful thing happens during the daylight, the stars are always there unchanged.
......And when I see them...
...they fill me with an oddly calm feeling.

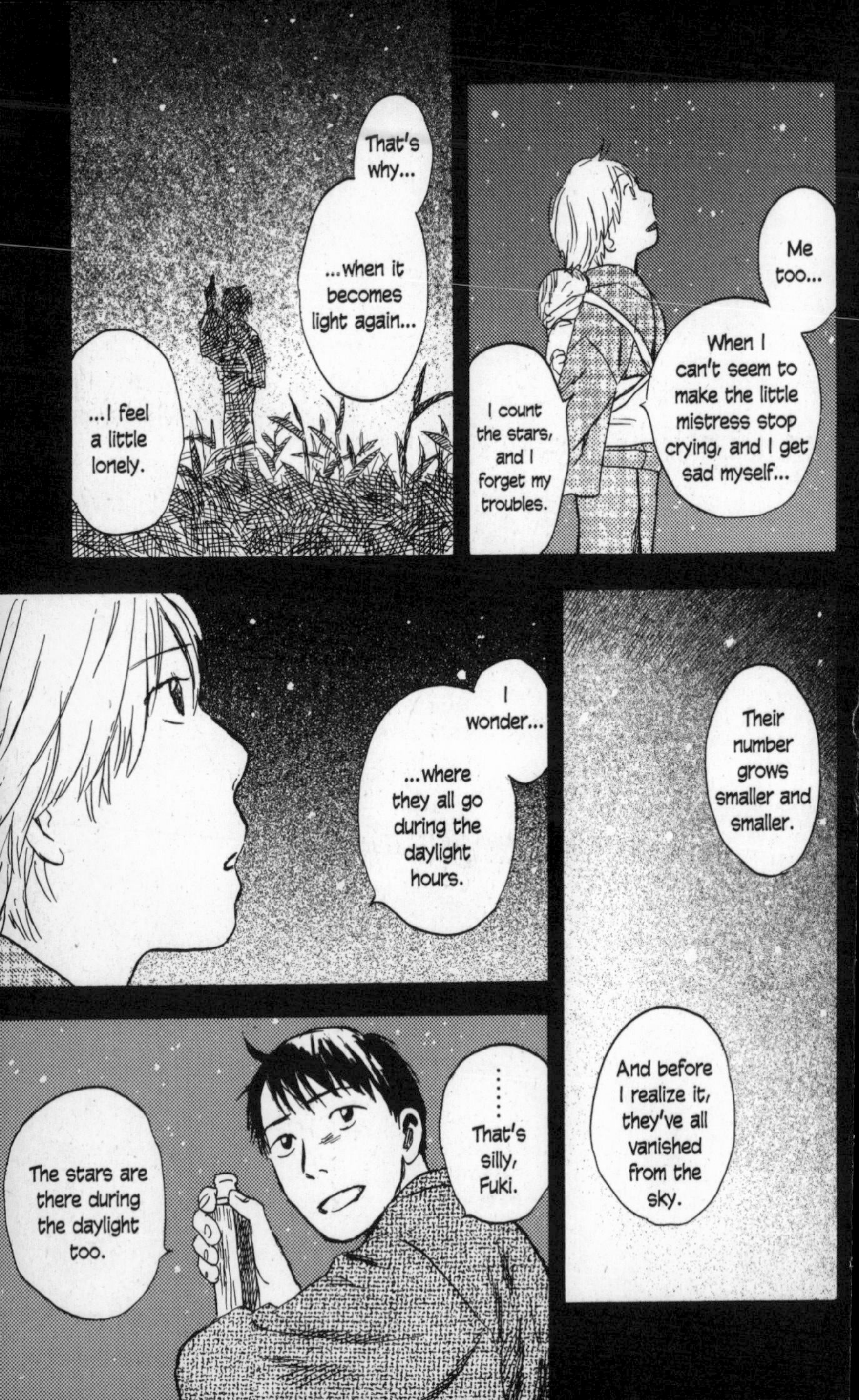
Me too...
When I can't seem to make the little mistress stop crying, and I get sad myself...
I count the stars, and I forget my troubles.
That's why...
...when it becomes light again...
...I feel a little lonely.
Their number grows smaller and smaller.
And before I realize it, they've all vanished from the sky.
I wonder...
...where they all go during the daylight hours.
......
That's silly, Fuki.
The stars are there during the daylight too.

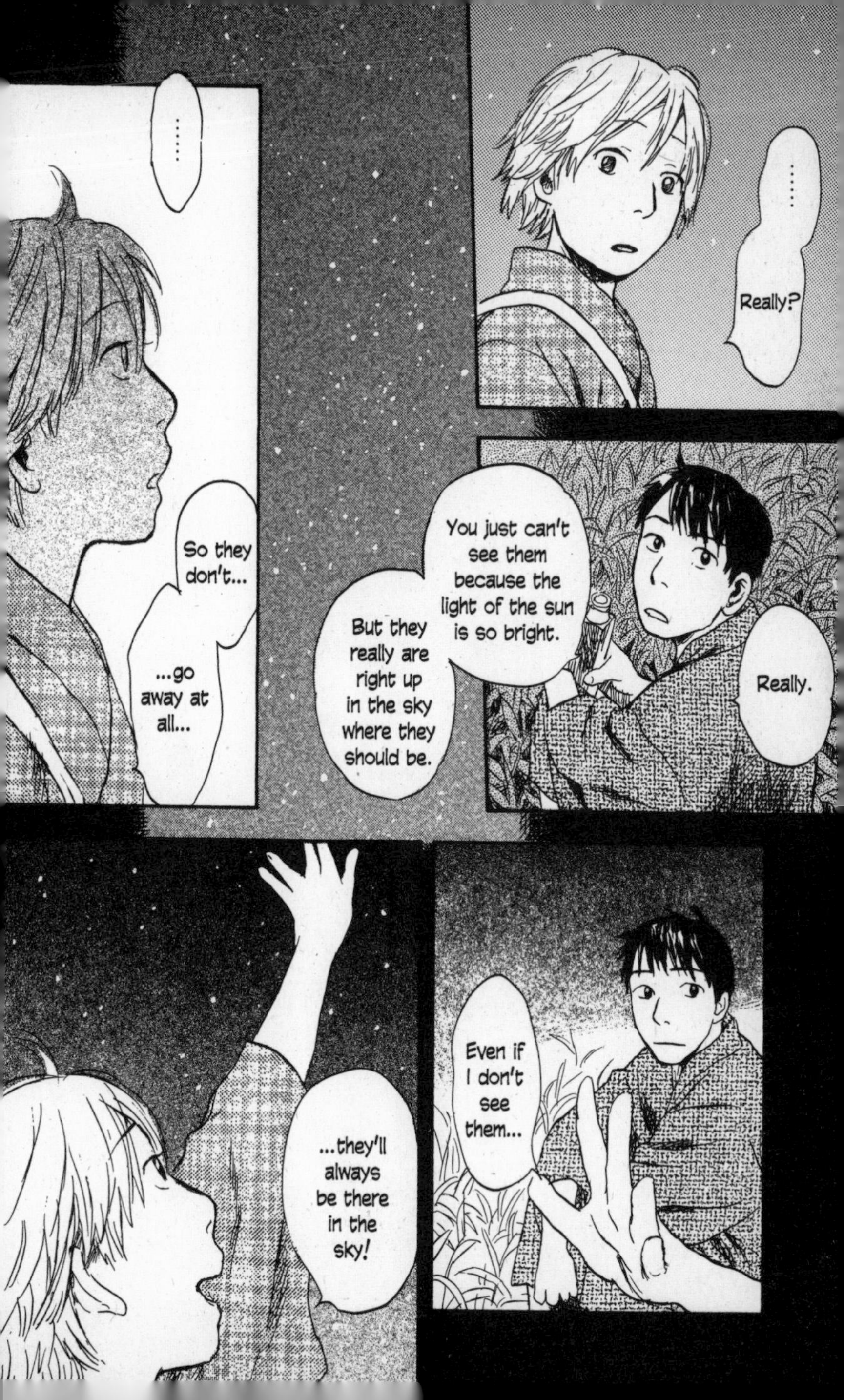
……
Really?
Really.
You just can't see them because the light of the sun is so bright.
But they really are right up in the sky where they should be.
……
So they don't...
...go away at all...
Even if I don't see them...
...they'll always be there in the sky!

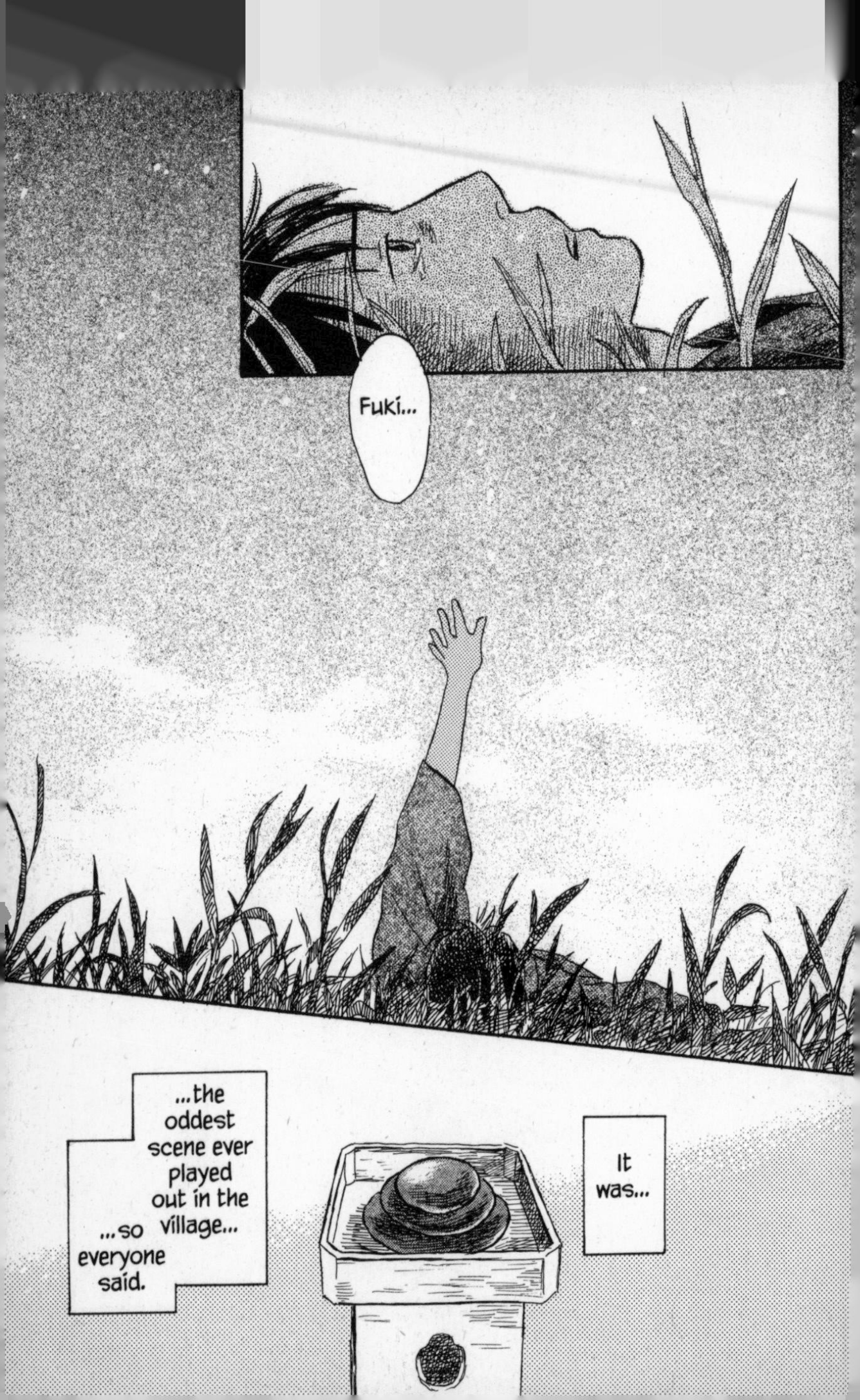
Fuki...
It was...
...the oddest scene ever played out in the village...
...so everyone said.

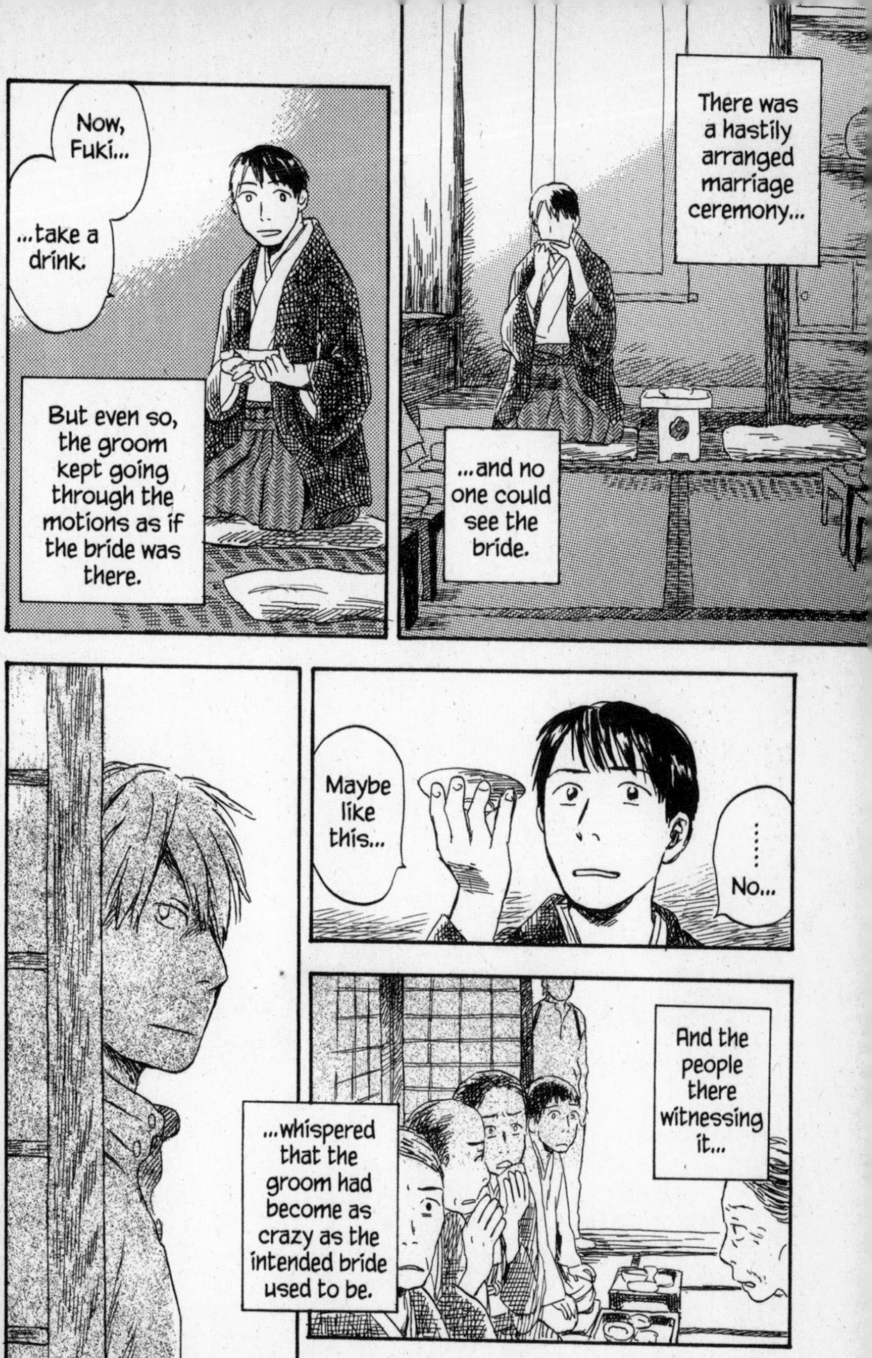
There was a hastily arranged marriage ceremony...
...and no one could see the bride.
Now, Fuki...
...take a drink.
But even so, the groom kept going through the motions as if the bride was there.
Maybe like this...
...... No...
And the people there witnessing it...
...whispered that the groom had become as crazy as the intended bride used to be.

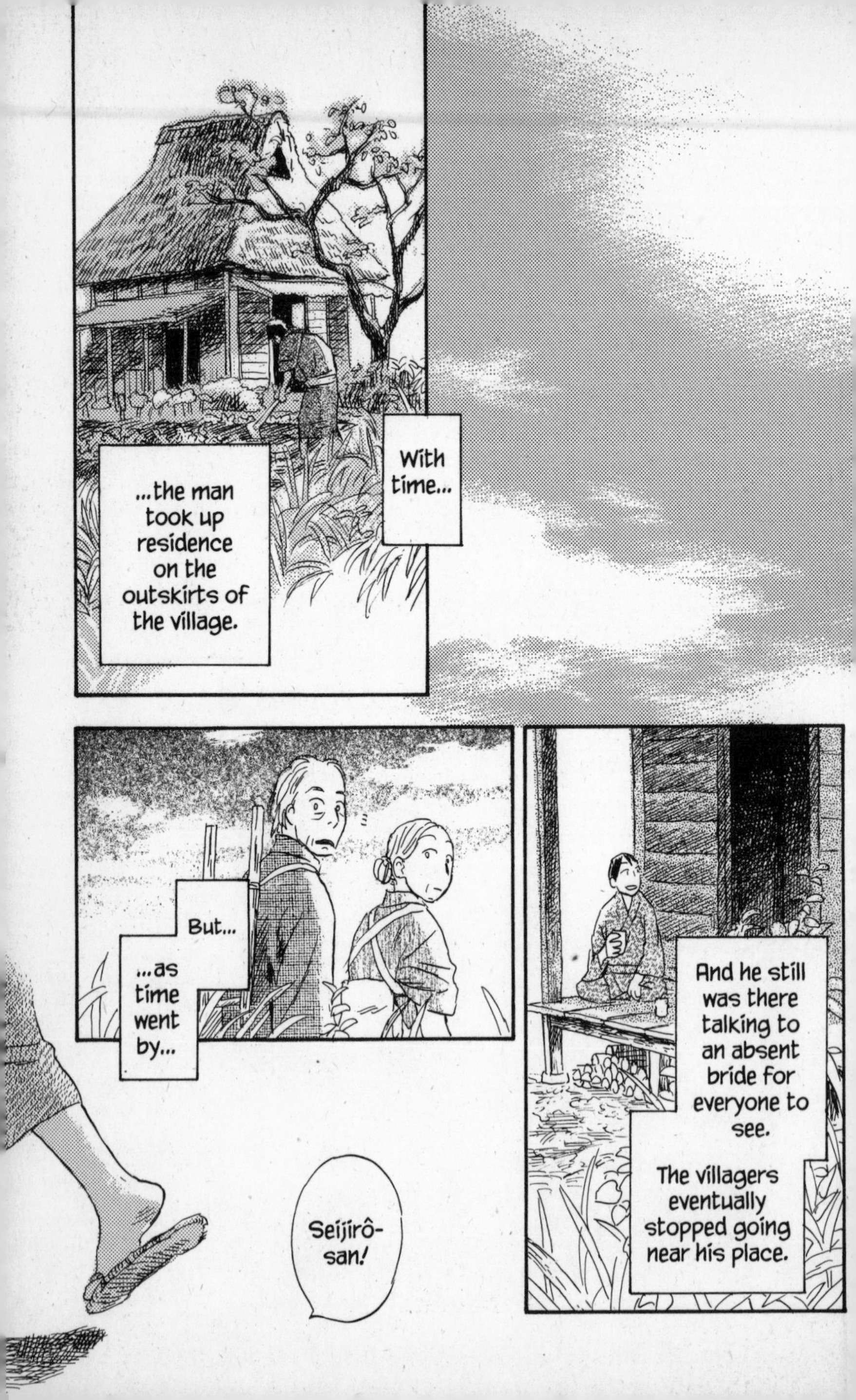
With time...
...the man took up residence on the outskirts of the village.
And he still was there talking to an absent bride for everyone to see.
The villagers eventually stopped going near his place.
But...
...as time went by...
Seijirô-san!

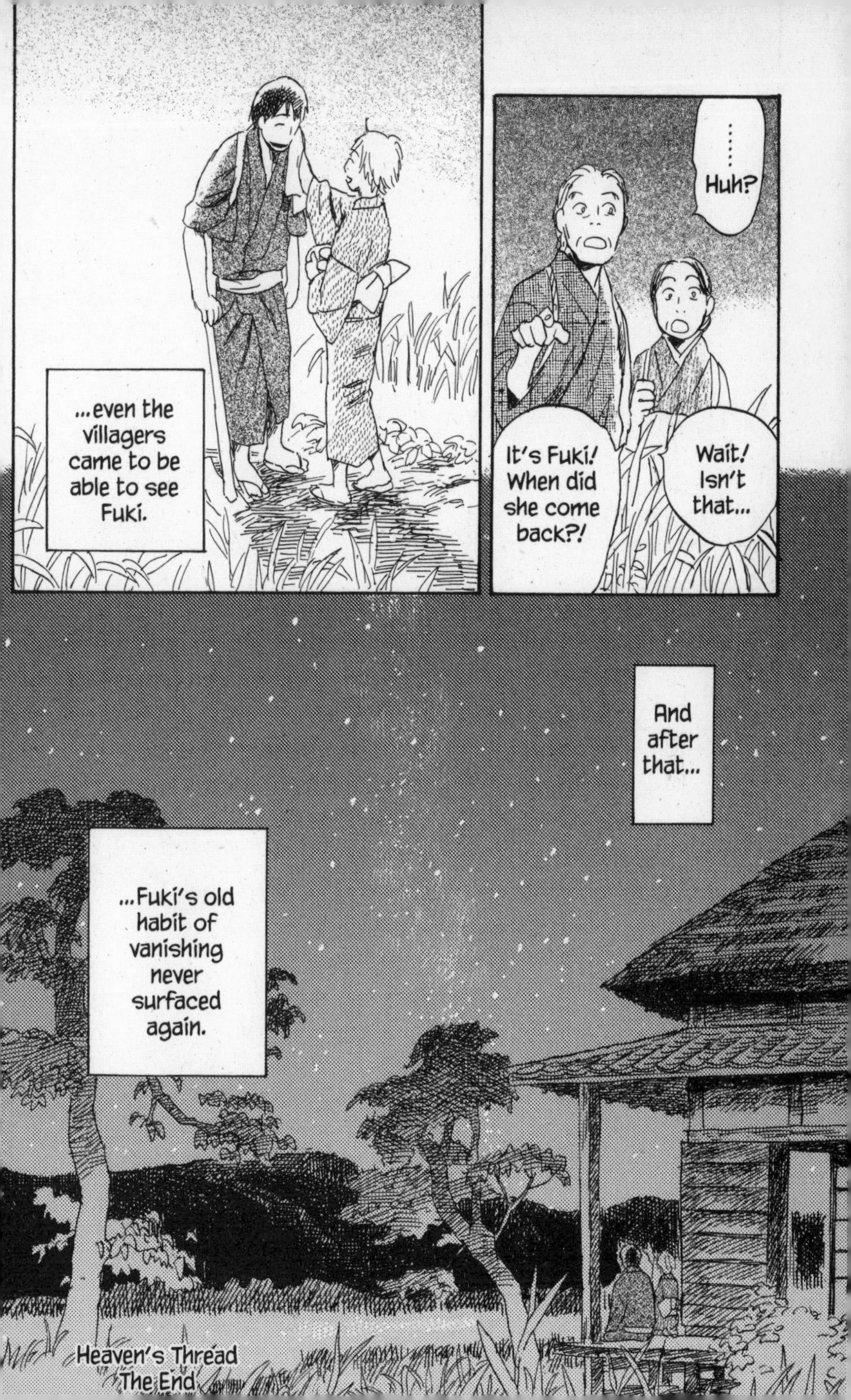

......Huh?
Wait! Isn't that...
It's Fuki! When did she come back?!
...even the villagers came to be able to see Fuki.
And after that...
...Fuki's old habit of vanishing never surfaced again.
Heaven's Thread The End

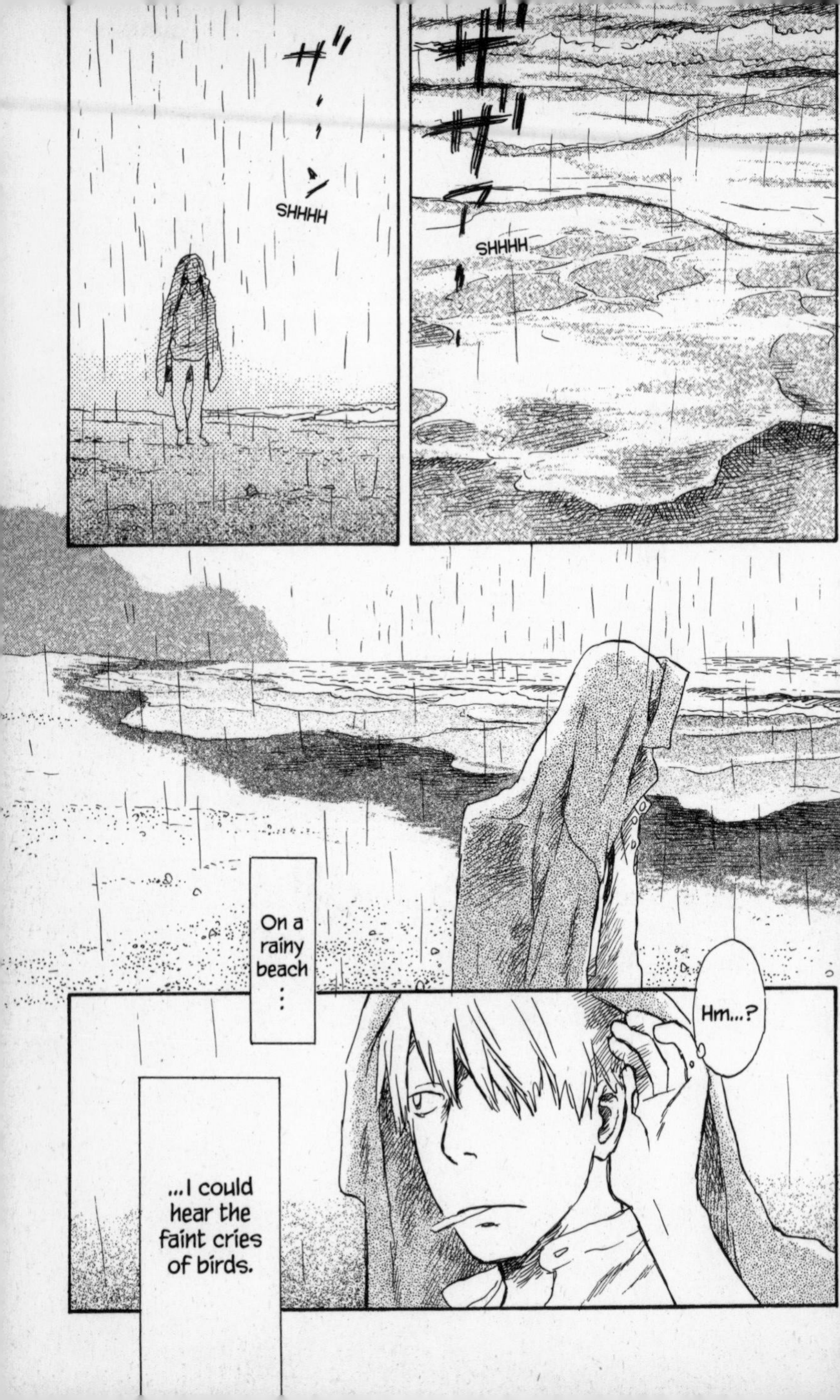
SHHHH
SHHHH
On a rainy beach...
Hm...?
...I could hear the faint cries of birds.

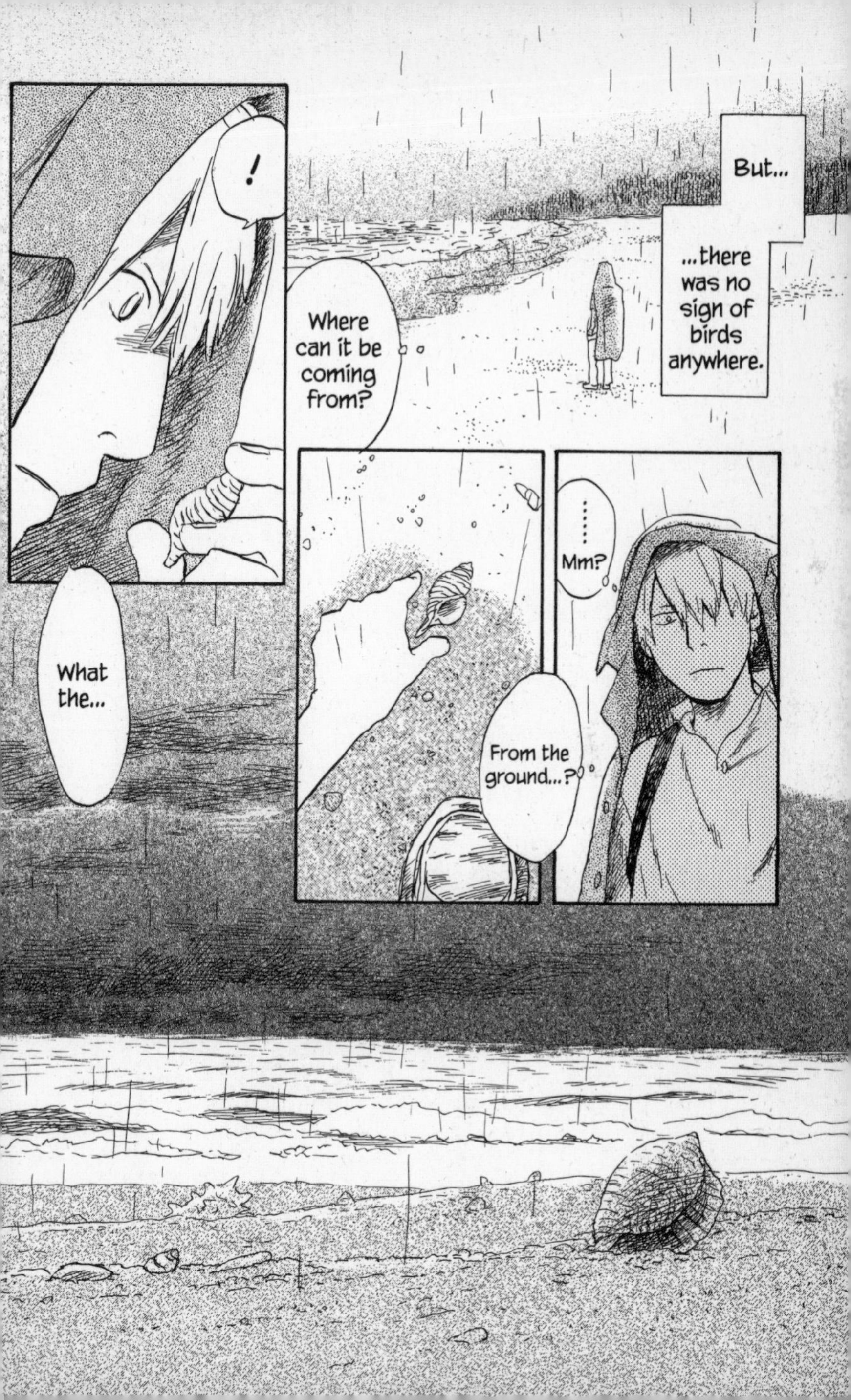
But...
...there was no sign of birds anywhere.
Where can it be coming from?
!
......
Mm?
From the ground...?
What the...

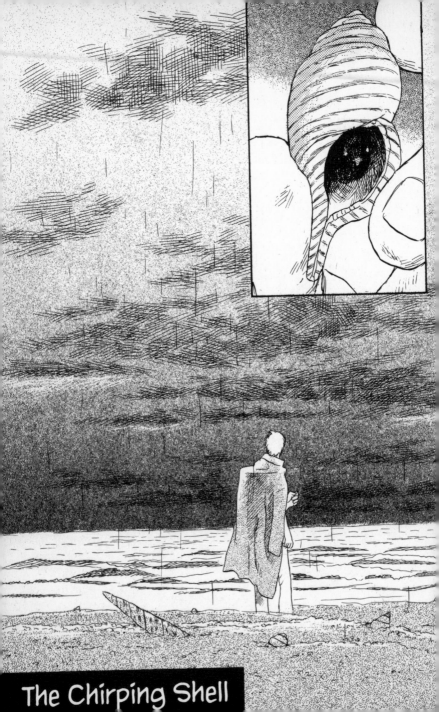

The Chirping Shell

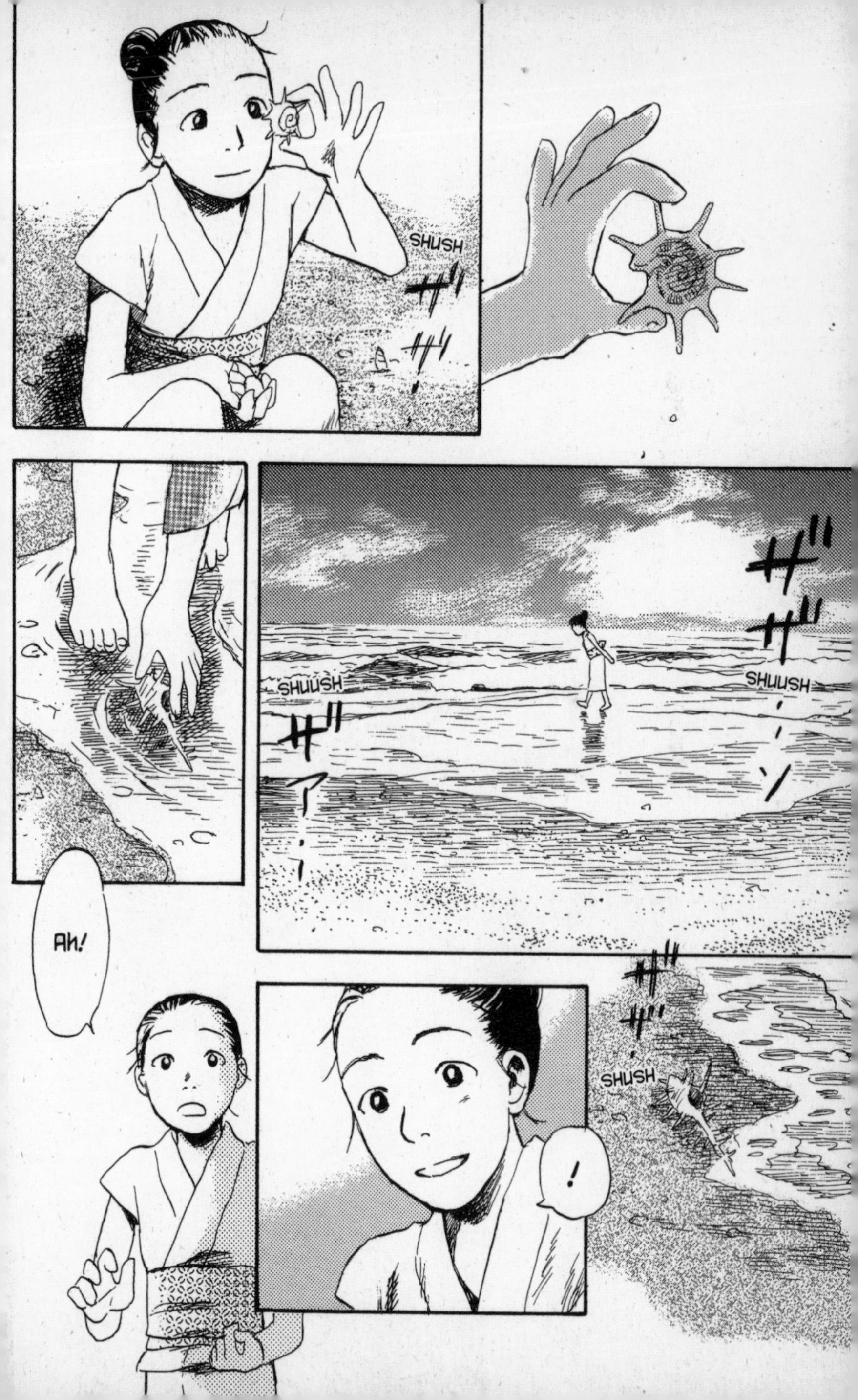
SHUSH
SHUUSH
SHUUSH
SHUSH
!
Ah!

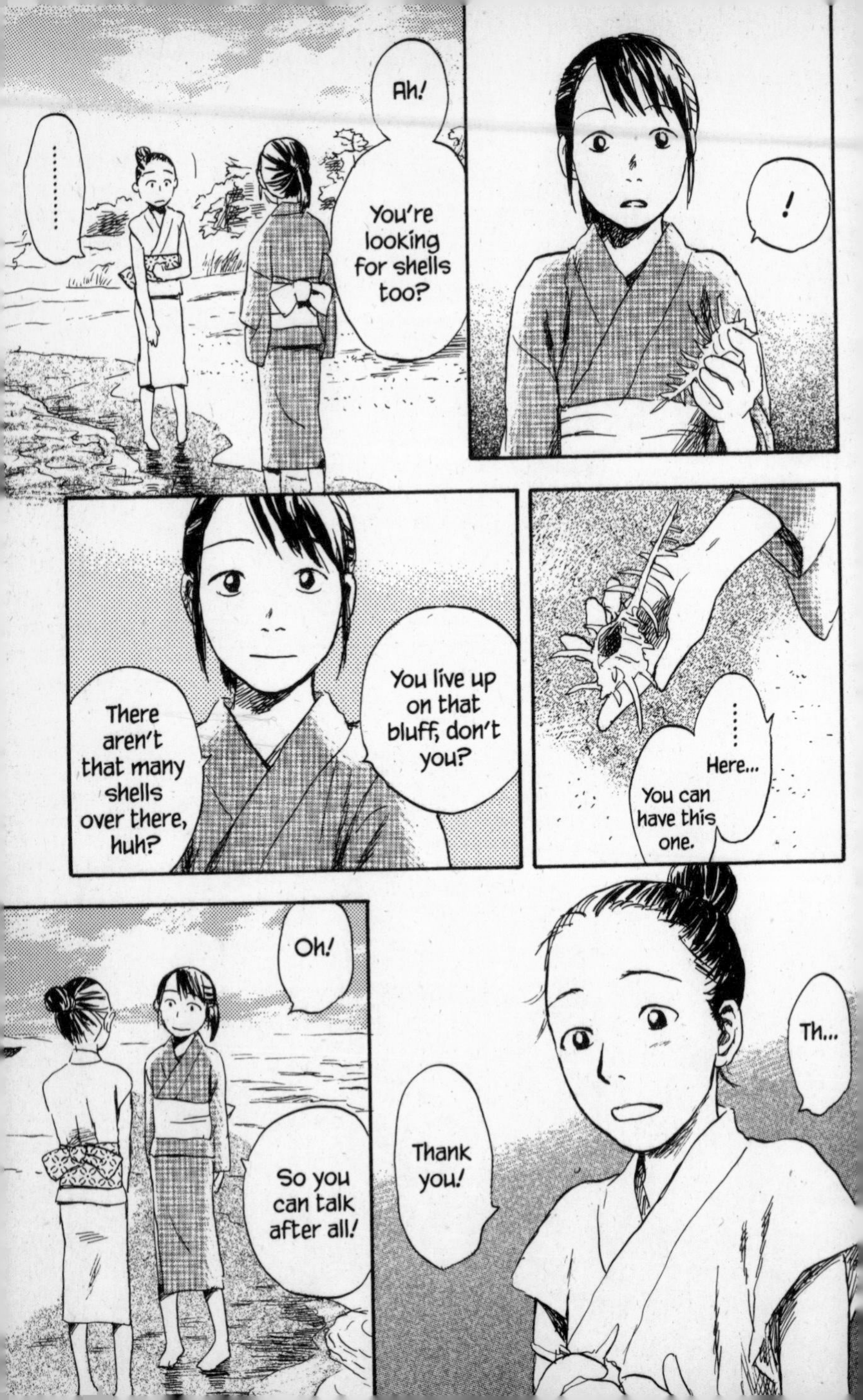
!
Ah!
You're looking for shells too?
......
......
Here...
You can have this one.
You live up on that bluff, don't you?
There aren't that many shells over there, huh?
Th...
Thank you!
Oh!
So you can talk after all!

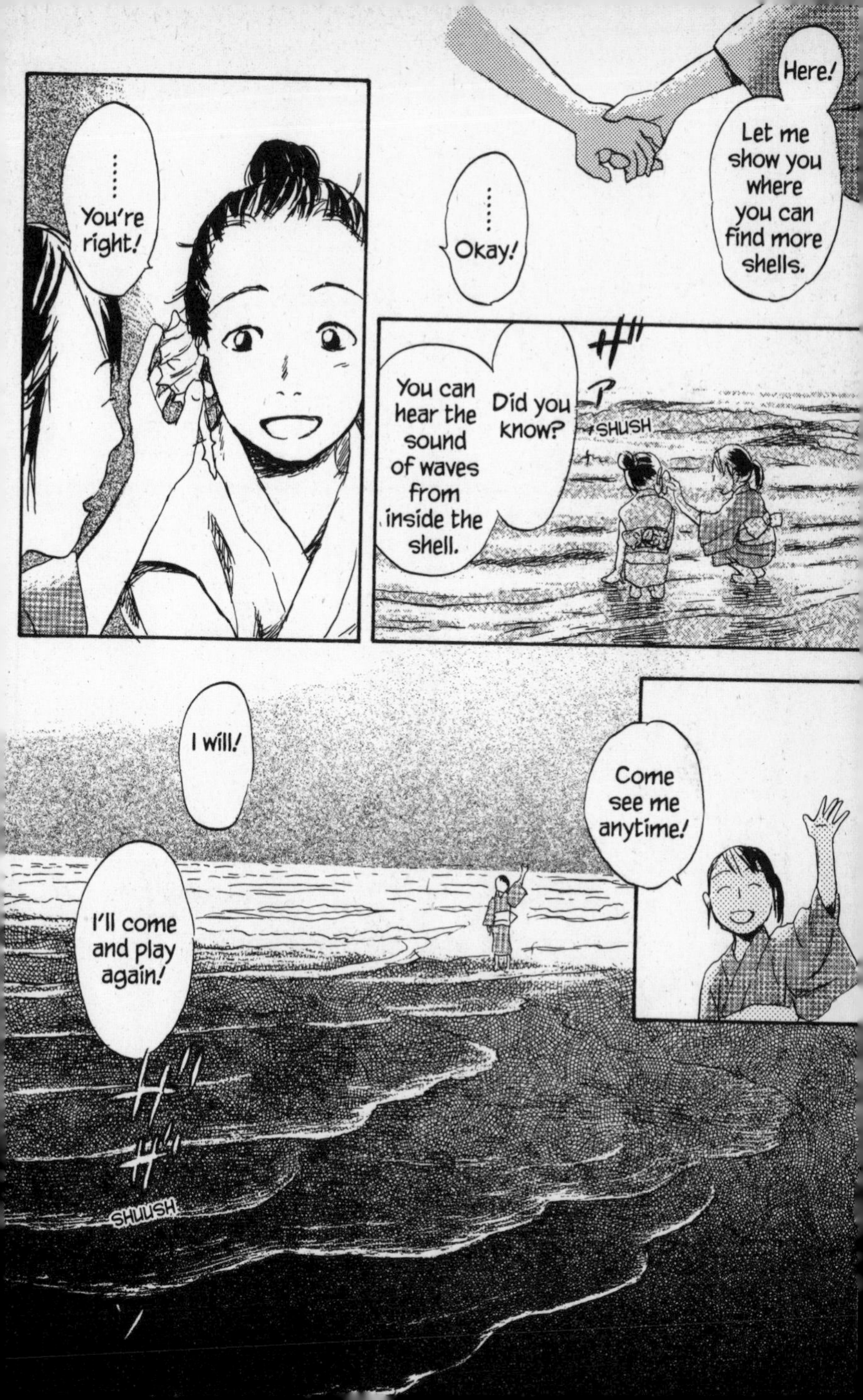
Here!
Let me show you where you can find more shells.
...... Okay!
Did you know?
You can hear the sound of waves from inside the shell.
SHUSH
...... You're right!
Come see me anytime!
I will!
I'll come and play again!
SHUUSH

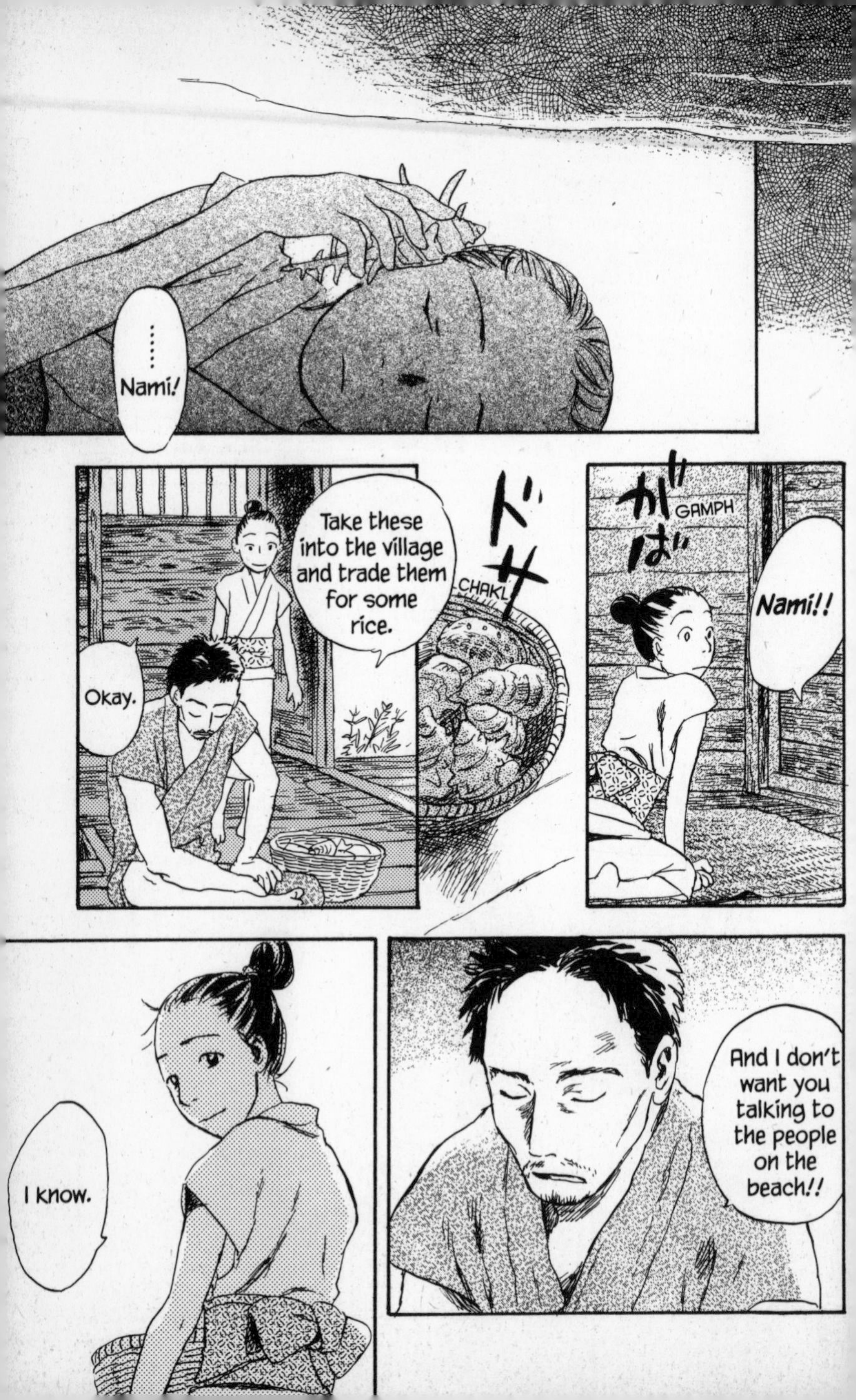
……
Nami!
がば
GAMPH
Nami!!
ドサ
CHAKL
Take these into the village and trade them for some rice.
Okay.
And I don't want you talking to the people on the beach!!
I know.

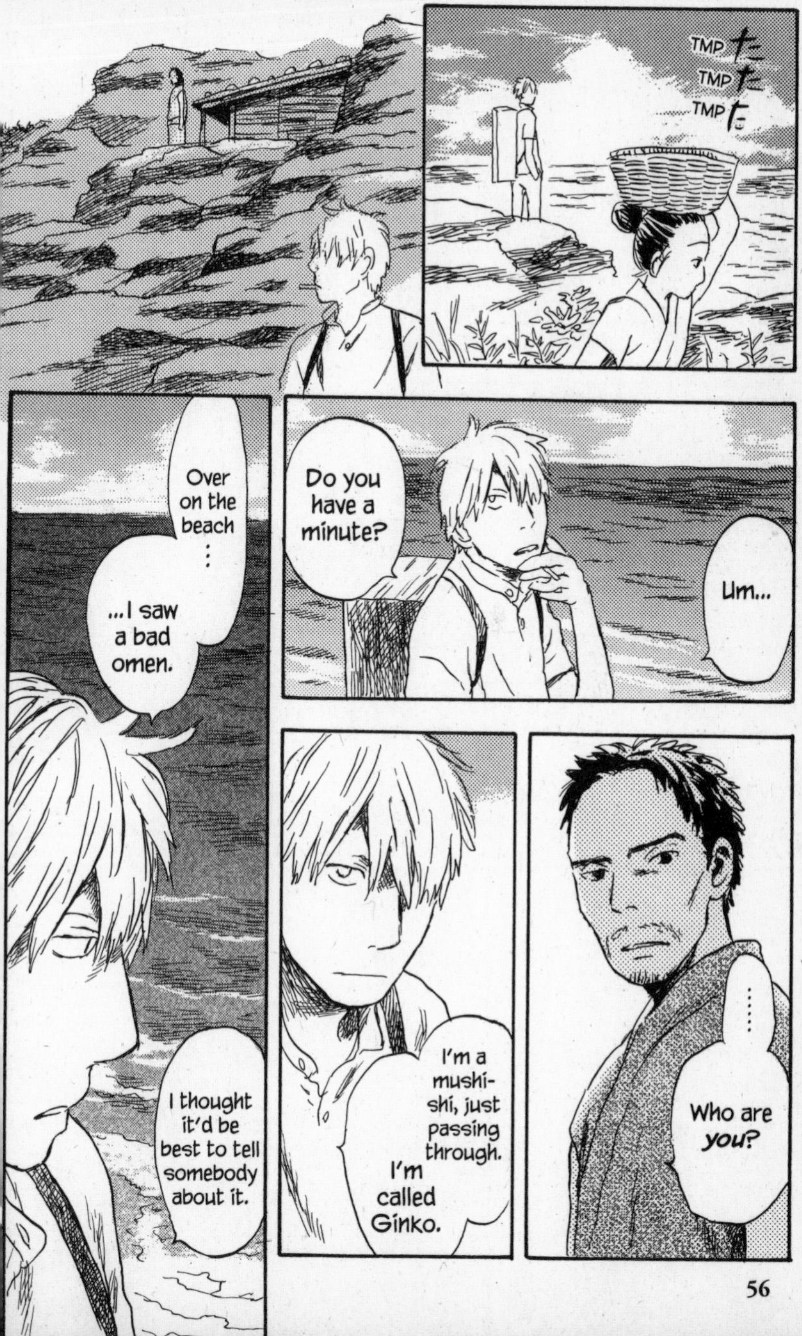
TMP
TMP
TMP
Um...
Do you have a minute?
......
Who are *you*?
I'm a mushi-shi, just passing through.
I'm called Ginko.
Over on the beach ...
...I saw a bad omen.
I thought it'd be best to tell somebody about it.

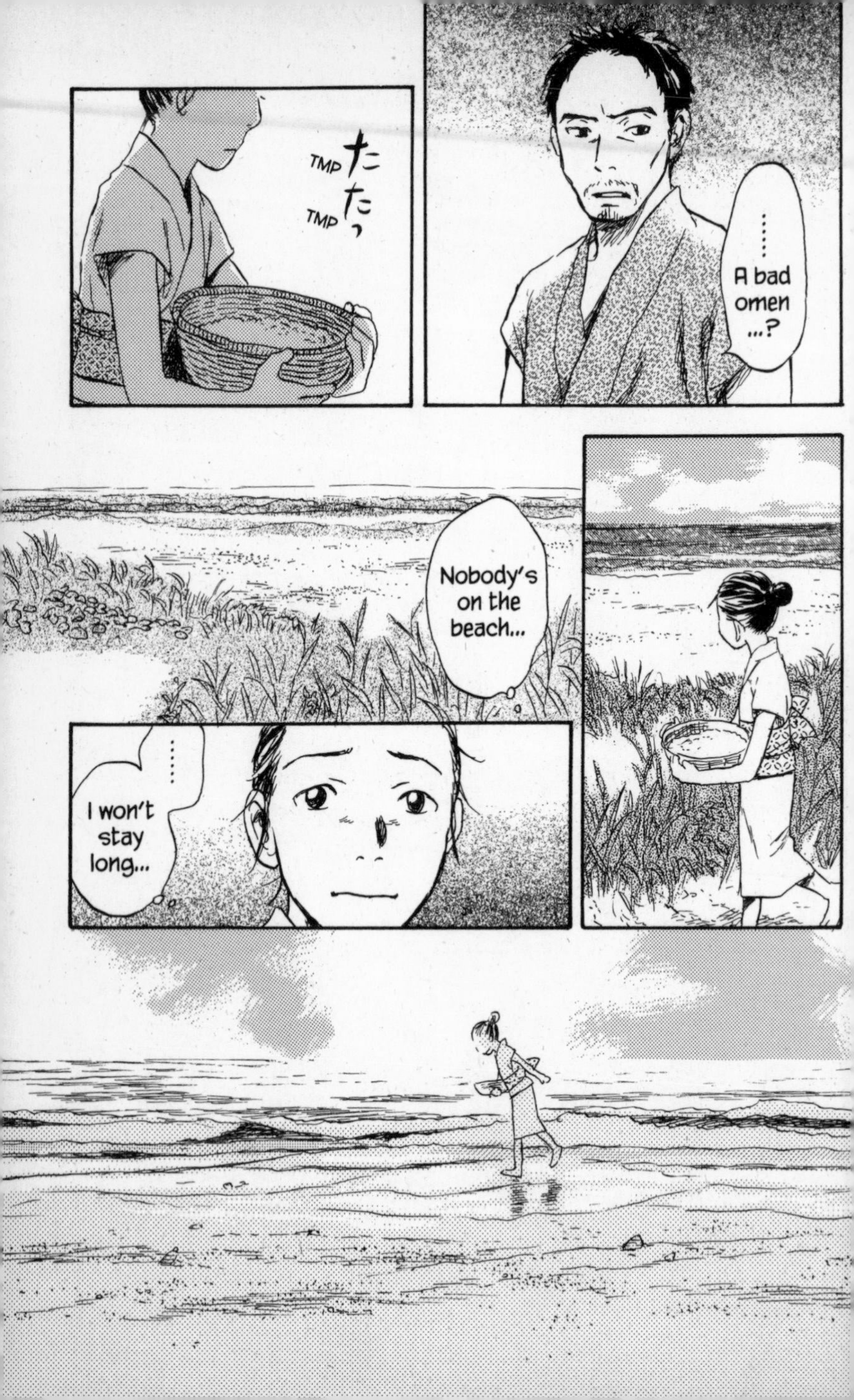

...... A bad omen ...?
たたっ
TMP TMP
Nobody's on the beach...
...... I won't stay long...

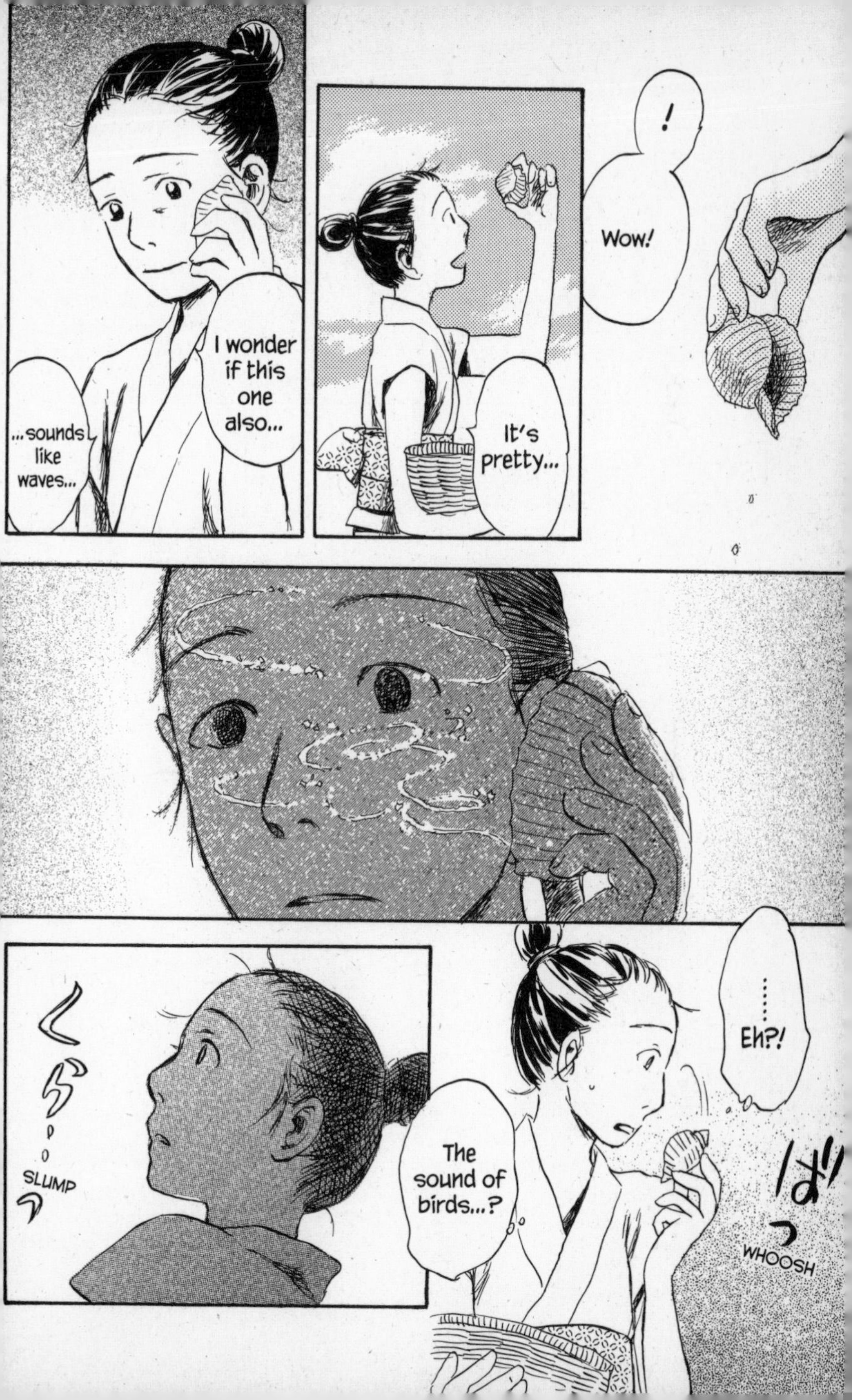
!
Wow!
It's pretty...
I wonder if this one also...
...sounds like waves...
......
Eh?!
ぱっ
WHOOSH
The sound of birds...?
くら
SLUMP

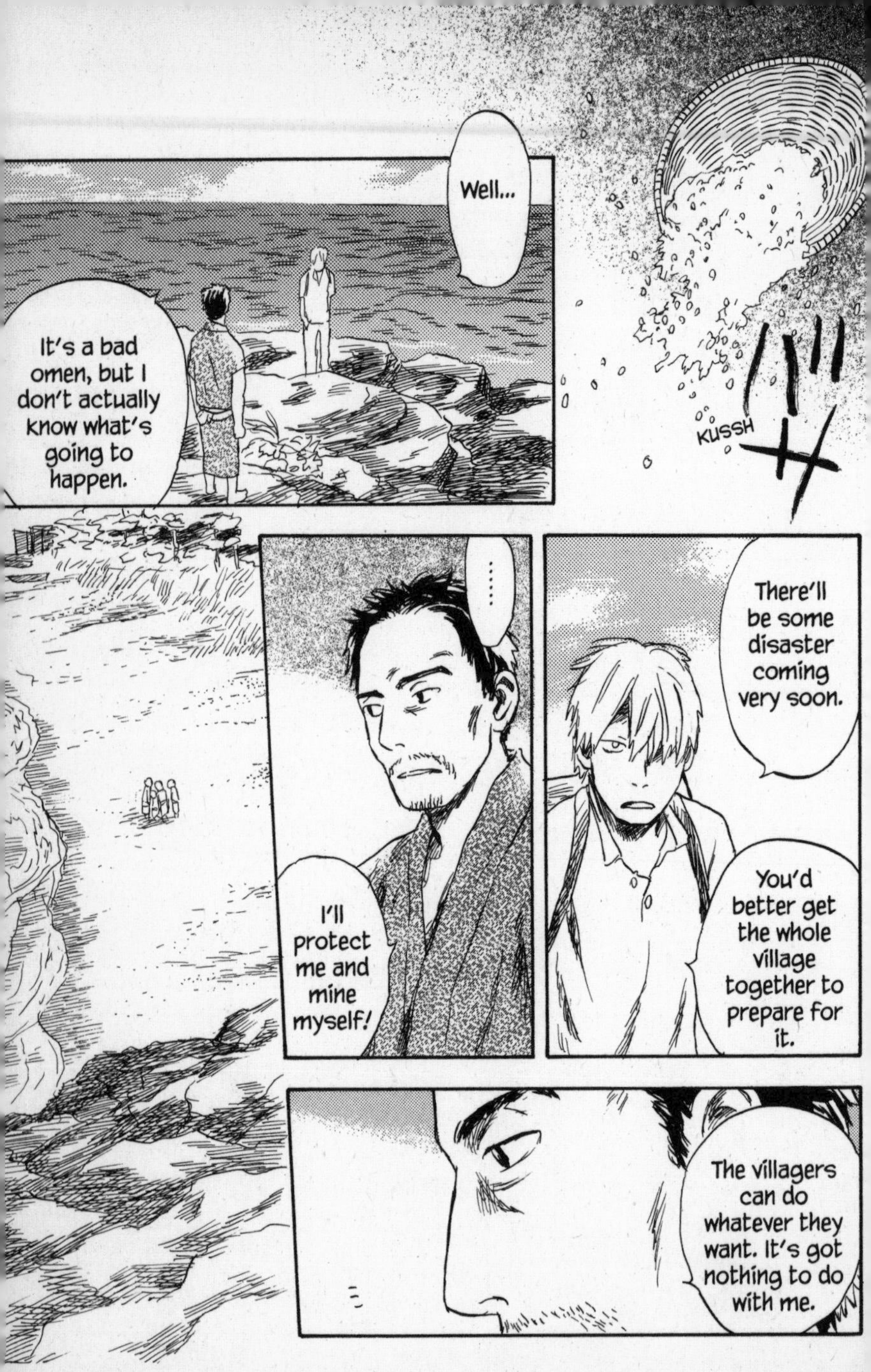
KUSSH
Well...
It's a bad omen, but I don't actually know what's going to happen.
There'll be some disaster coming very soon.
You'd better get the whole village together to prepare for it.
......
I'll protect me and mine myself!
The villagers can do whatever they want. It's got nothing to do with me.

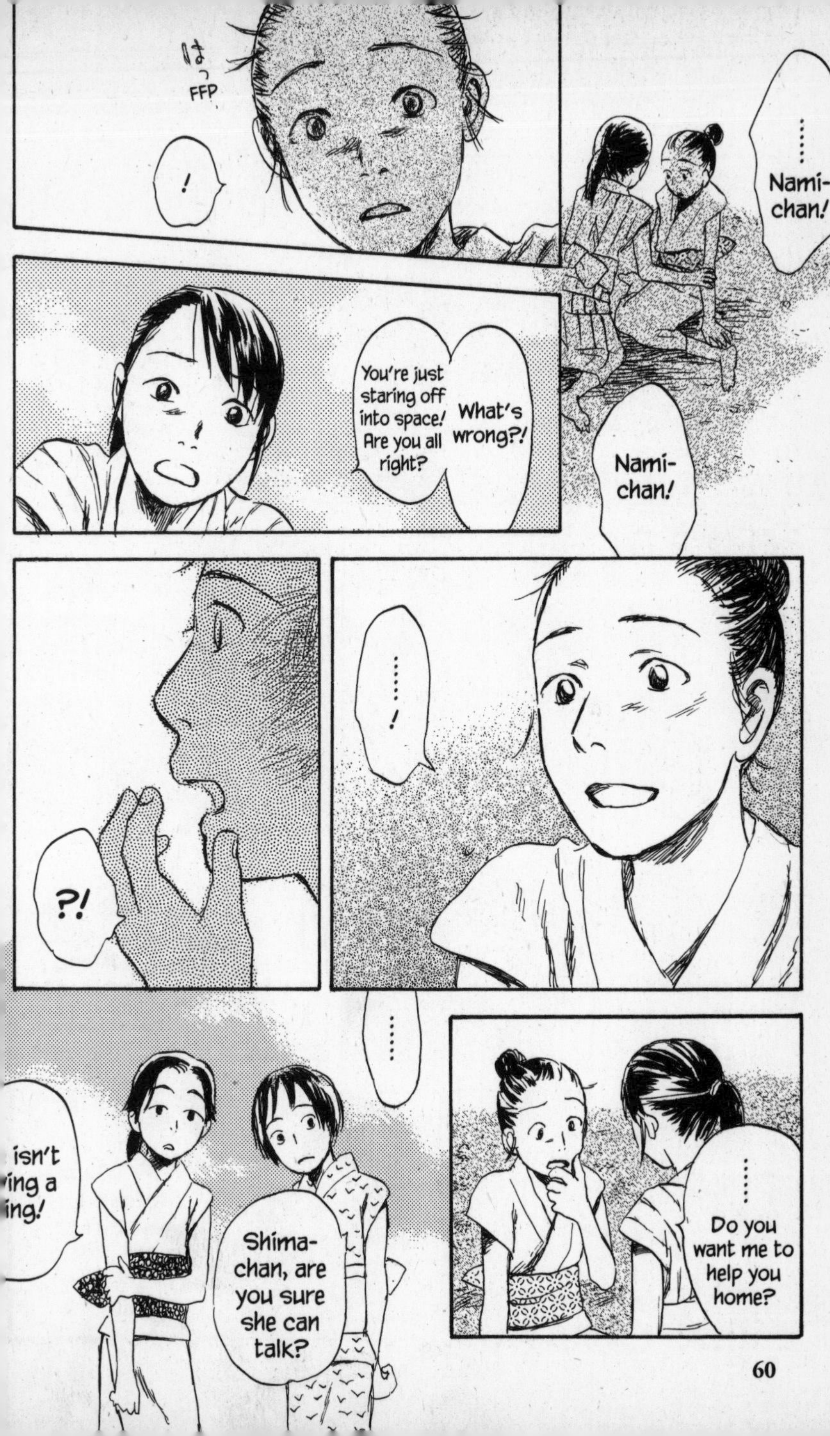

......
Nami-chan!
Nami-chan!
はっ FFP
!
What's wrong?!
You're just staring off into space! Are you all right?
......!
?!
......
Do you want me to help you home?
......
Shima-chan, are you sure she can talk?
isn't ing a ing!

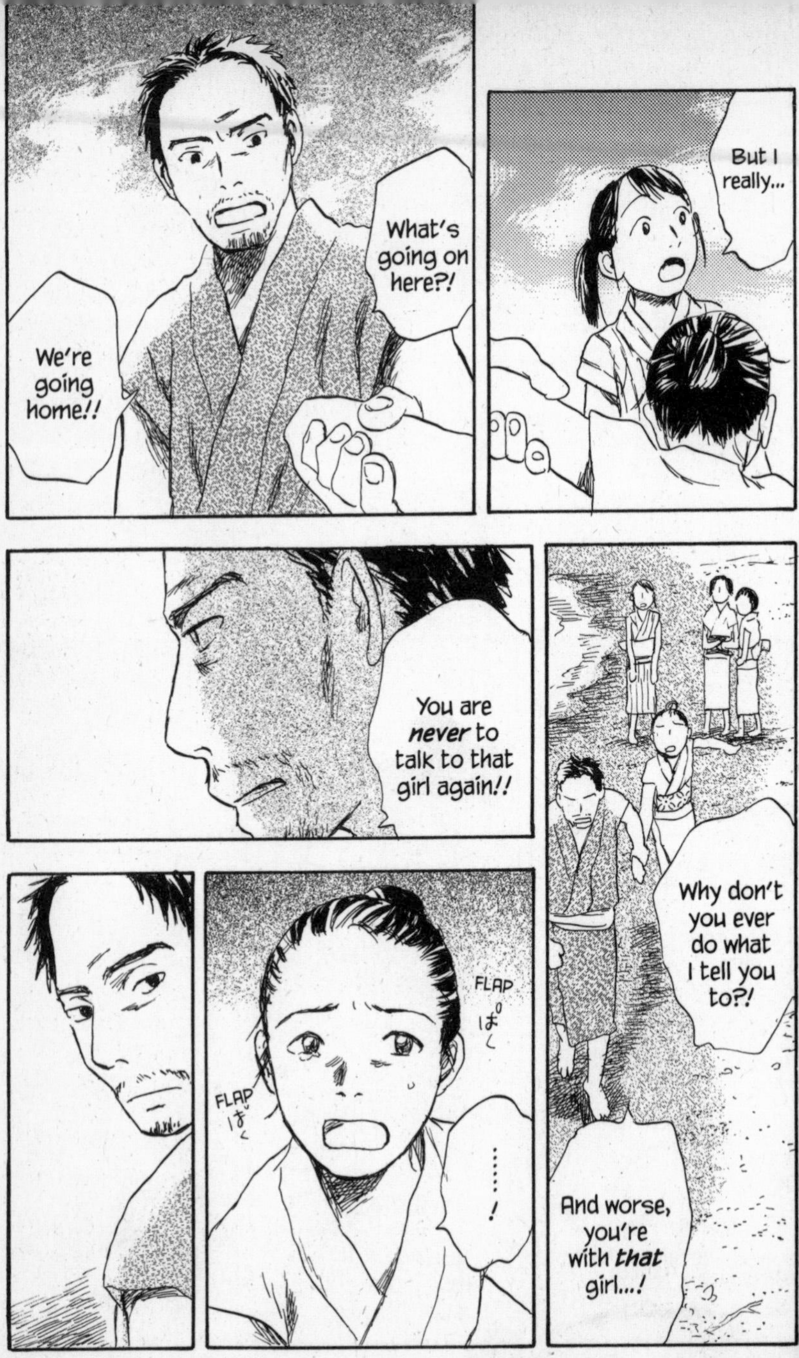

But I really...
What's going on here?!
We're going home!!
Why don't you ever do what I tell you to?!
And worse, you're with *that* girl...!
You are *never* to talk to that girl again!!
FLAP
ぱく
FLAP
ぱく
......!

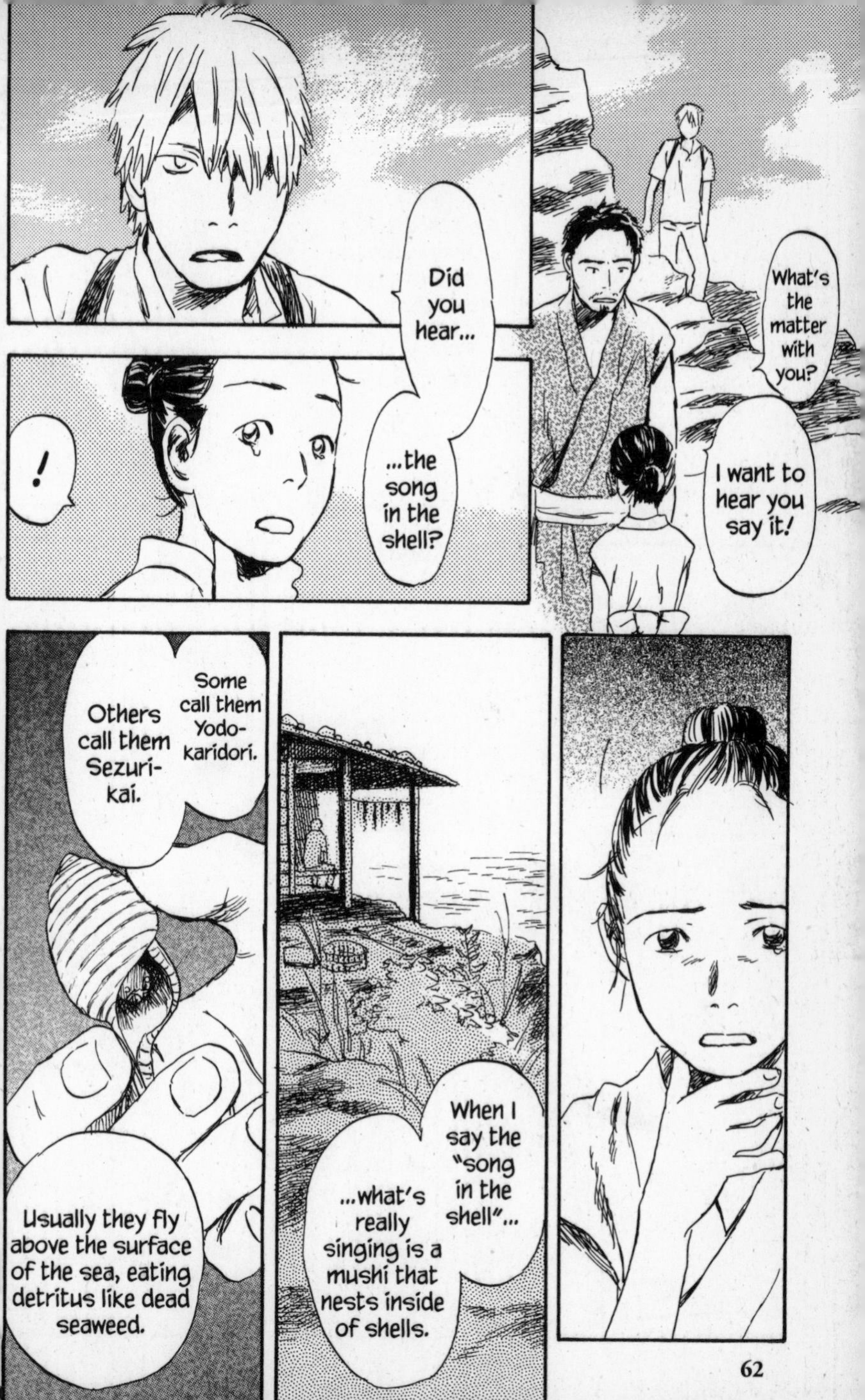
What's the matter with you?
I want to hear you say it!
Did you hear...
...the song in the shell?
!
When I say the "song in the shell"...
...what's really singing is a mushi that nests inside of shells.
Some call them Yodo-karidori.
Others call them Sezuri-kai.
Usually they fly above the surface of the sea, eating detritus like dead seaweed.

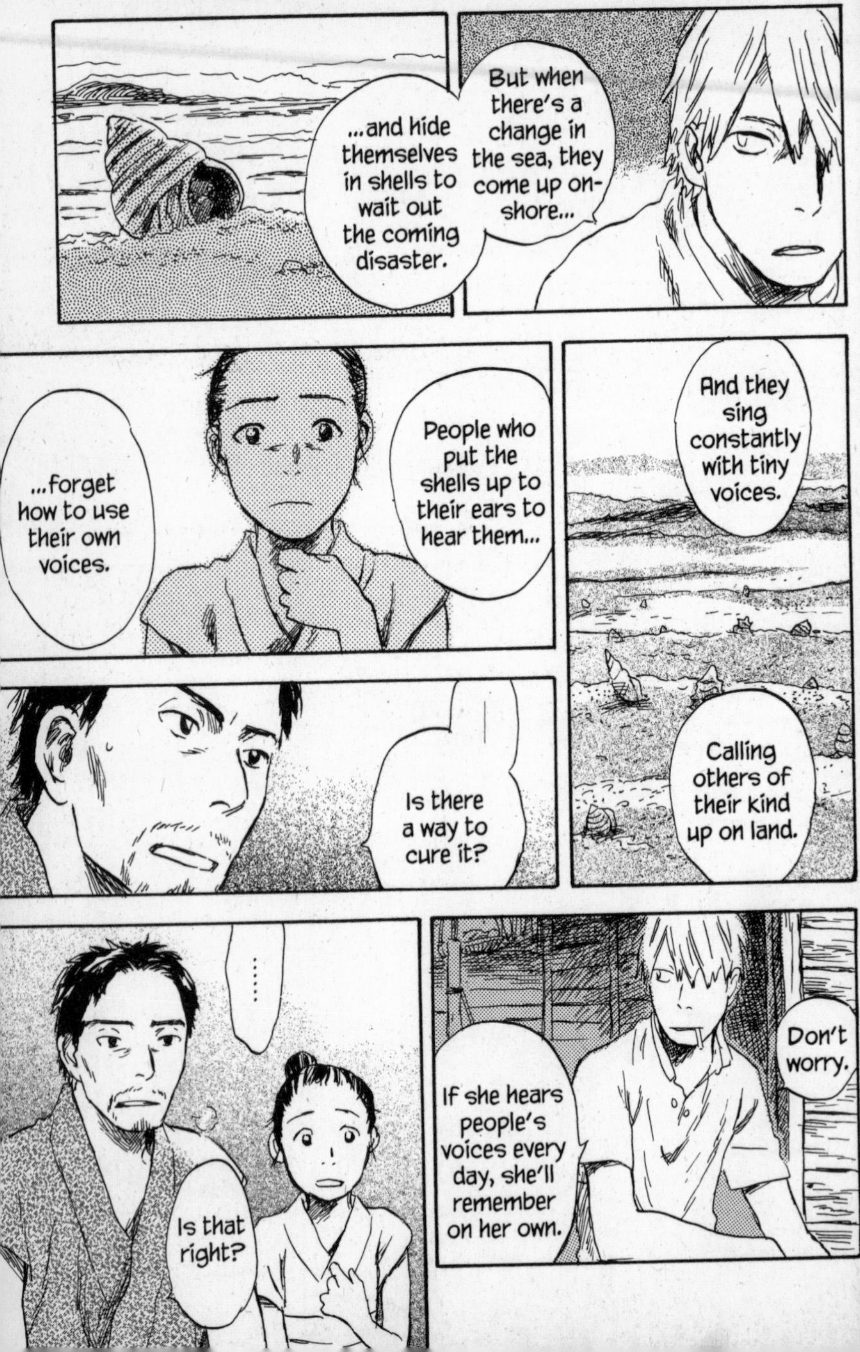
But when there's a change in the sea, they come up on-shore...
...and hide themselves in shells to wait out the coming disaster.
And they sing constantly with tiny voices.
Calling others of their kind up on land.
People who put the shells up to their ears to hear them...
...forget how to use their own voices.
Is there a way to cure it?
Don't worry.
If she hears people's voices every day, she'll remember on her own.
......
Is that right?

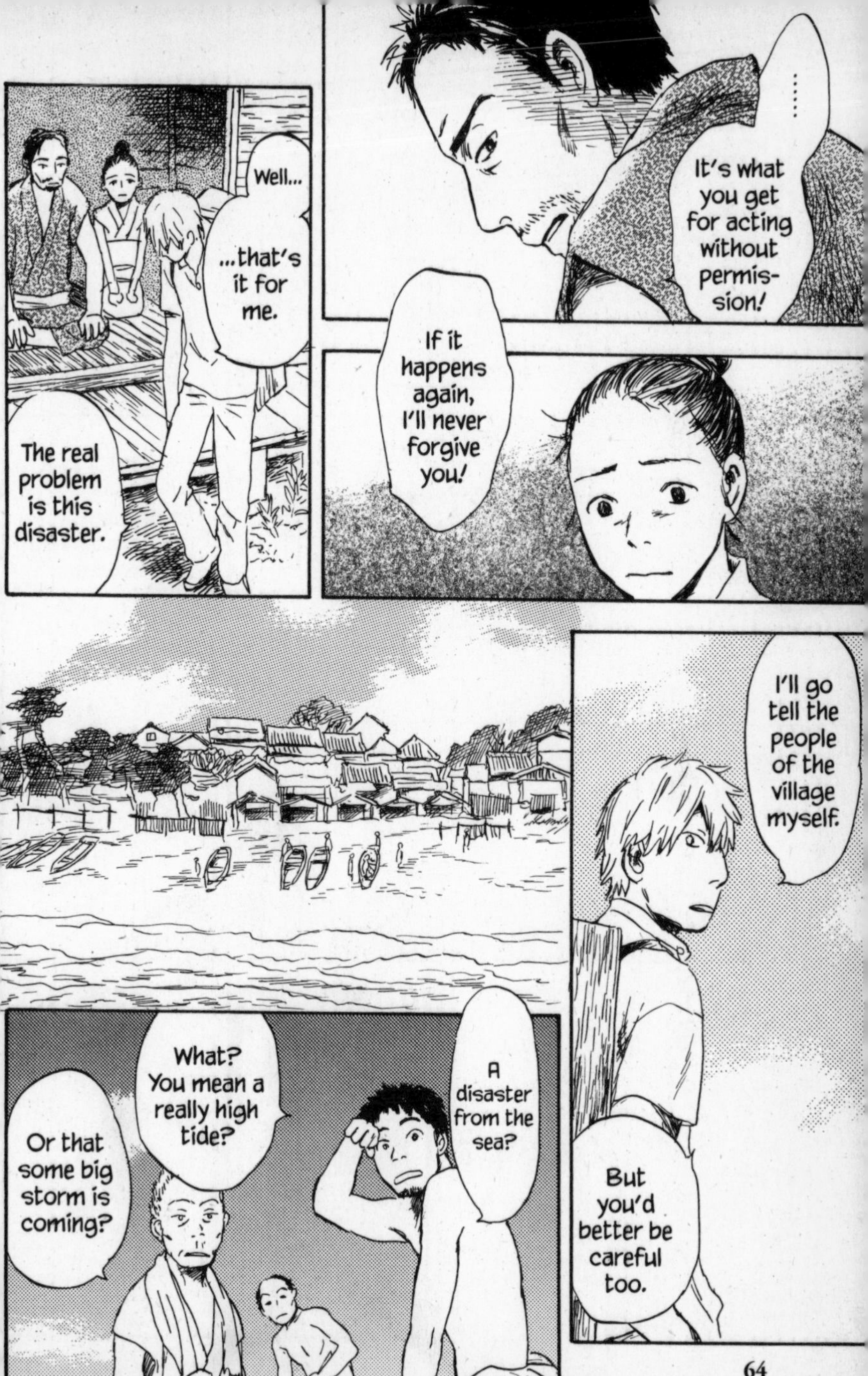
......
It's what you get for acting without permission!
If it happens again, I'll never forgive you!
Well...
...that's it for me.
The real problem is this disaster.
I'll go tell the people of the village myself.
But you'd better be careful too.
A disaster from the sea?
What? You mean a really high tide?
Or that some big storm is coming?

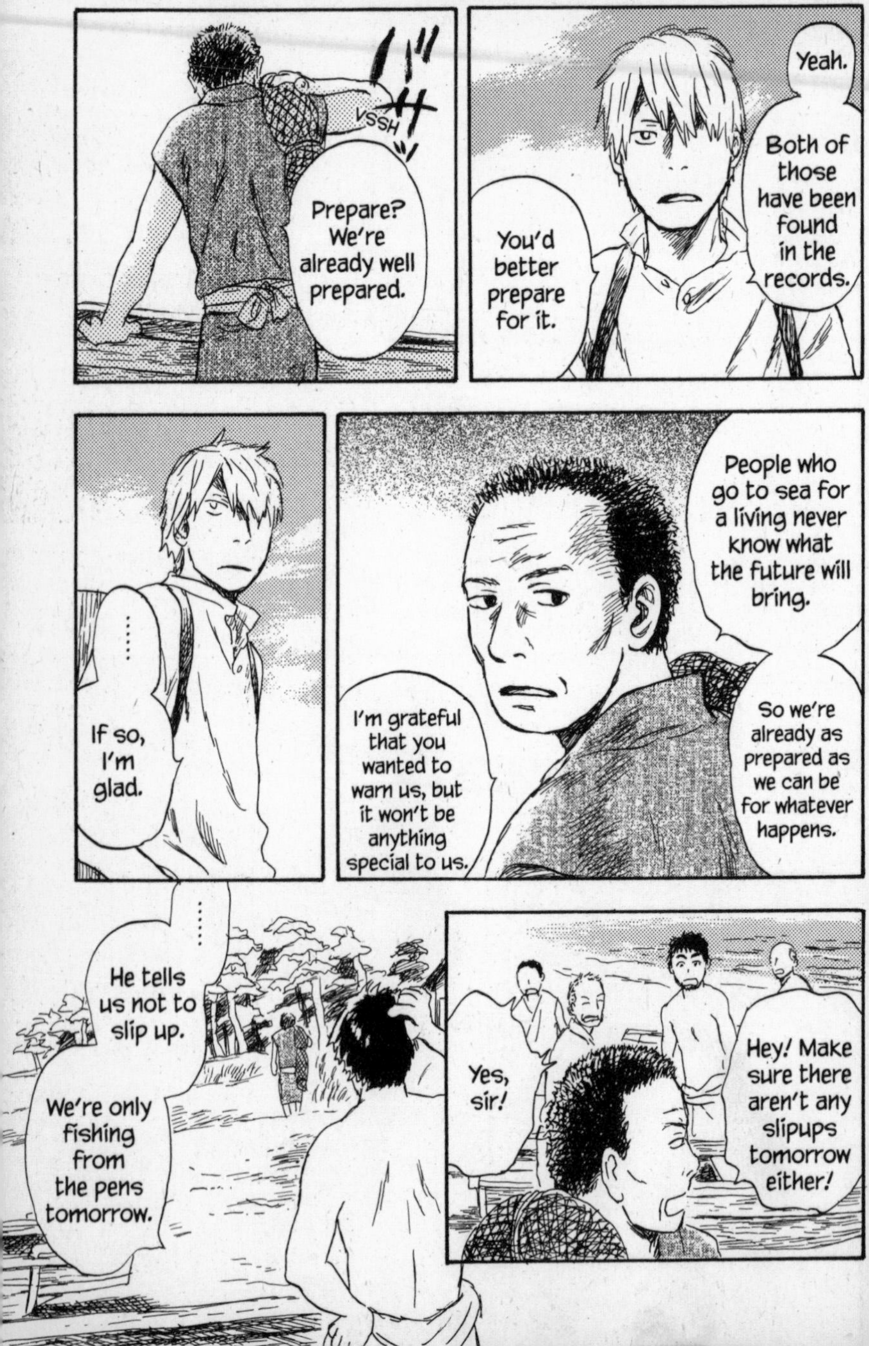
Yeah.
Both of those have been found in the records.
You'd better prepare for it.
VSSH
Prepare? We're already well prepared.
People who go to sea for a living never know what the future will bring.
So we're already as prepared as we can be for whatever happens.
I'm grateful that you wanted to warn us, but it won't be anything special to us.
......
If so, I'm glad.
Hey! Make sure there aren't any slipups tomorrow either!
Yes, sir!
......
He tells us not to slip up.
We're only fishing from the pens tomorrow.

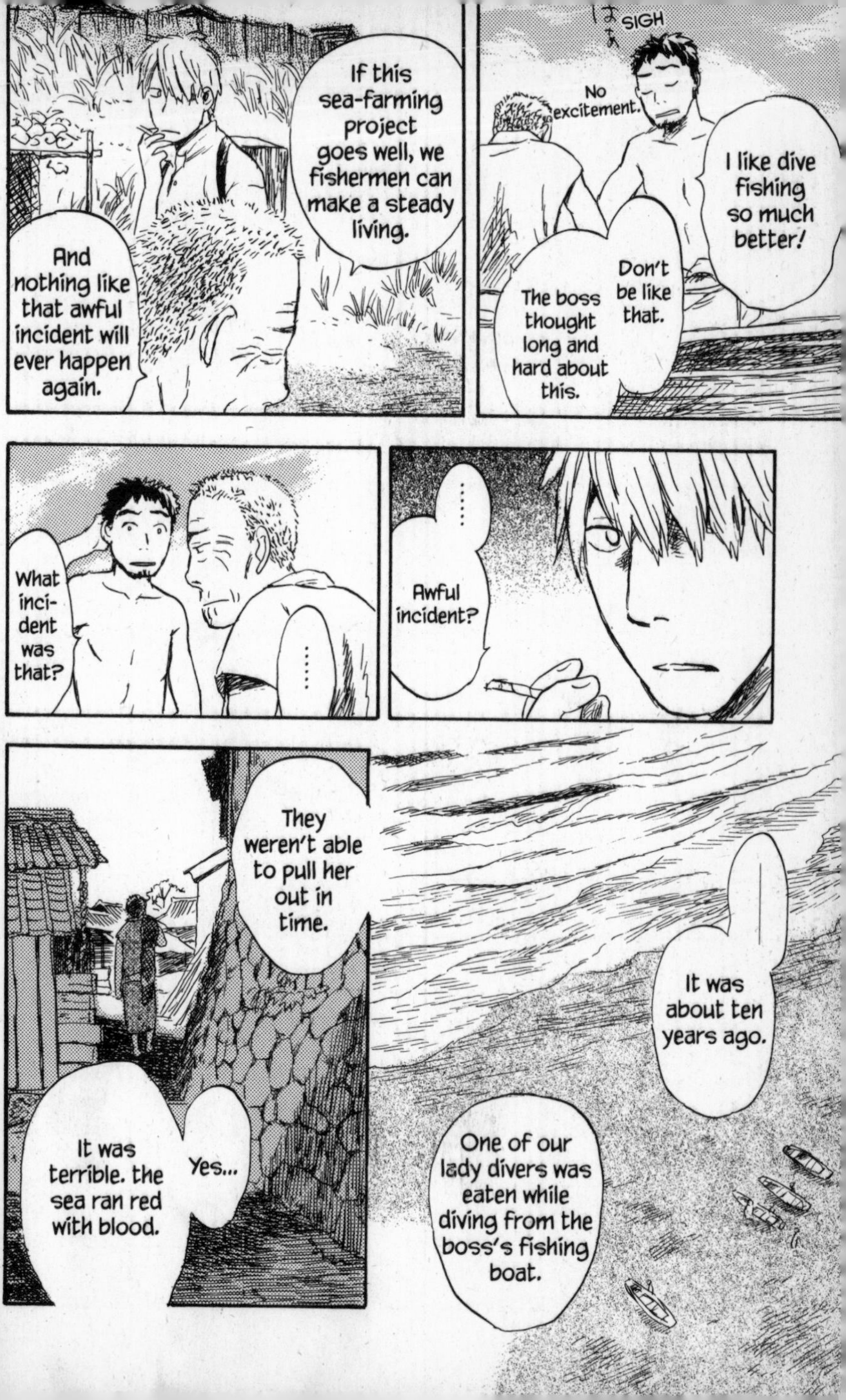
SIGH
No excitement.
I like dive fishing so much better!
Don't be like that.
The boss thought long and hard about this.
If this sea-farming project goes well, we fishermen can make a steady living.
And nothing like that awful incident will ever happen again.
……
Awful incident?
What incident was that?
……
It was about ten years ago.
One of our lady divers was eaten while diving from the boss's fishing boat.
They weren't able to pull her out in time.
Yes...
It was terrible. the sea ran red with blood.

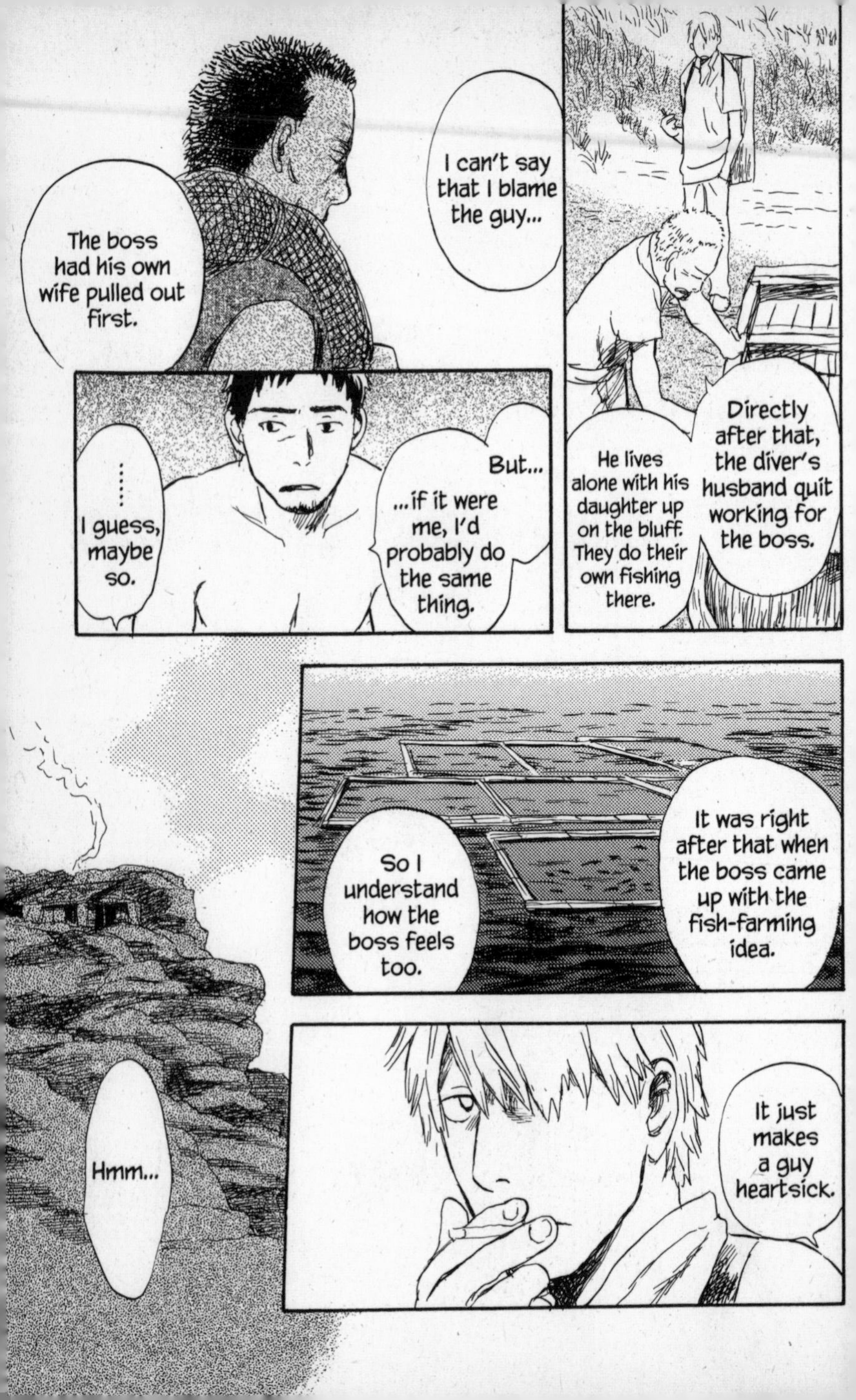
Directly after that, the diver's husband quit working for the boss.
He lives alone with his daughter up on the bluff. They do their own fishing there.
I can't say that I blame the guy...
The boss had his own wife pulled out first.
But...
...if it were me, I'd probably do the same thing.
...... I guess, maybe so.
It was right after that when the boss came up with the fish-farming idea.
So I understand how the boss feels too.
It just makes a guy heartsick.
Hmm...

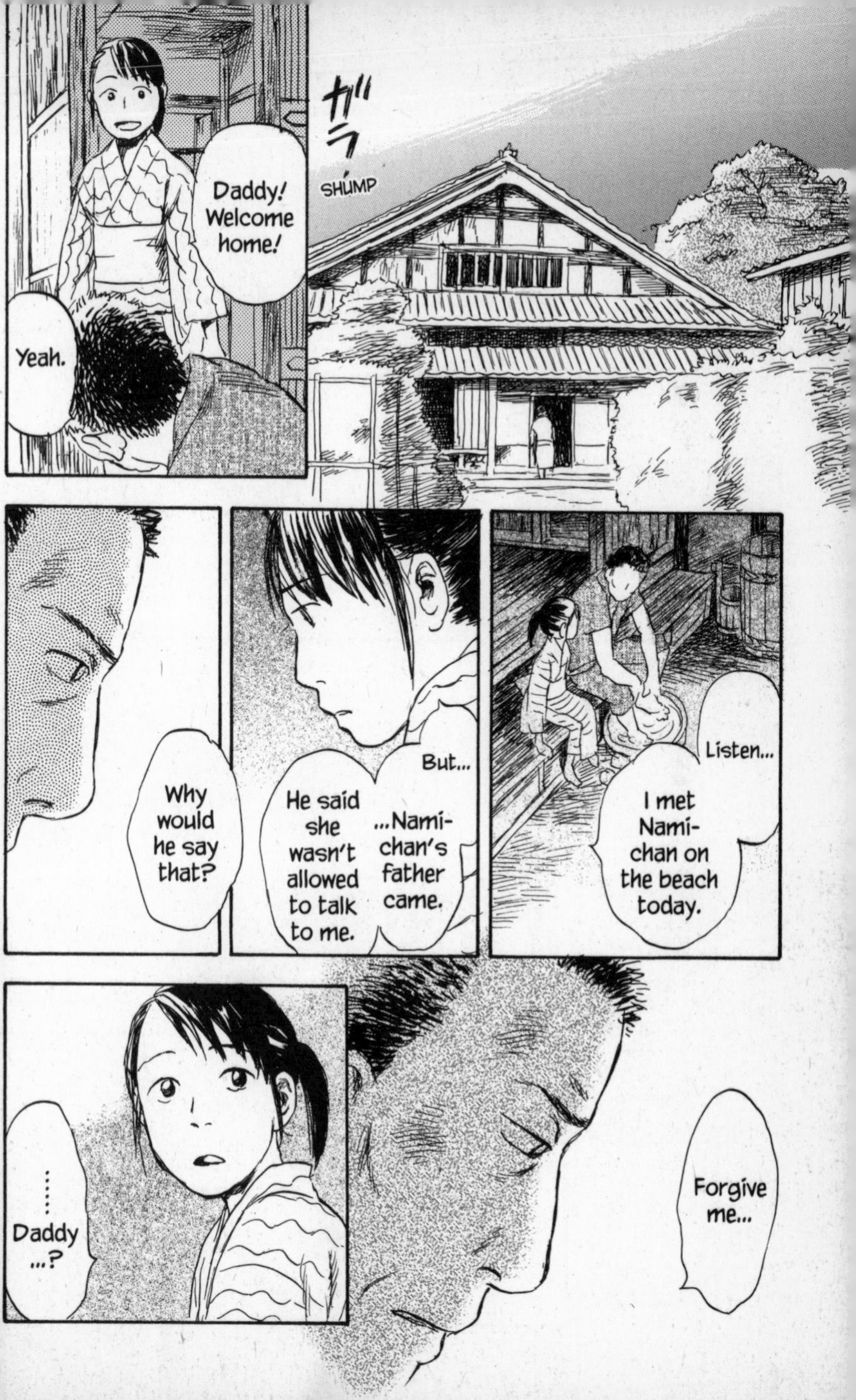
ガラ
SHUMP
Daddy! Welcome home!
Yeah.
Listen...
I met Nami-chan on the beach today.
But...
...Nami-chan's father came.
He said she wasn't allowed to talk to me.
Why would he say that?
Forgive me...
...... Daddy ...?

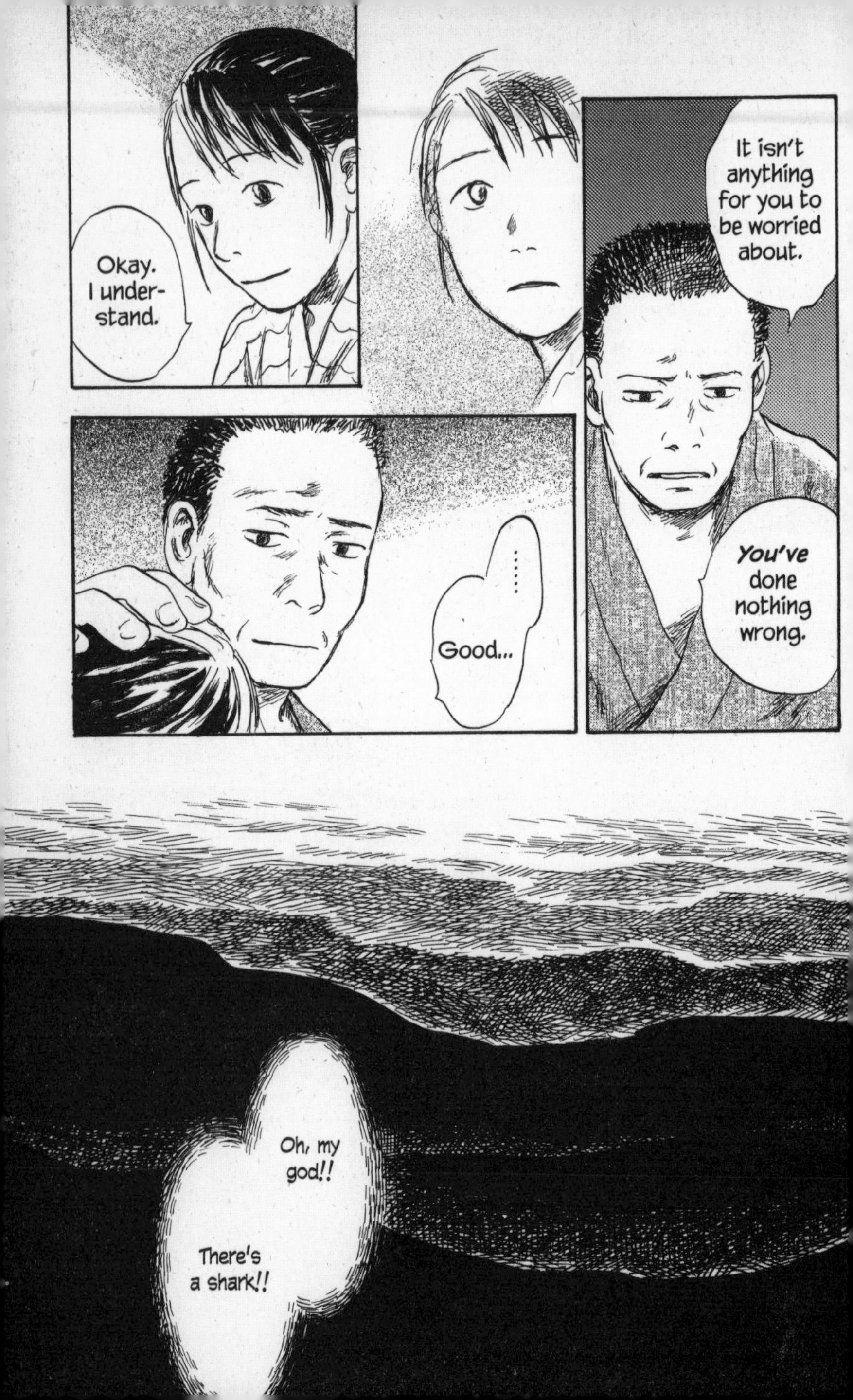
It isn't anything for you to be worried about.
You've done nothing wrong.
Okay. I understand.
......
Good...
Oh, my god!!
There's a shark!!

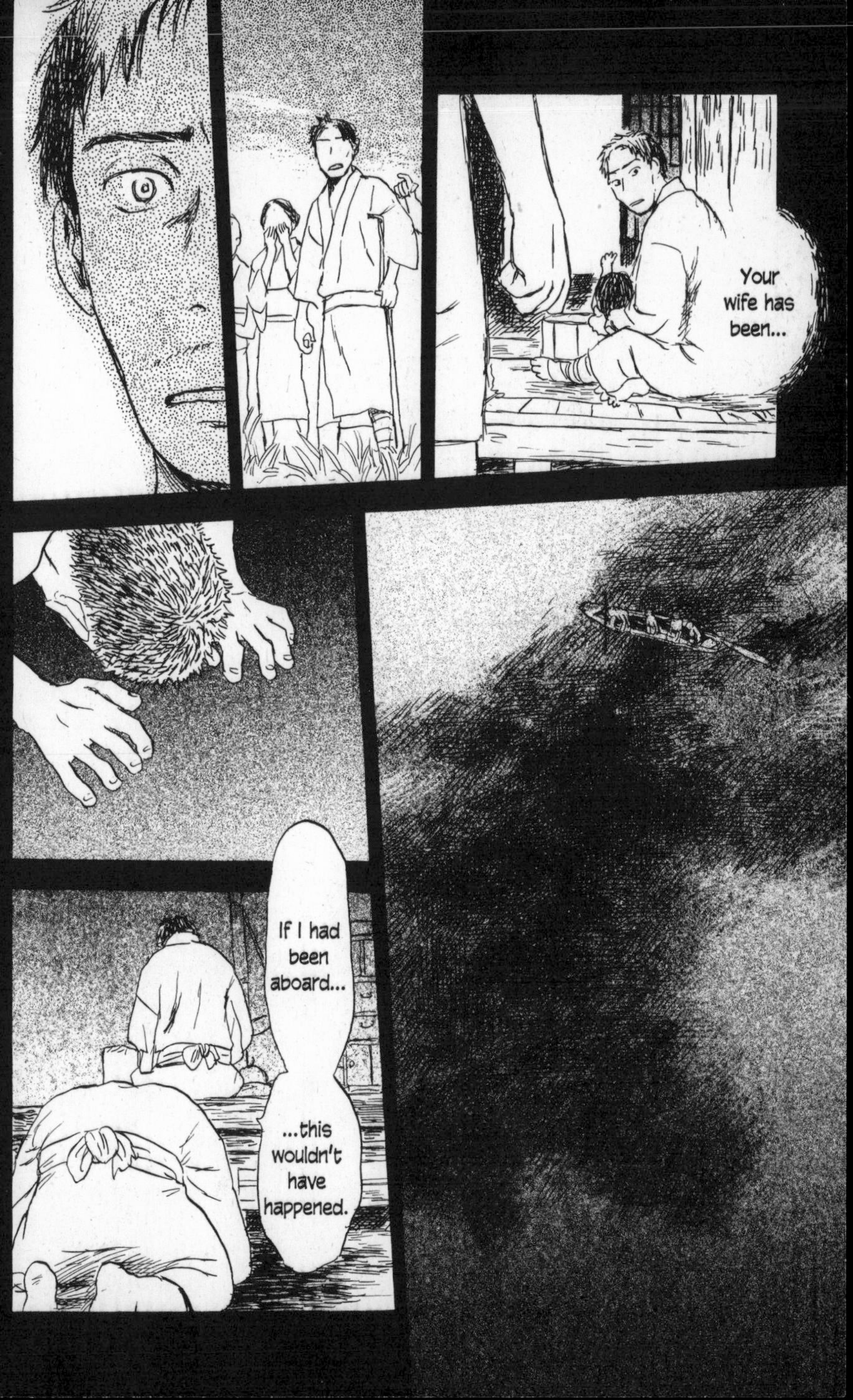
Your wife has been...
If I had been aboard...
...this wouldn't have happened.

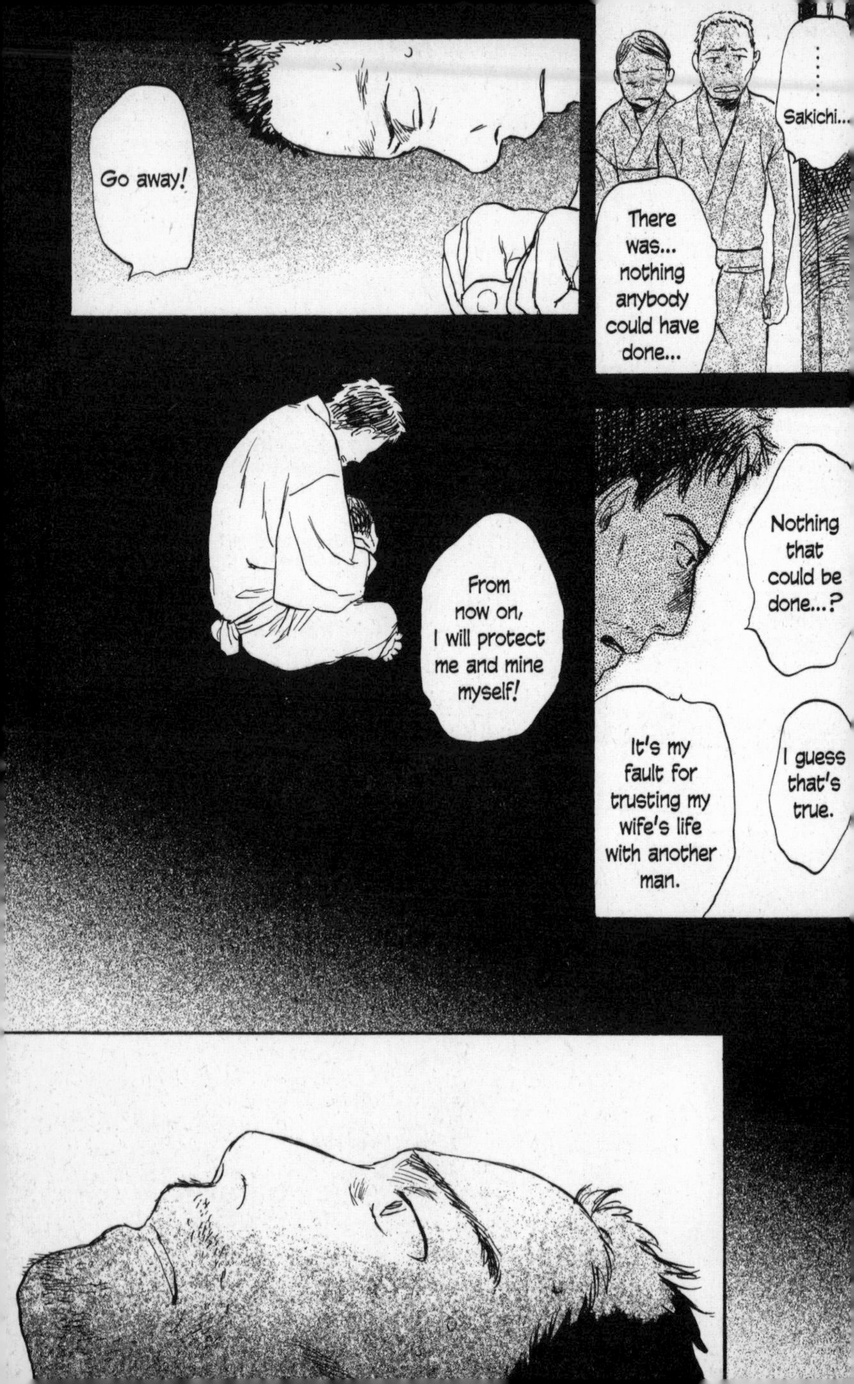

......
Sakichi...
There was... nothing anybody could have done...
Go away!
Nothing that could be done...?
I guess that's true.
It's my fault for trusting my wife's life with another man.
From now on, I will protect me and mine myself!

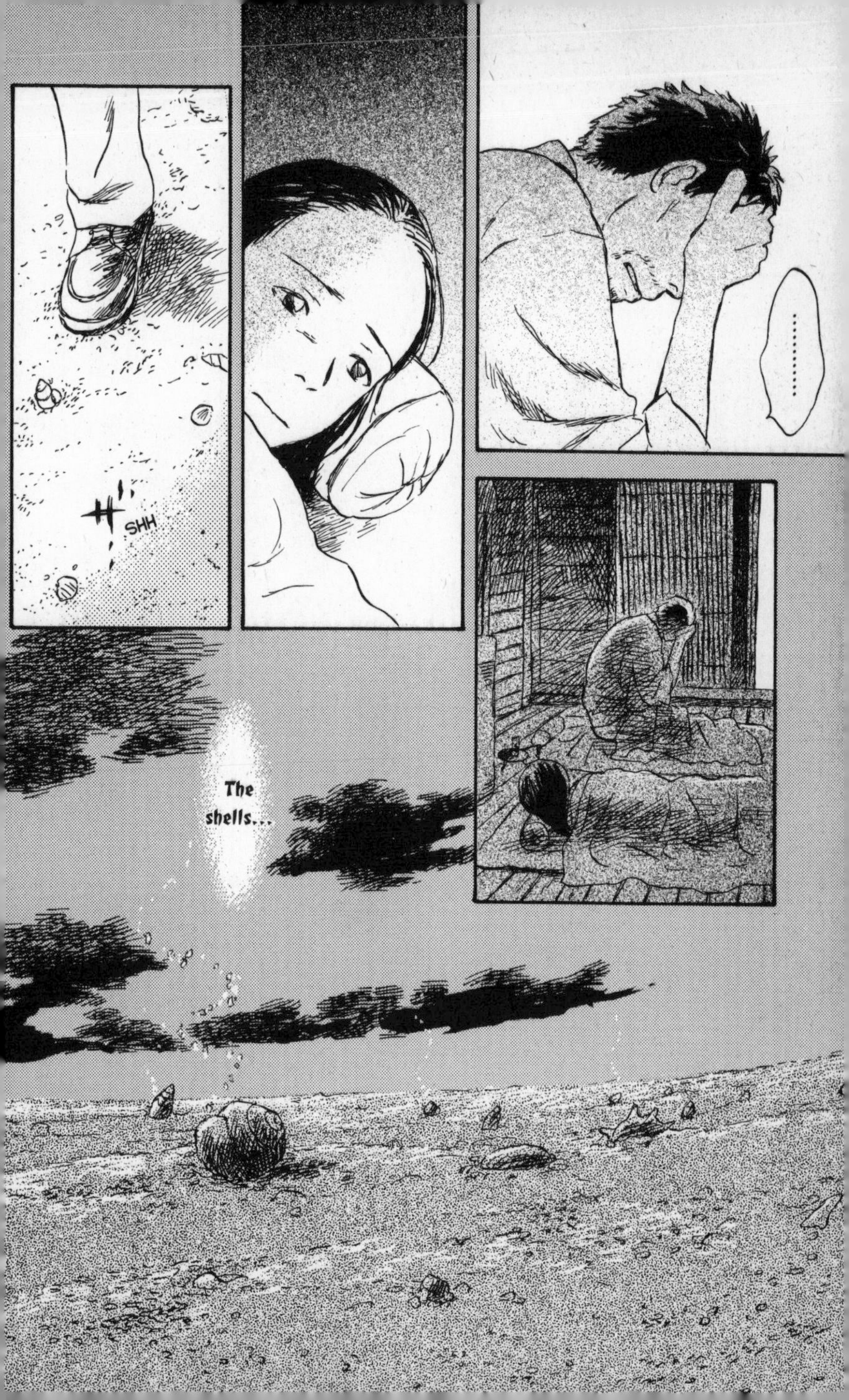
……
SHH
The shells...

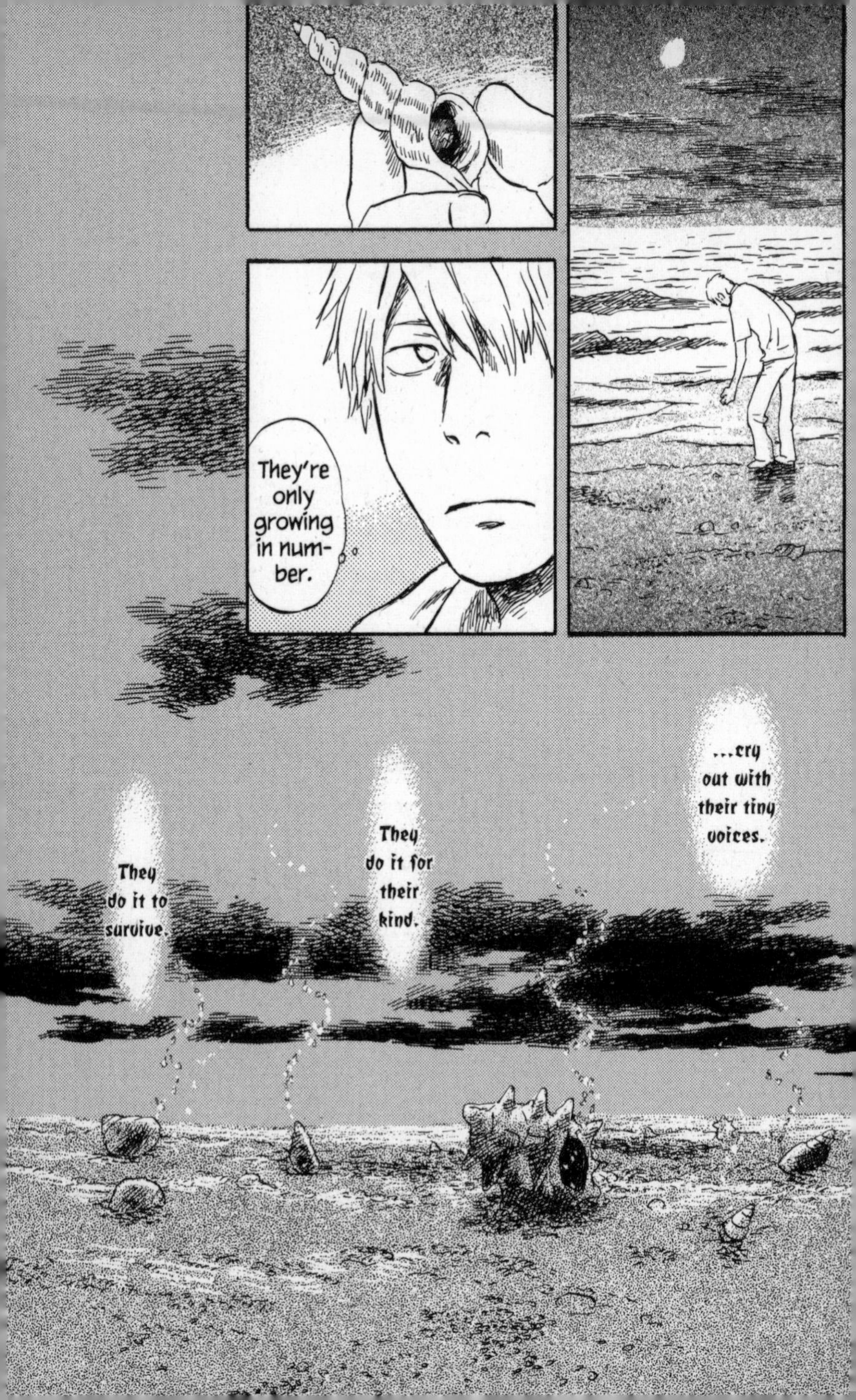
They're only growing in num-ber.
...cry out with their tiny voices.
They do it for their kind.
They do it to survive.

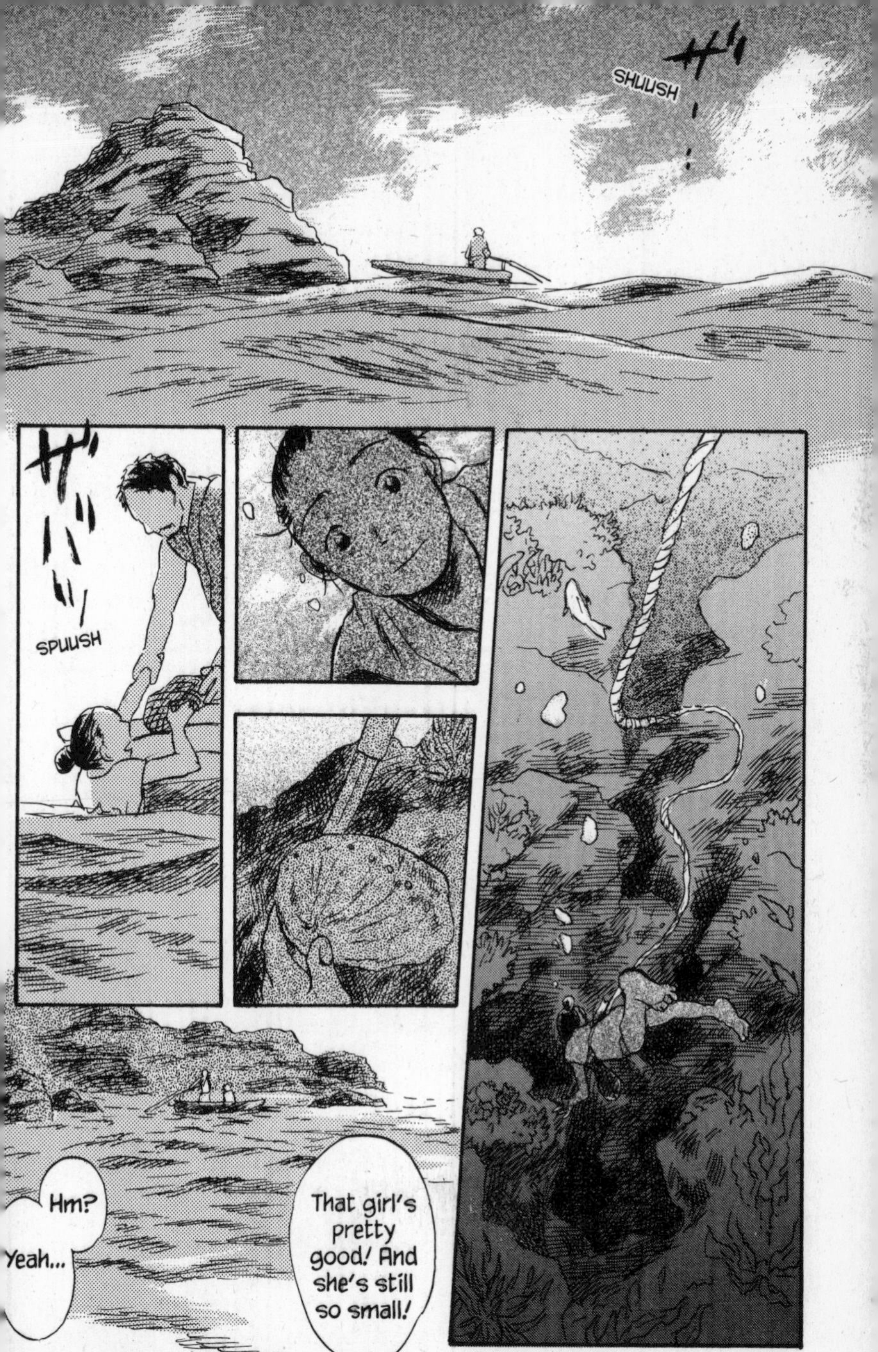
SHUUSH
SPUUSH
That girl's pretty good! And she's still so small!
Hm?
Yeah...

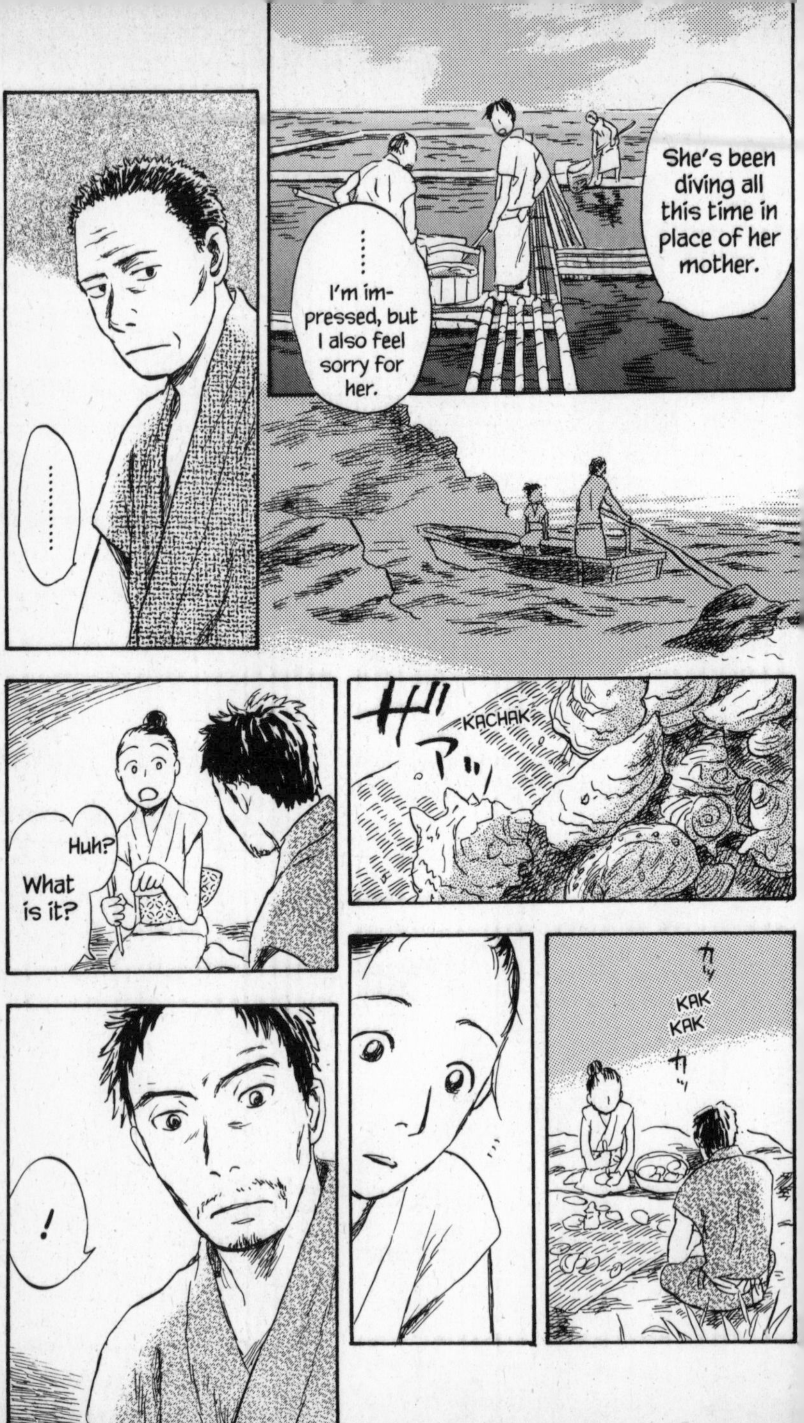
She's been diving all this time in place of her mother.
...... I'm impressed, but I also feel sorry for her.
......
ザアッ
KACHAK
Huh? What is it?
カッ
KAK KAK
カッ
!

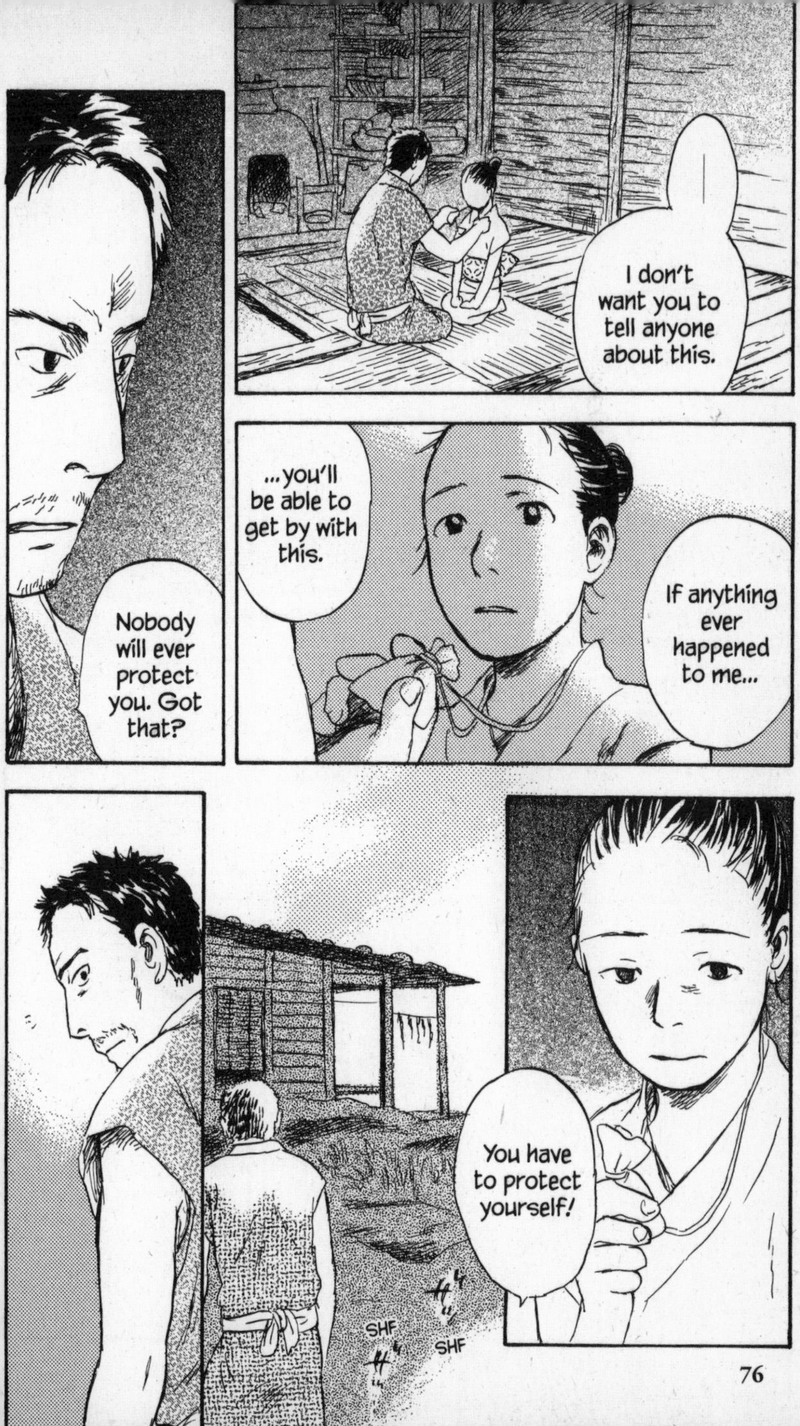
I don't want you to tell anyone about this.
If anything ever happened to me...
...you'll be able to get by with this.
Nobody will ever protect you. Got that?
You have to protect yourself!
SHF
SHF

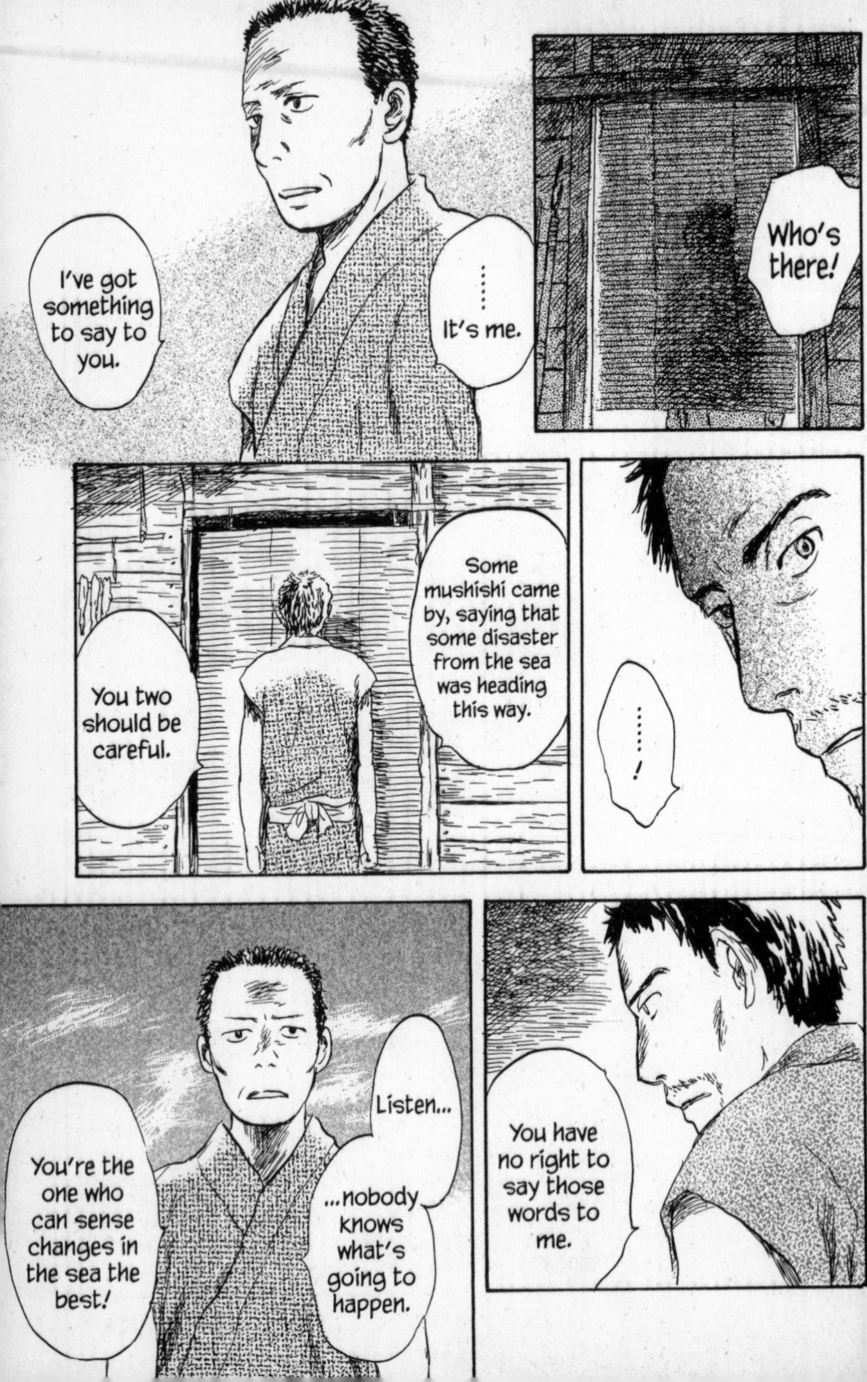
Who's there!
......It's me.
I've got something to say to you.
......!
Some mushishi came by, saying that some disaster from the sea was heading this way.
You two should be careful.
You have no right to say those words to me.
Listen...
...nobody knows what's going to happen.
You're the one who can sense changes in the sea the best!

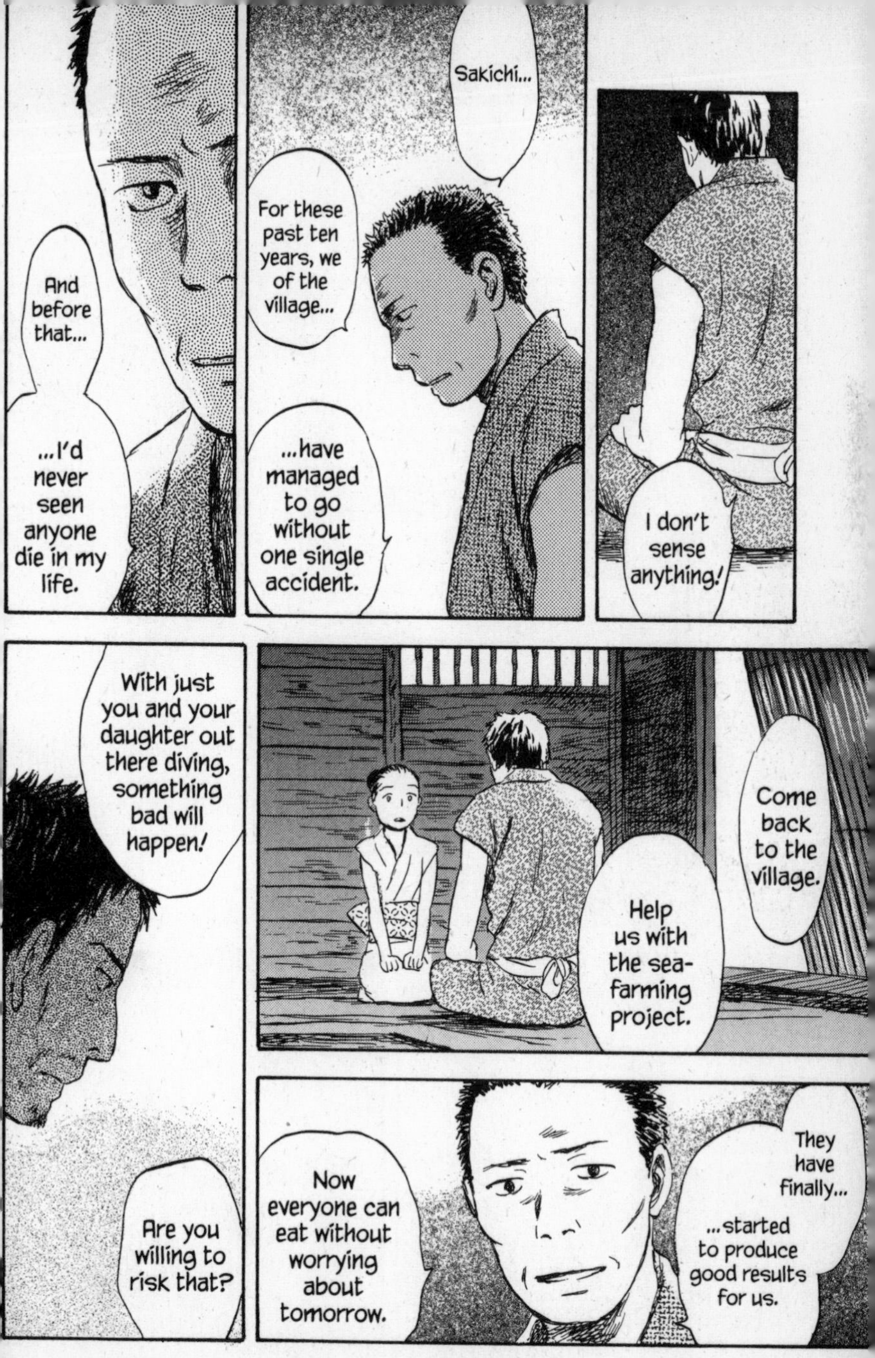
I don't sense anything!
Sakichi...
For these past ten years, we of the village...
...have managed to go without one single accident.
And before that...
...I'd never seen anyone die in my life.
Come back to the village.
Help us with the sea-farming project.
They have finally...
...started to produce good results for us.
Now everyone can eat without worrying about tomorrow.
With just you and your daughter out there diving, something bad will happen!
Are you willing to risk that?

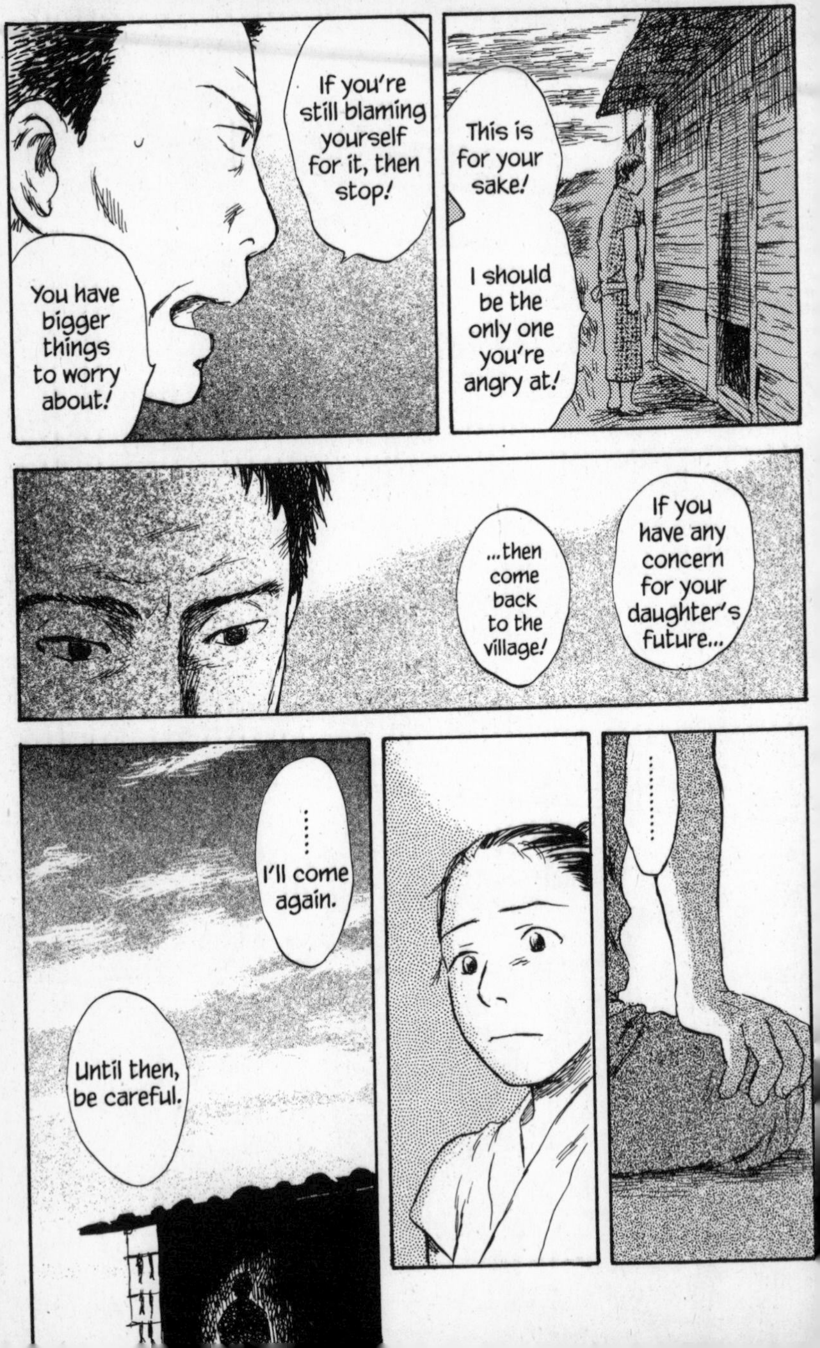
This is for your sake!
I should be the only one you're angry at!
If you're still blaming yourself for it, then stop!
You have bigger things to worry about!
If you have any concern for your daughter's future...
...then come back to the village!
......
......
I'll come again.
Until then, be careful.

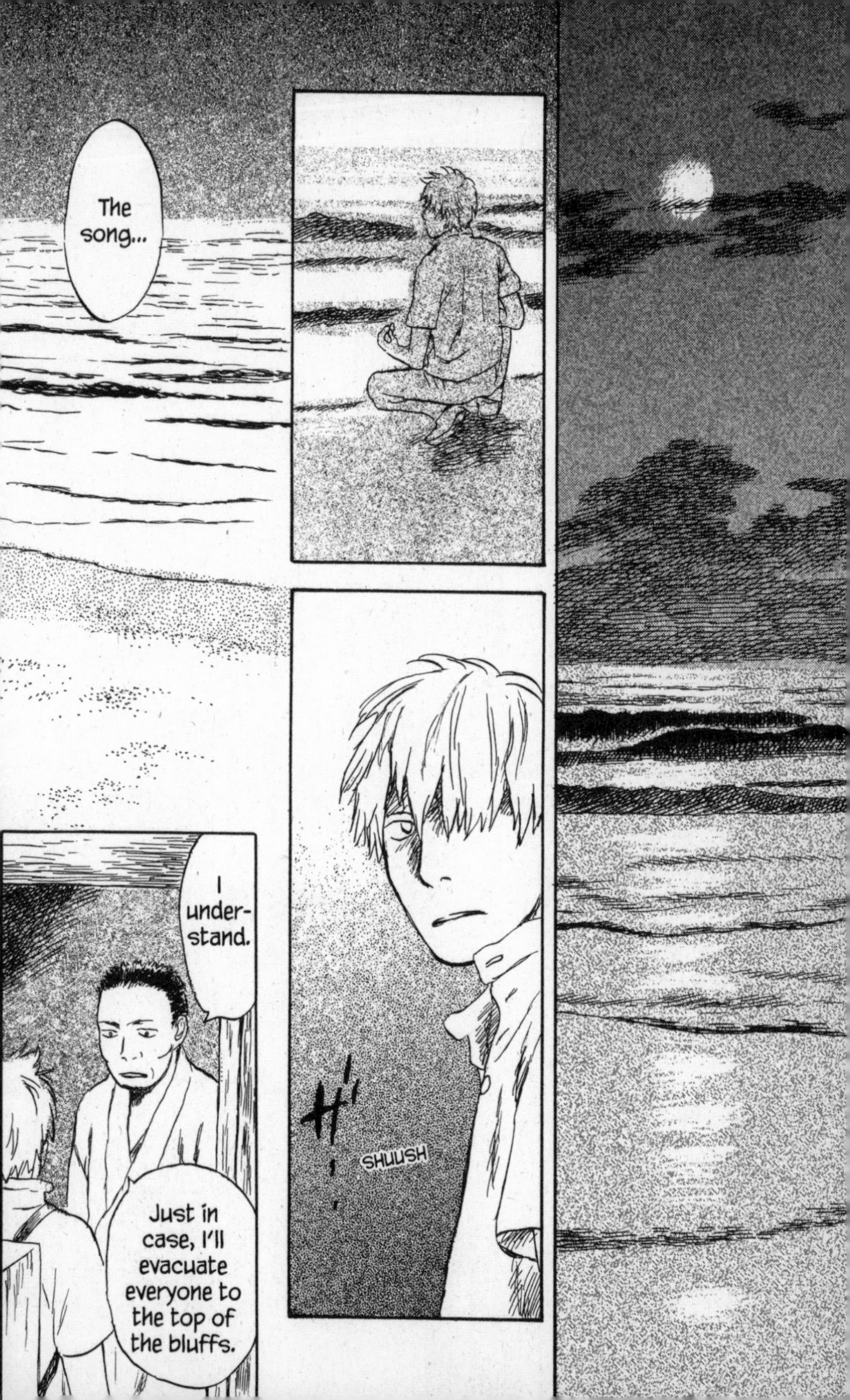
The song...
SHUUSH
I under-stand.
Just in case, I'll evacuate everyone to the top of the bluffs.

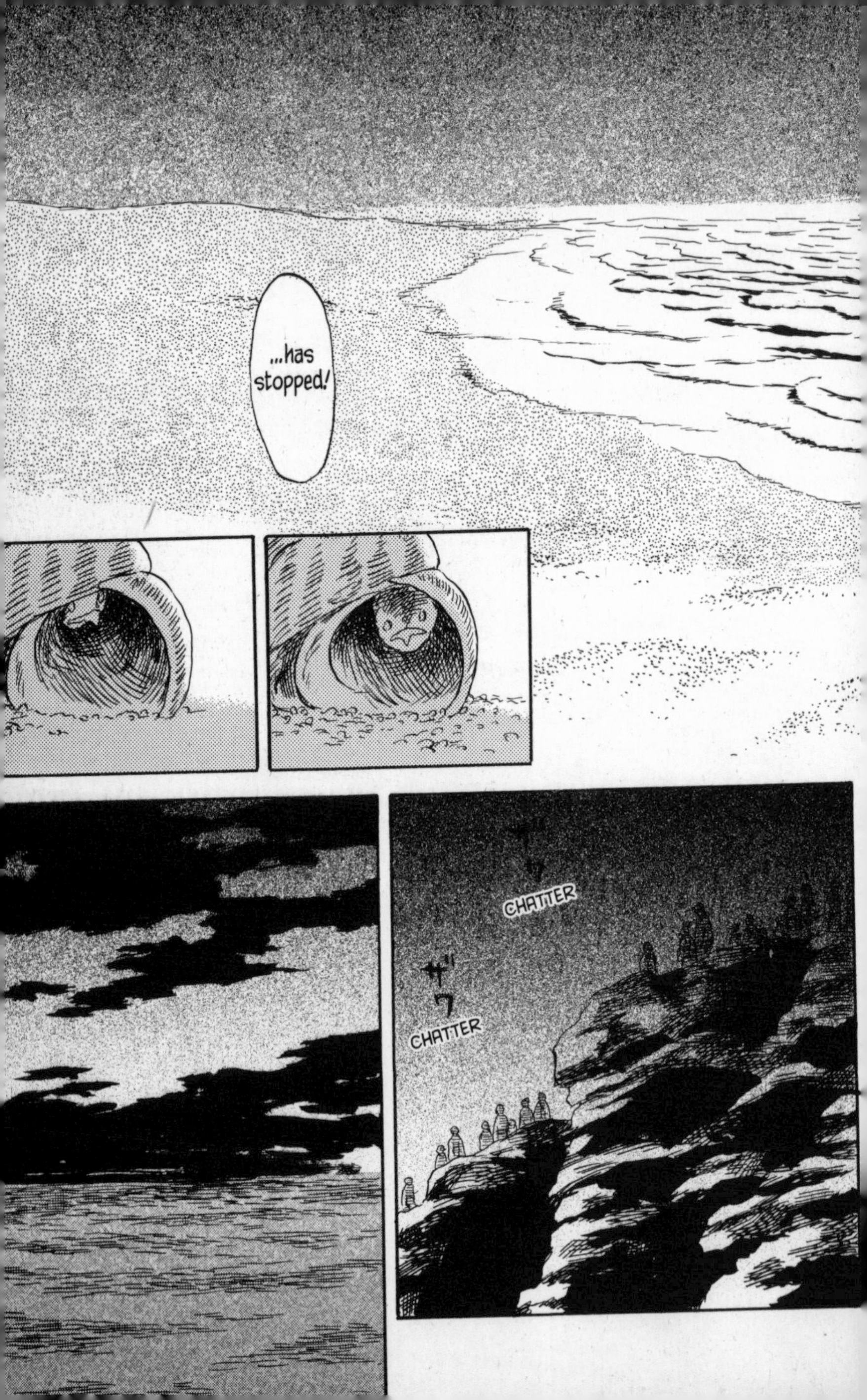
...has stopped!
CHATTER
ザワ
CHATTER

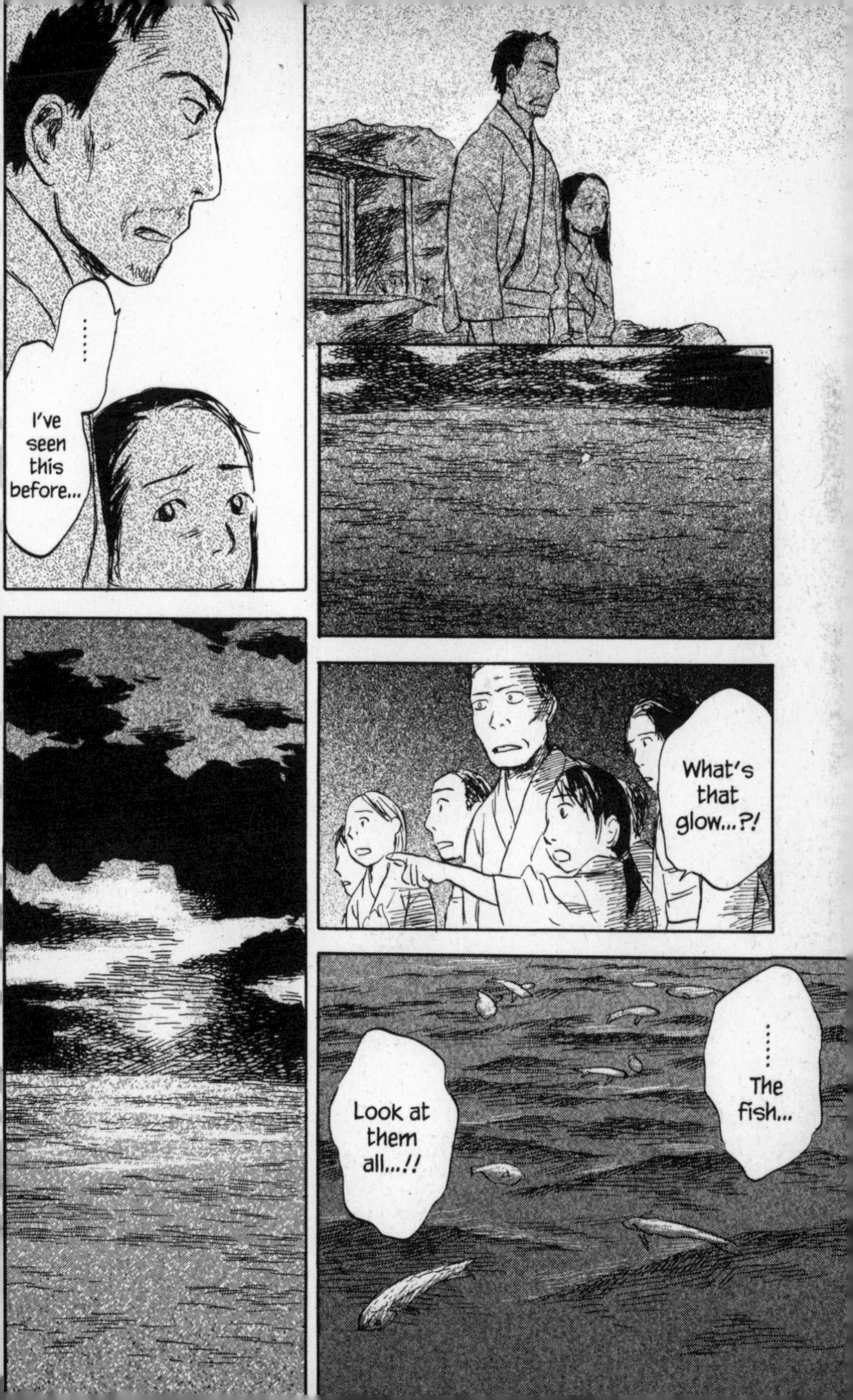
......
I've seen this before...
What's that glow...?!
...... The fish...
Look at them all...!!

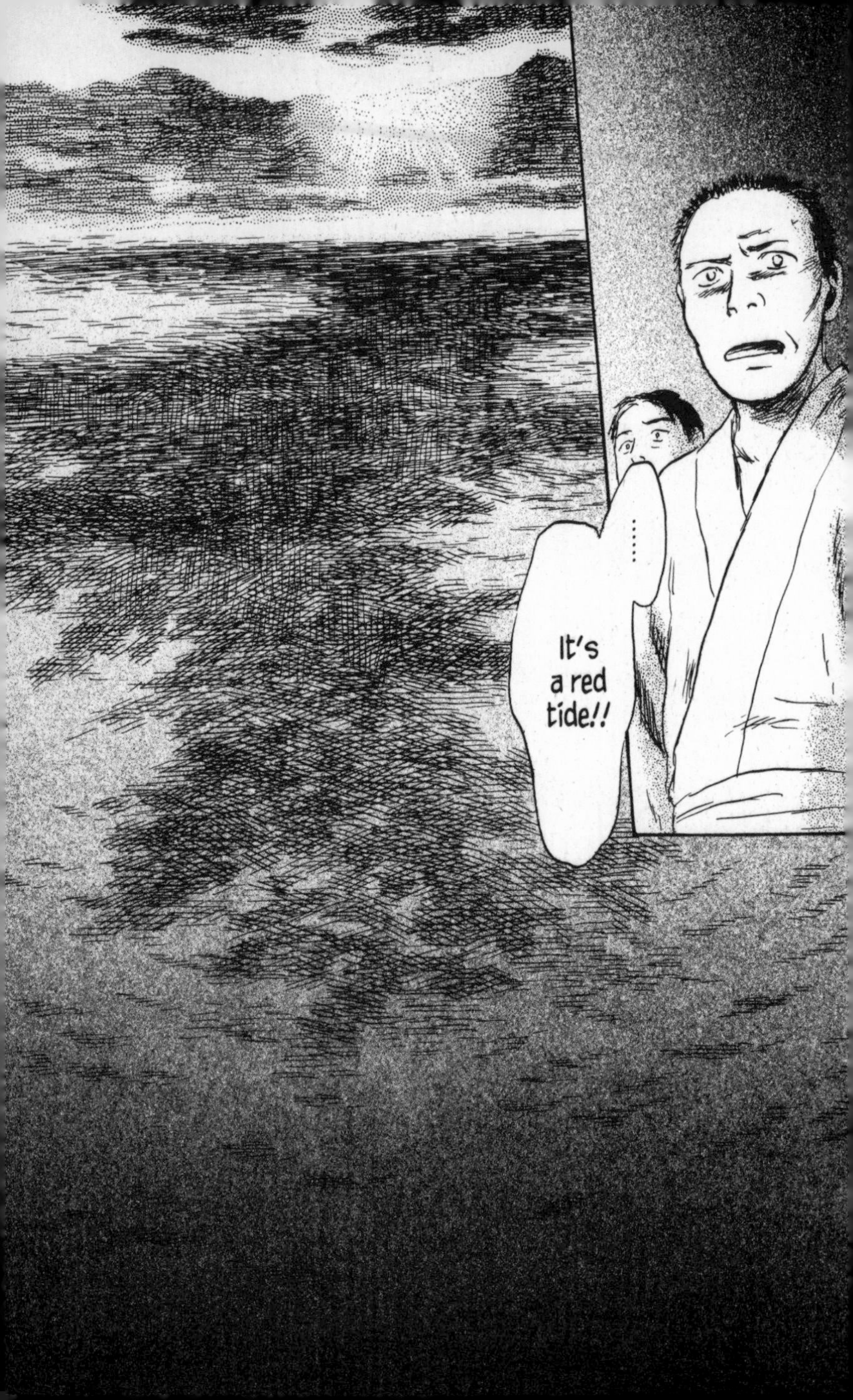
......
It's a red tide!!

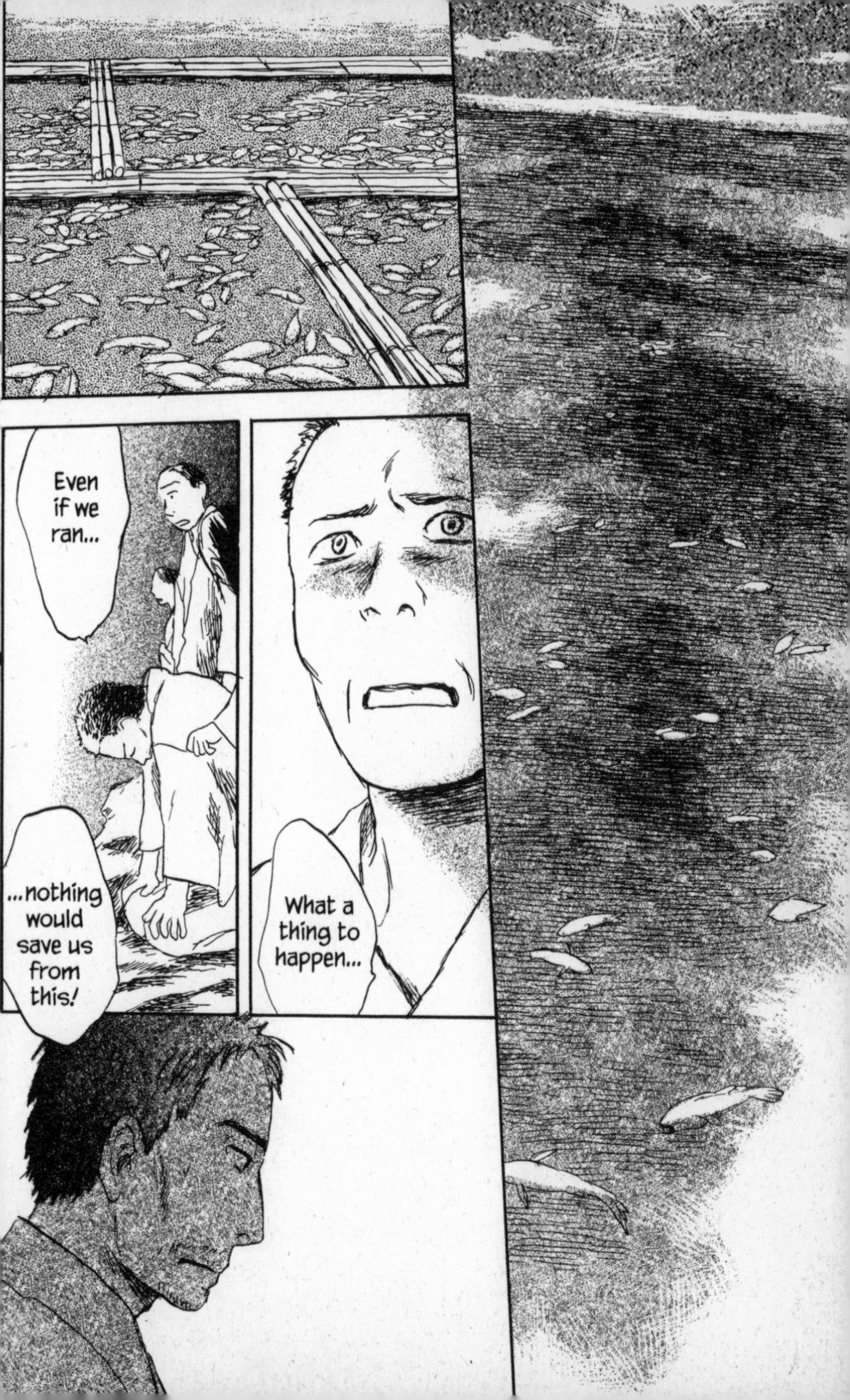

What a thing to happen...
Even if we ran...
...nothing would save us from this!

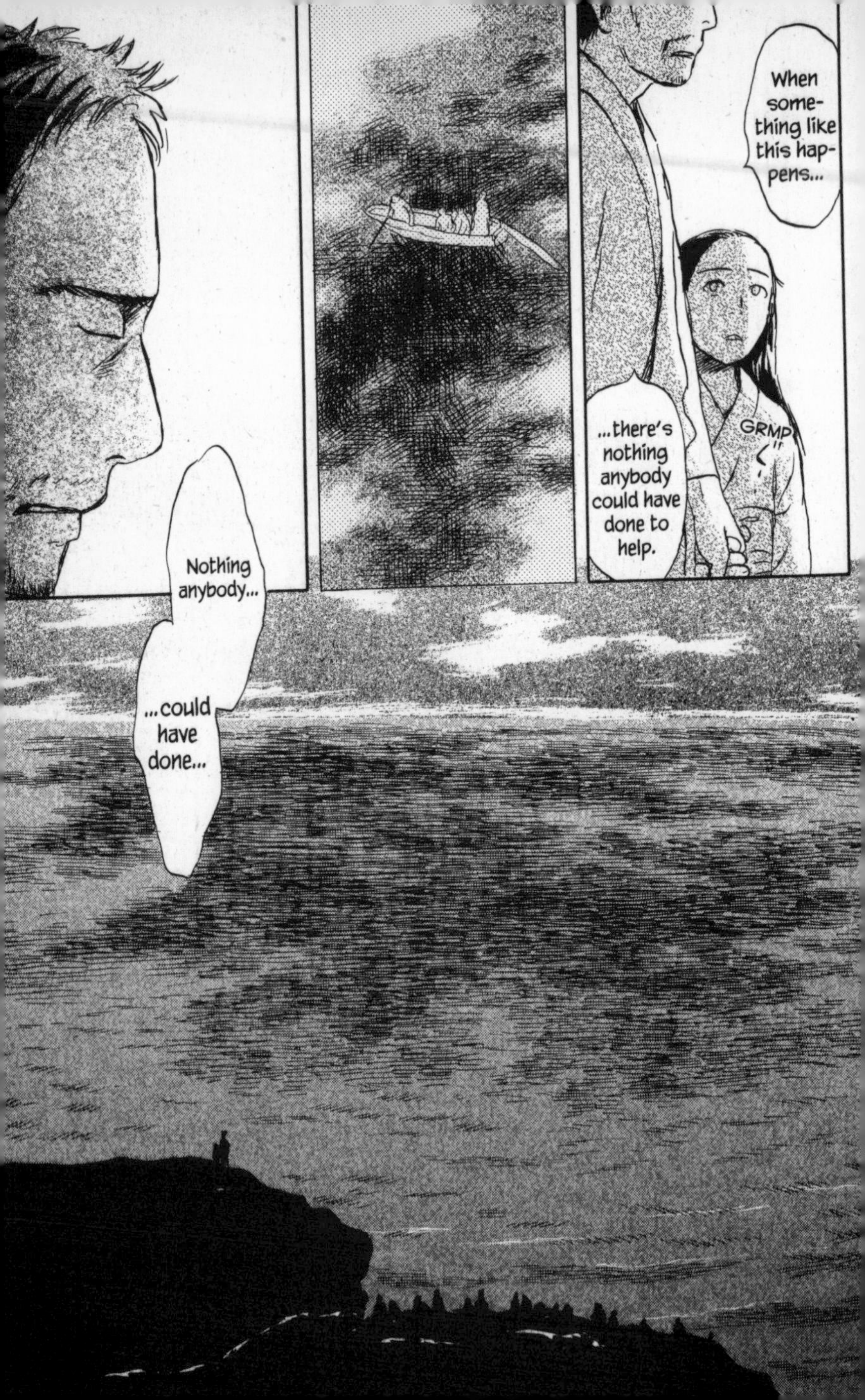
When something like this happens...
...there's nothing anybody could have done to help.
GRMP
Nothing anybody...
...could have done...

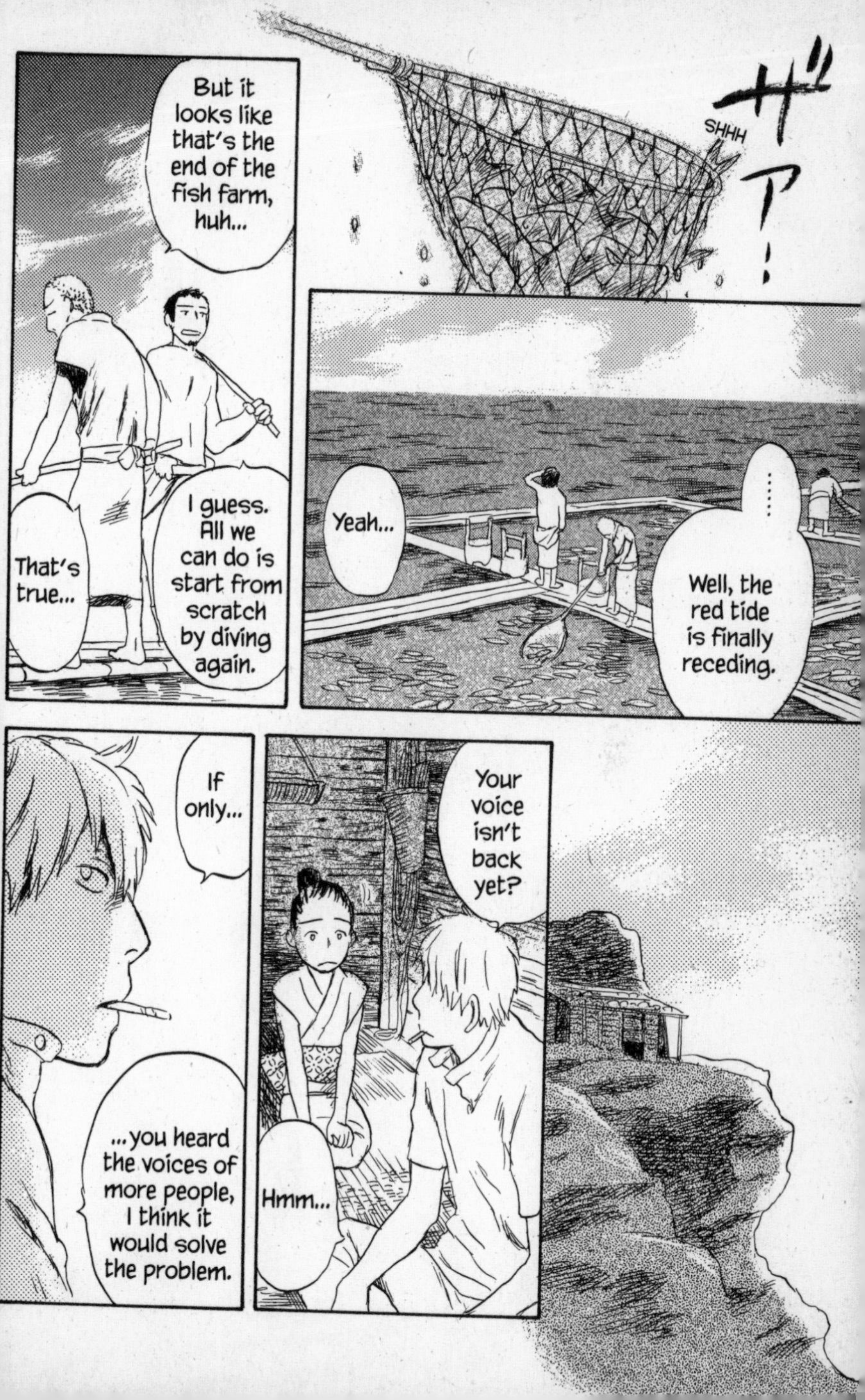
SHHH
......
Well, the red tide is finally receding.
Yeah...
But it looks like that's the end of the fish farm, huh...
I guess. All we can do is start from scratch by diving again.
That's true...
Your voice isn't back yet?
Hmm...
If only...
...you heard the voices of more people, I think it would solve the problem.

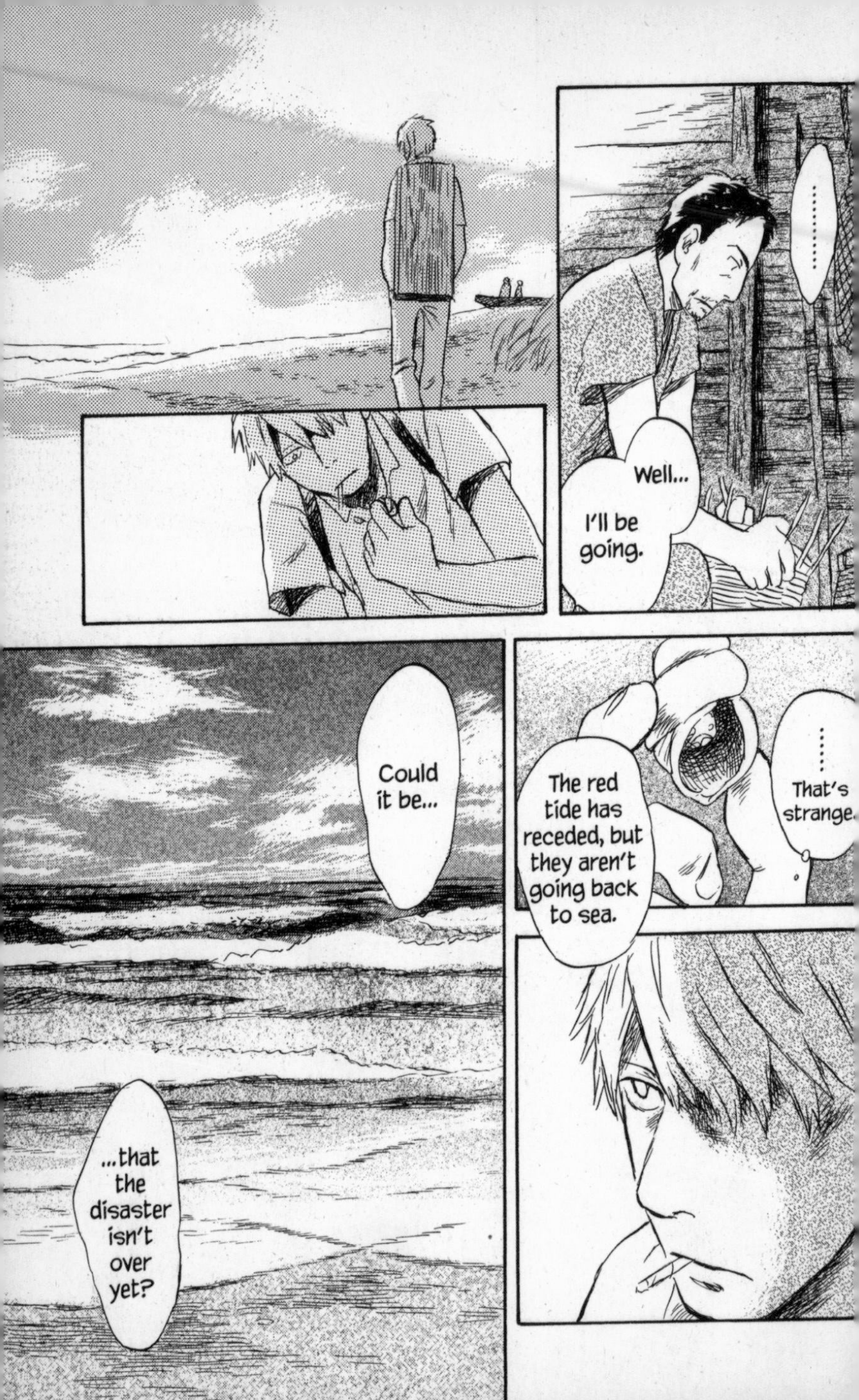
……
Well…
I'll be going.
……
That's strange.
The red tide has receded, but they aren't going back to sea.
Could it be…
…that the disaster isn't over yet?

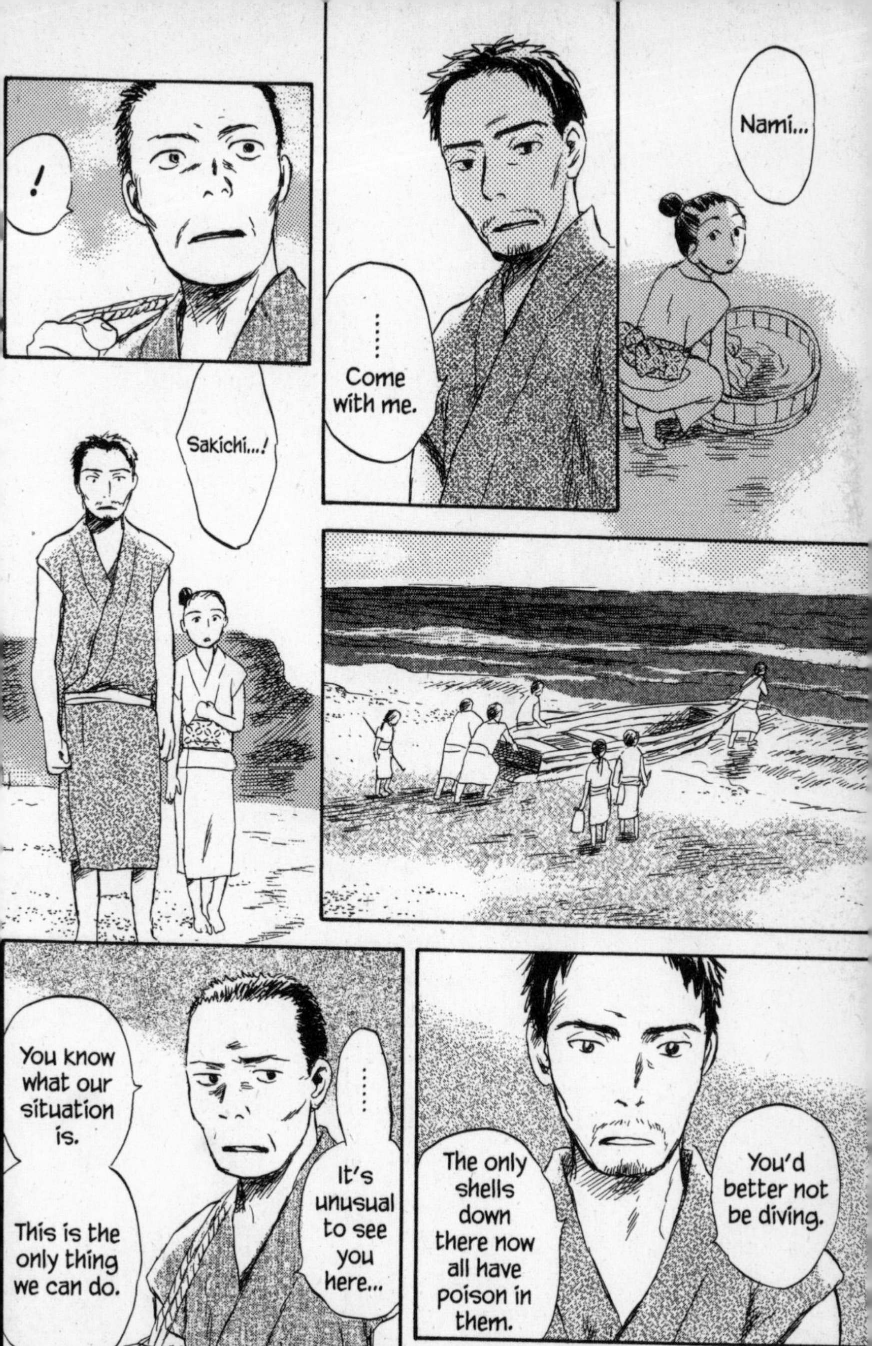
Nami...
......
Come with me.
!
Sakichi...!
You'd better not be diving.
The only shells down there now all have poison in them.
......
It's unusual to see you here...
You know what our situation is.
This is the only thing we can do.

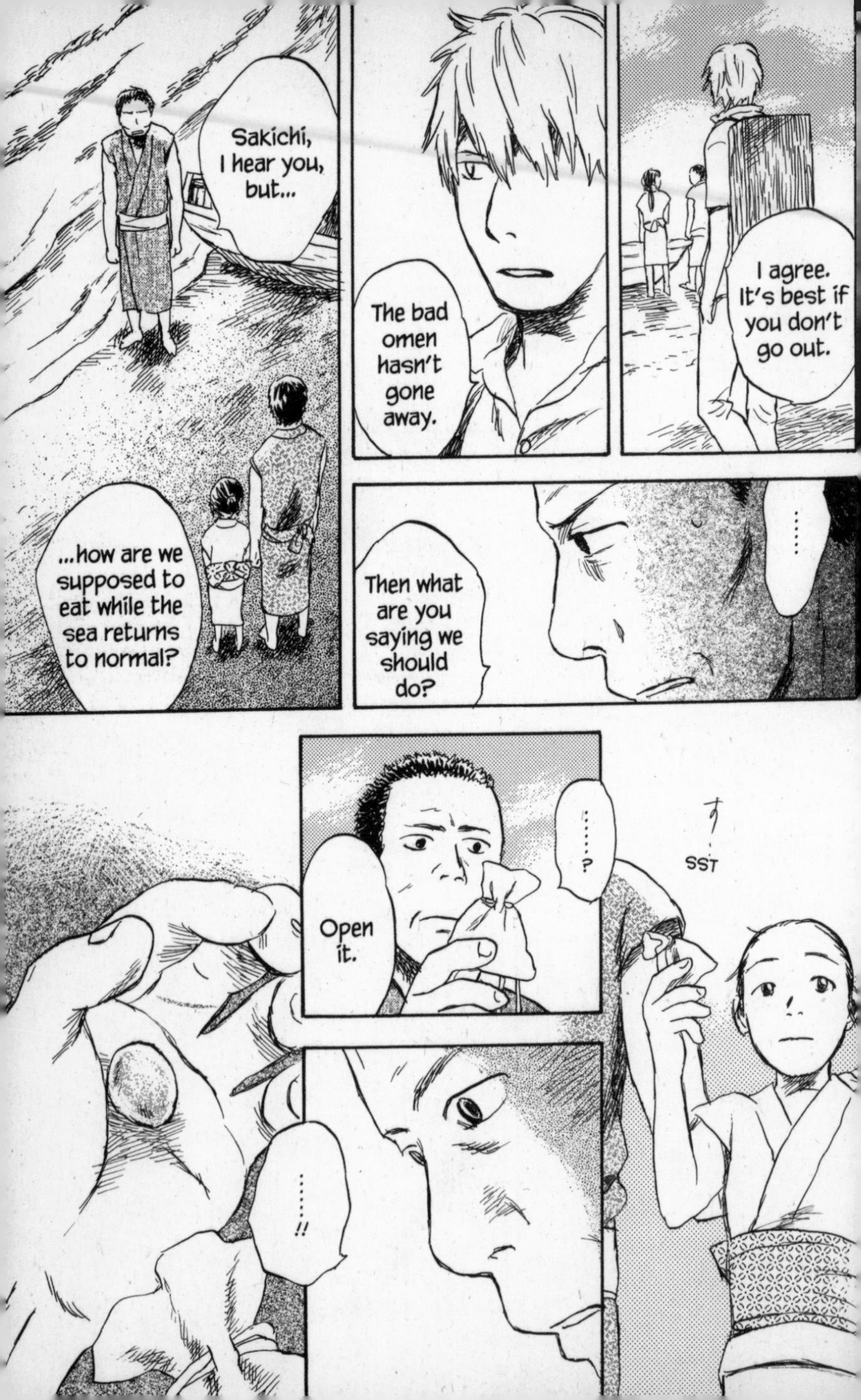
I agree. It's best if you don't go out.
The bad omen hasn't gone away.
......
Then what are you saying we should do?
Sakichi, I hear you, but...
...how are we supposed to eat while the sea returns to normal?
す
SST
......?
Open it.
......!!

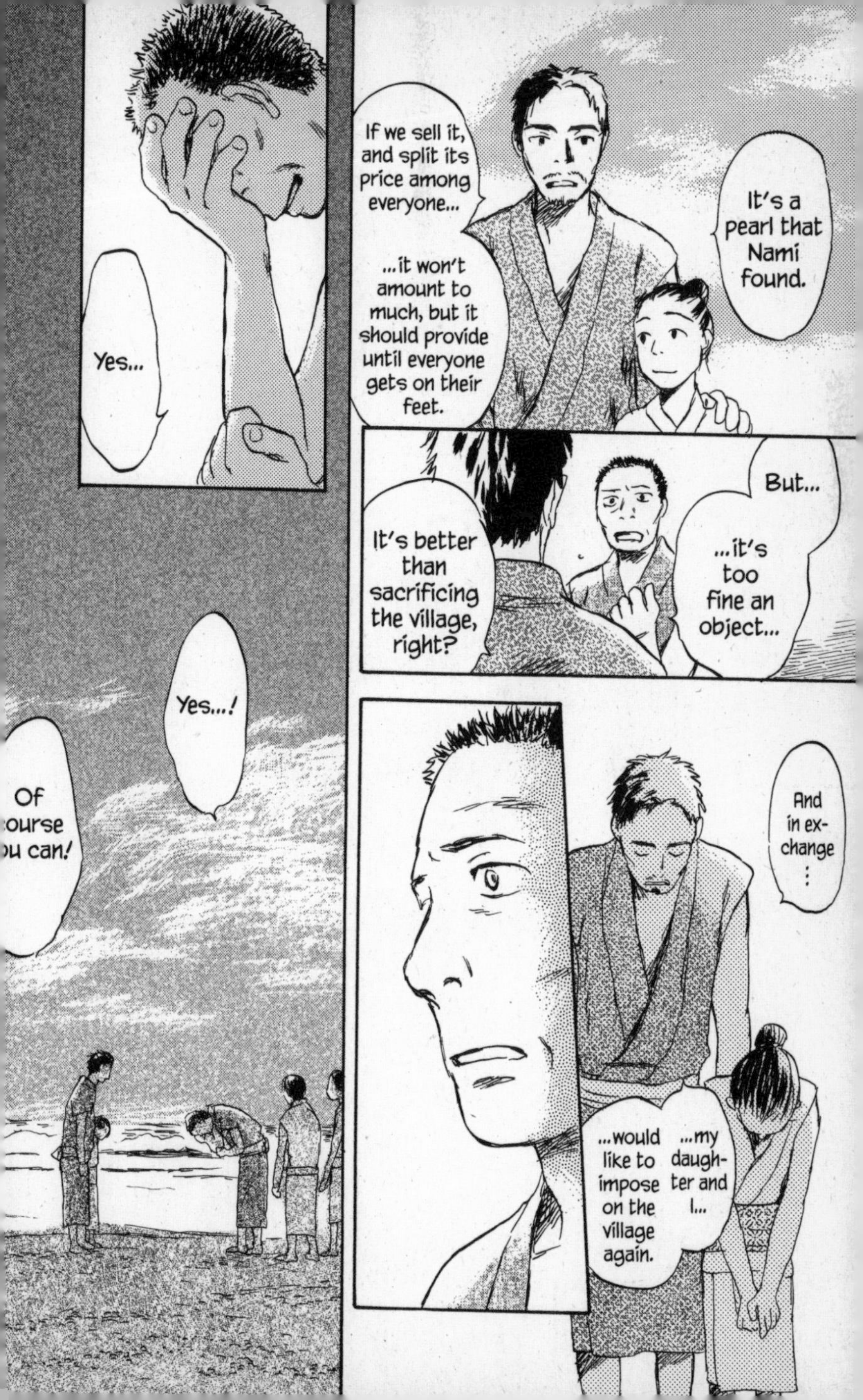
It's a pearl that Nami found.
If we sell it, and split its price among everyone...
...it won't amount to much, but it should provide until everyone gets on their feet.
But...
...it's too fine an object...
It's better than sacrificing the village, right?
And in exchange...
...my daughter and I...
...would like to impose on the village again.
Yes...
Yes...!
Of
ourse
u can!

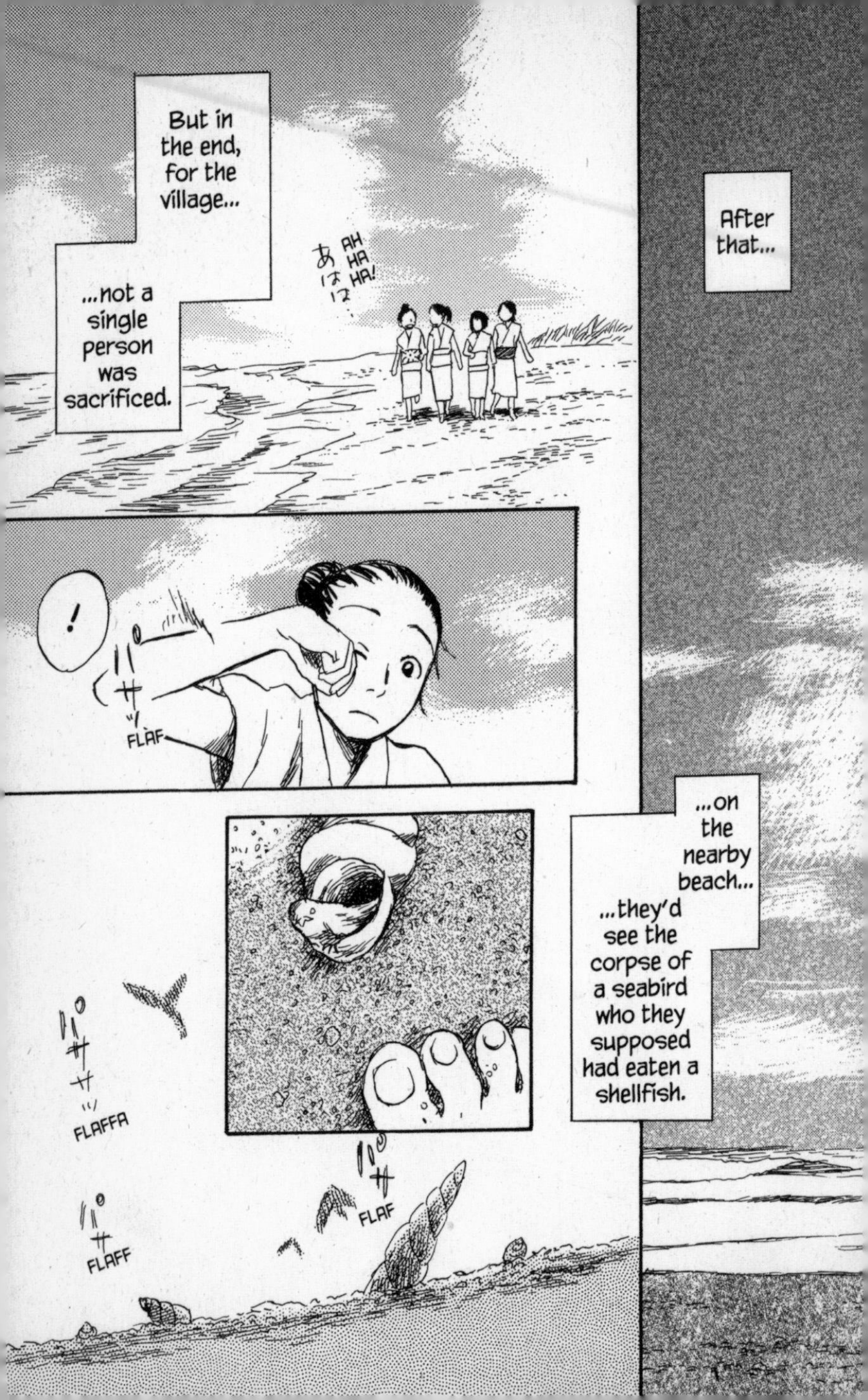
After that...
...on the nearby beach...
...they'd see the corpse of a seabird who they supposed had eaten a shellfish.
But in the end, for the village...
...not a single person was sacrificed.
あはは
AH HA HA!
!
パサッ
FLAF
パサッ
FLAFFA
パサ
FLAF
パサ
FLAFF

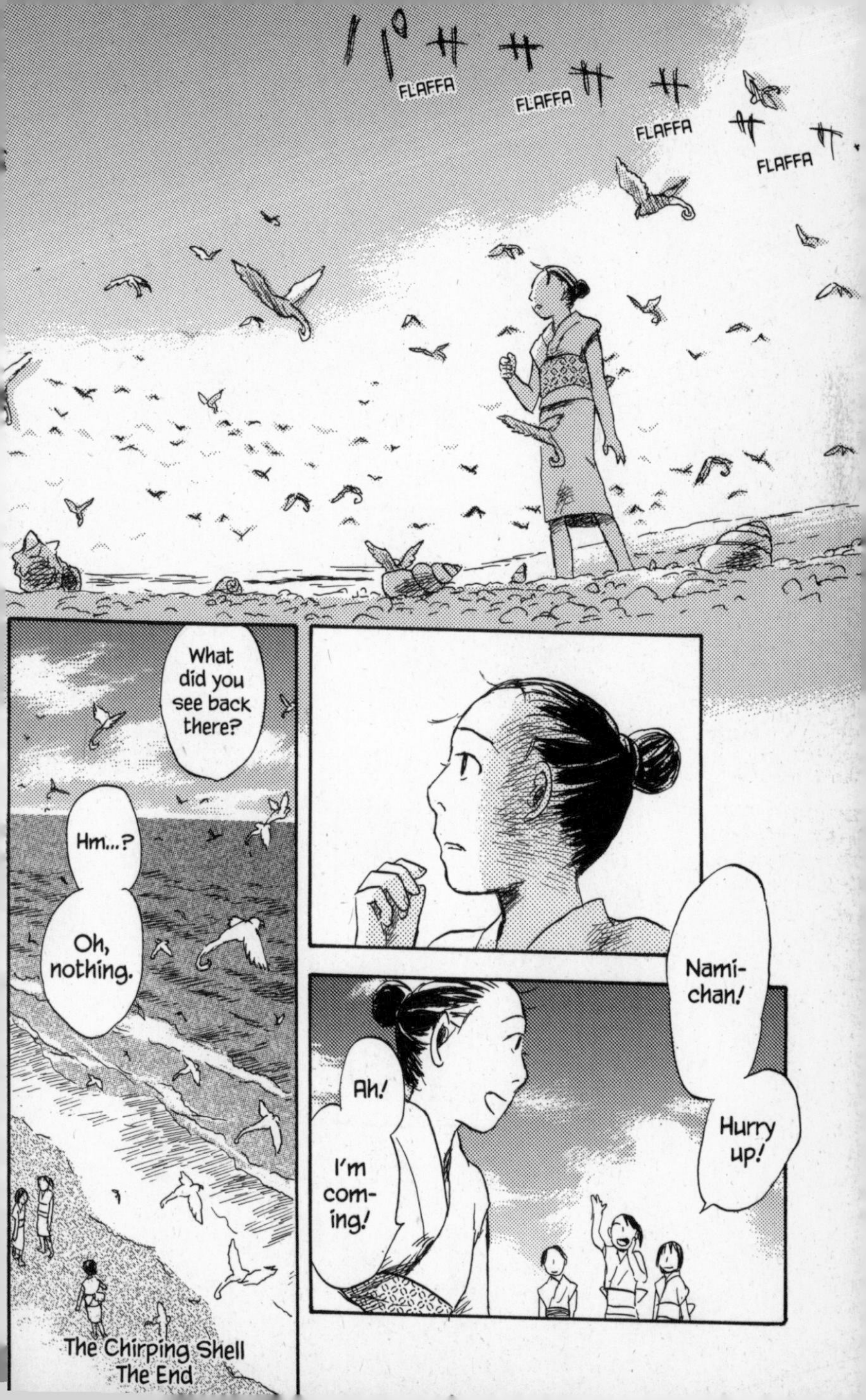
FLAFFA
FLAFFA
FLAFFA
FLAFFA
Nami-chan!
Hurry up!
Ah!
I'm com-ing!
What did you see back there?
Hm...?
Oh, nothing.
The Chirping Shell
The End

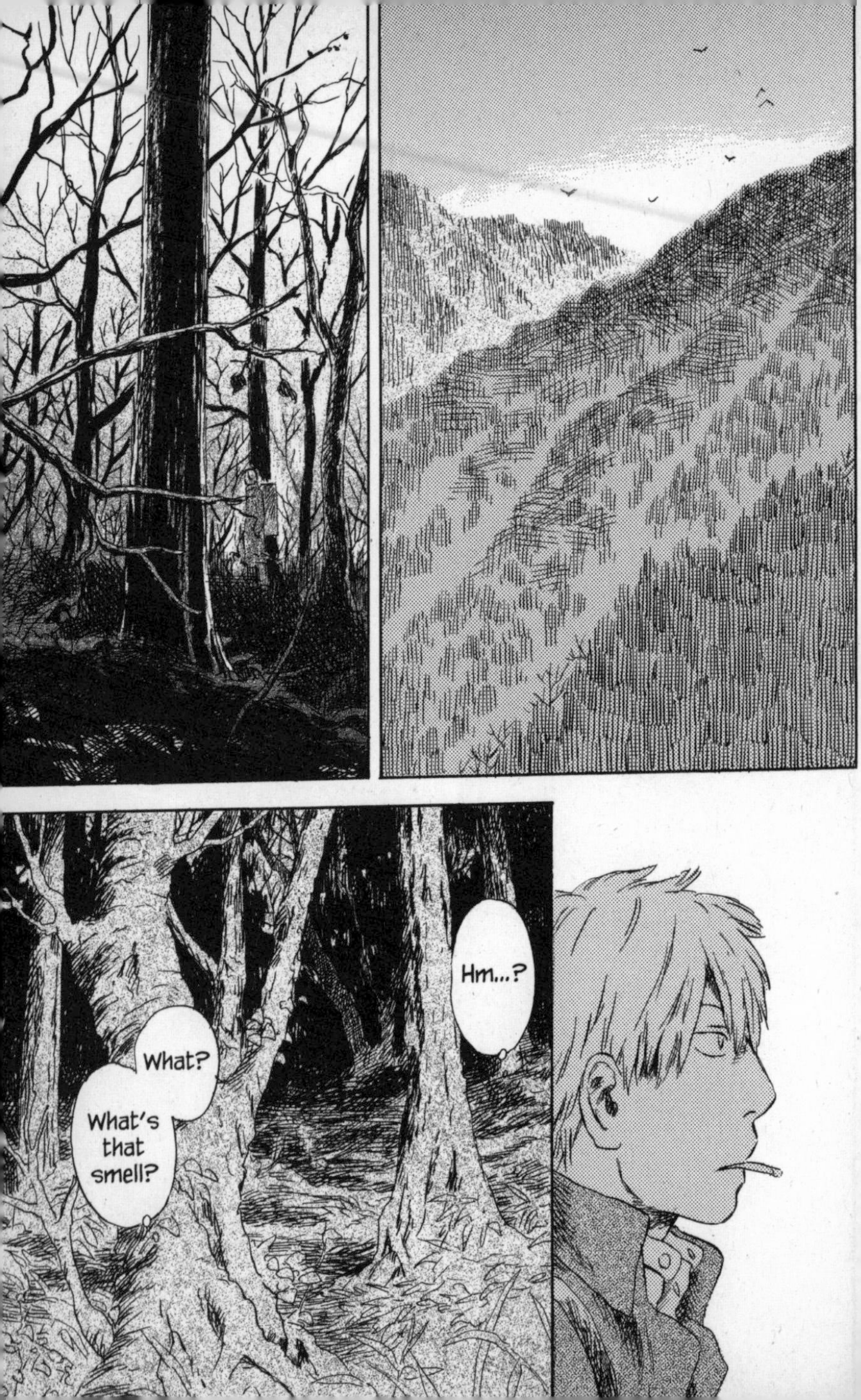
Hm...?
What?
What's that smell?

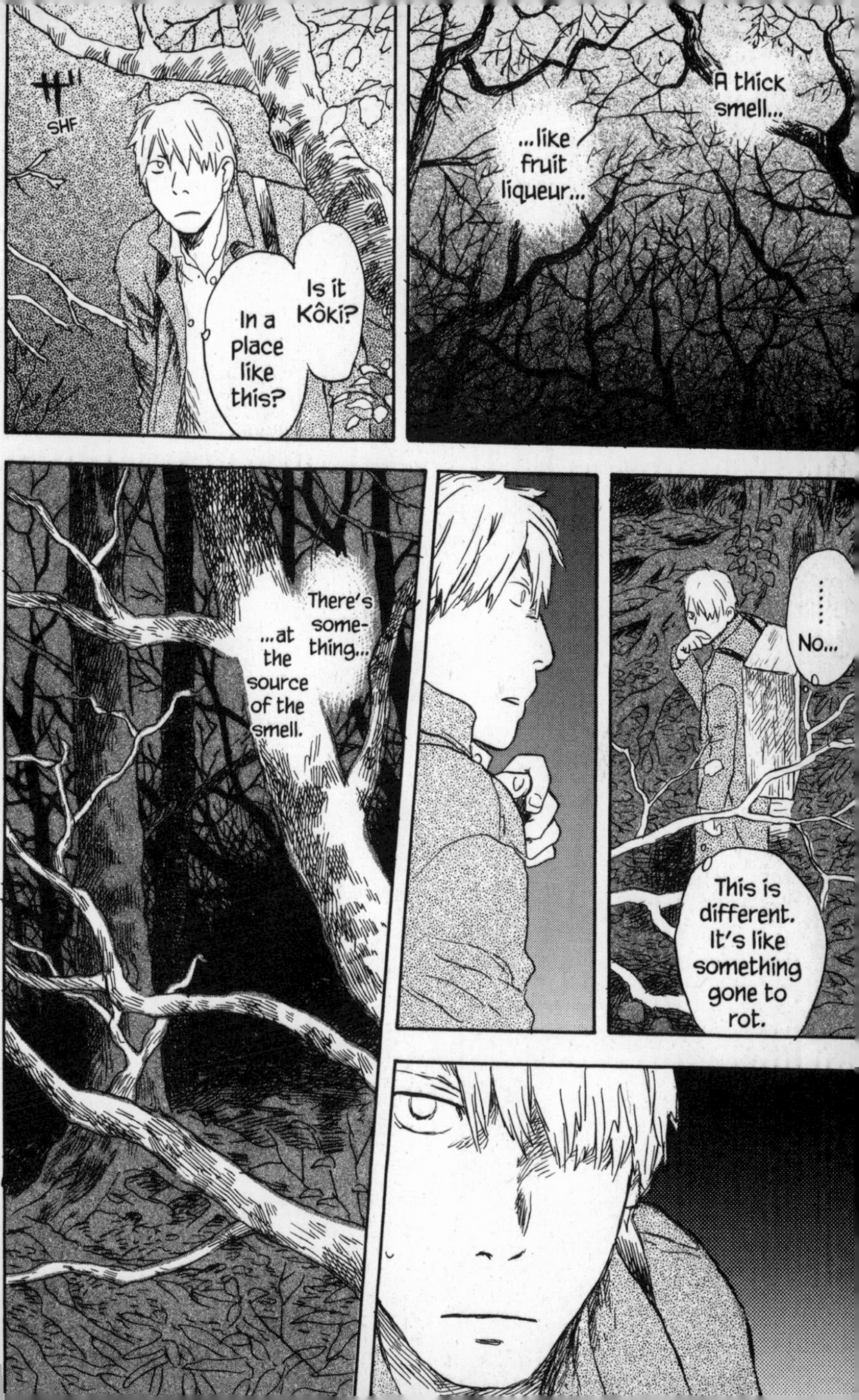
A thick smell...
...like fruit liqueur...
SHF
Is it Kôki?
In a place like this?
......
No...
This is different. It's like something gone to rot.
There's something...
...at the source of the smell.

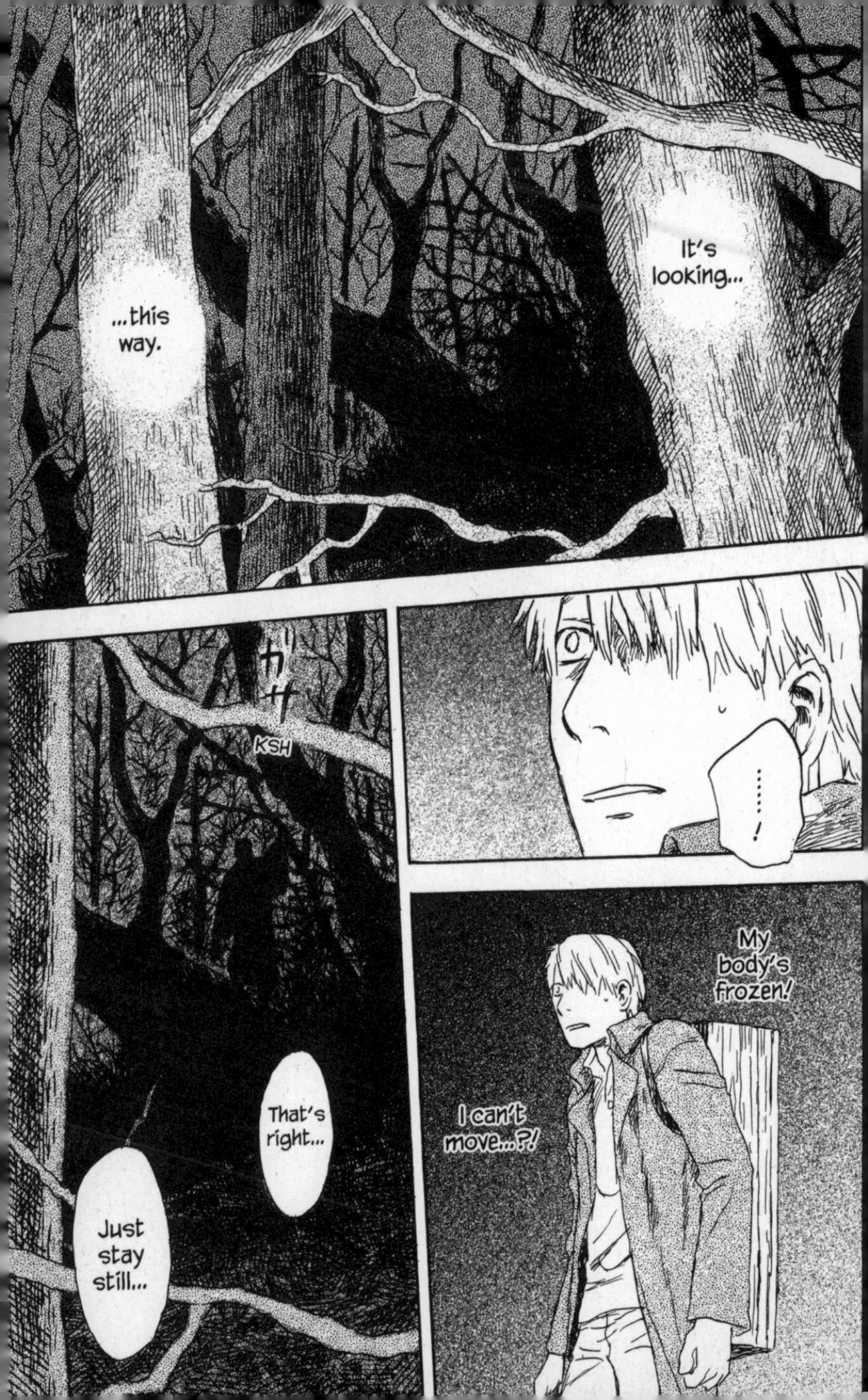
It's looking...
...this way.
......!
My body's frozen!
I can't move...?!
KSH
That's right...
Just stay still...

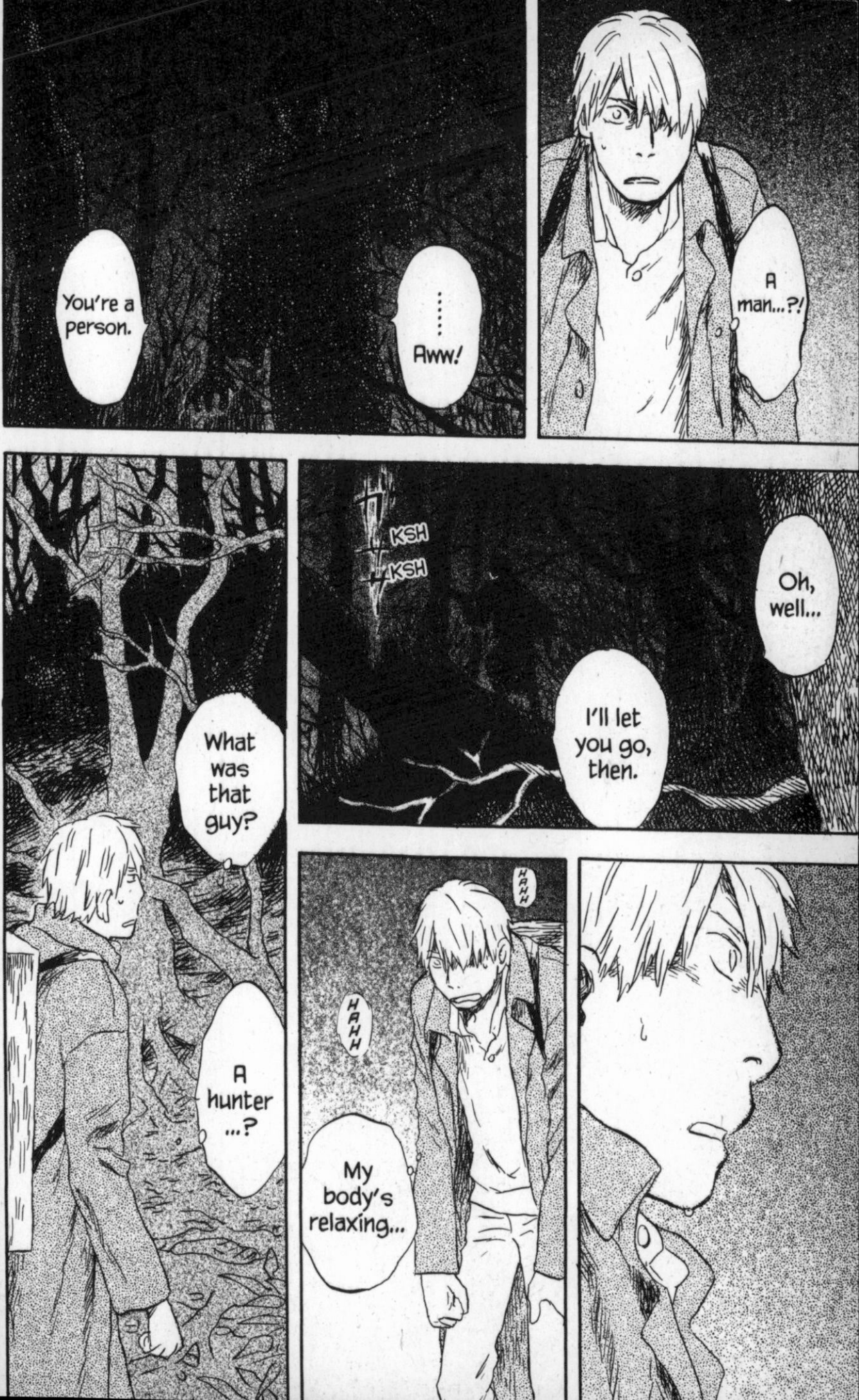
A man...?!
......
Aww!
You're a person.
KSH
KSH
Oh, well...
I'll let you go, then.
HAHH
HAHH
My body's relaxing...
What was that guy?
A hunter ...?

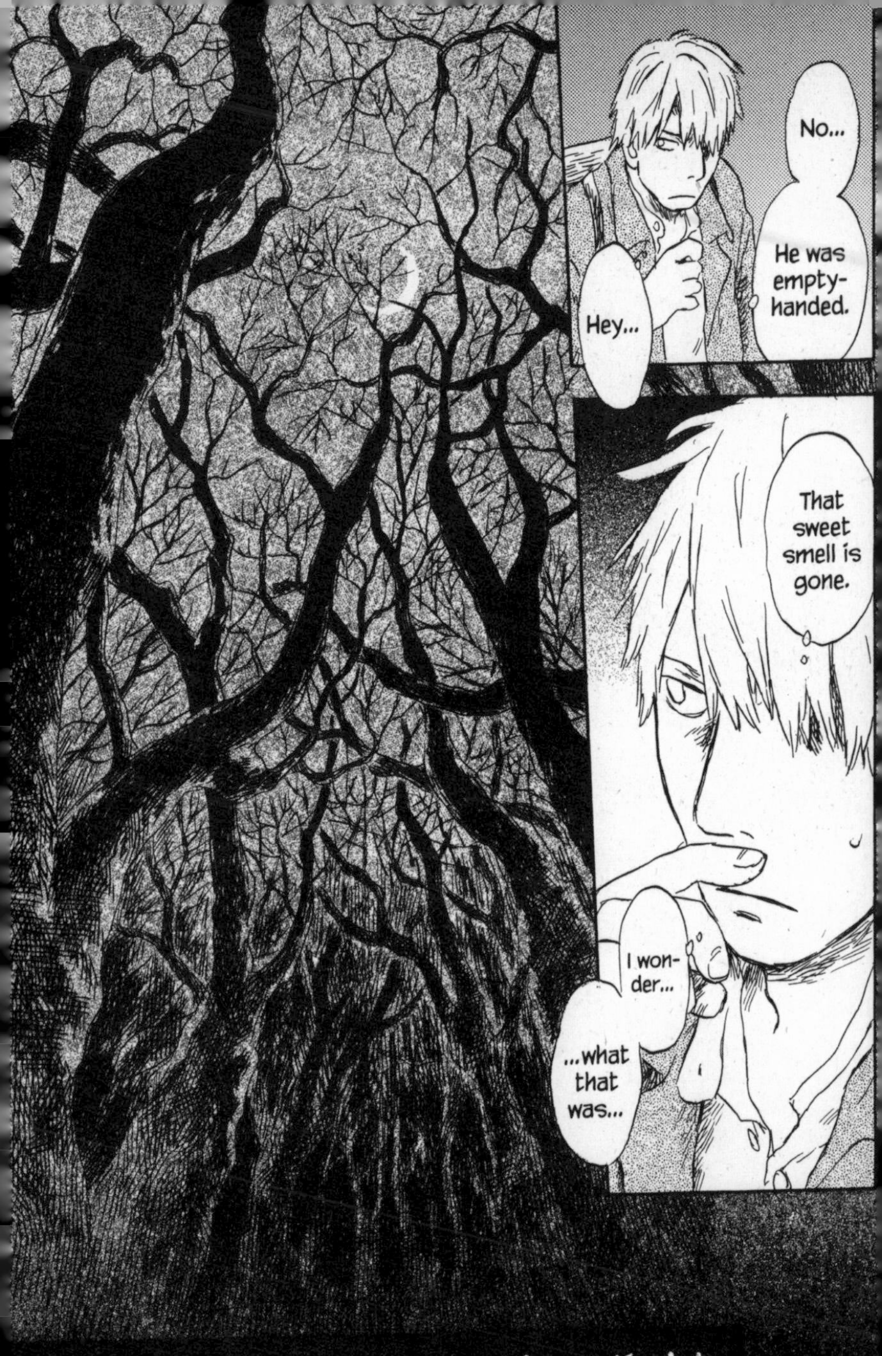
No...
He was empty-handed.
Hey...
That sweet smell is gone.
I wonder...
...what that was...

The Hand That Pets the Night

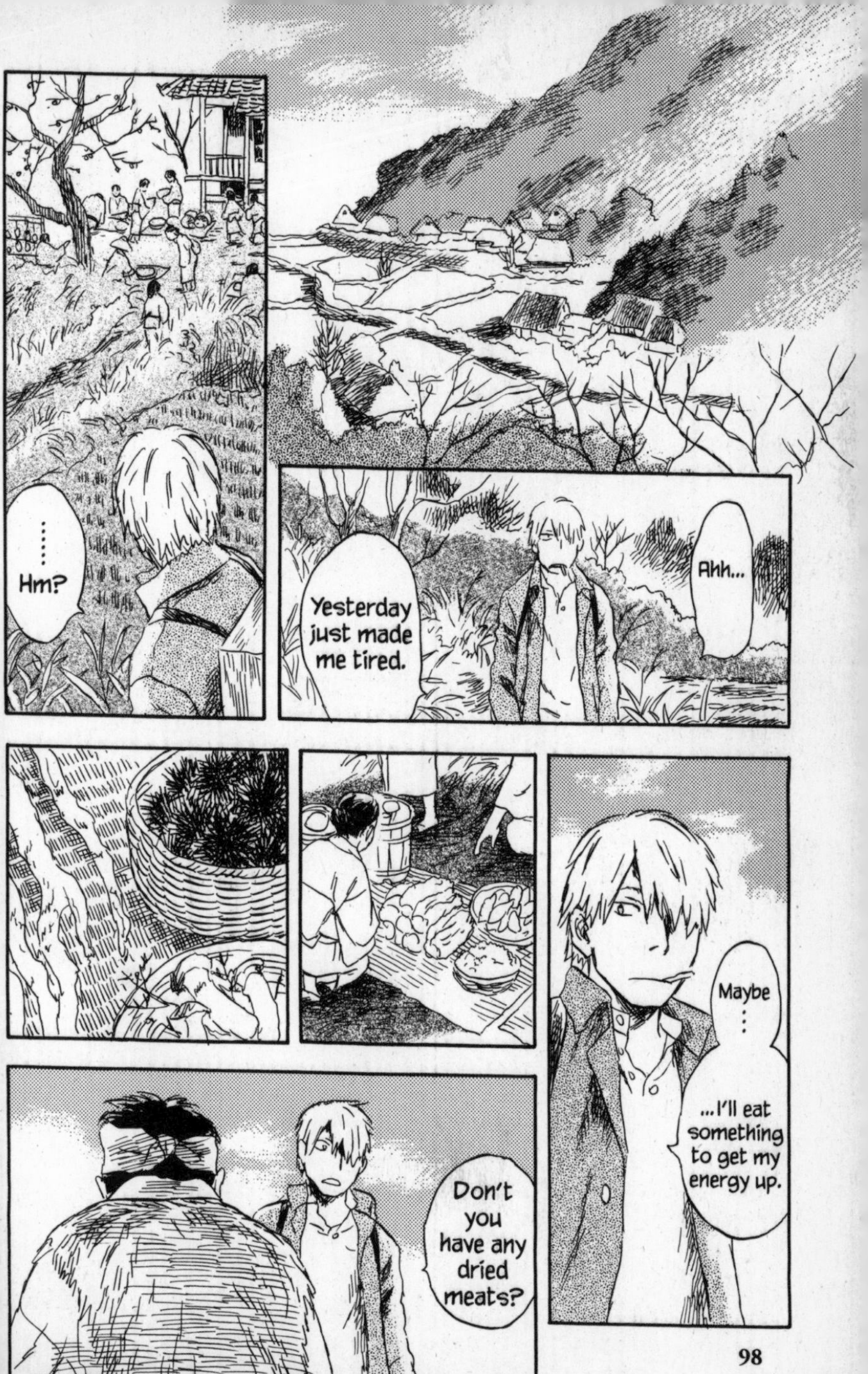
Ahh...
Yesterday just made me tired.
...... Hm?
Maybe ...
...I'll eat something to get my energy up.
Don't you have any dried meats?

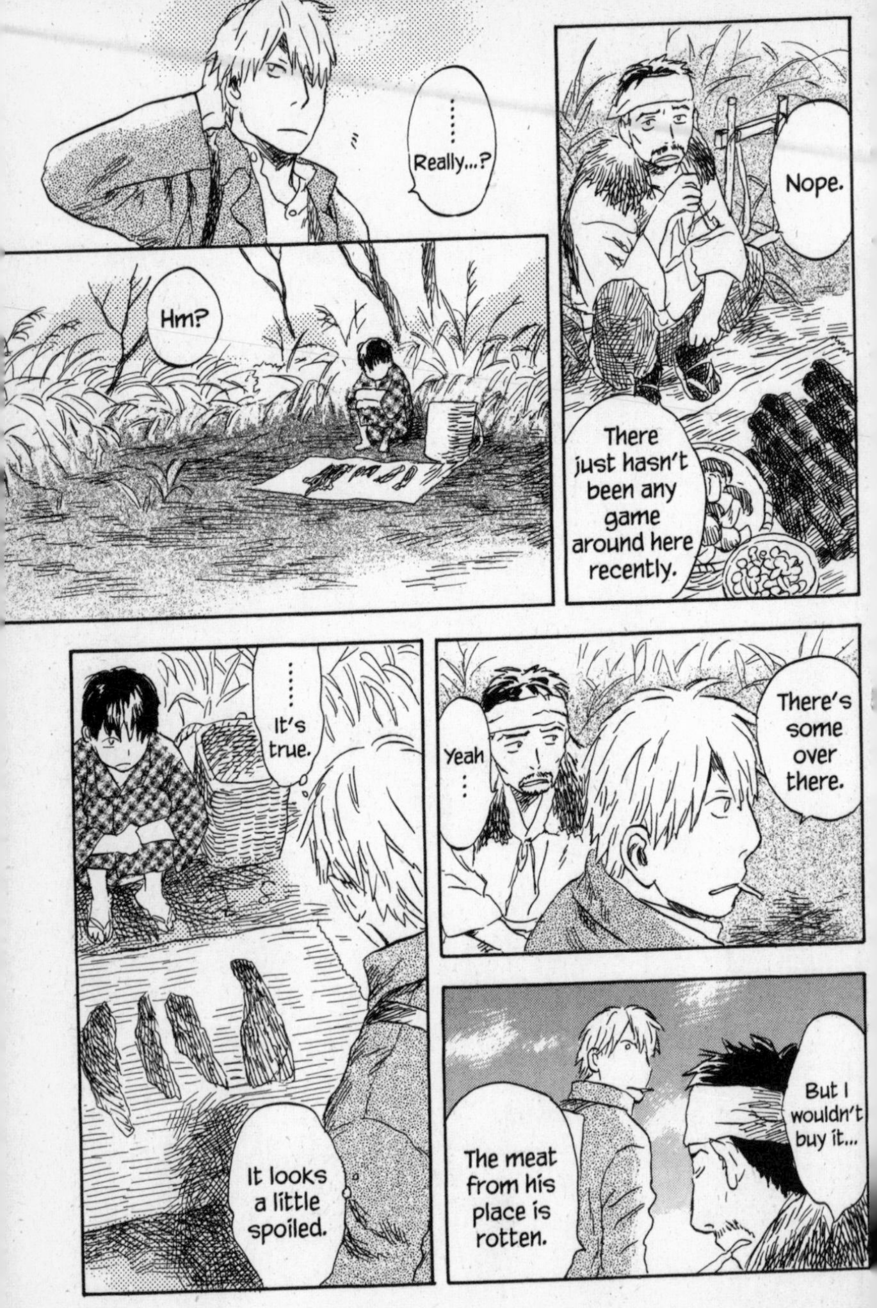
Nope.
There just hasn't been any game around here recently.
......Really...?
Hm?
There's some over there.
Yeah...
But I wouldn't buy it...
The meat from his place is rotten.
......It's true.
It looks a little spoiled.

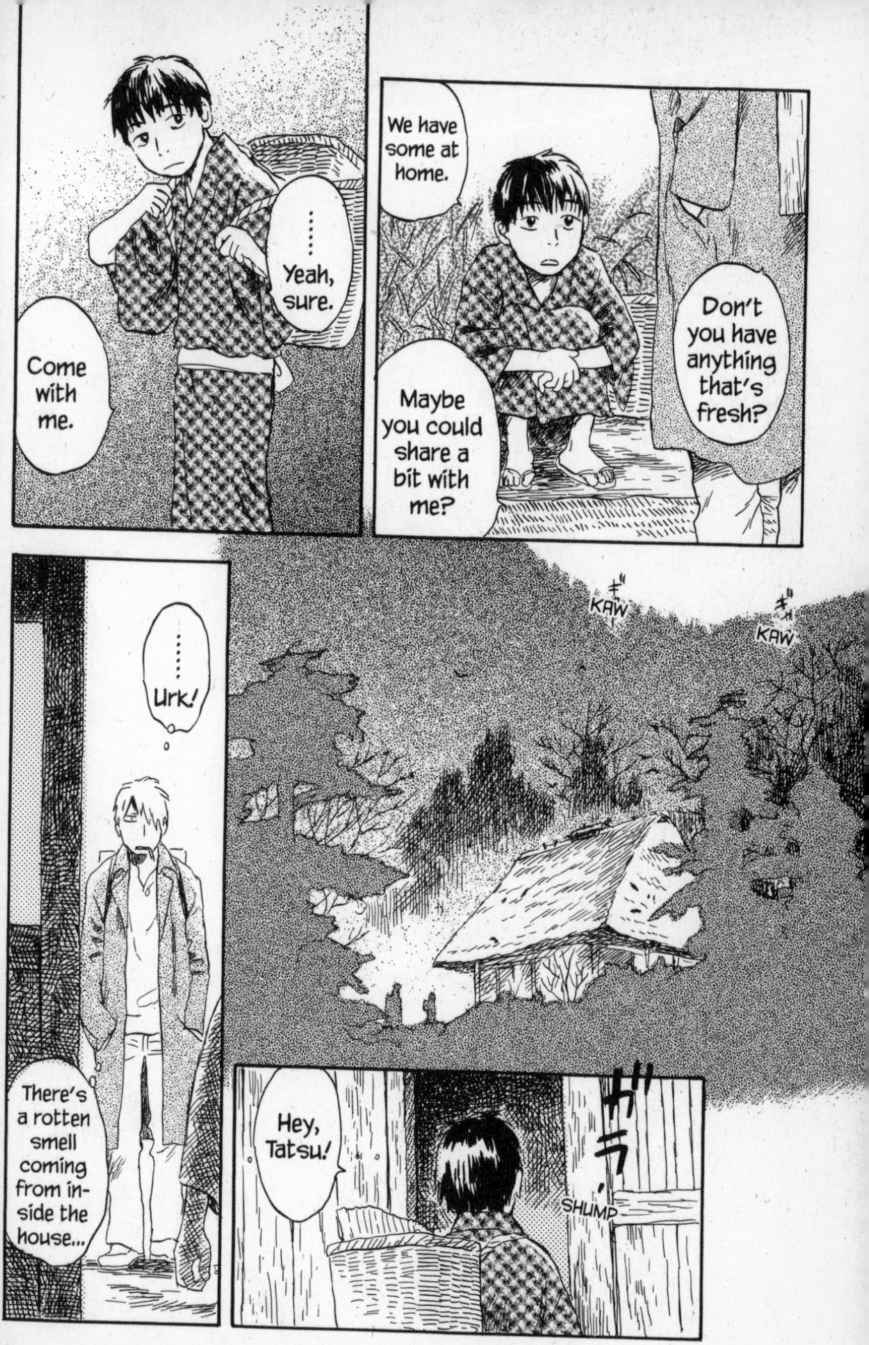
Don't you have anything that's fresh?
We have some at home.
Maybe you could share a bit with me?
...... Yeah, sure.
Come with me.
KAW
KAW
SHUMP
Hey, Tatsu!
...... Urk!
There's a rotten smell coming from inside the house...

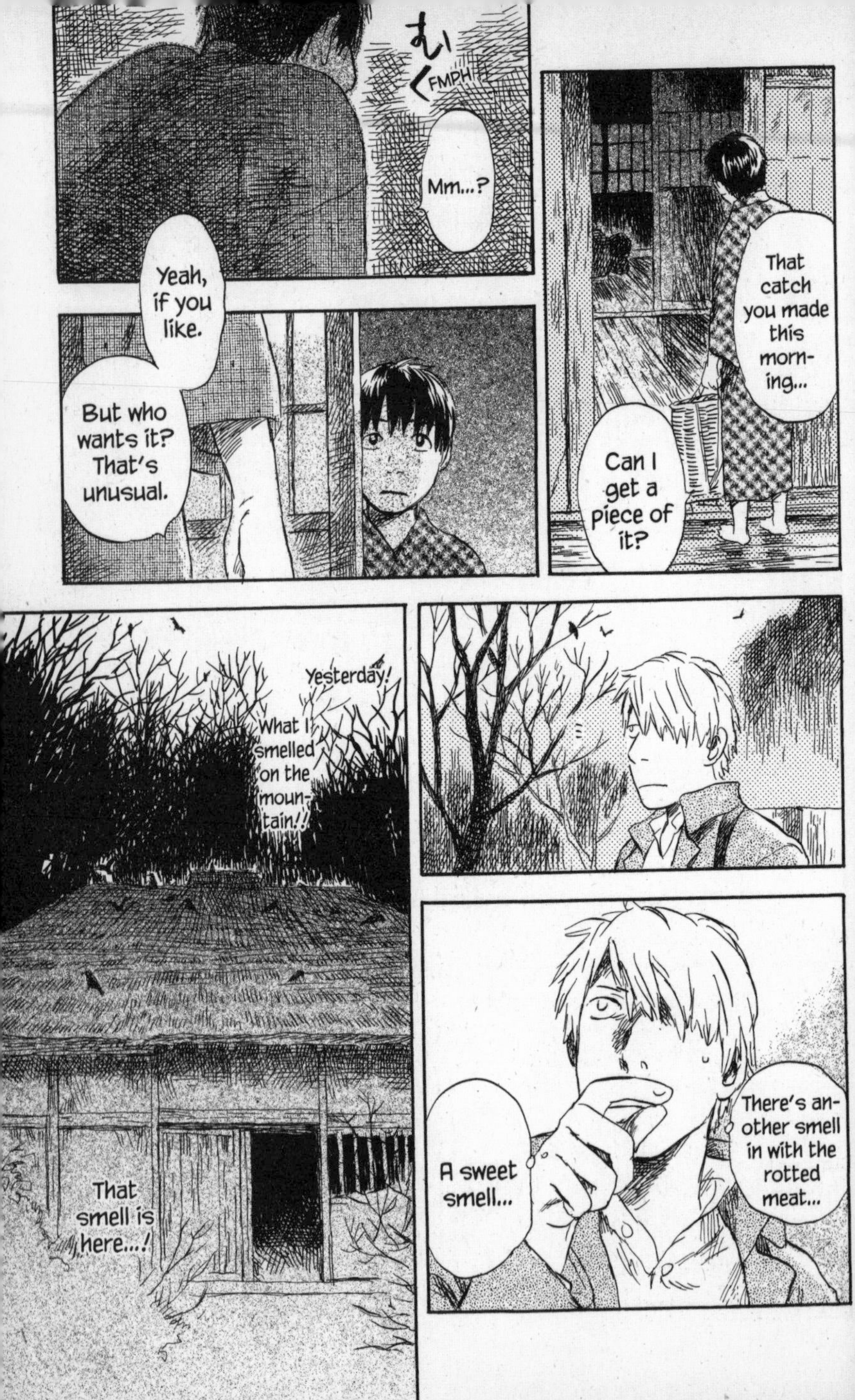
That catch you made this morning...
Can I get a piece of it?
むく FMPH
Mm...?
Yeah, if you like.
But who wants it? That's unusual.
There's another smell in with the rotted meat...
A sweet smell...
Yesterday!
What I smelled on the mountain!
That smell is here...!

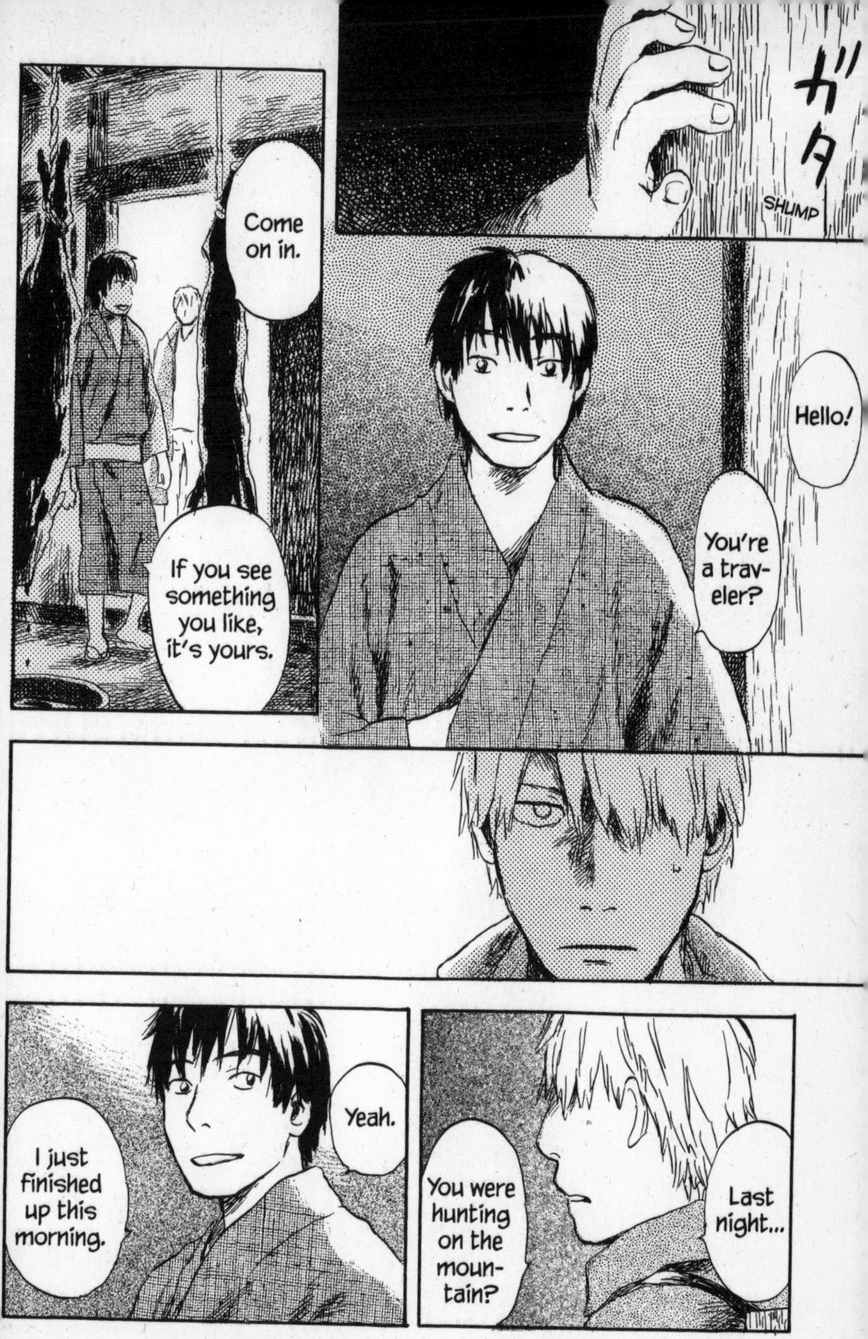
ガタ
SHUMP
Hello!
You're a traveler?
Come on in.
If you see something you like, it's yours.
Last night...
You were hunting on the mountain?
Yeah.
I just finished up this morning.

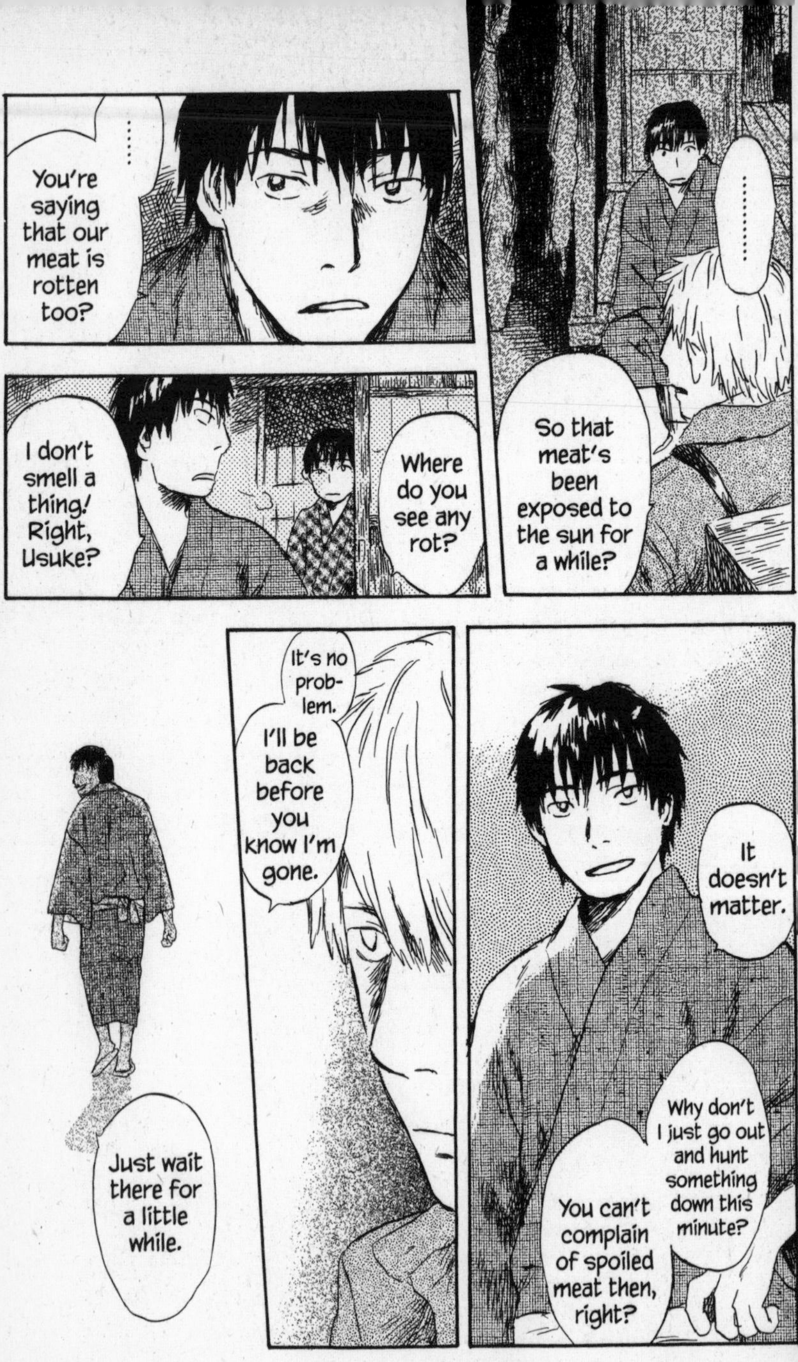
......
So that meat's been exposed to the sun for a while?
......
You're saying that our meat is rotten too?
Where do you see any rot?
I don't smell a thing! Right, Usuke?
It doesn't matter.
Why don't I just go out and hunt something down this minute?
You can't complain of spoiled meat then, right?
It's no problem.
I'll be back before you know I'm gone.
Just wait there for a little while.

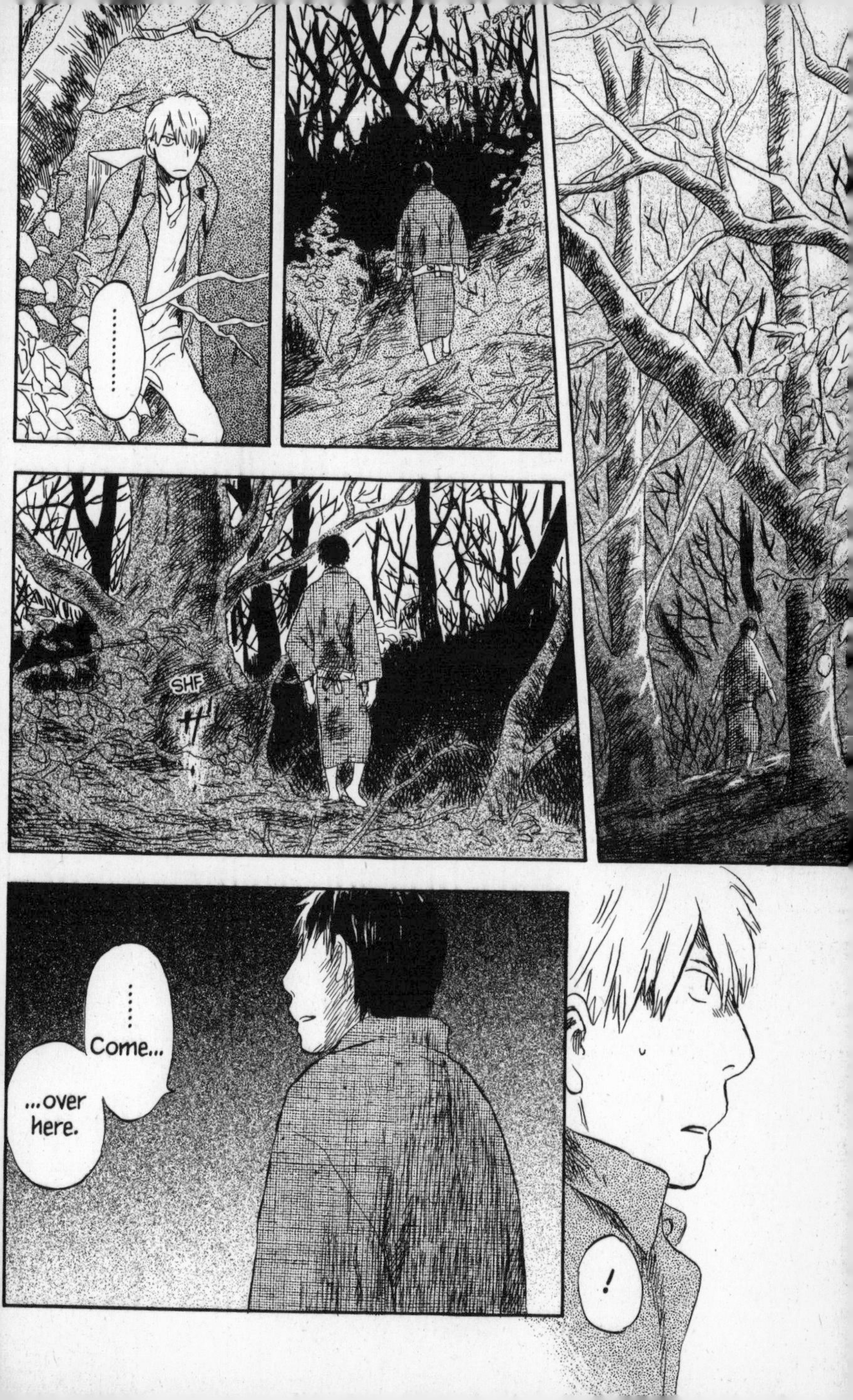
......
SHF
......
Come...
...over here.
!

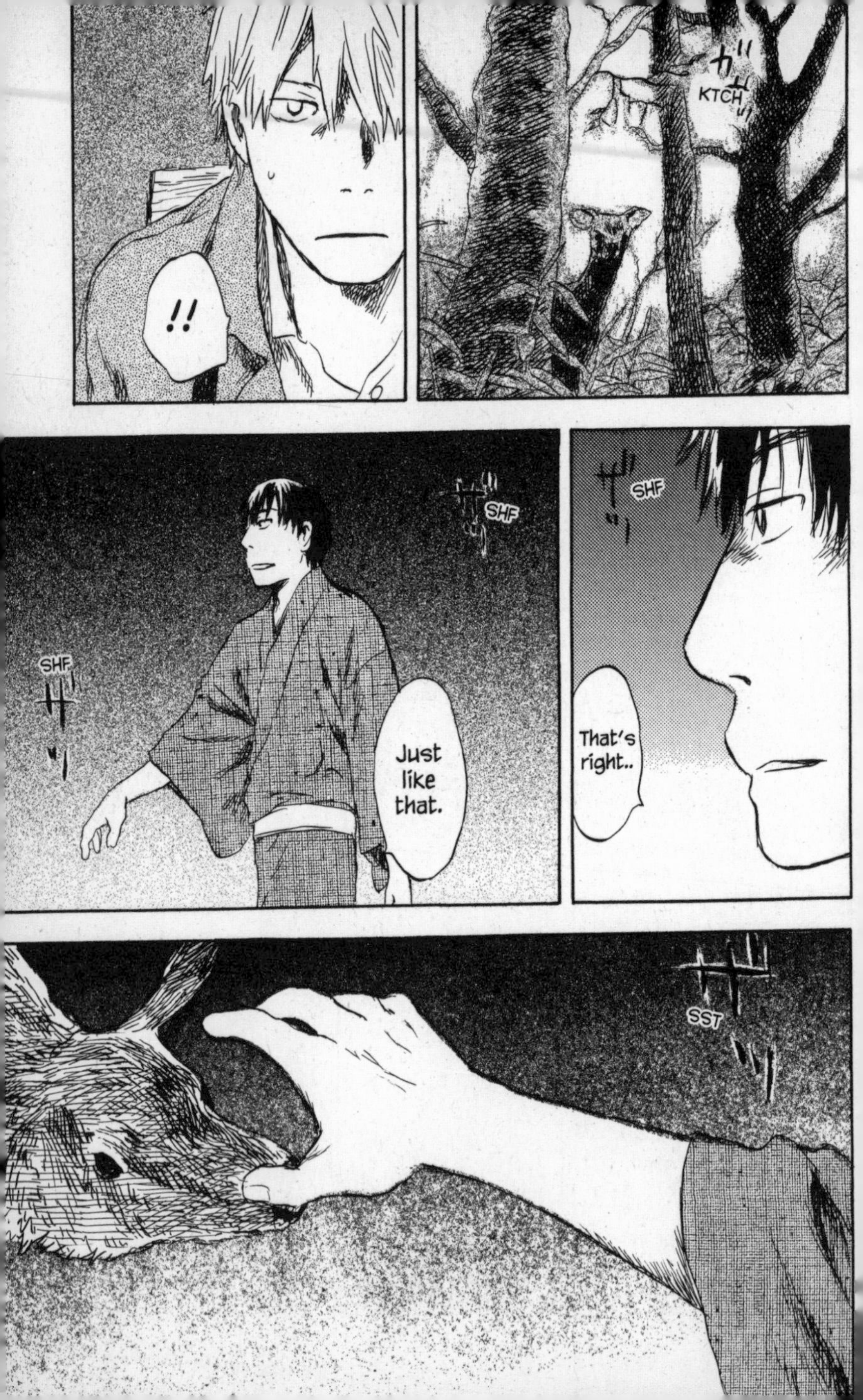
KTCH
!!
SHF
That's right..
SHF
SHF
Just like that.
SST

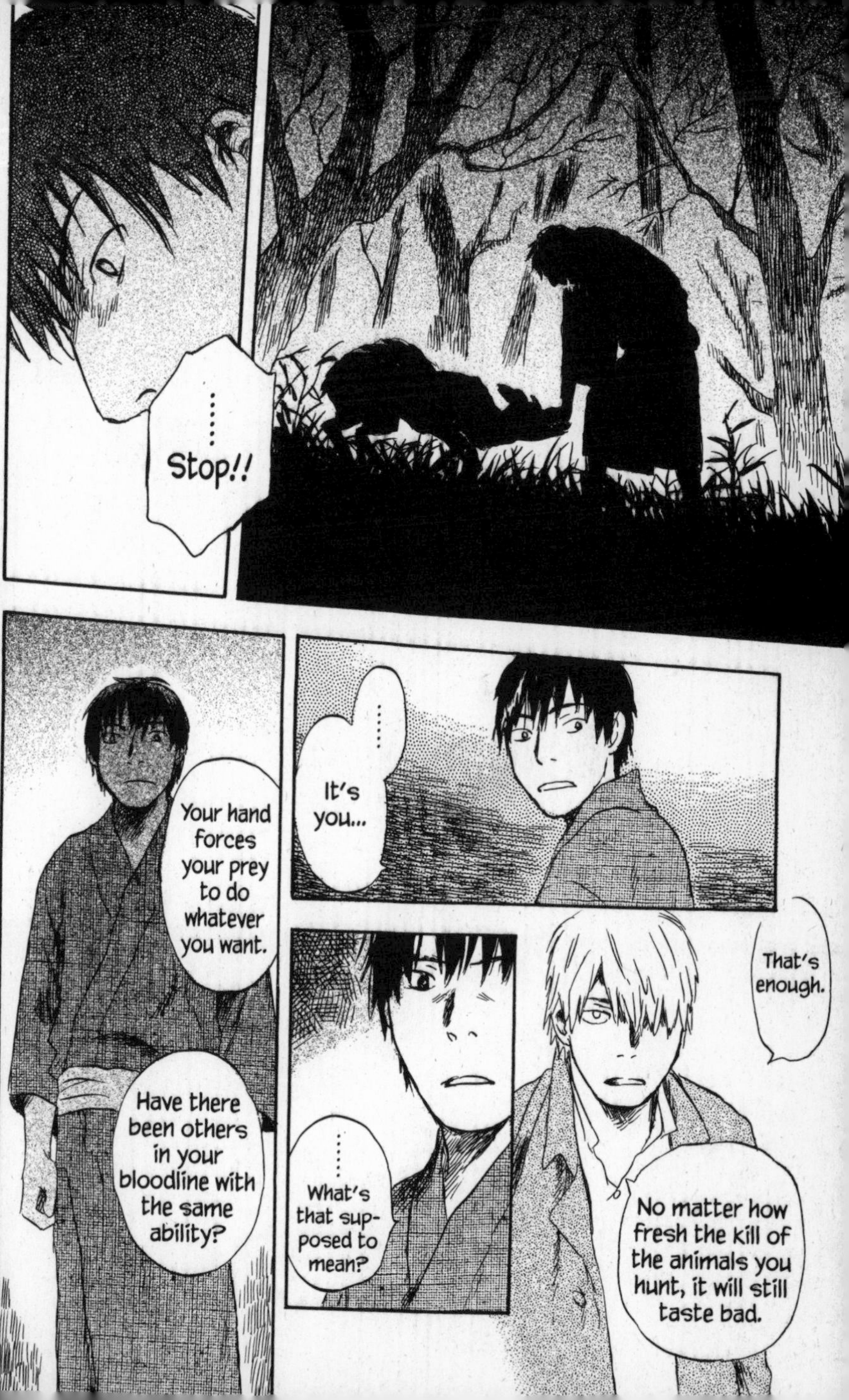

...... Stop!!
...... It's you...
That's enough.
No matter how fresh the kill of the animals you hunt, it will still taste bad.
...... What's that sup-posed to mean?
Your hand forces your prey to do whatever you want.
Have there been others in your bloodline with the same ability?

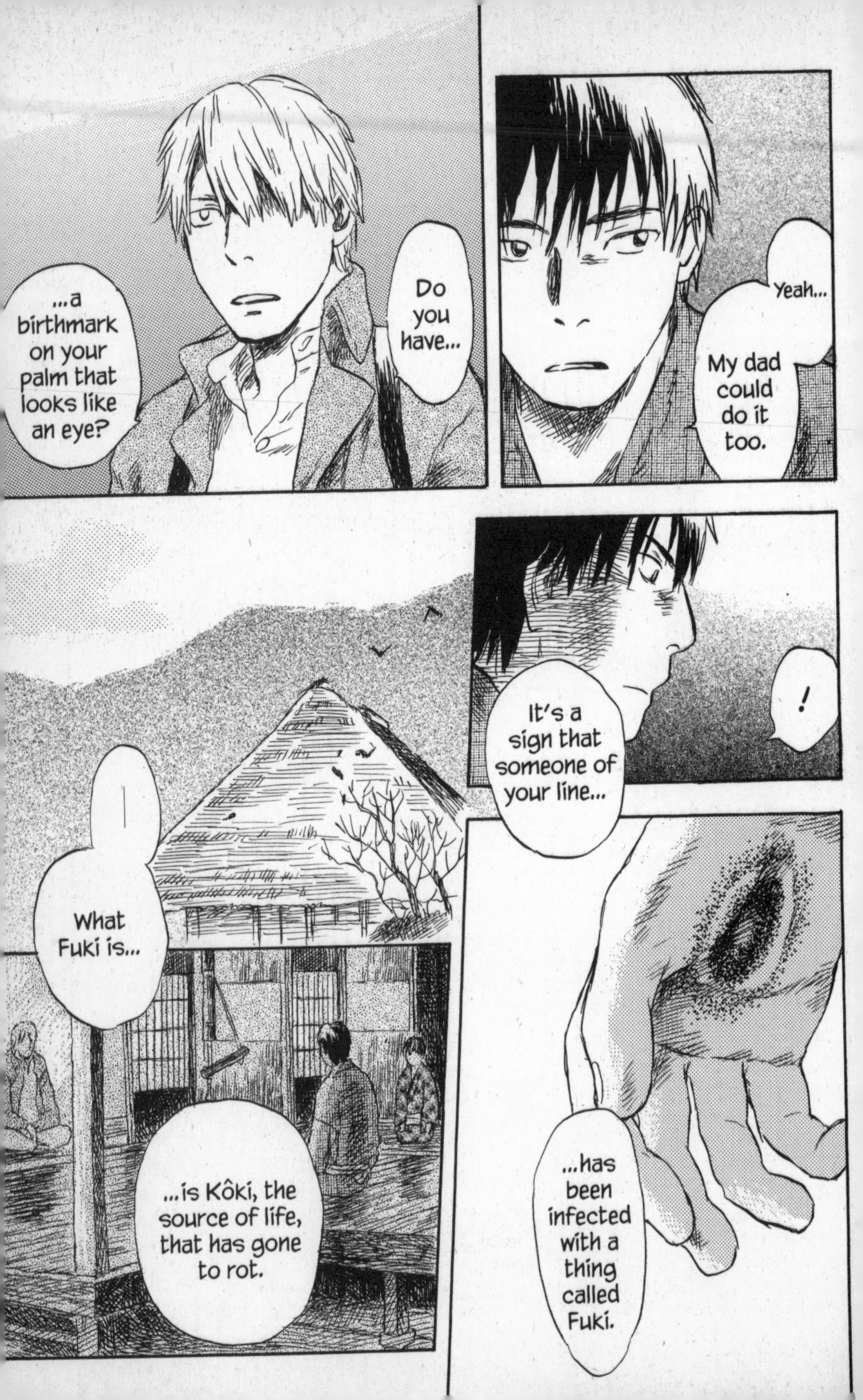

Yeah...
My dad could do it too.
Do you have...
...a birthmark on your palm that looks like an eye?
!
It's a sign that someone of your line...
...has been infected with a thing called Fuki.
What Fuki is...
...is Kôki, the source of life, that has gone to rot.

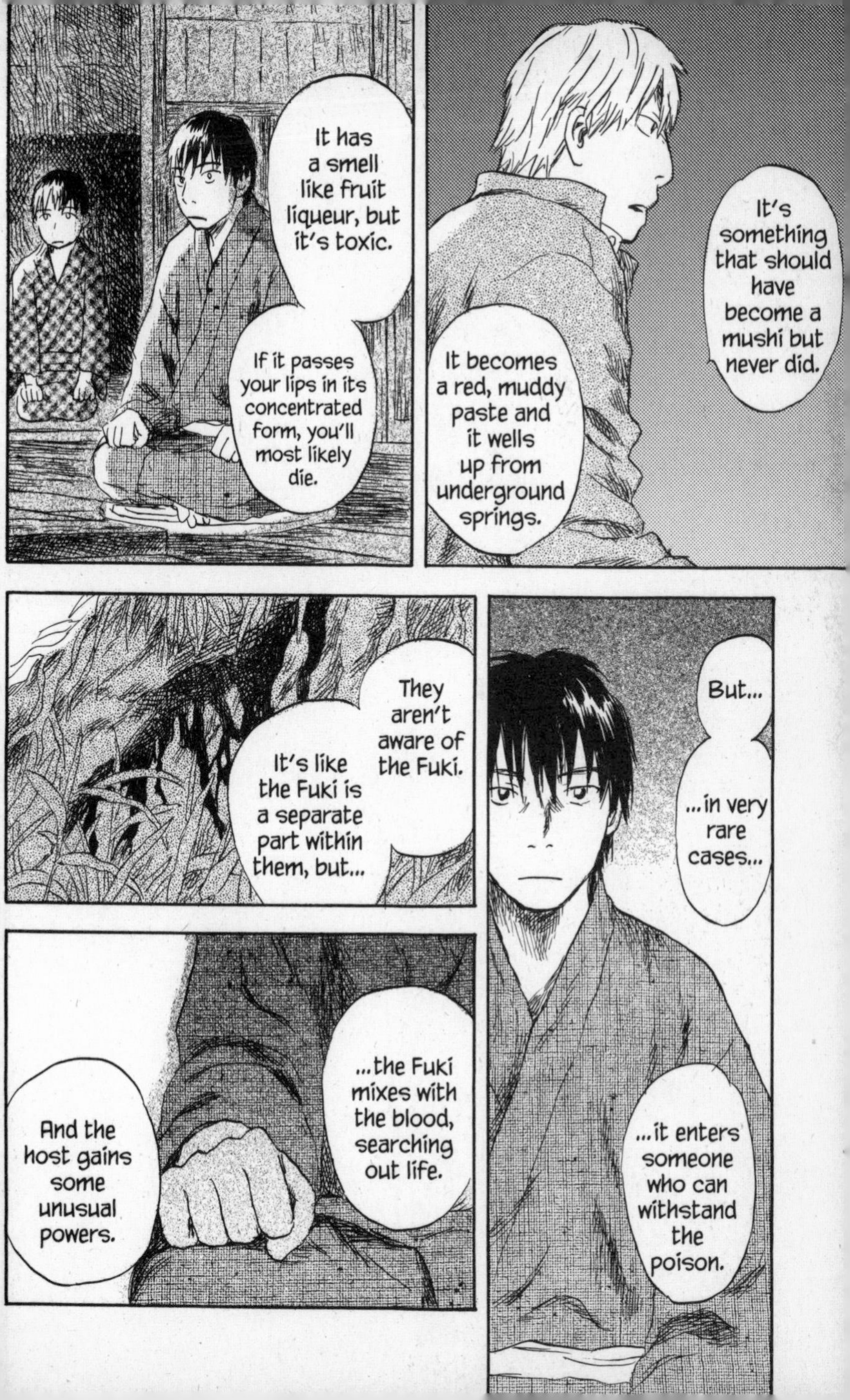
It's something that should have become a mushi but never did.
It becomes a red, muddy paste and it wells up from underground springs.
It has a smell like fruit liqueur, but it's toxic.
If it passes your lips in its concentrated form, you'll most likely die.
But...
...in very rare cases...
...it enters someone who can withstand the poison.
They aren't aware of the Fuki.
It's like the Fuki is a separate part within them, but...
...the Fuki mixes with the blood, searching out life.
And the host gains some unusual powers.

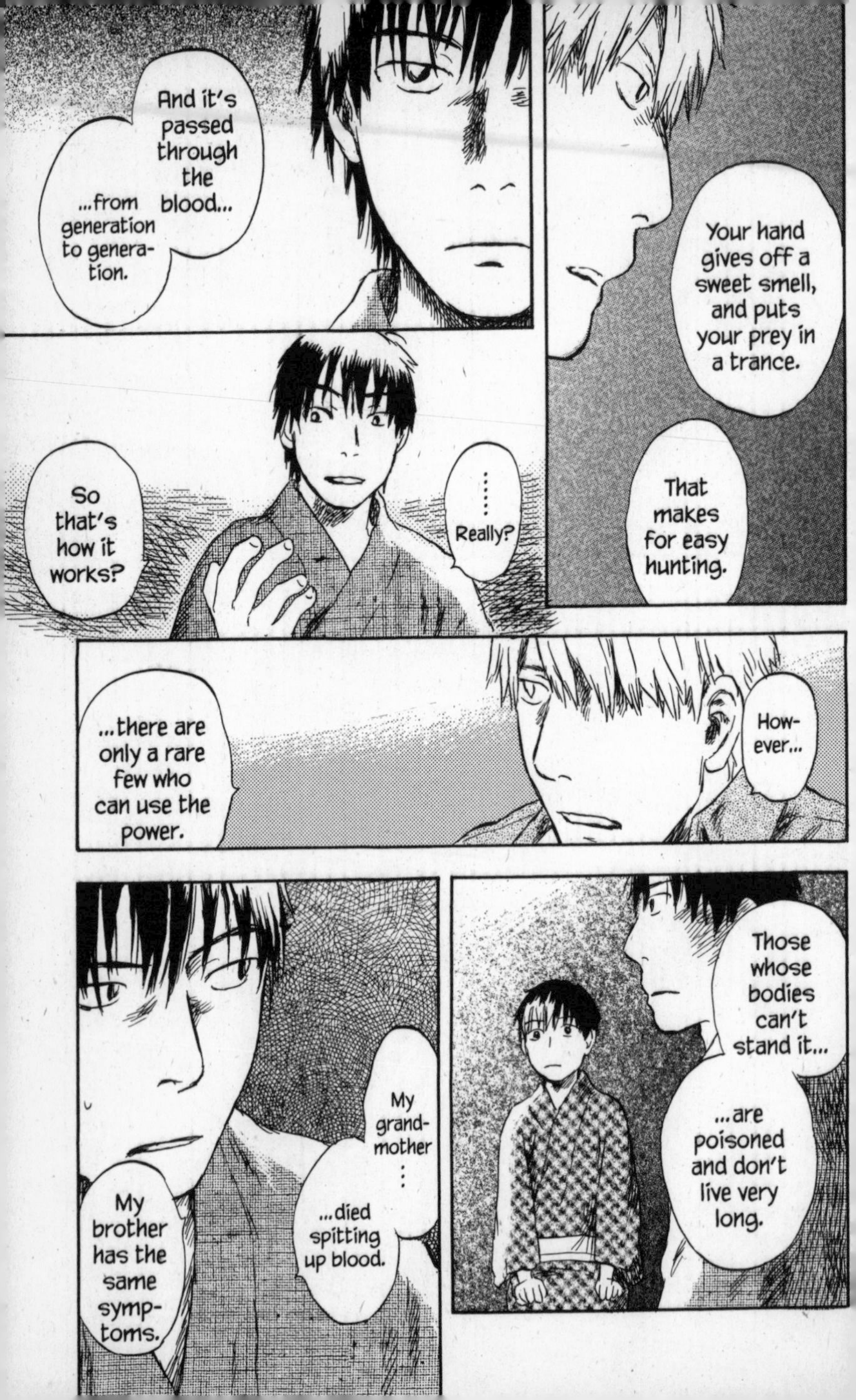
Your hand gives off a sweet smell, and puts your prey in a trance.
That makes for easy hunting.
And it's passed through the blood...
...from generation to generation.
......Really?
So that's how it works?
However...
...there are only a rare few who can use the power.
Those whose bodies can't stand it...
...are poisoned and don't live very long.
My grandmother...
...died spitting up blood.
My brother has the same symptoms.

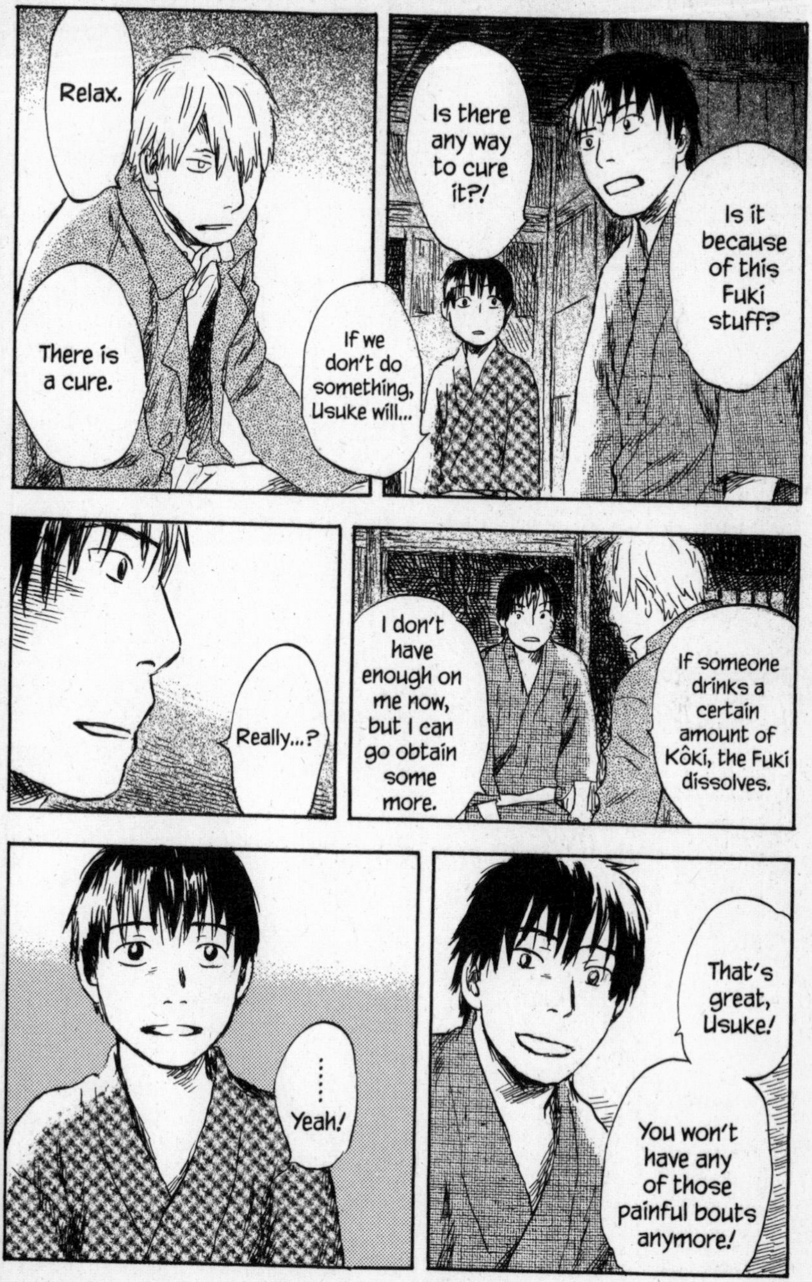
Is it because of this Fuki stuff?
Is there any way to cure it?!
If we don't do something, Usuke will...
Relax.
There is a cure.
If someone drinks a certain amount of Kôki, the Fuki dissolves.
I don't have enough on me now, but I can go obtain some more.
Really...?
That's great, Usuke!
You won't have any of those painful bouts anymore!
......
Yeah!

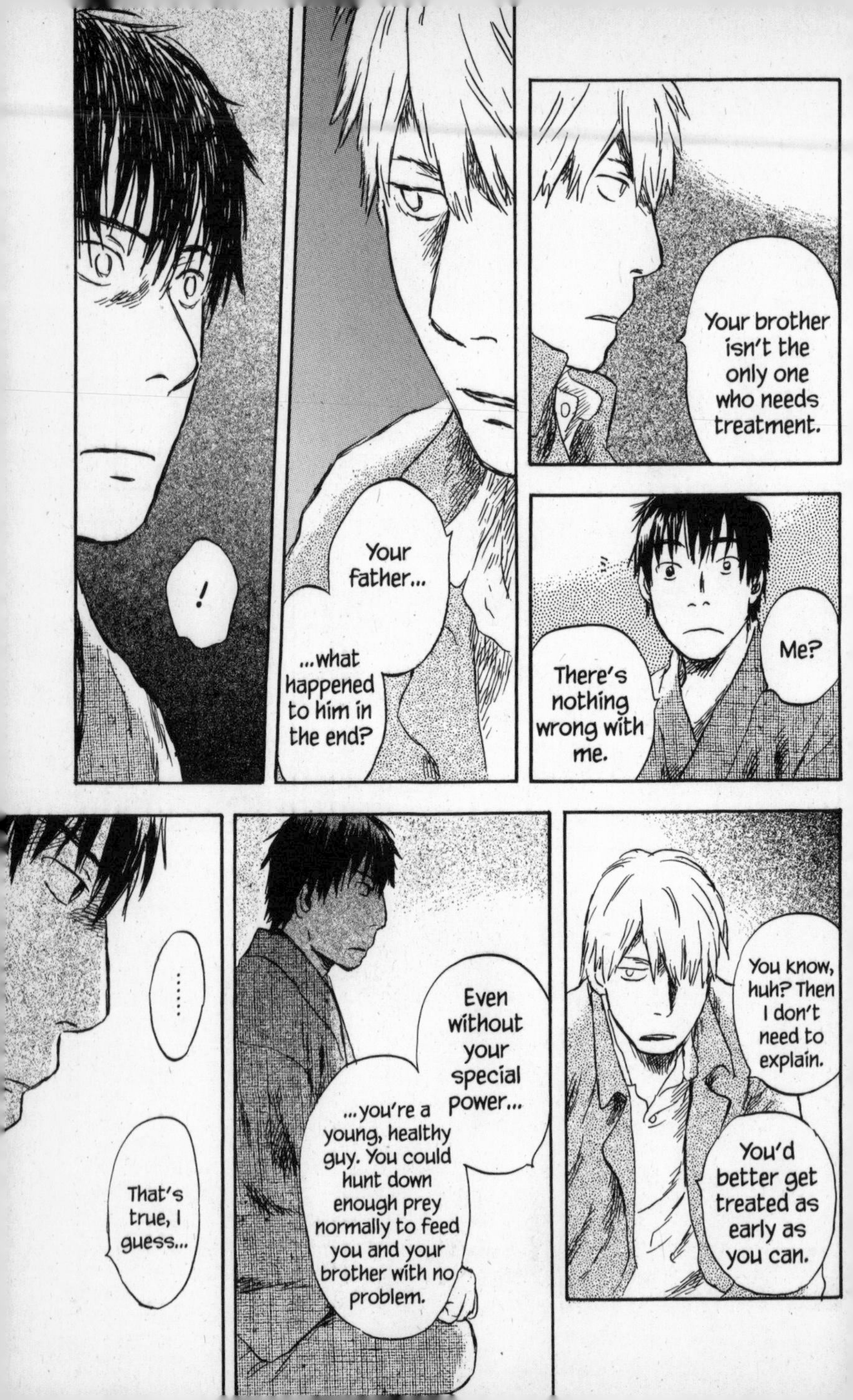
Your brother isn't the only one who needs treatment.
Me?
There's nothing wrong with me.
Your father...
...what happened to him in the end?
!
You know, huh? Then I don't need to explain.
You'd better get treated as early as you can.
Even without your special power...
...you're a young, healthy guy. You could hunt down enough prey normally to feed you and your brother with no problem.
......
That's true, I guess...

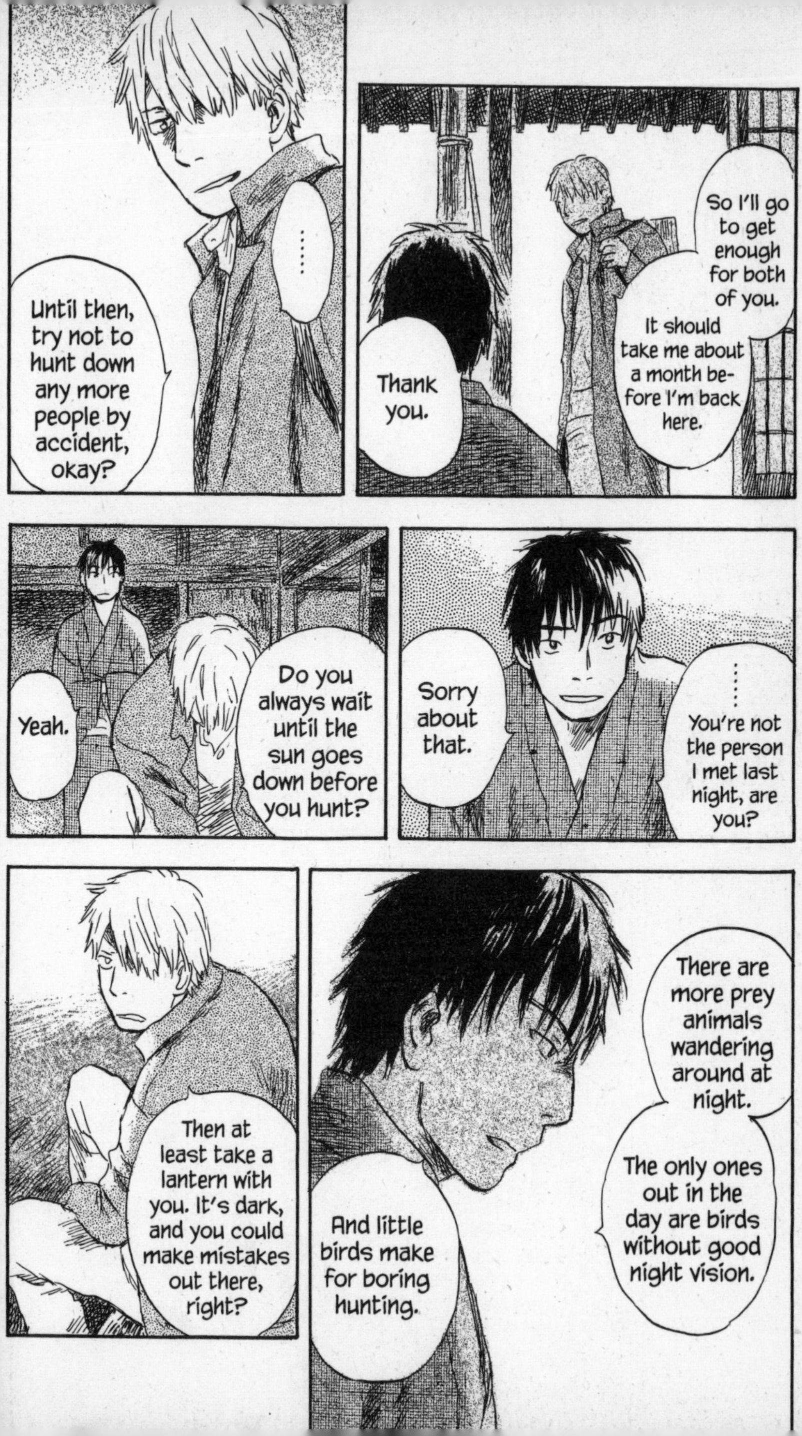
So I'll go to get enough for both of you.
It should take me about a month before I'm back here.
Thank you.
......
Until then, try not to hunt down any more people by accident, okay?
......
You're not the person I met last night, are you?
Sorry about that.
Do you always wait until the sun goes down before you hunt?
Yeah.
There are more prey animals wandering around at night.
The only ones out in the day are birds without good night vision.
And little birds make for boring hunting.
Then at least take a lantern with you. It's dark, and you could make mistakes out there, right?

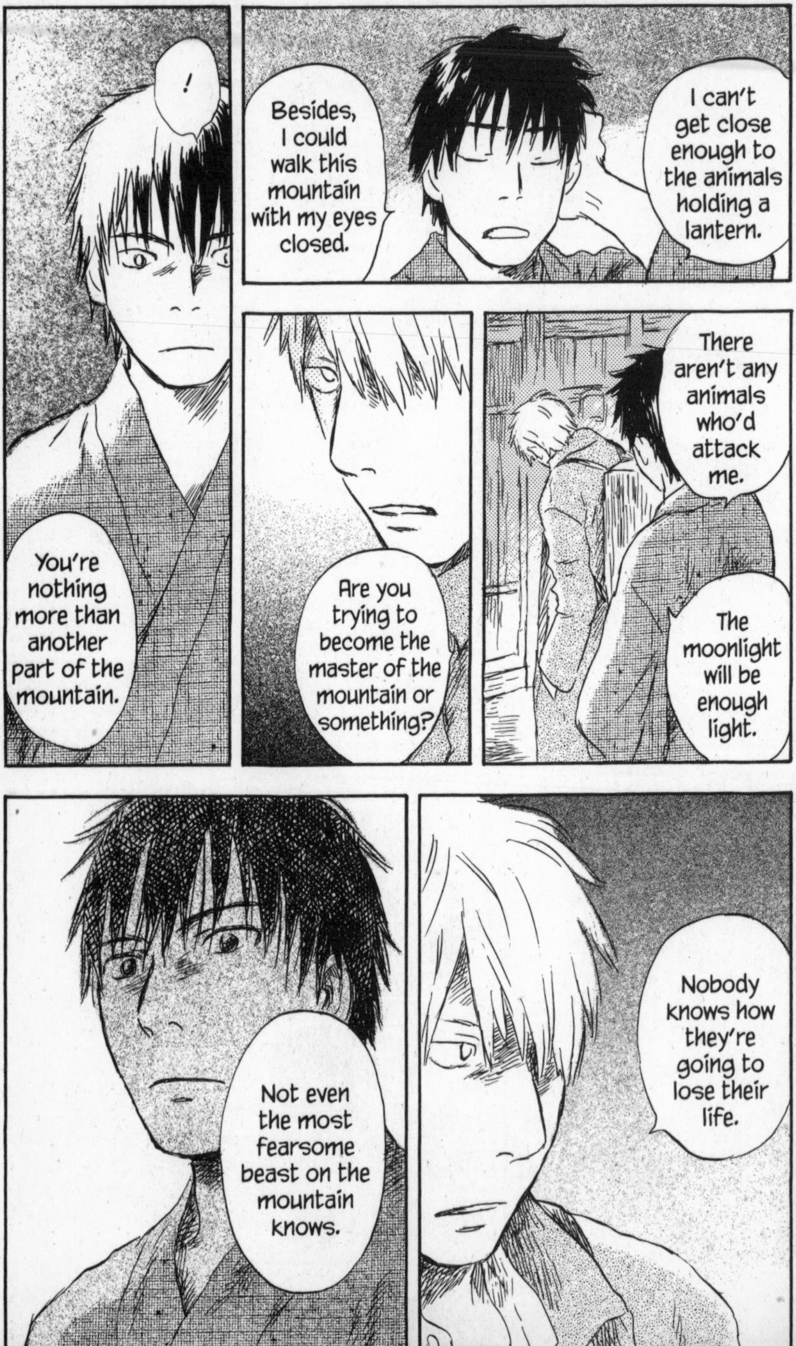
I can't get close enough to the animals holding a lantern.
Besides, I could walk this mountain with my eyes closed.
There aren't any animals who'd attack me.
The moonlight will be enough light.
Are you trying to become the master of the mountain or something?
!
You're nothing more than another part of the mountain.
Nobody knows how they're going to lose their life.
Not even the most fearsome beast on the mountain knows.

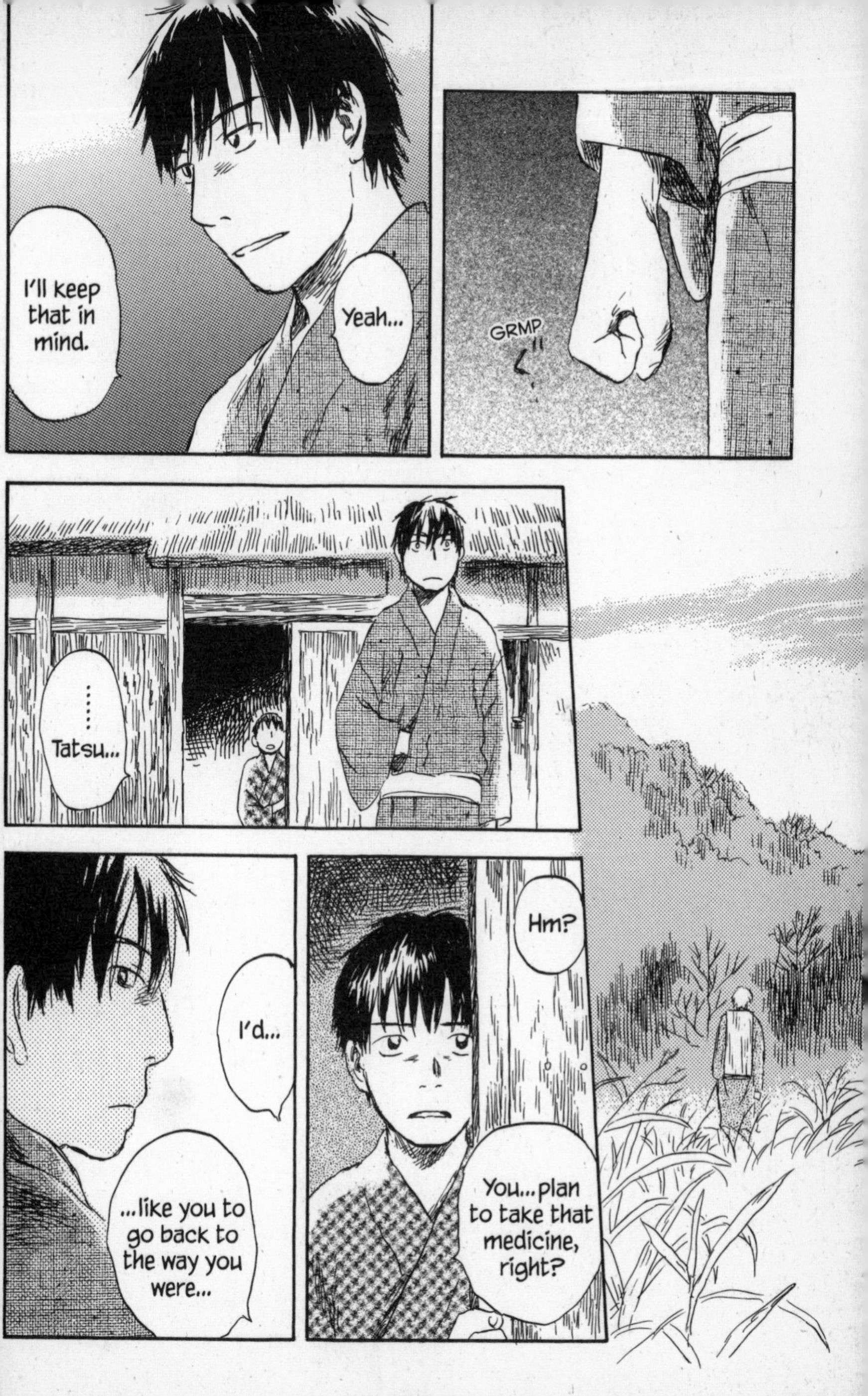
GRMP
Yeah...
I'll keep that in mind.
......
Tatsu...
Hm?
You...plan to take that medicine, right?
I'd...
...like you to go back to the way you were...

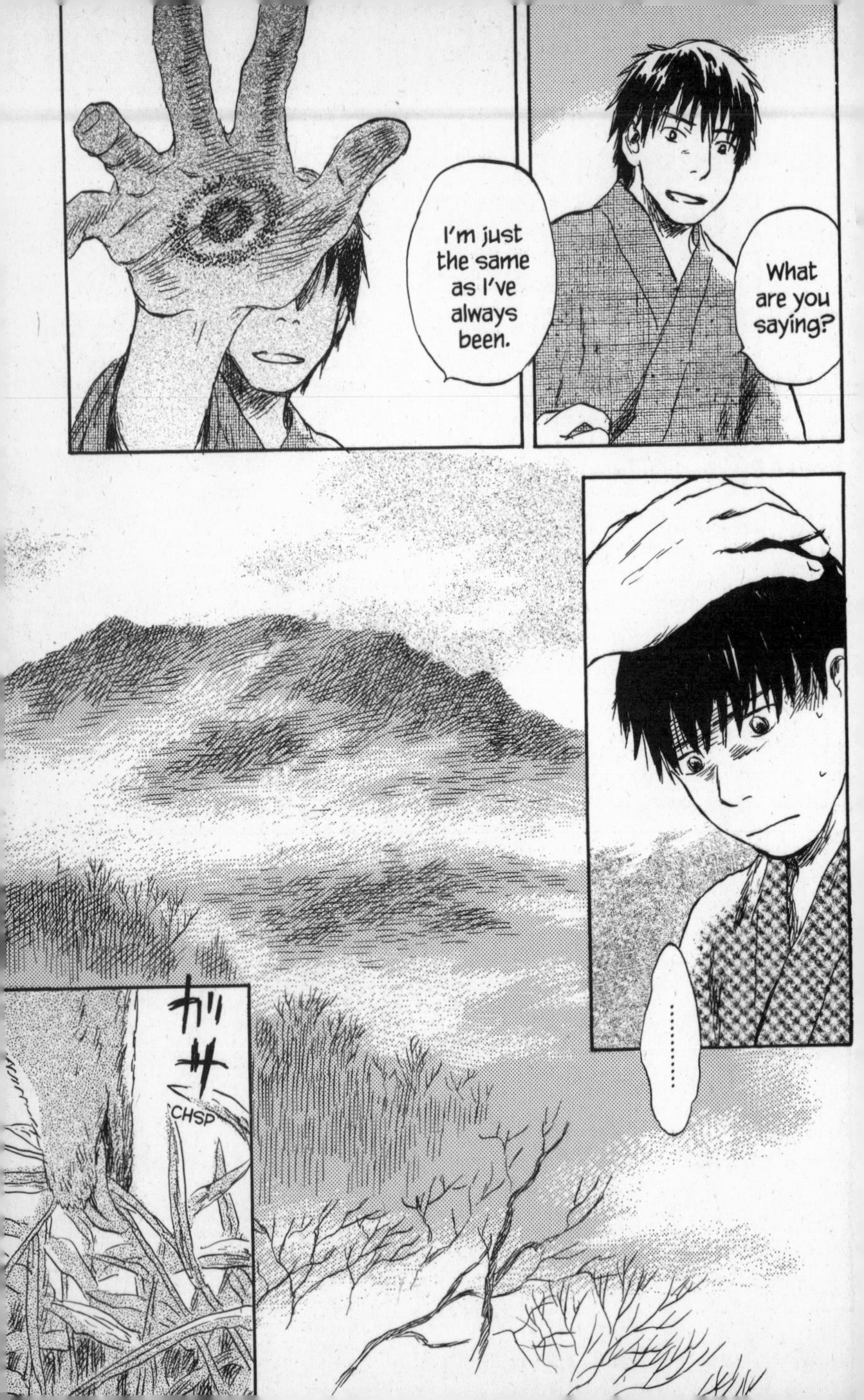
What are you saying?
I'm just the same as I've always been.
......
カサ
CHSP

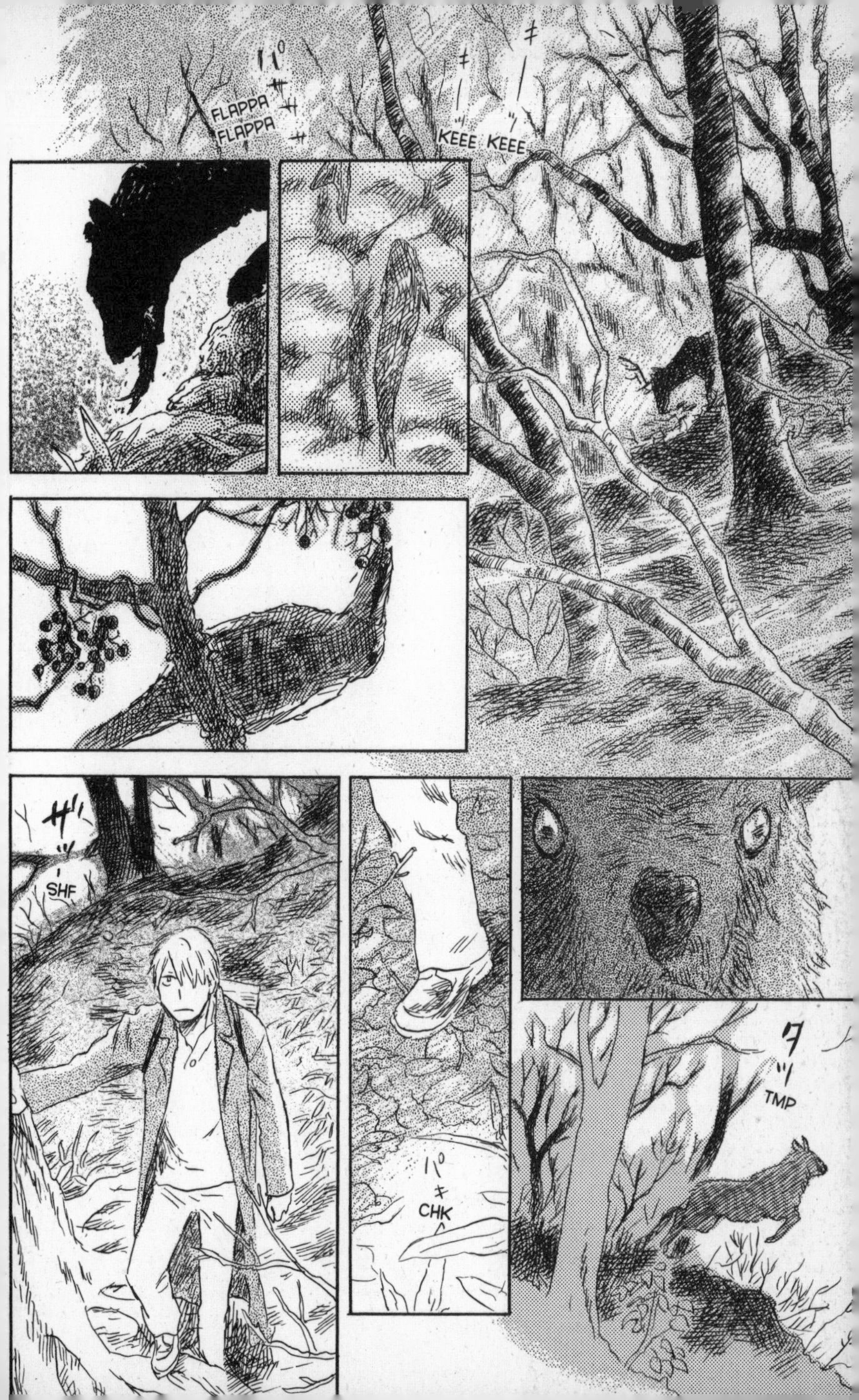
キーッ
KEEE KEEE
バサッ
FLAPPA FLAPPA
ザッ
SHF
パキ
CHK
タッ
TMP

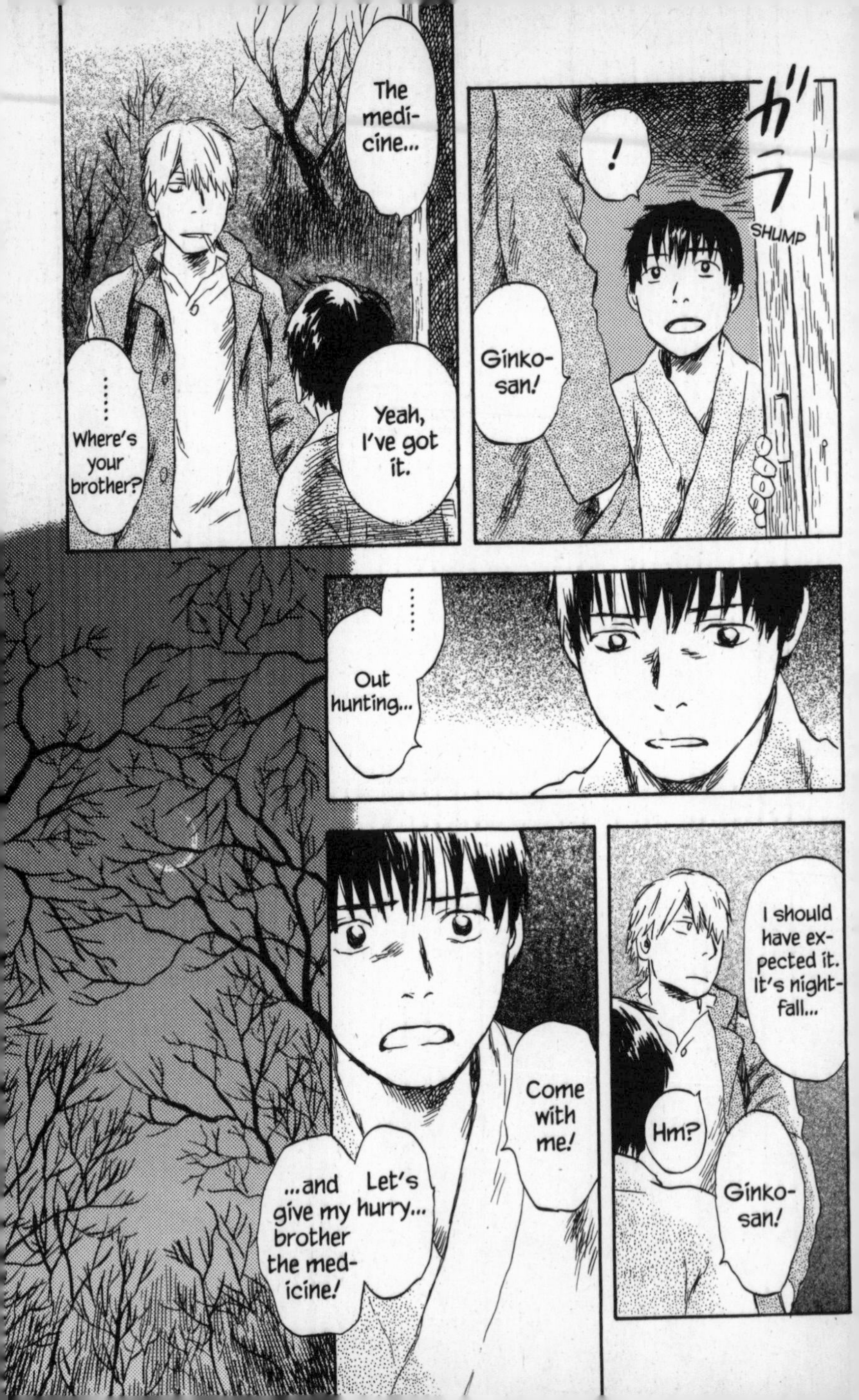
ガラ
SHUMP
!
Ginko-san!
The medi-cine...
Yeah, I've got it.
...... Where's your brother?
...... Out hunting...
I should have ex-pected it. It's night-fall...
Hm?
Ginko-san!
Come with me!
Let's hurry...
...and give my brother the med-icine!

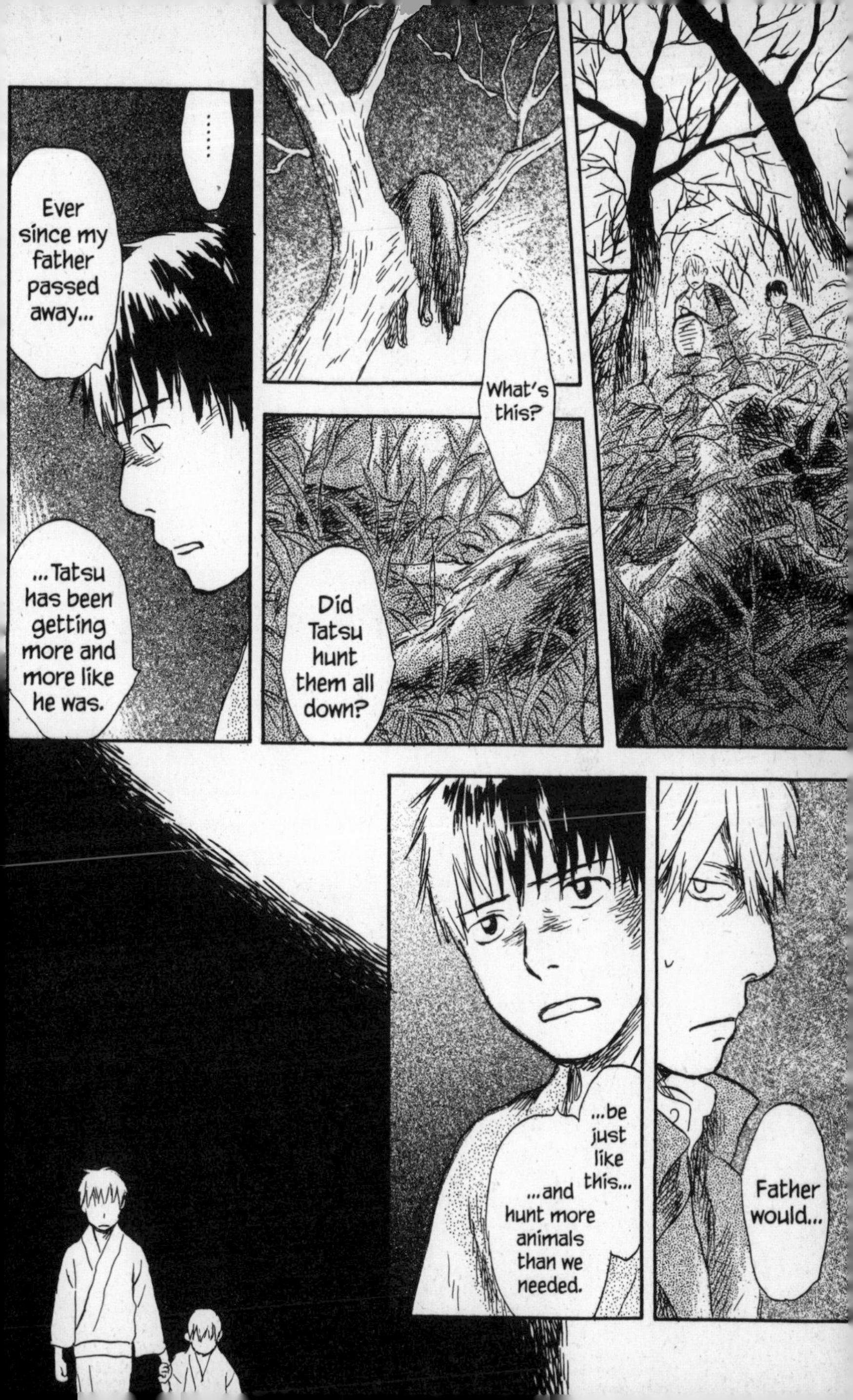
What's this?
Did Tatsu hunt them all down?
......
Ever since my father passed away...
...Tatsu has been getting more and more like he was.
Father would...
...be just like this...
...and hunt more animals than we needed.

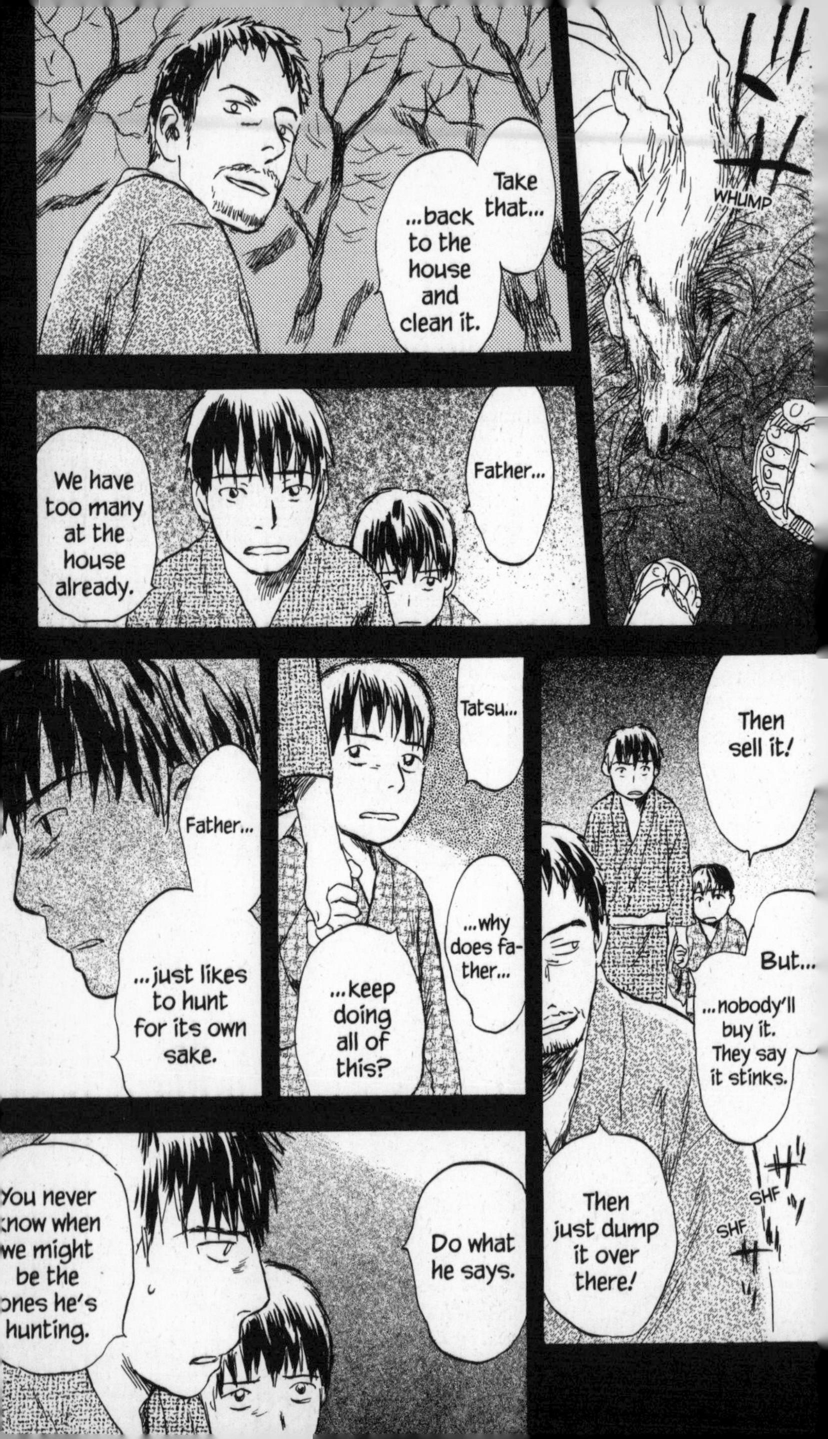
WHUMP
Take that...
...back to the house and clean it.
Father...
We have too many at the house already.
Then sell it!
But...
...nobody'll buy it. They say it stinks.
SHF
SHF
Then just dump it over there!
Tatsu...
...why does father...
...keep doing all of this?
Father...
...just likes to hunt for its own sake.
Do what he says.
You never know when we might be the ones he's hunting.

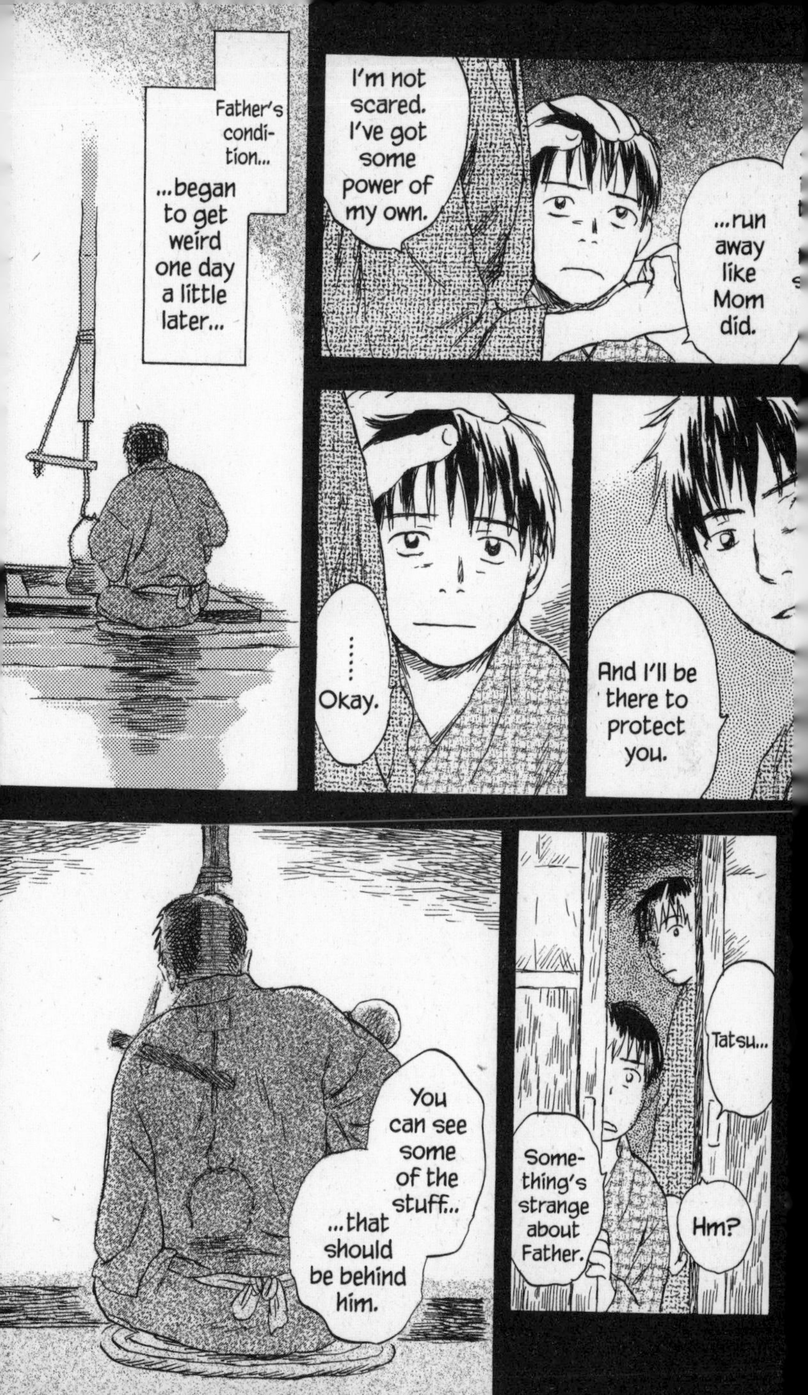
...run away like Mom did.
I'm not scared. I've got some power of my own.
And I'll be there to protect you.
......Okay.
Father's condition...
...began to get weird one day a little later...
Tatsu...
Hm?
Something's strange about Father.
You can see some of the stuff...
...that should be behind him.

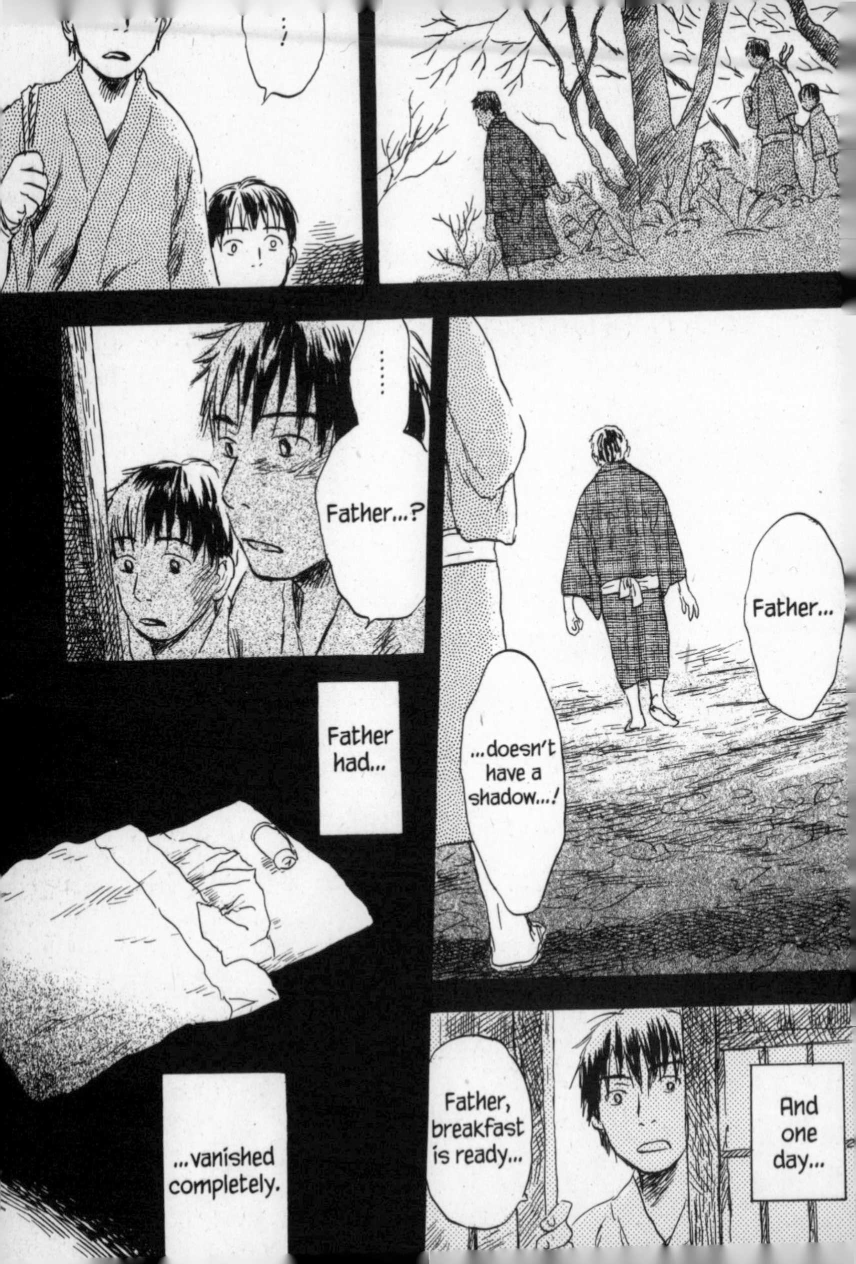
!
Father...
...doesn't have a shadow...!
And one day...
Father, breakfast is ready...
......
Father...?
Father had...
...vanished completely.

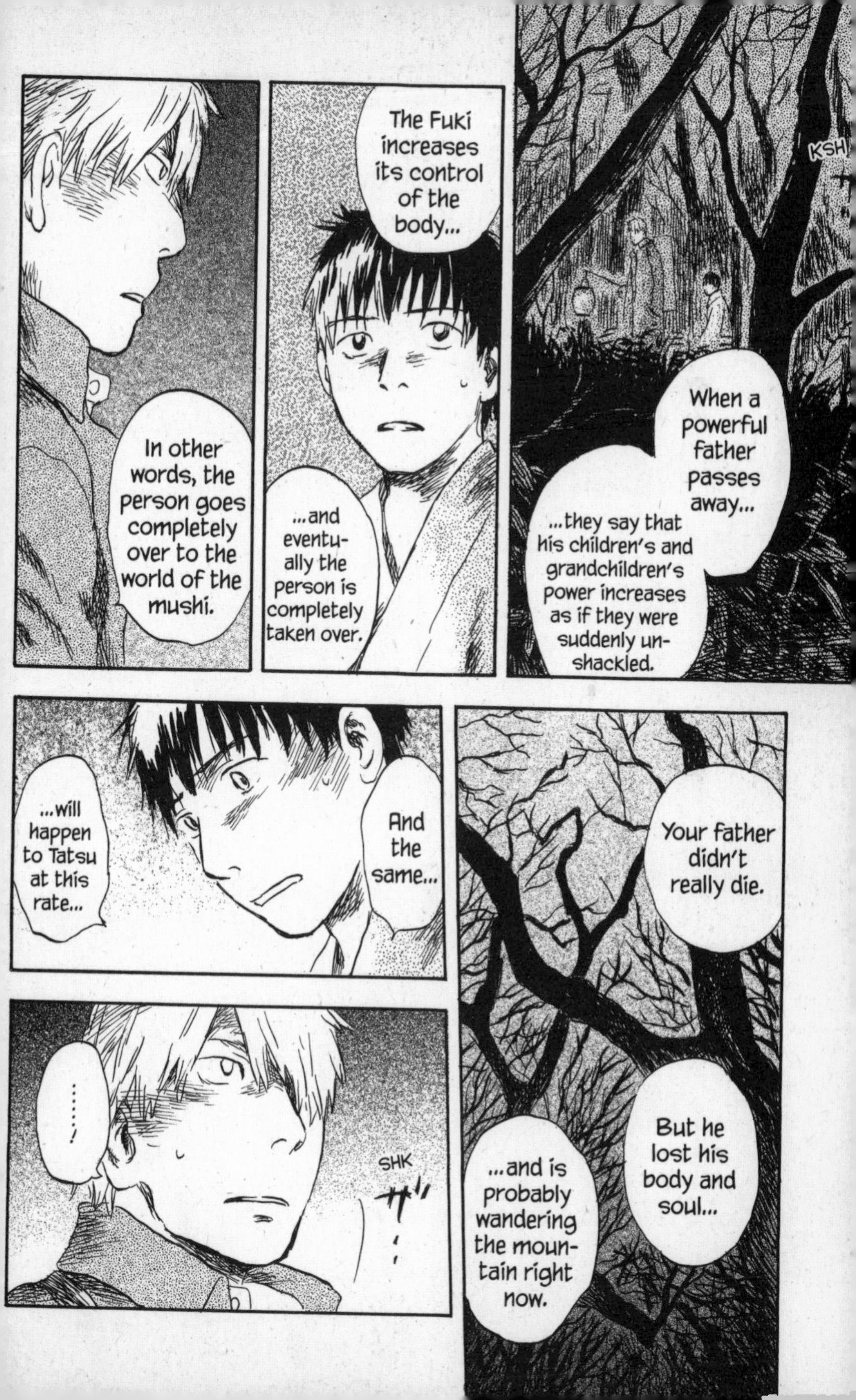
KSH
When a powerful father passes away...
...they say that his children's and grandchildren's power increases as if they were suddenly unshackled.
The Fuki increases its control of the body...
...and eventually the person is completely taken over.
In other words, the person goes completely over to the world of the mushi.
Your father didn't really die.
But he lost his body and soul...
...and is probably wandering the mountain right now.
And the same...
...will happen to Tatsu at this rate...
......!
SHK

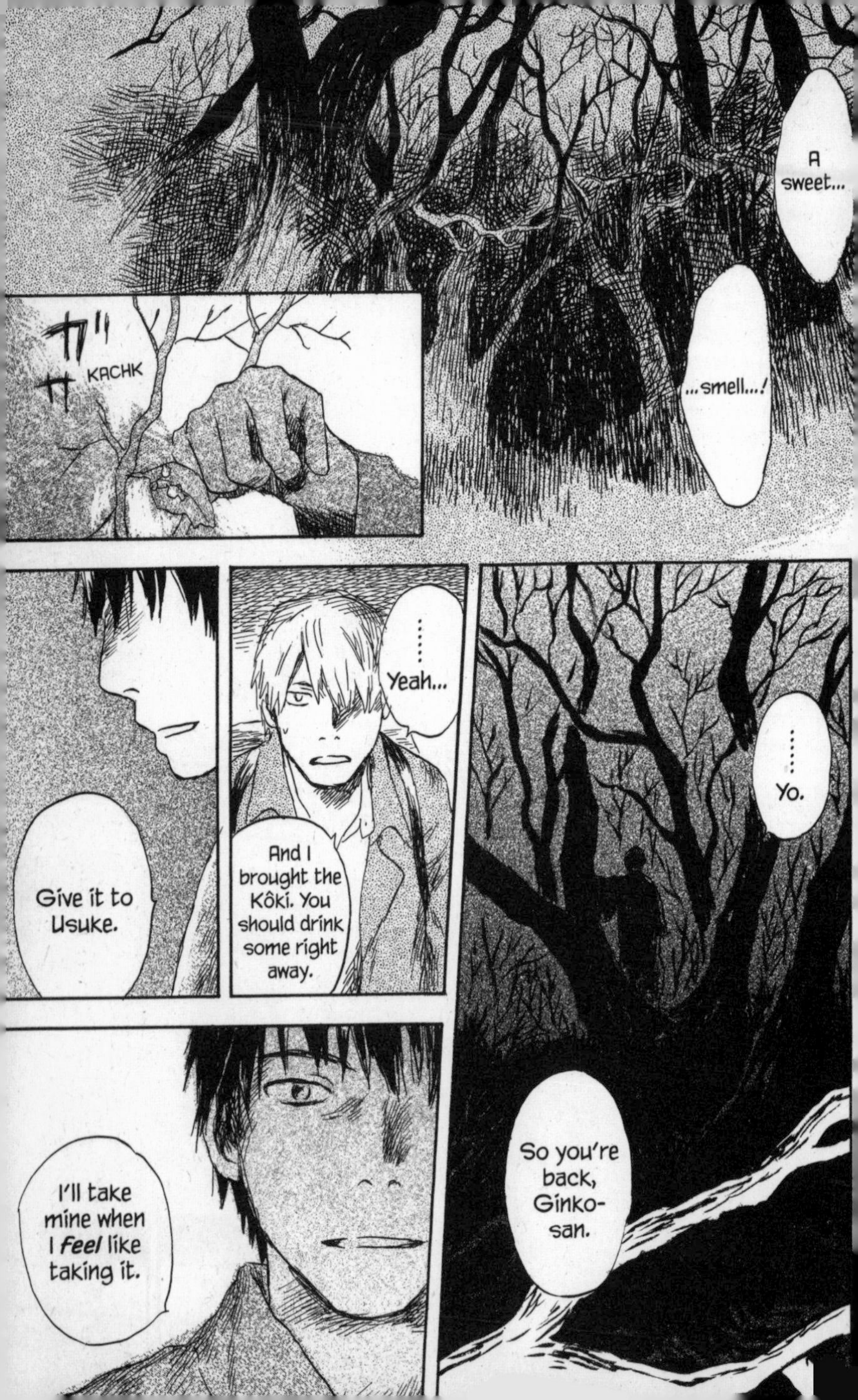

A sweet...
...smell...!
KACHK
......Yo.
So you're back, Ginko-san.
......Yeah...
And I brought the Kôki. You should drink some right away.
Give it to Usuke.
I'll take mine when I *feel* like taking it.

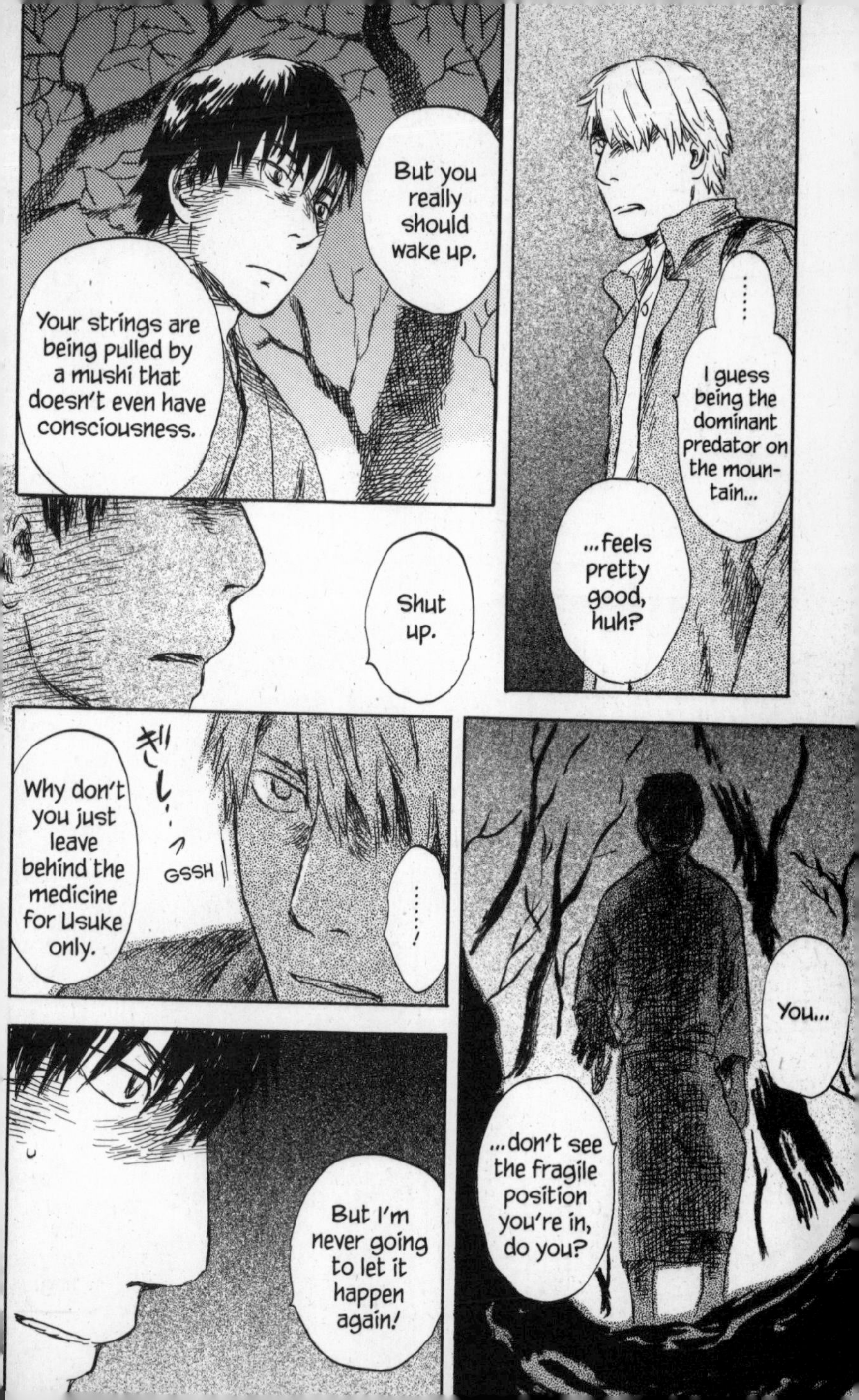
......
I guess being the dominant predator on the mountain...
...feels pretty good, huh?
But you really should wake up.
Your strings are being pulled by a mushi that doesn't even have consciousness.
Shut up.
You...
...don't see the fragile position you're in, do you?
GSSH
......!
Why don't you just leave behind the medicine for Usuke only.
But I'm never going to let it happen again!

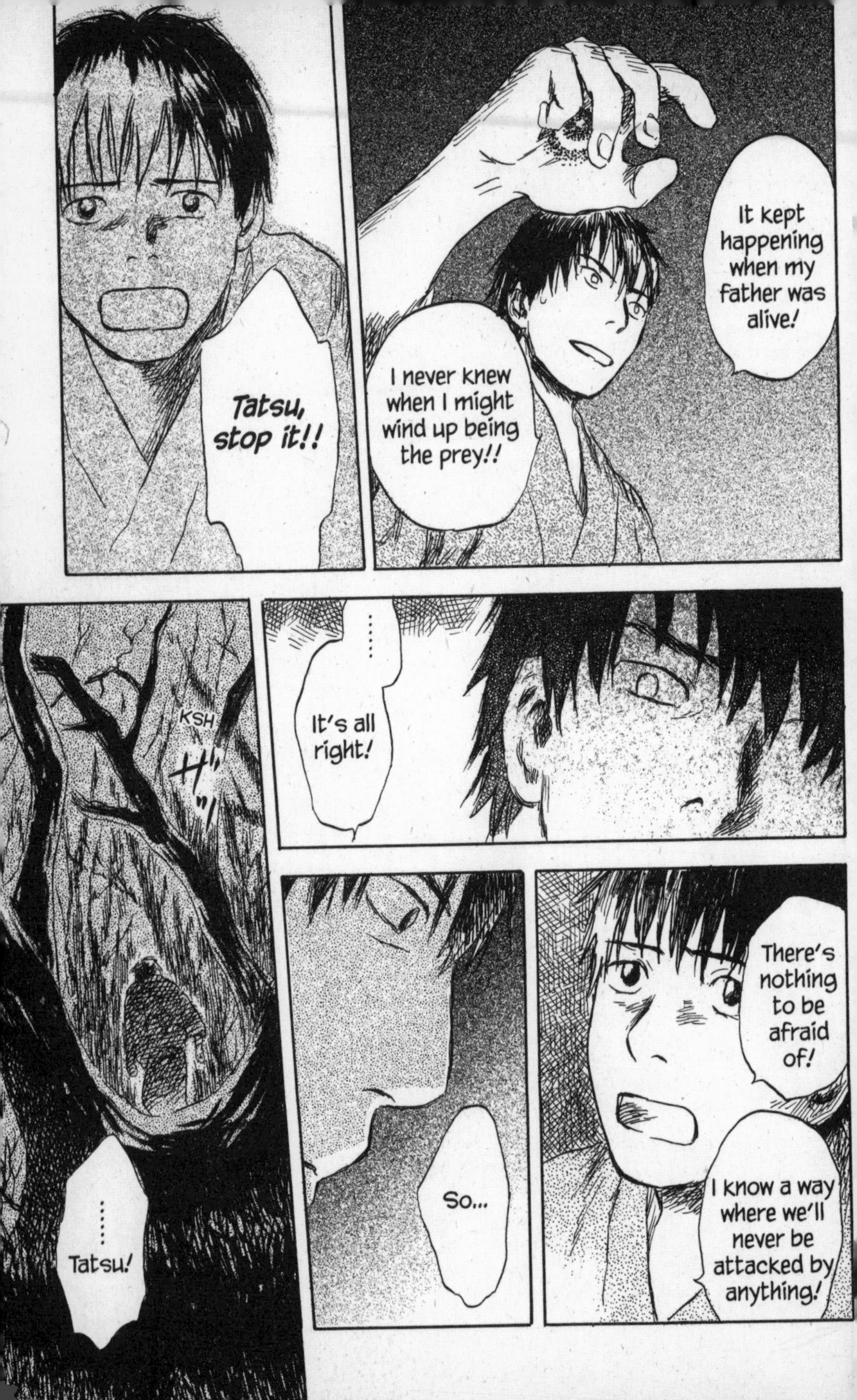
It kept happening when my father was alive!
I never knew when I might wind up being the prey!!
Tatsu, stop it!!
......
It's all right!
There's nothing to be afraid of!
I know a way where we'll never be attacked by anything!
So...
KSH
......
Tatsu!

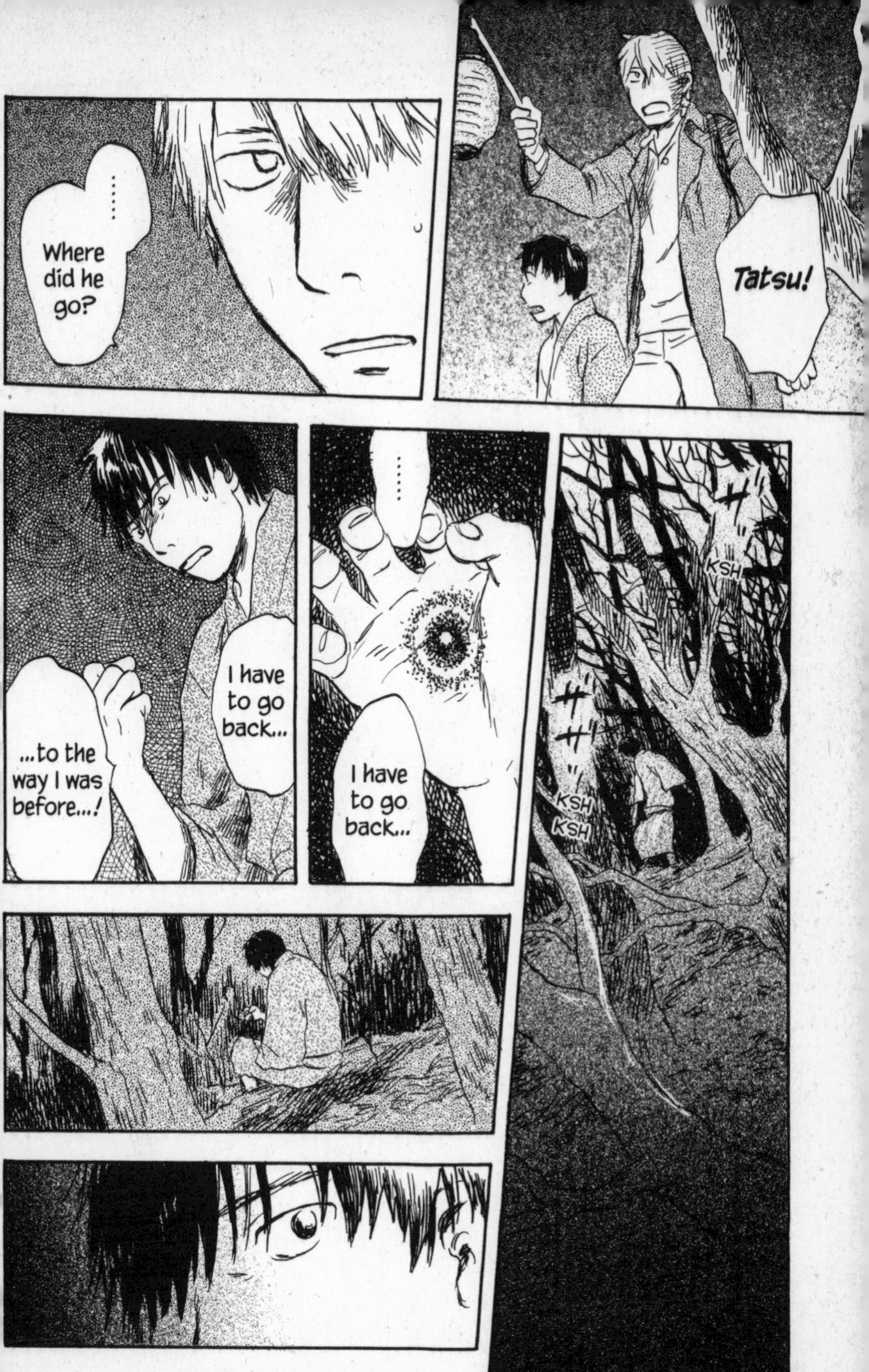
Tatsu!
......
Where did he go?
KSH
KSH
KSH
......
I have to go back...
I have to go back...
...to the way I was before...!

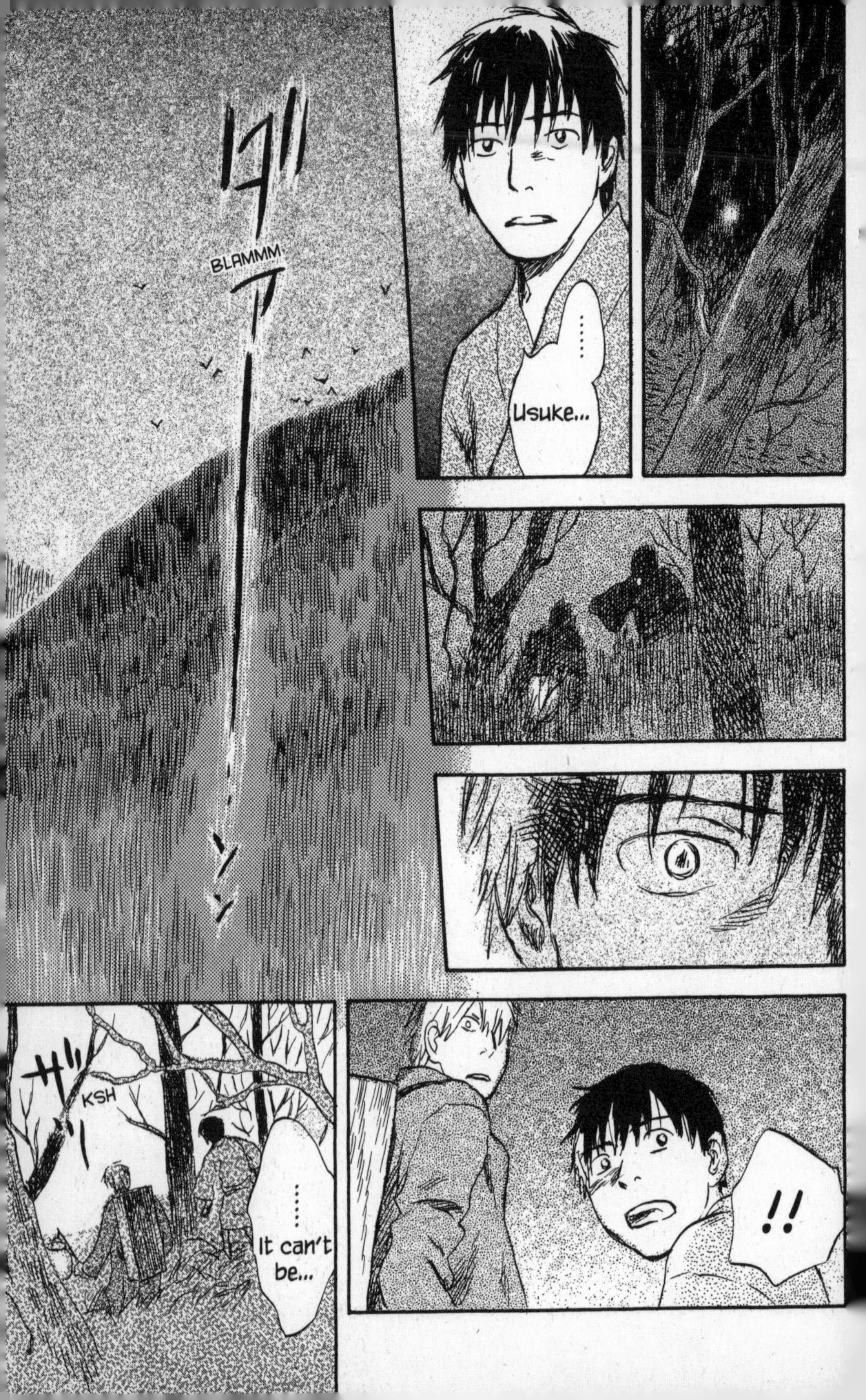
.....
Usuke...
BLAMMM
!!
KSH
.....
It can't be...

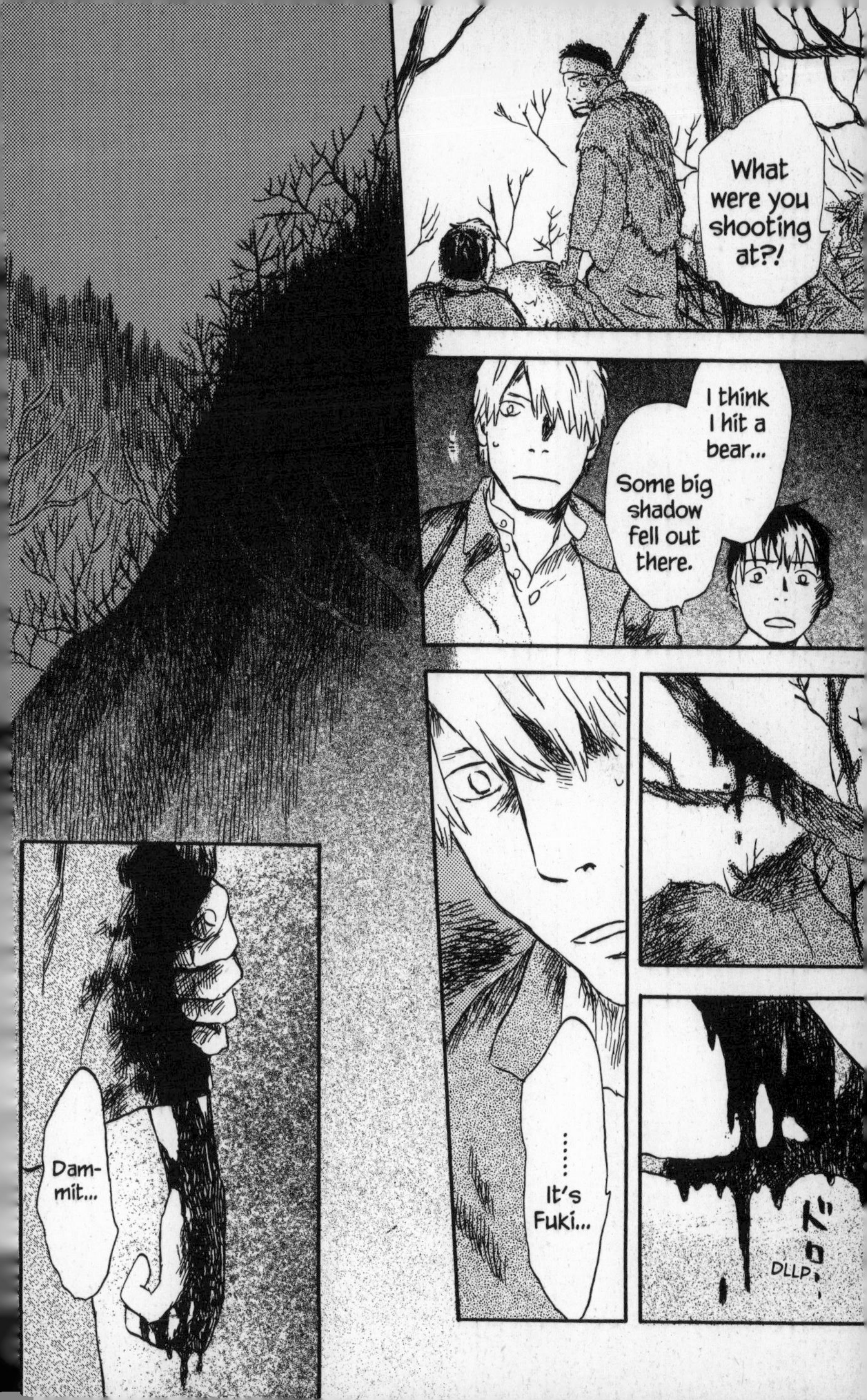
What were you shooting at?!
I think I hit a bear...
Some big shadow fell out there.
ドロ
DLLP
......
It's Fuki...
Dam-mit...

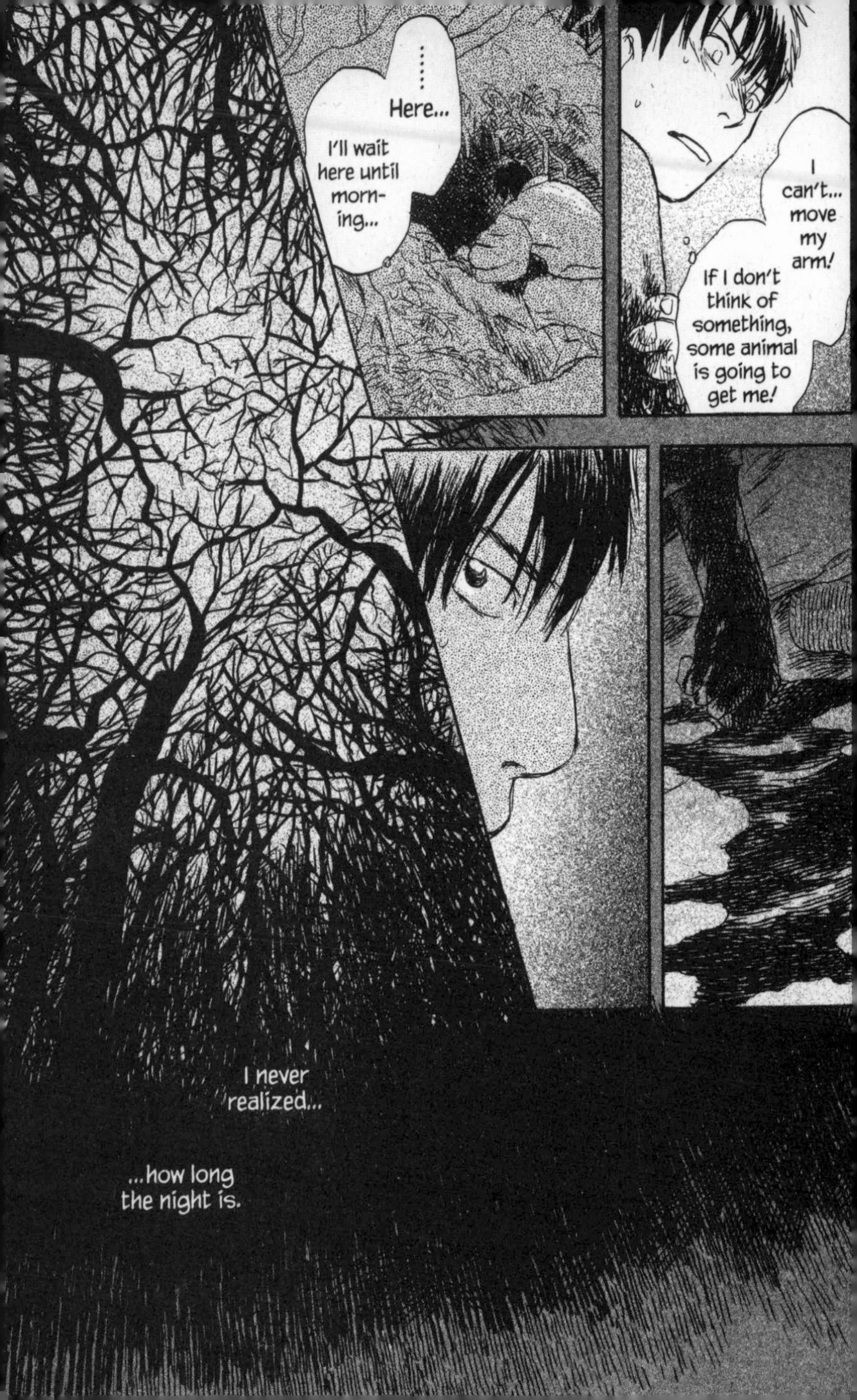
I can't... move my arm!
If I don't think of something, some animal is going to get me!
...... Here...
I'll wait here until morn-ing...
I never realized...
...how long the night is.

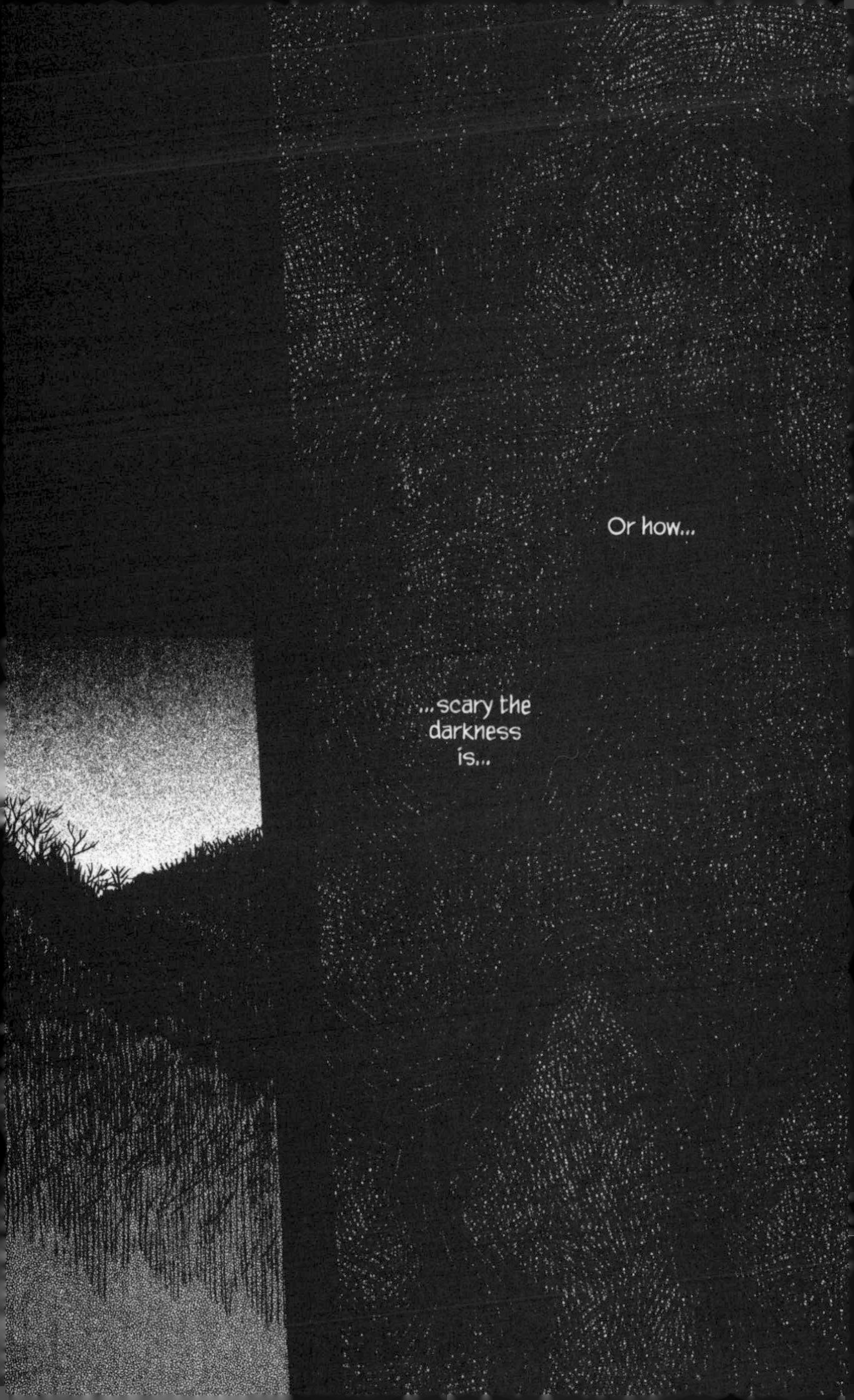
Or how...
...scary the darkness is...

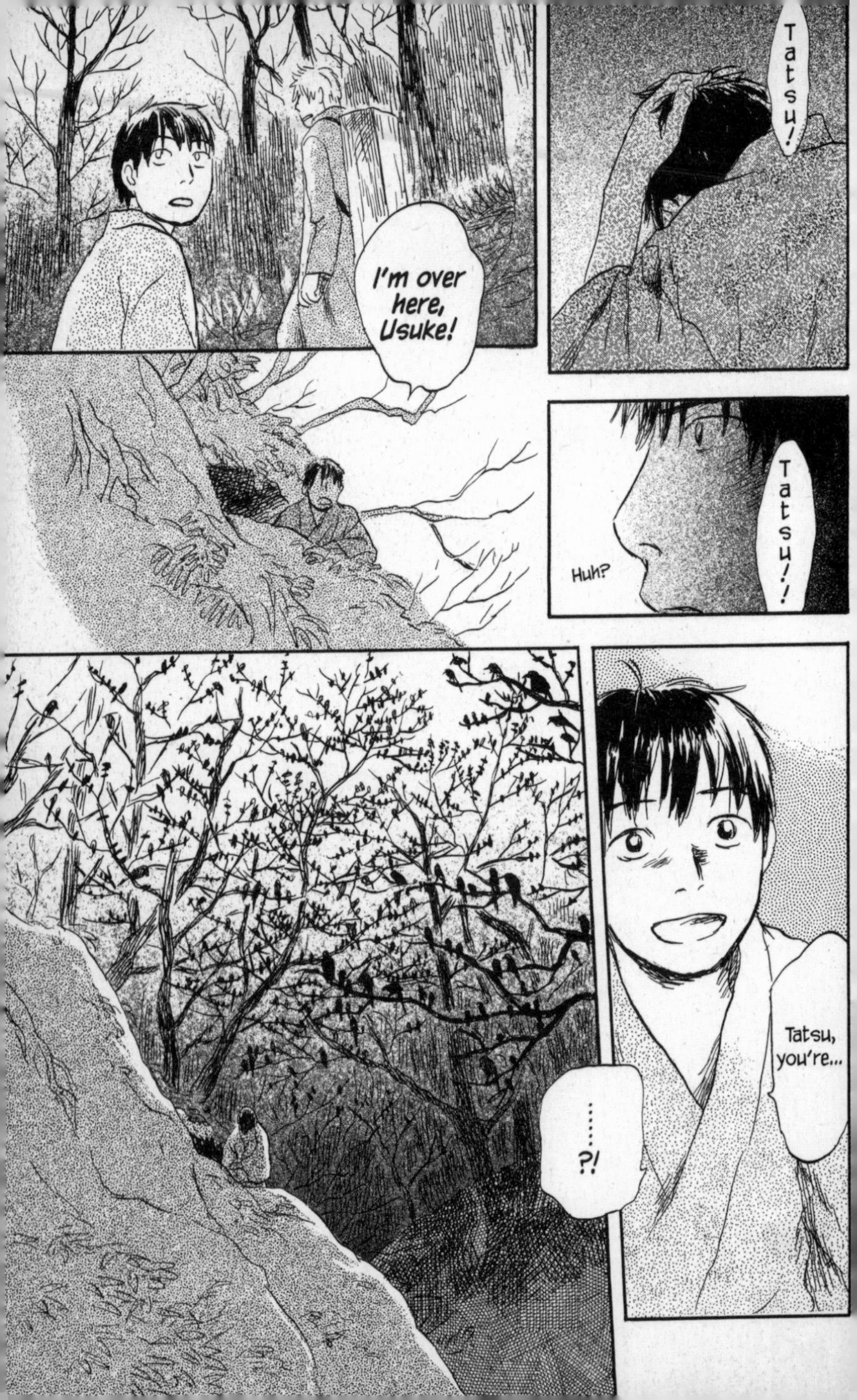
Tatsu!
I'm over here, Usuke!
Tatsu!!
Huh?
Tatsu, you're...
......?!

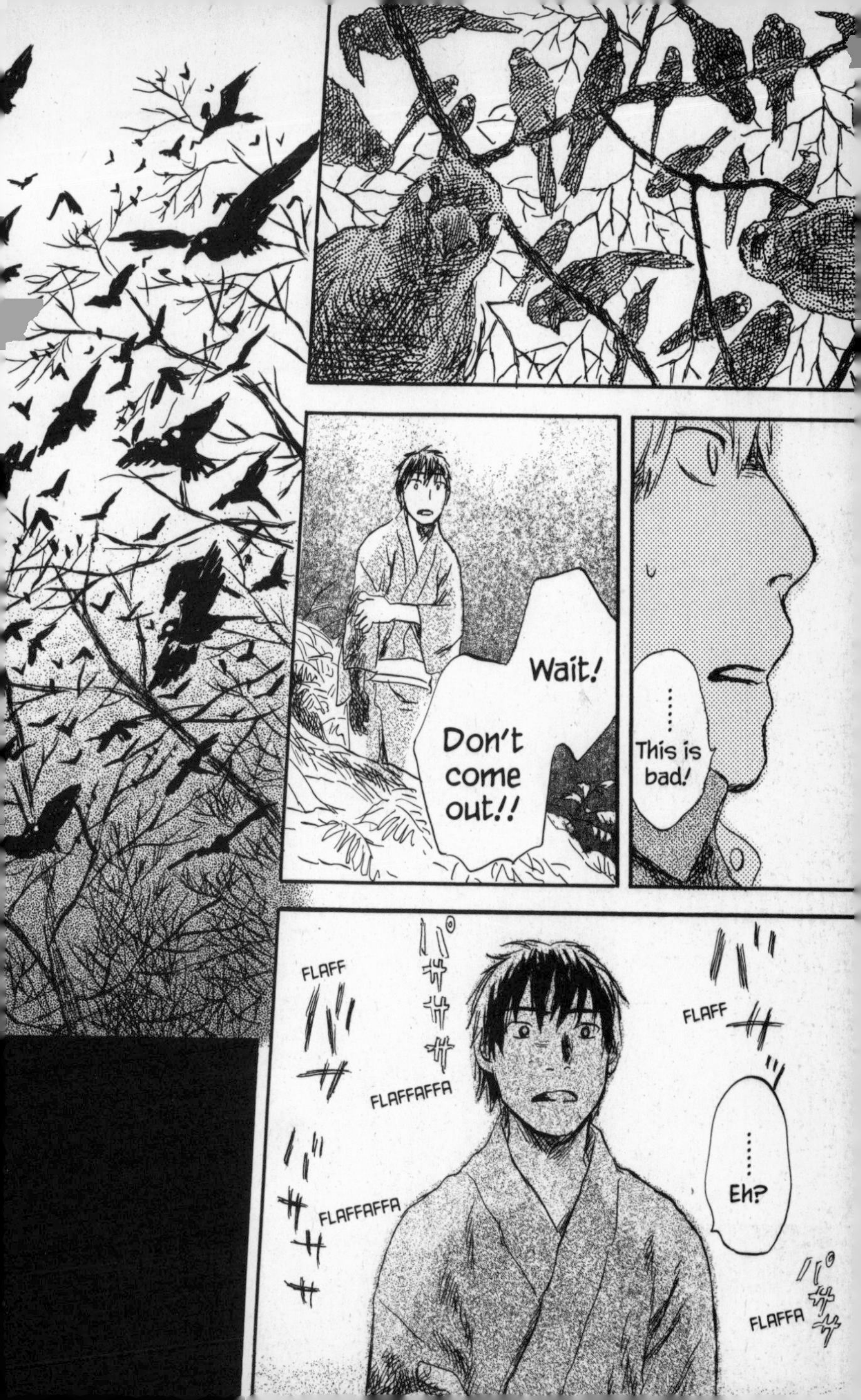
......This is bad!
Wait! Don't come out!!
FLAFF
......Eh?
FLAFFA
FLAFF
FLAFFAFFA
FLAFFAFFA

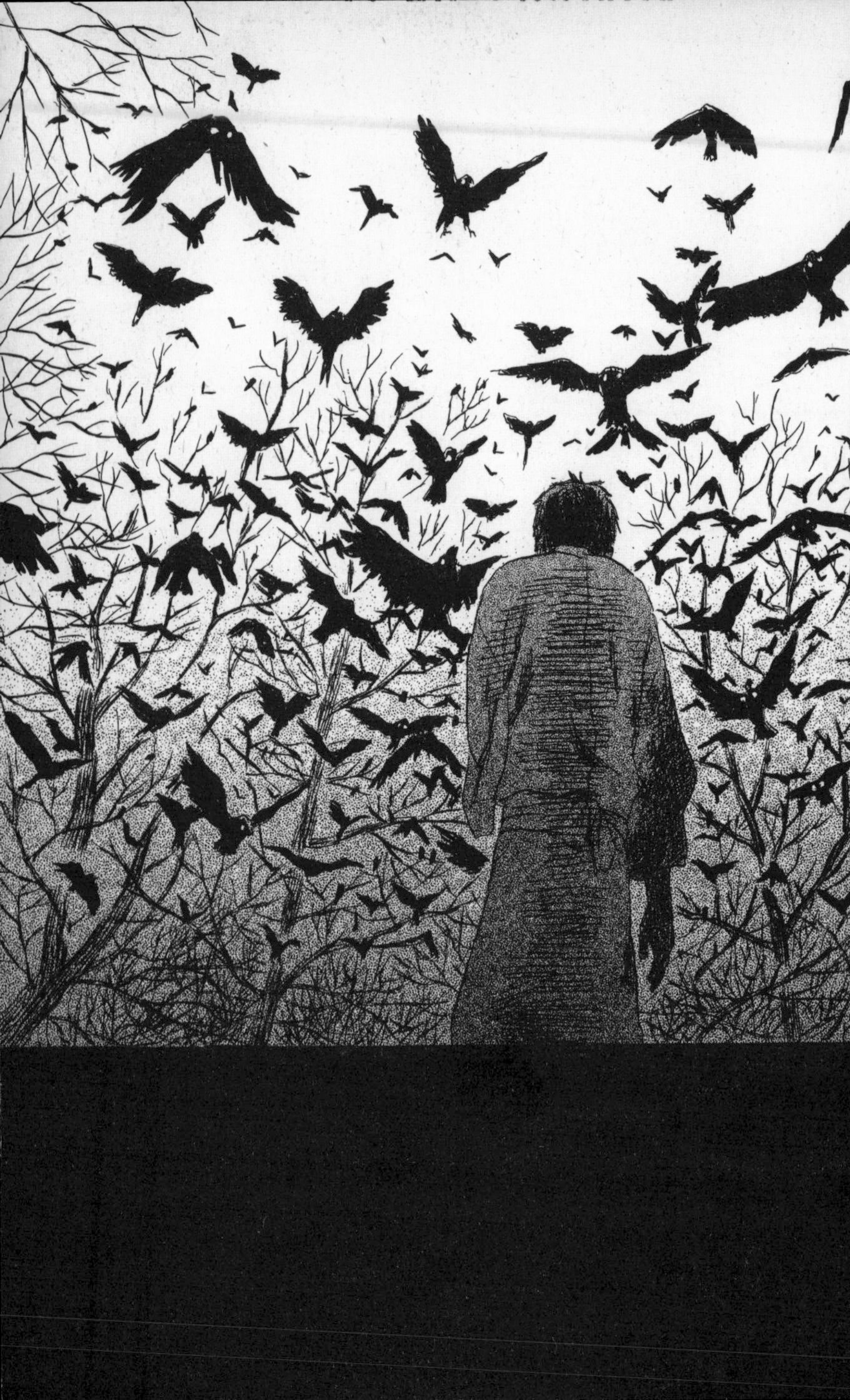

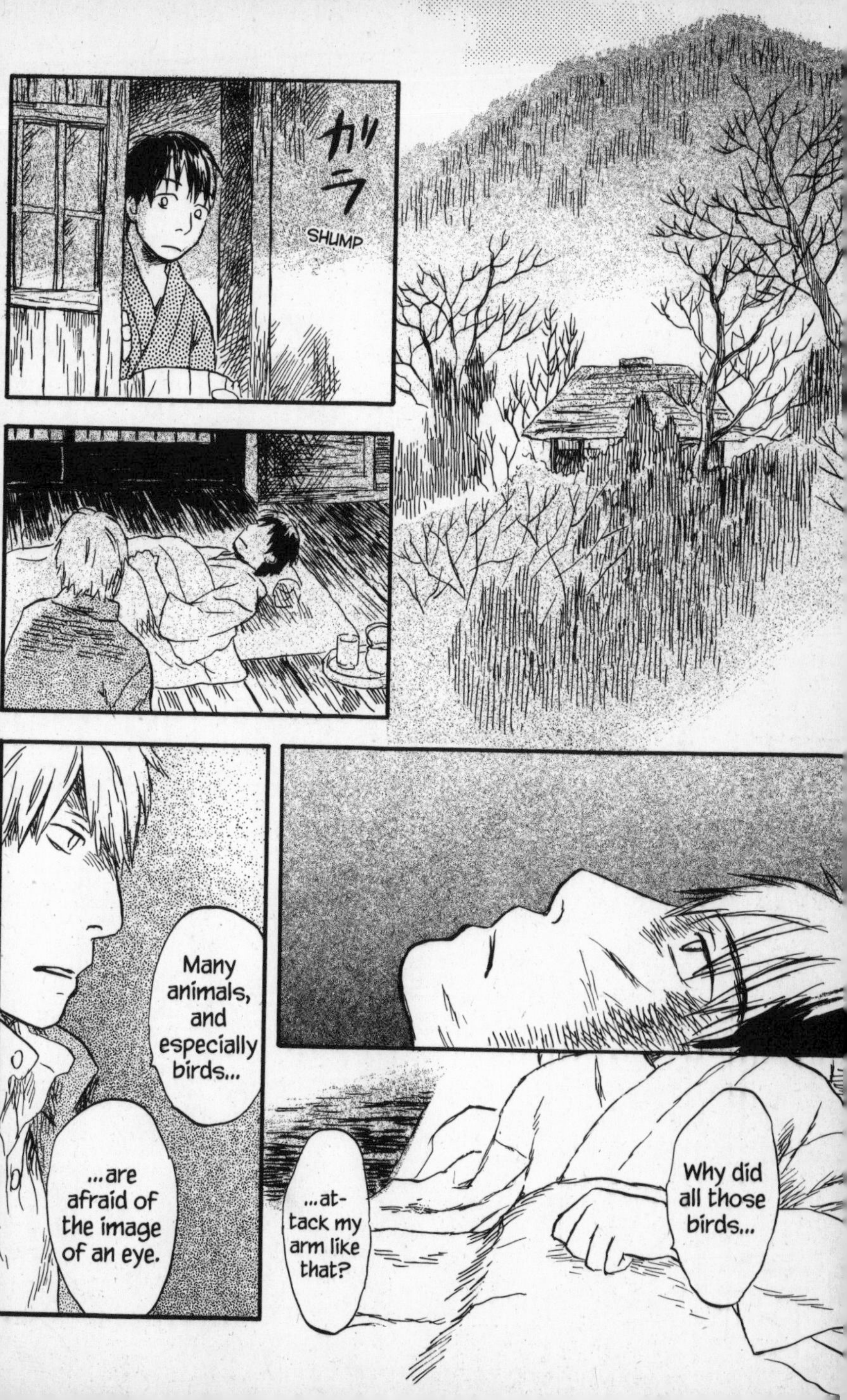

ガラ
SHUMP
Why did all those birds...
...at-tack my arm like that?
Many animals, and especially birds...
...are afraid of the image of an eye.

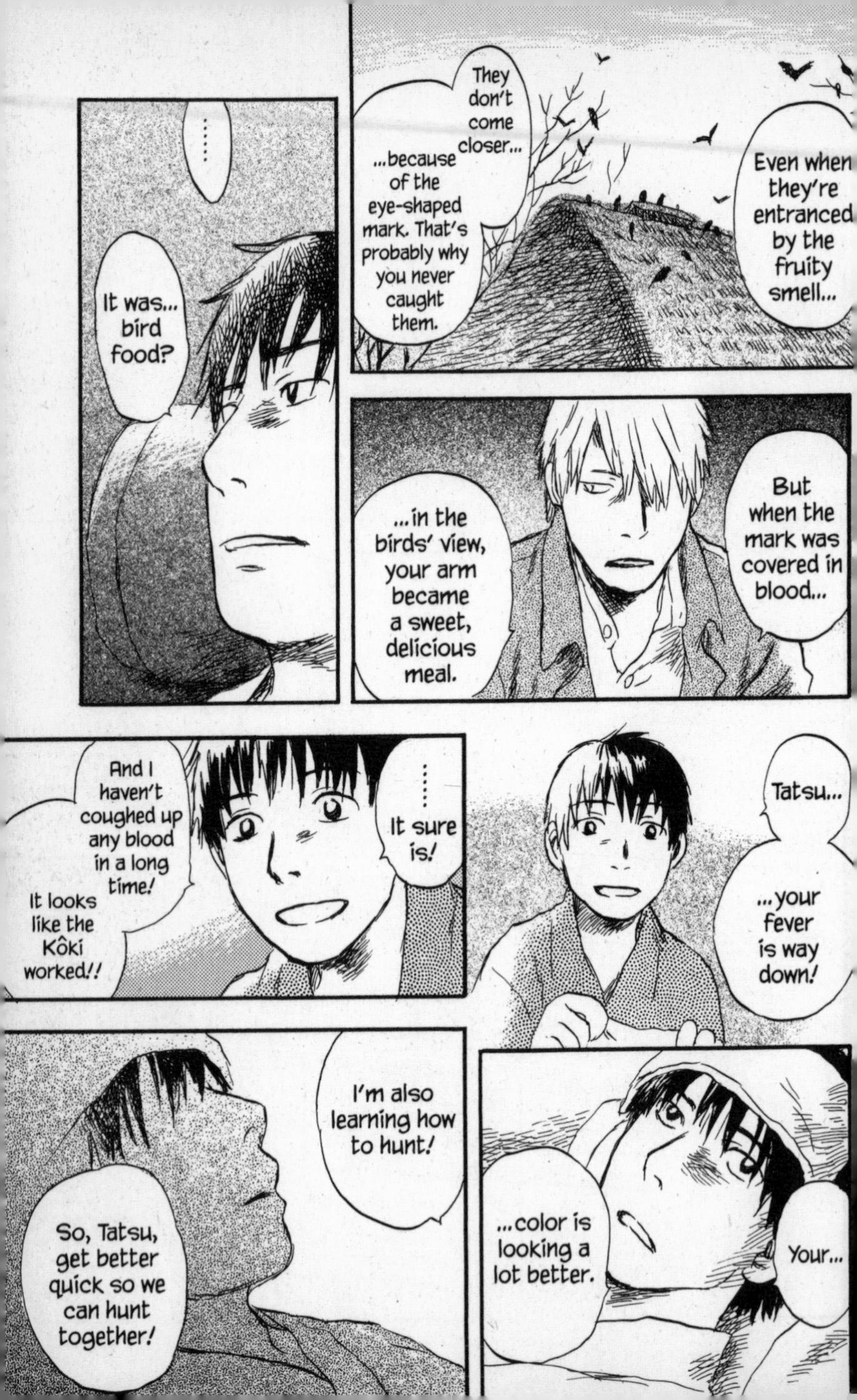
Even when they're entranced by the fruity smell...
They don't come closer...
...because of the eye-shaped mark. That's probably why you never caught them.
But when the mark was covered in blood...
...in the birds' view, your arm became a sweet, delicious meal.
......
It was... bird food?
Tatsu...
...your fever is way down!
......
It sure is!
And I haven't coughed up any blood in a long time!
It looks like the Kôki worked!!
Your...
...color is looking a lot better.
I'm also learning how to hunt!
So, Tatsu, get better quick so we can hunt together!

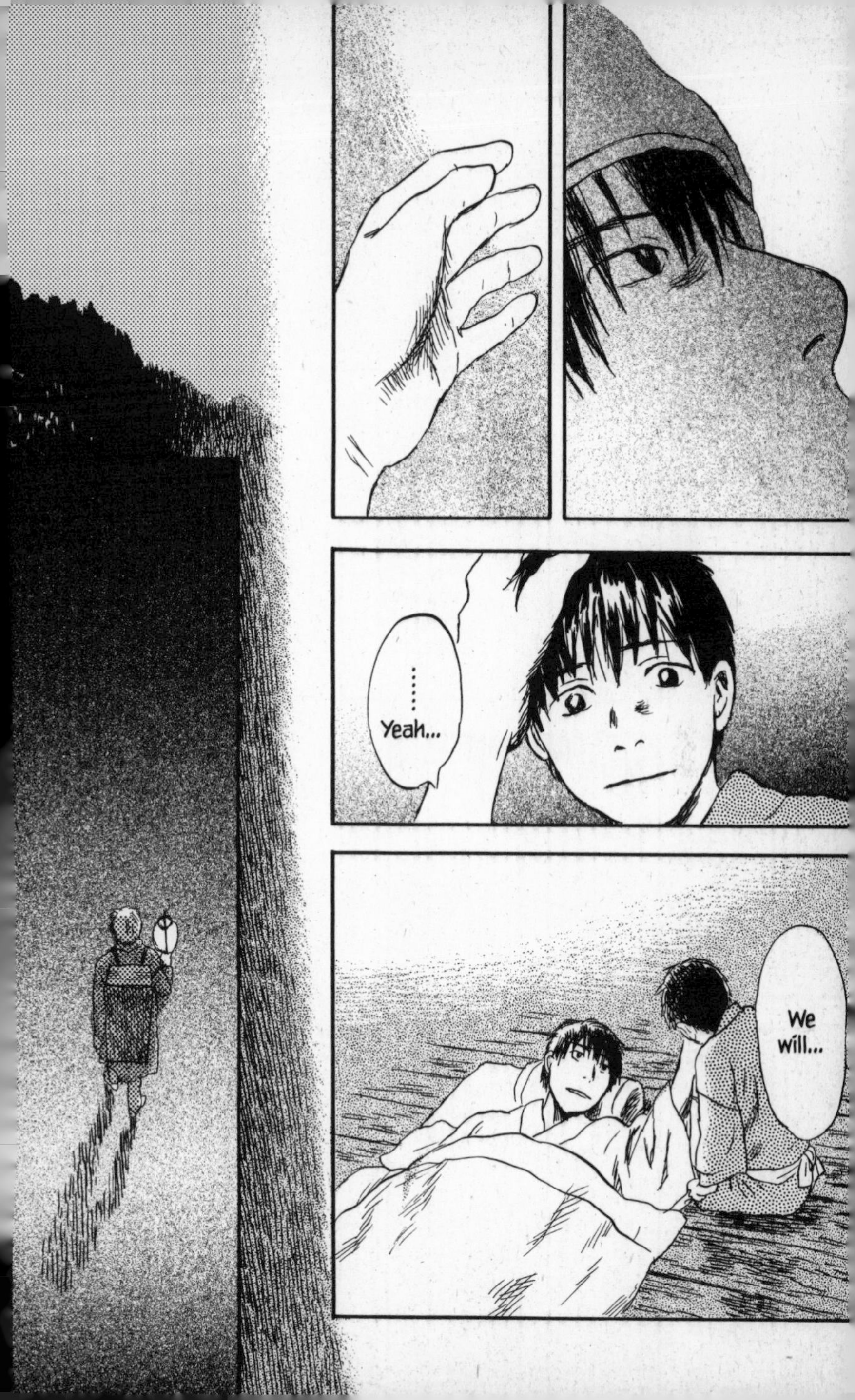
……Yeah…
We will…

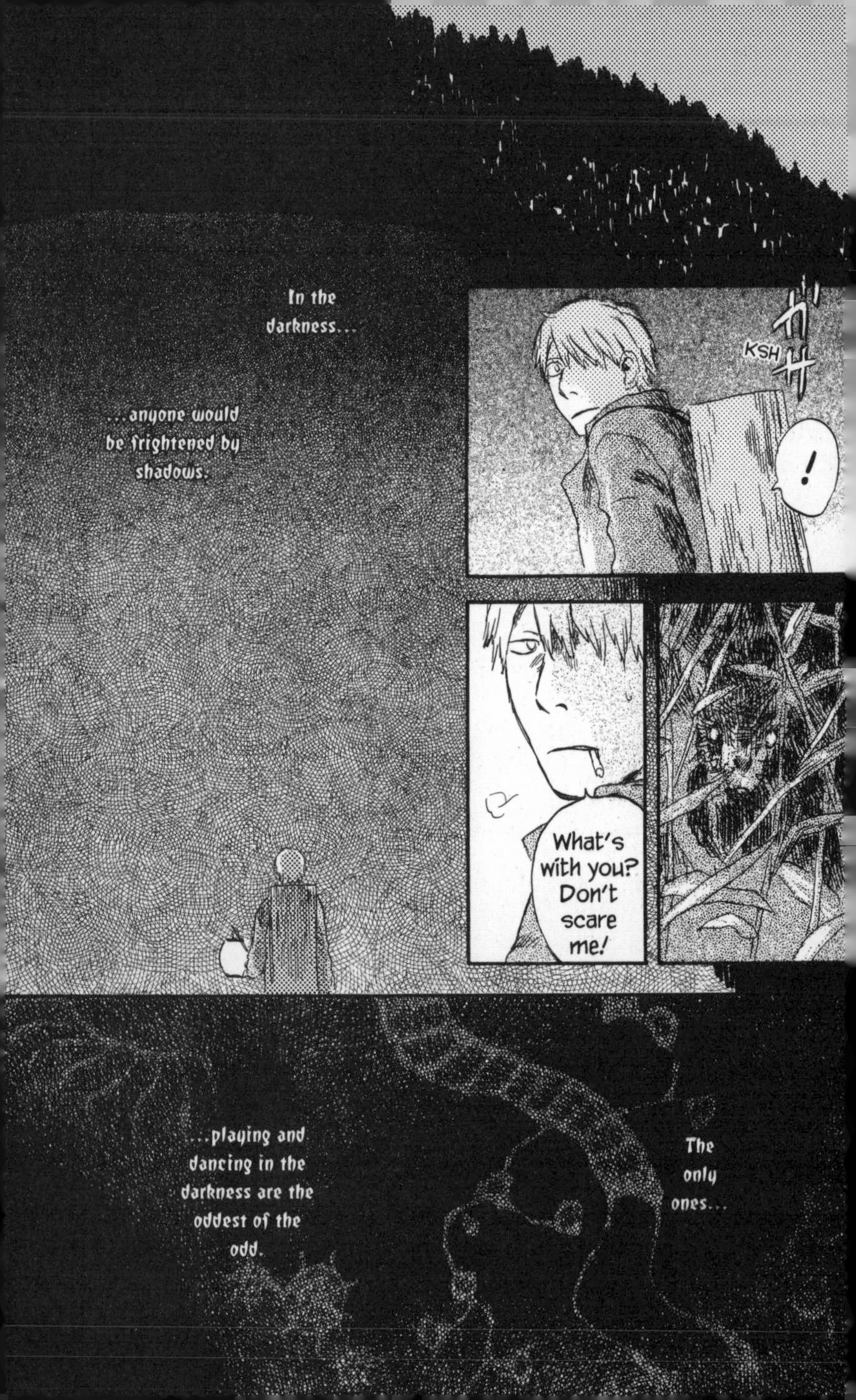

ガサ
KSH
!
What's with you? Don't scare me!
In the darkness...
...anyone would be frightened by shadows.
The only ones...
...playing and dancing in the darkness are the oddest of the odd.

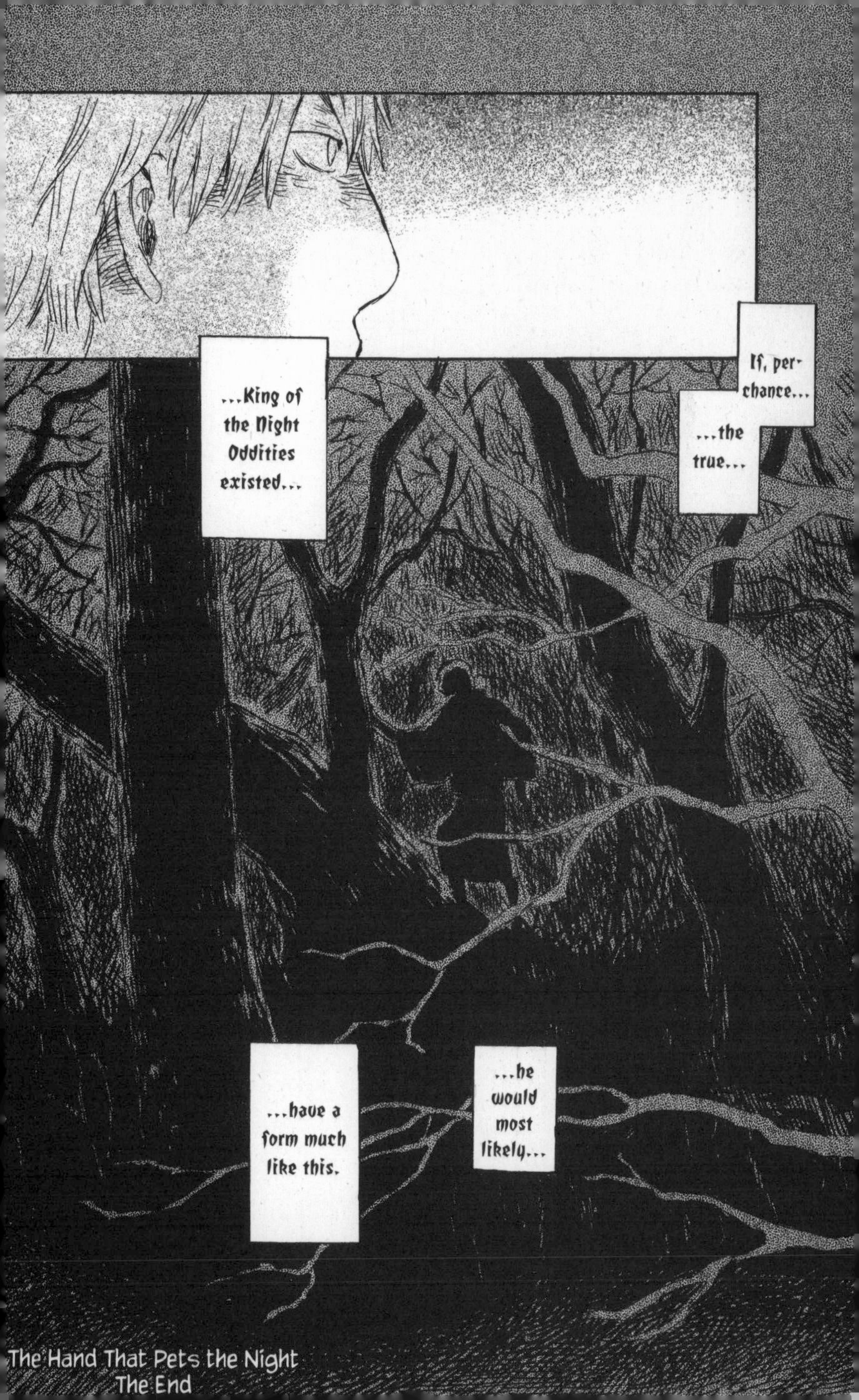
If, perchance...
...the true...
...King of the Night Oddities existed...
...he would most likely...
...have a form much like this.
The Hand That Pets the Night
The End

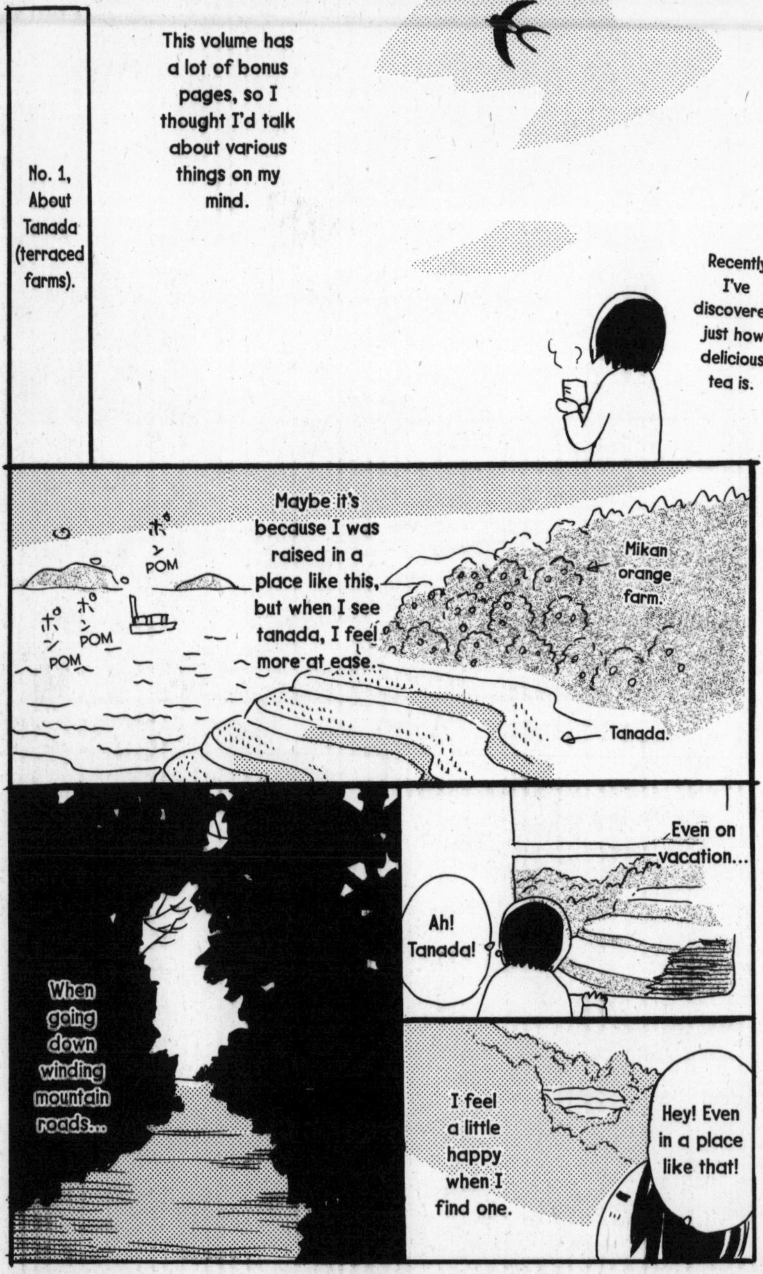

This volume has a lot of bonus pages, so I thought I'd talk about various things on my mind.
Recently I've discovered just how delicious tea is.
No. 1, About Tanada (terraced farms).
Maybe it's because I was raised in a place like this, but when I see tanada, I feel more at ease.
Mikan orange farm.
Tanada.
ポン POM
ポン POM
ポン POM
Even on vacation...
Ah! Tanada!
Hey! Even in a place like that!
I feel a little happy when I find one.
When going down winding mountain roads...

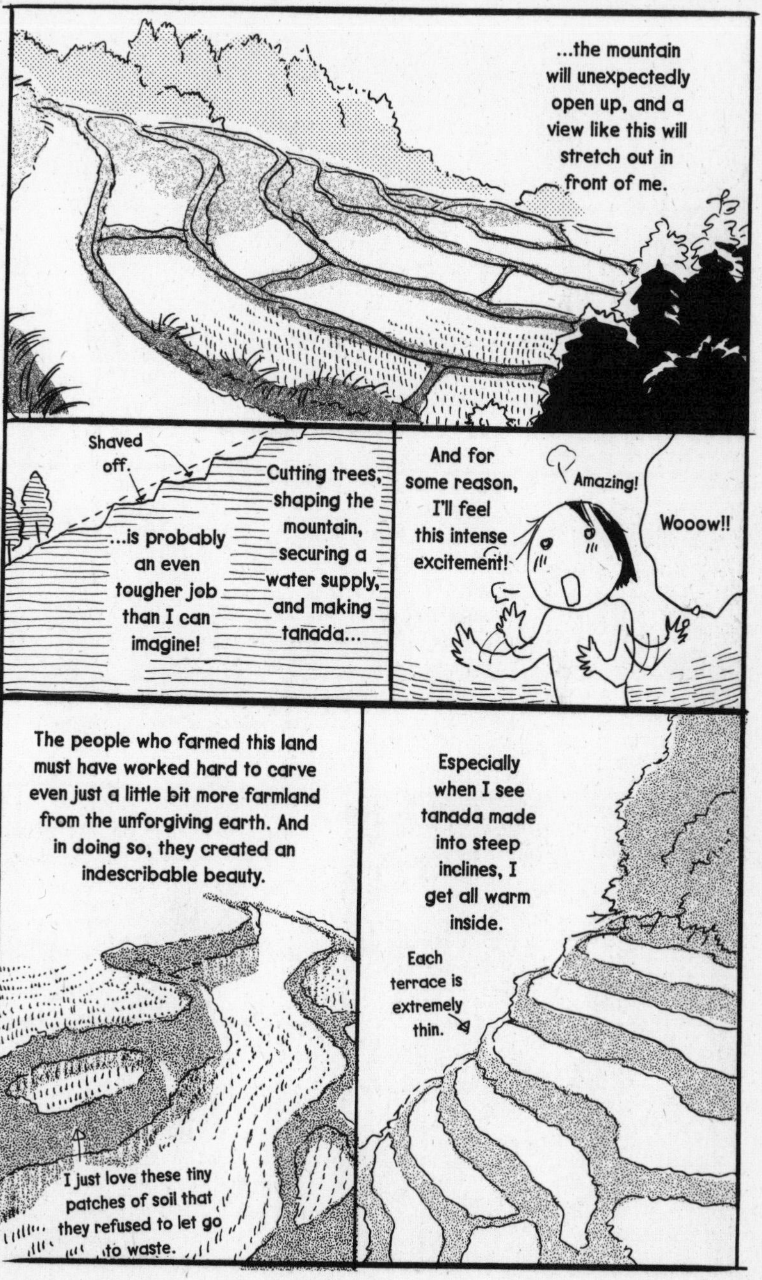
...the mountain will unexpectedly open up, and a view like this will stretch out in front of me.
Wooow!!
Amazing!
And for some reason, I'll feel this intense excitement!
Cutting trees, shaping the mountain, securing a water supply, and making tanada...
Shaved off.
...is probably an even tougher job than I can imagine!
Especially when I see tanada made into steep inclines, I get all warm inside.
Each terrace is extremely thin.
The people who farmed this land must have worked hard to carve even just a little bit more farmland from the unforgiving earth. And in doing so, they created an indescribable beauty.
I just love these tiny patches of soil that they refused to let go to waste.

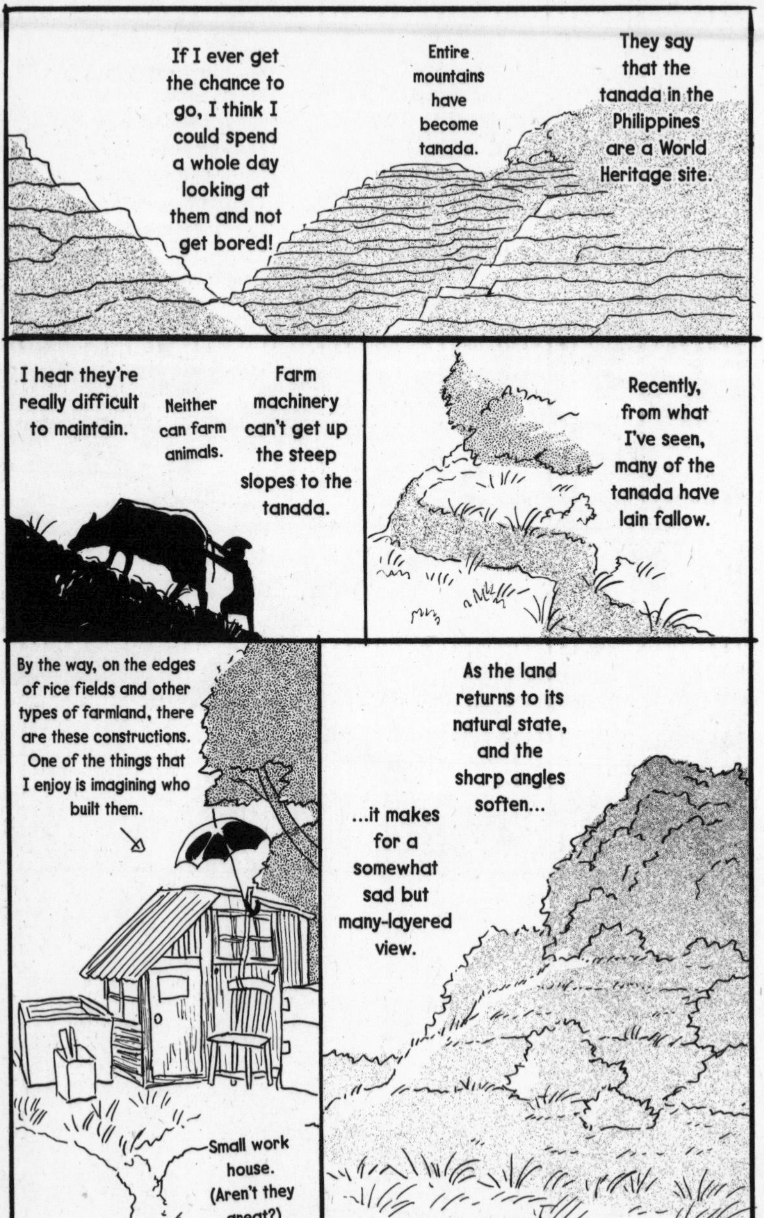
They say that the tanada in the Philippines are a World Heritage site.
Entire mountains have become tanada.
If I ever get the chance to go, I think I could spend a whole day looking at them and not get bored!
Recently, from what I've seen, many of the tanada have lain fallow.
Farm machinery can't get up the steep slopes to the tanada.
Neither can farm animals.
I hear they're really difficult to maintain.
As the land returns to its natural state, and the sharp angles soften...
...it makes for a somewhat sad but many-layered view.
By the way, on the edges of rice fields and other types of farmland, there are these constructions. One of the things that I enjoy is imagining who built them.
Small work house. (Aren't they great?)

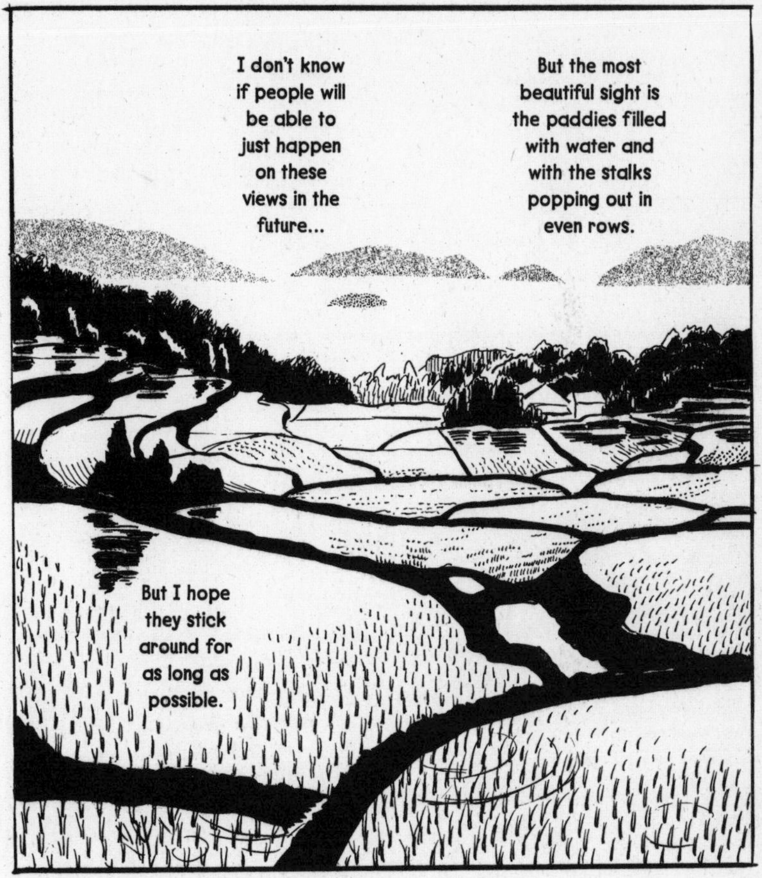
But the most beautiful sight is the paddies filled with water and with the stalks popping out in even rows.
I don't know if people will be able to just happen on these views in the future...
But I hope they stick around for as long as possible.

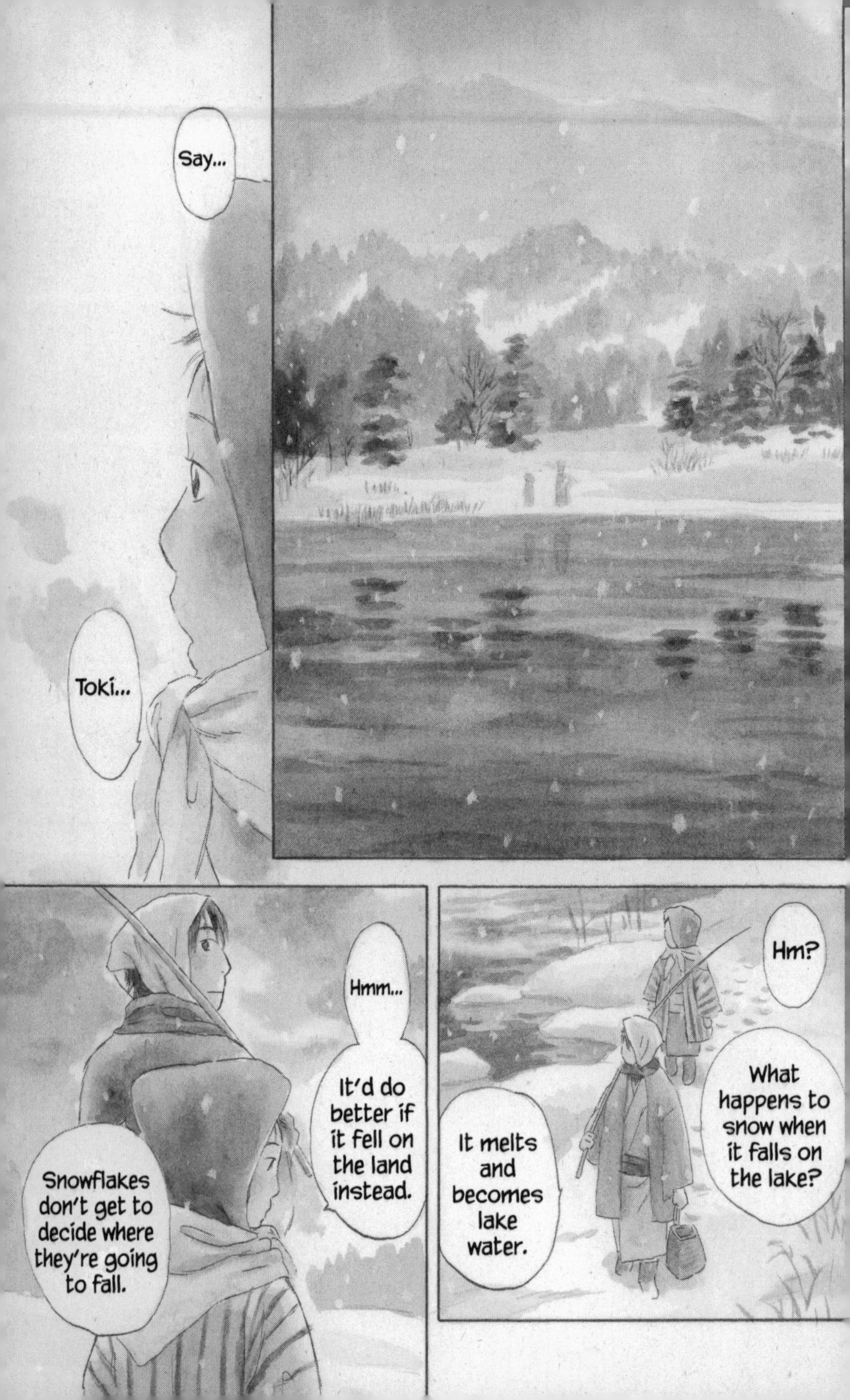
Say...
Toki...
Hm?
What happens to snow when it falls on the lake?
It melts and becomes lake water.
Hmm...
It'd do better if it fell on the land instead.
Snowflakes don't get to decide where they're going to fall.

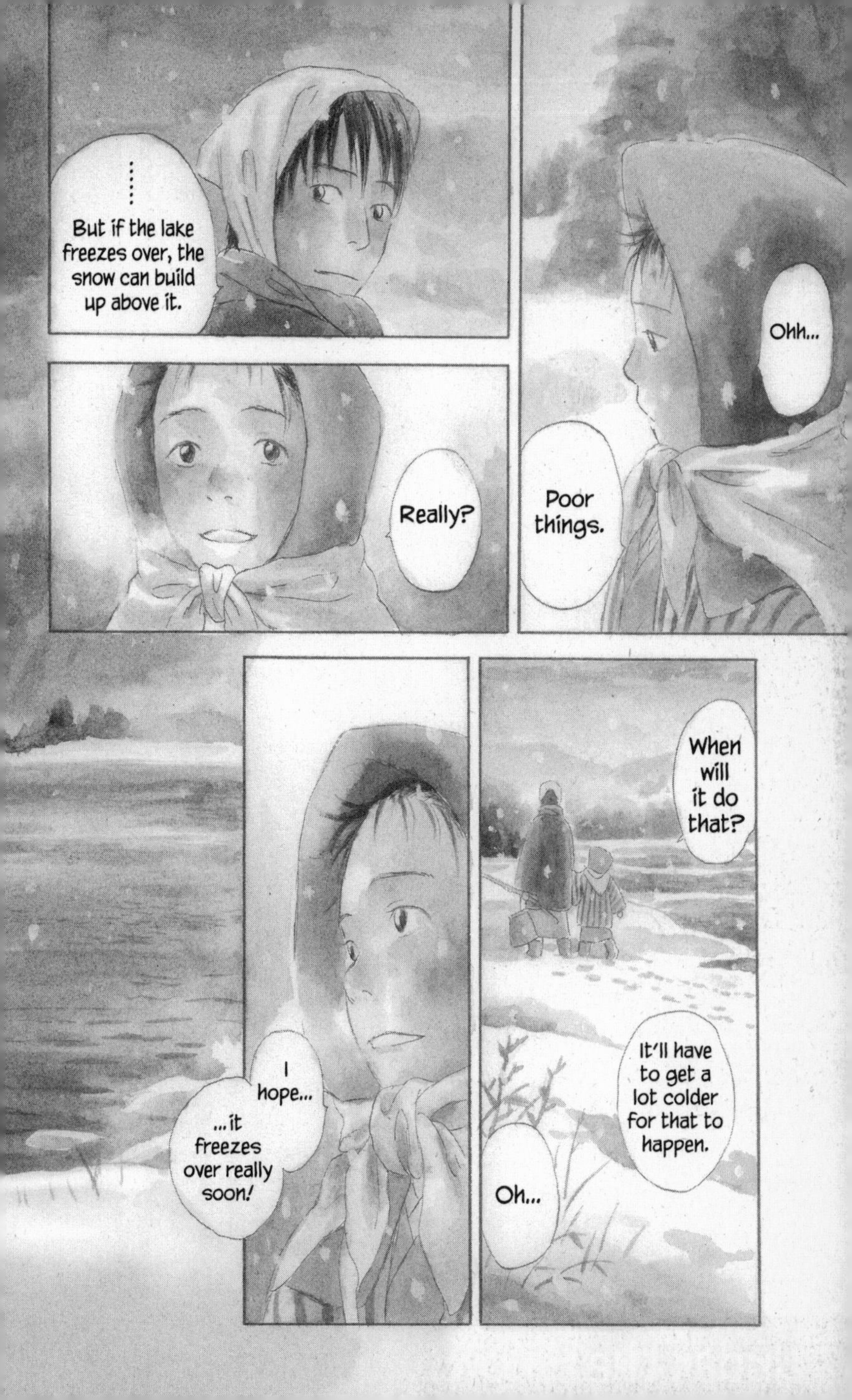
Ohh...
Poor things.
......
But if the lake freezes over, the snow can build up above it.
Really?
When will it do that?
It'll have to get a lot colder for that to happen.
Oh...
I hope...
...it freezes over really soon!

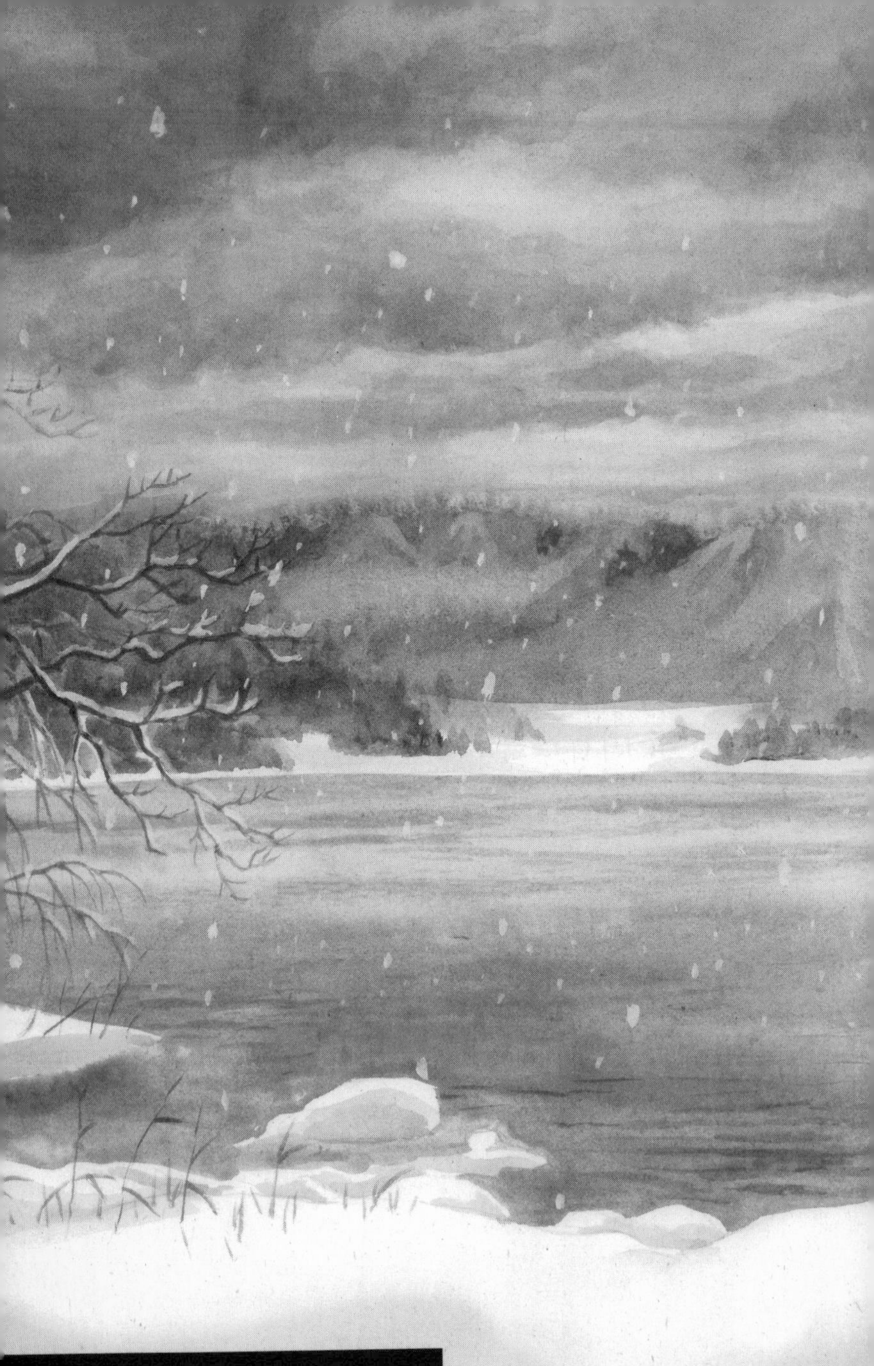

Under the Snow

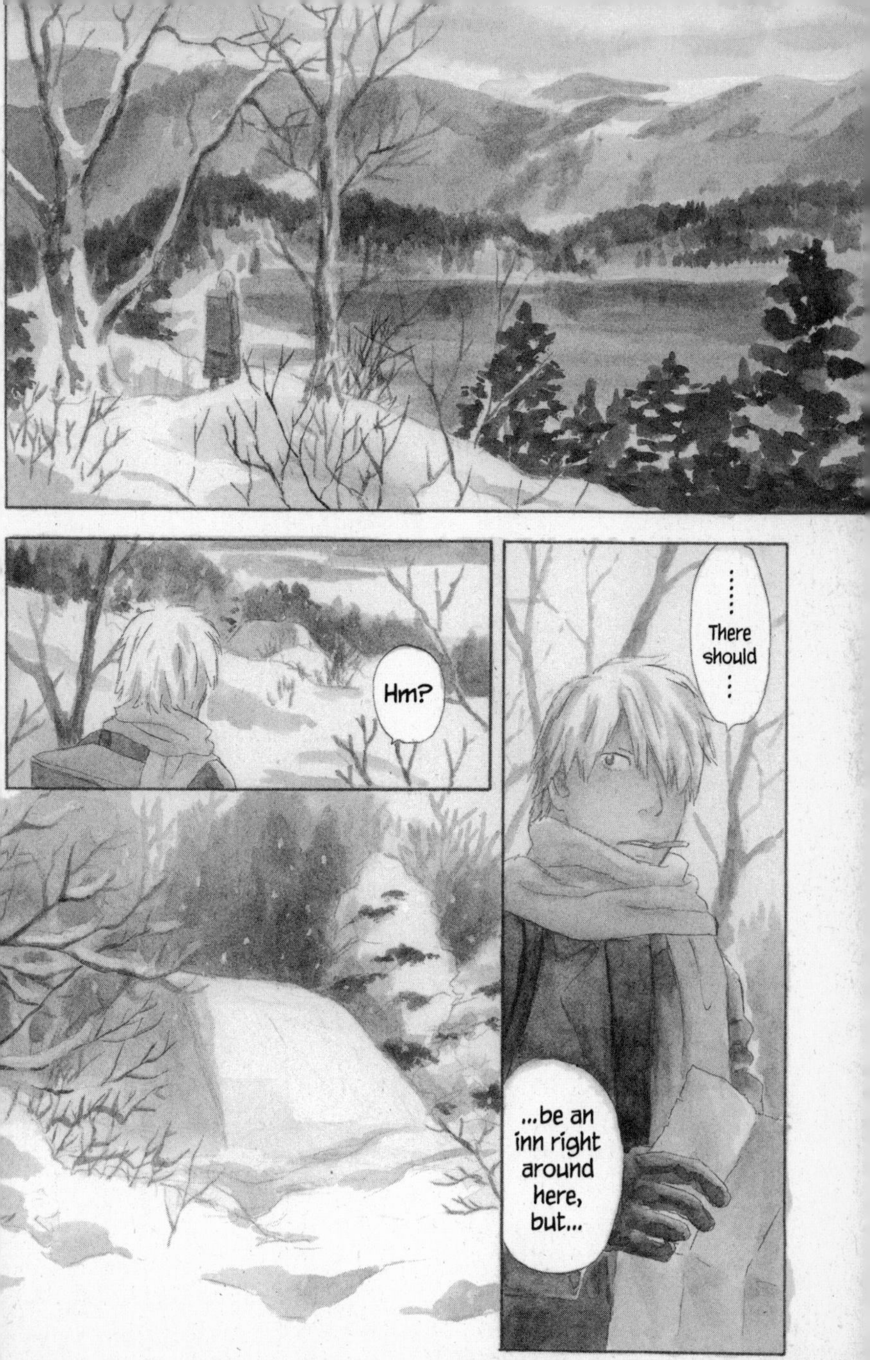
...... There should ...
...be an inn right around here, but...
Hm?

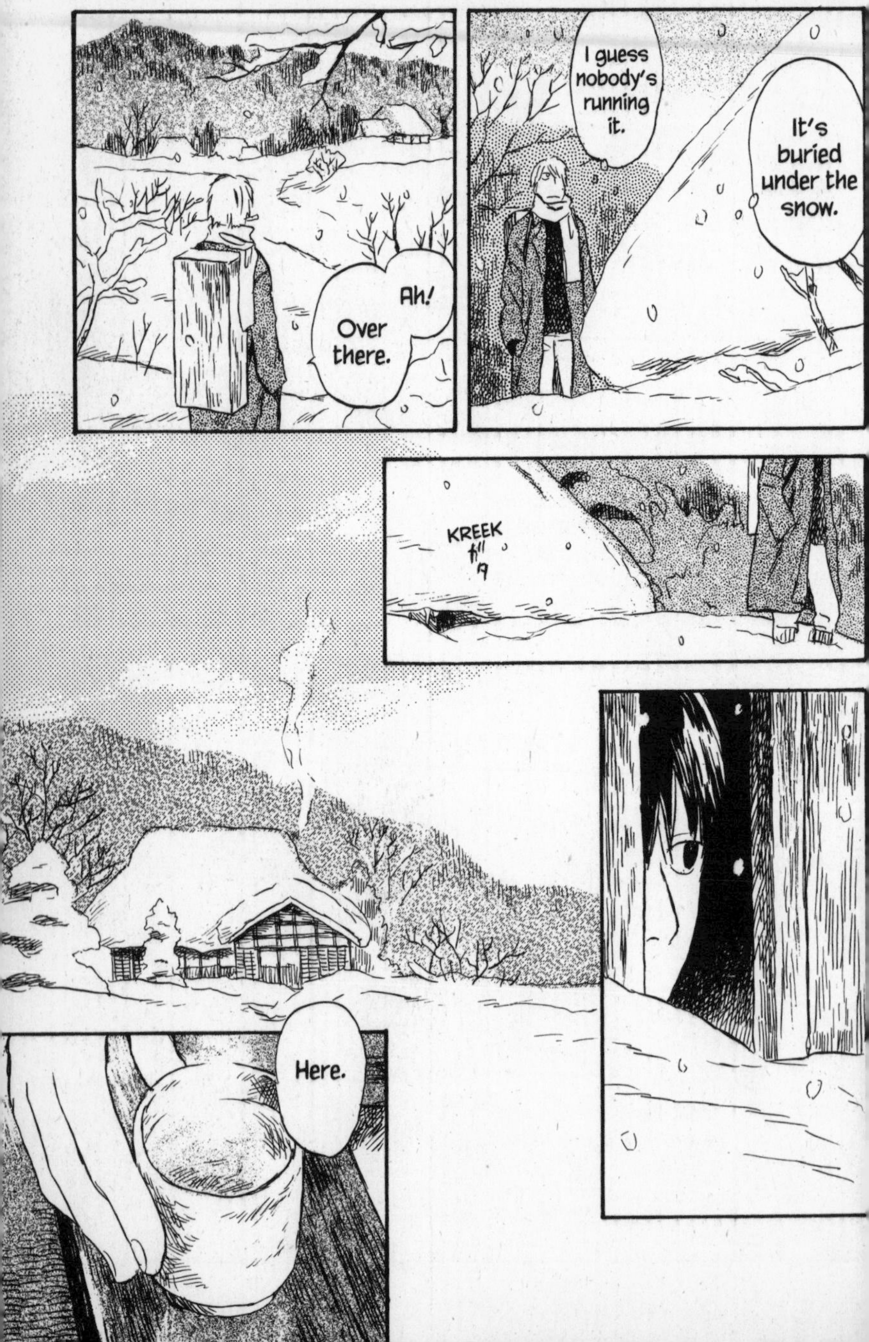

It's buried under the snow.
I guess nobody's running it.
Ah!
Over there.
KREEK
Here.

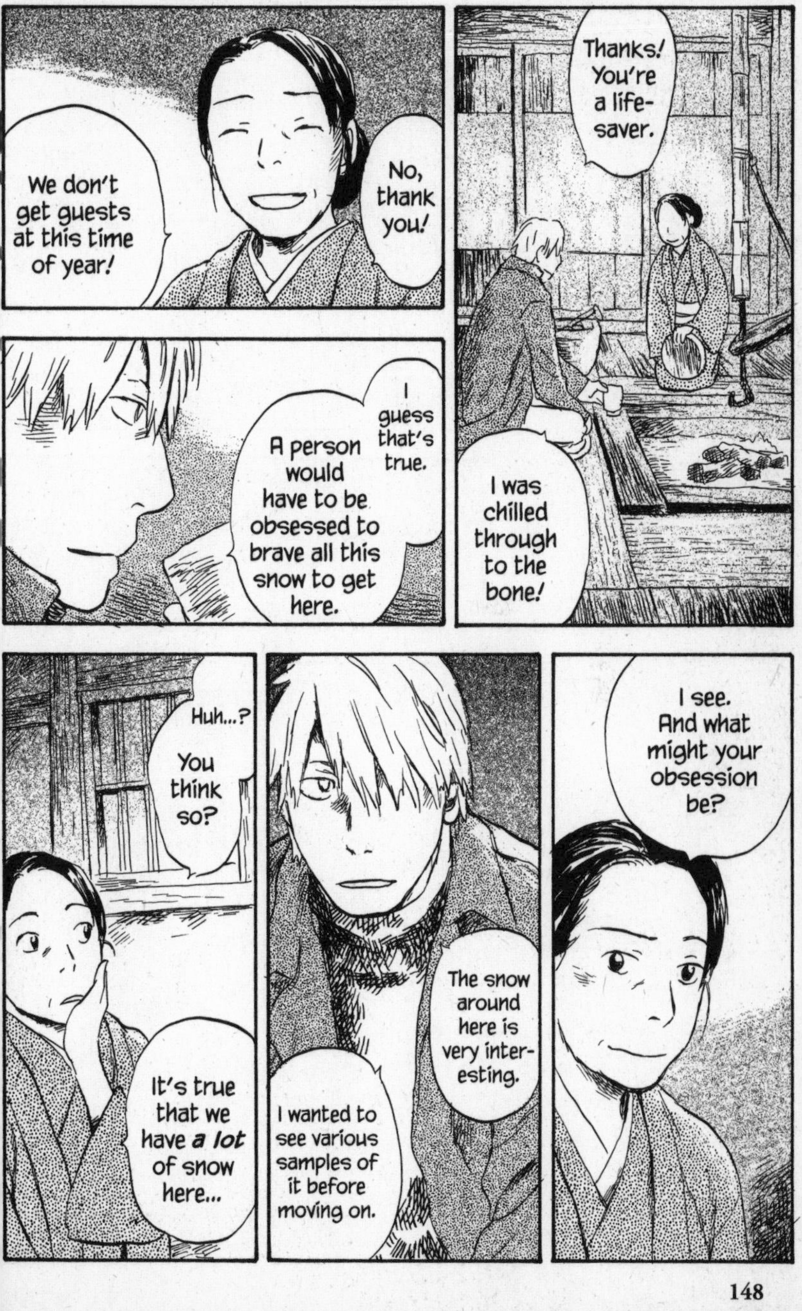

Thanks! You're a life-saver.
I was chilled through to the bone!
No, thank you!
We don't get guests at this time of year!
I guess that's true.
A person would have to be obsessed to brave all this snow to get here.
I see. And what might your obsession be?
The snow around here is very interesting.
I wanted to see various samples of it before moving on.
Huh...?
You think so?
It's true that we have *a lot* of snow here...

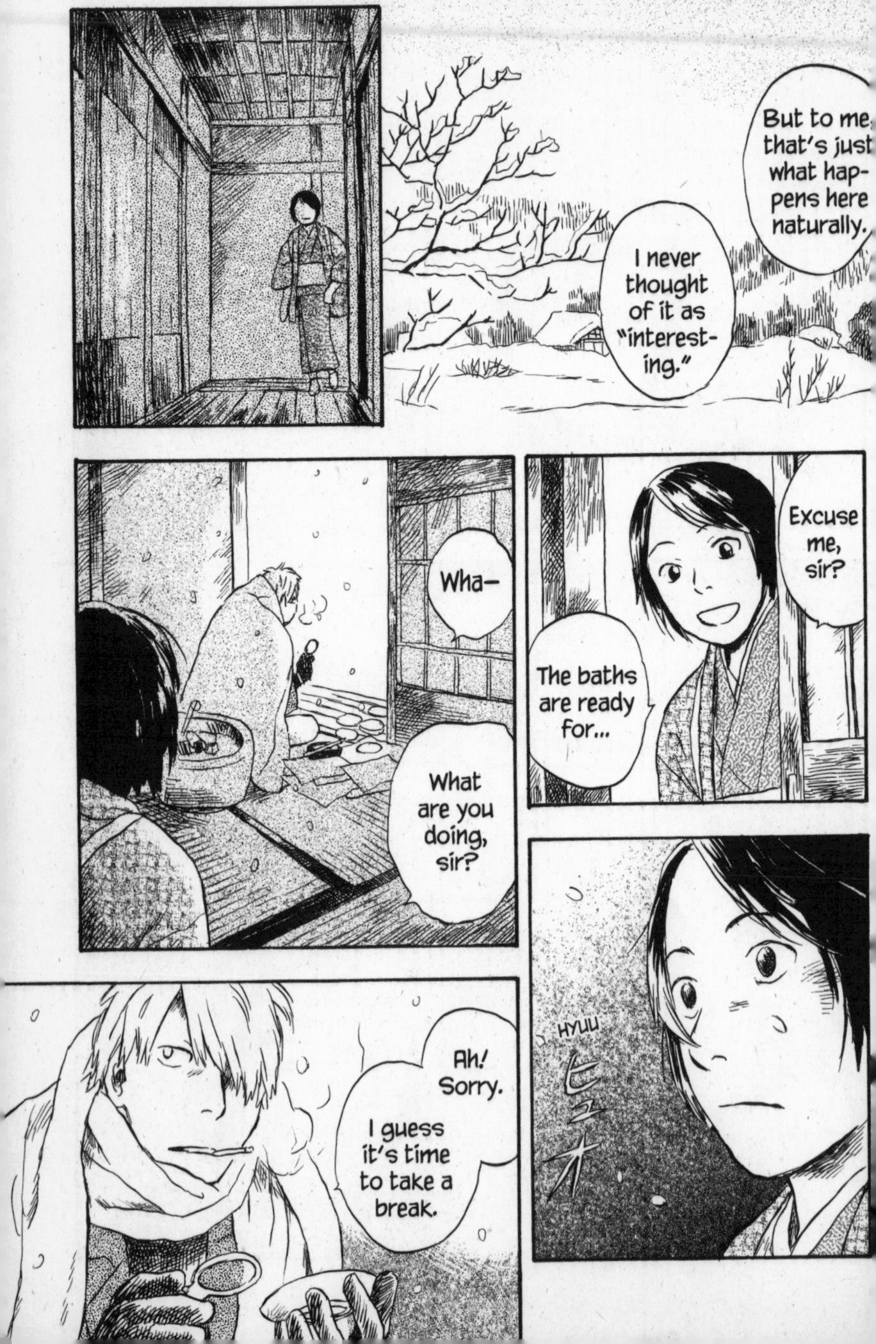
But to me, that's just what happens here naturally.
I never thought of it as "interesting."
Excuse me, sir?
The baths are ready for...
Wha–
What are you doing, sir?
HYUU
ヒュオ
Ah! Sorry.
I guess it's time to take a break.

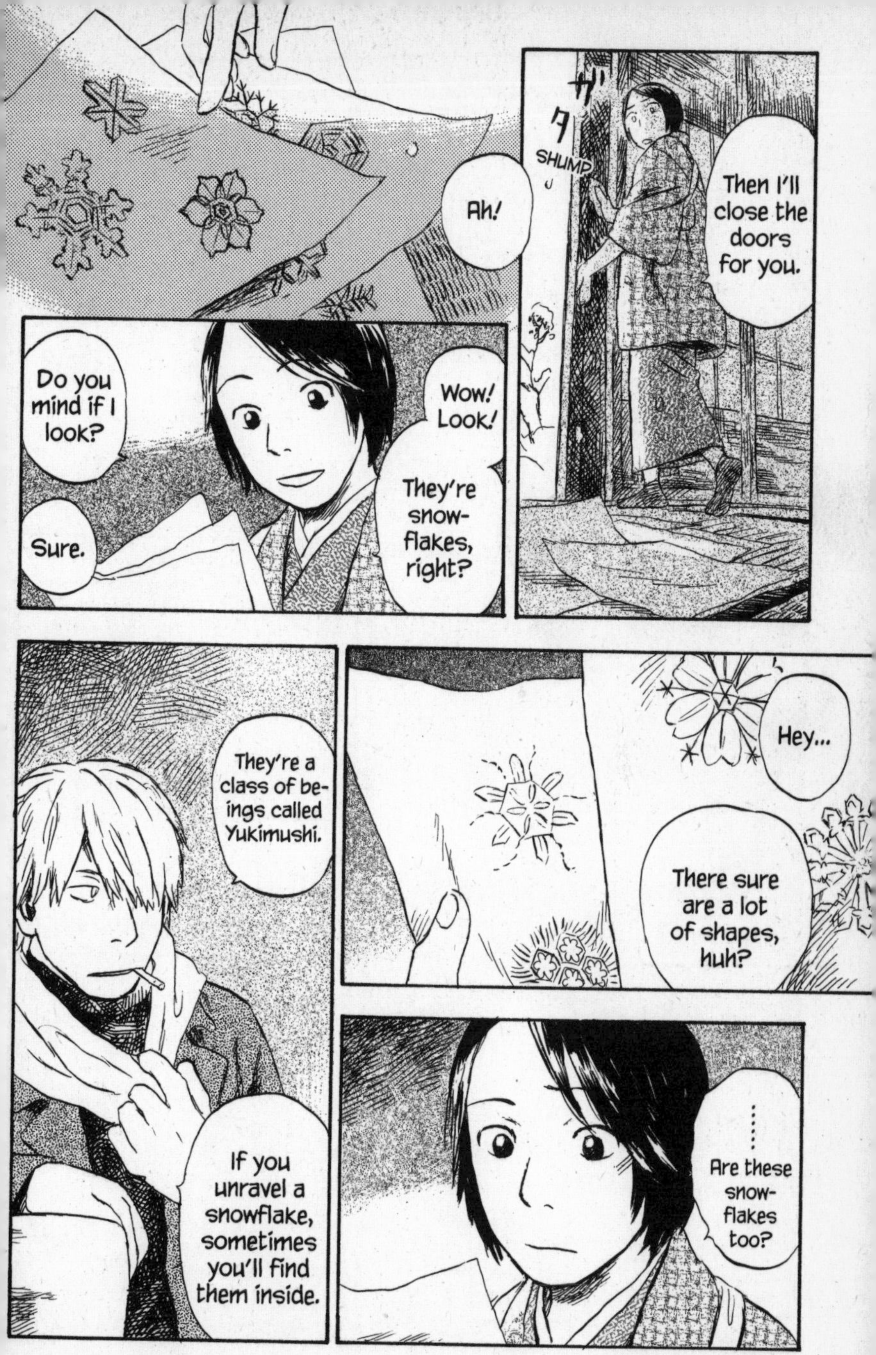
Then I'll close the doors for you.
SHUMP
Ah!
Wow! Look!
They're snow-flakes, right?
Do you mind if I look?
Sure.
Hey...
There sure are a lot of shapes, huh?
......
Are these snow-flakes too?
They're a class of be-ings called Yukimushi.
If you unravel a snowflake, sometimes you'll find them inside.

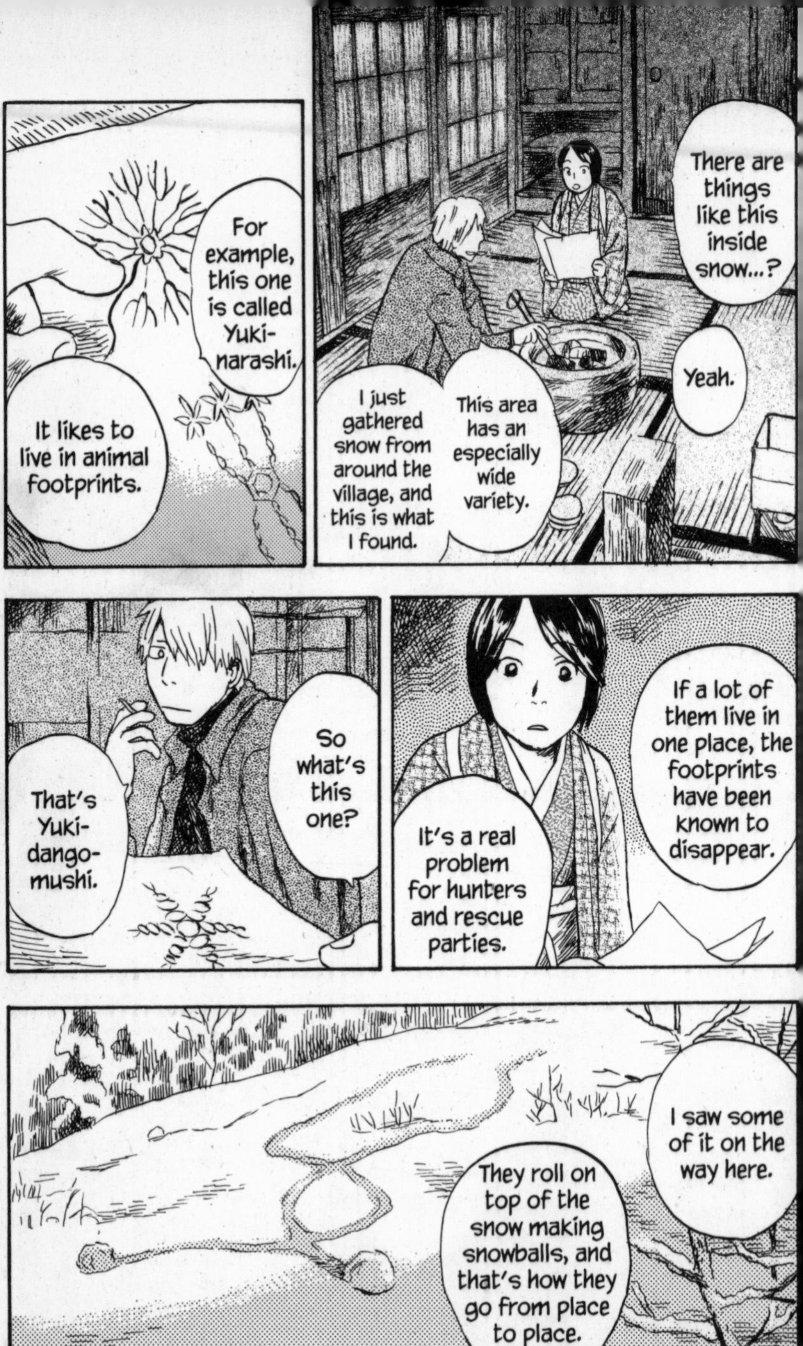
There are things like this inside snow...?
Yeah.
This area has an especially wide variety.
I just gathered snow from around the village, and this is what I found.
For example, this one is called Yuki-narashi.
It likes to live in animal footprints.
If a lot of them live in one place, the footprints have been known to disappear.
It's a real problem for hunters and rescue parties.
So what's this one?
That's Yuki-dangomushi.
I saw some of it on the way here.
They roll on top of the snow making snowballs, and that's how they go from place to place.

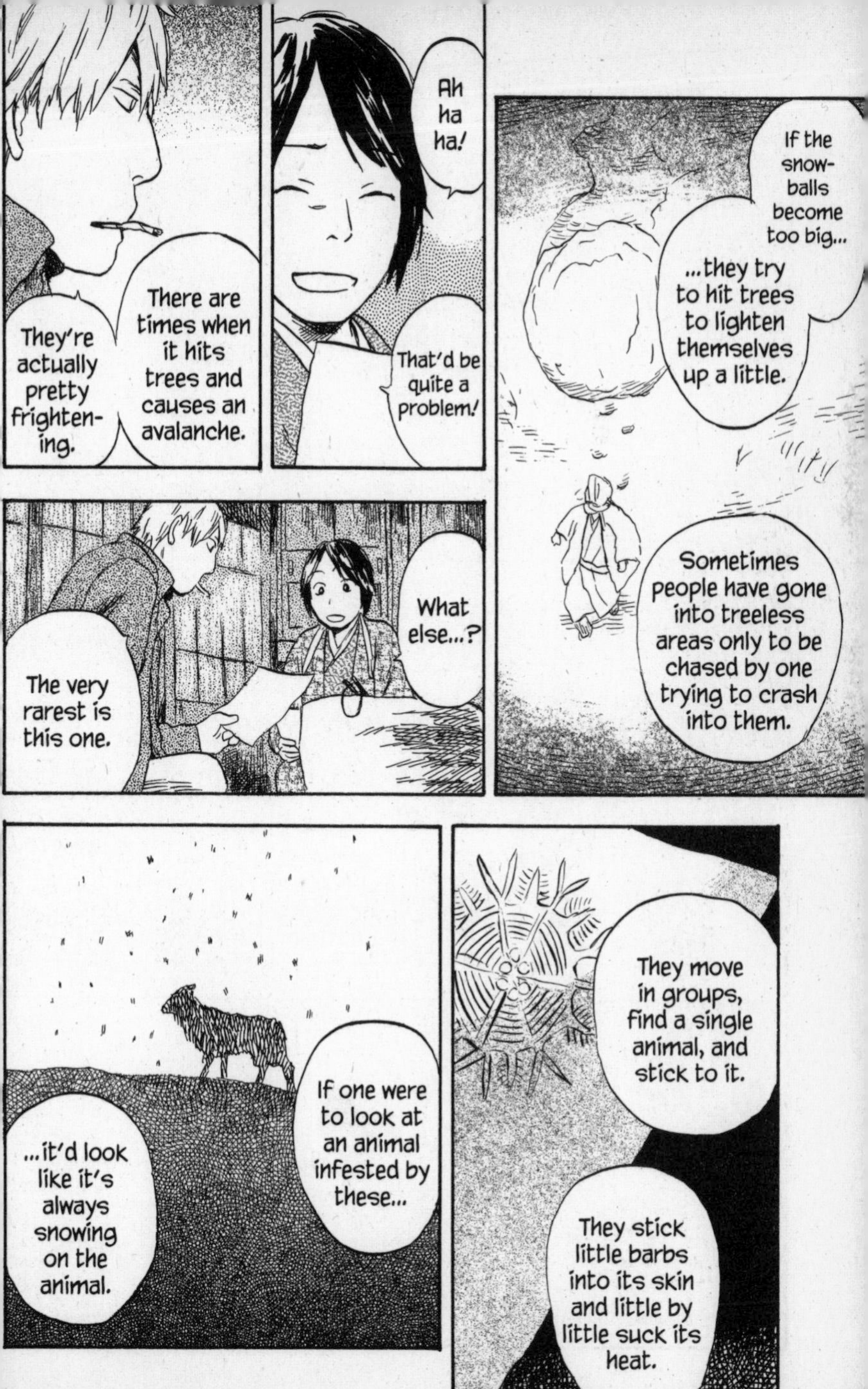

If the snowballs become too big...
...they try to hit trees to lighten themselves up a little.
Sometimes people have gone into treeless areas only to be chased by one trying to crash into them.
Ah ha ha!
That'd be quite a problem!
There are times when it hits trees and causes an avalanche.
They're actually pretty frightening.
What else...?
The very rarest is this one.
They move in groups, find a single animal, and stick to it.
They stick little barbs into its skin and little by little suck its heat.
If one were to look at an animal infested by these...
...it'd look like it's always snowing on the animal.

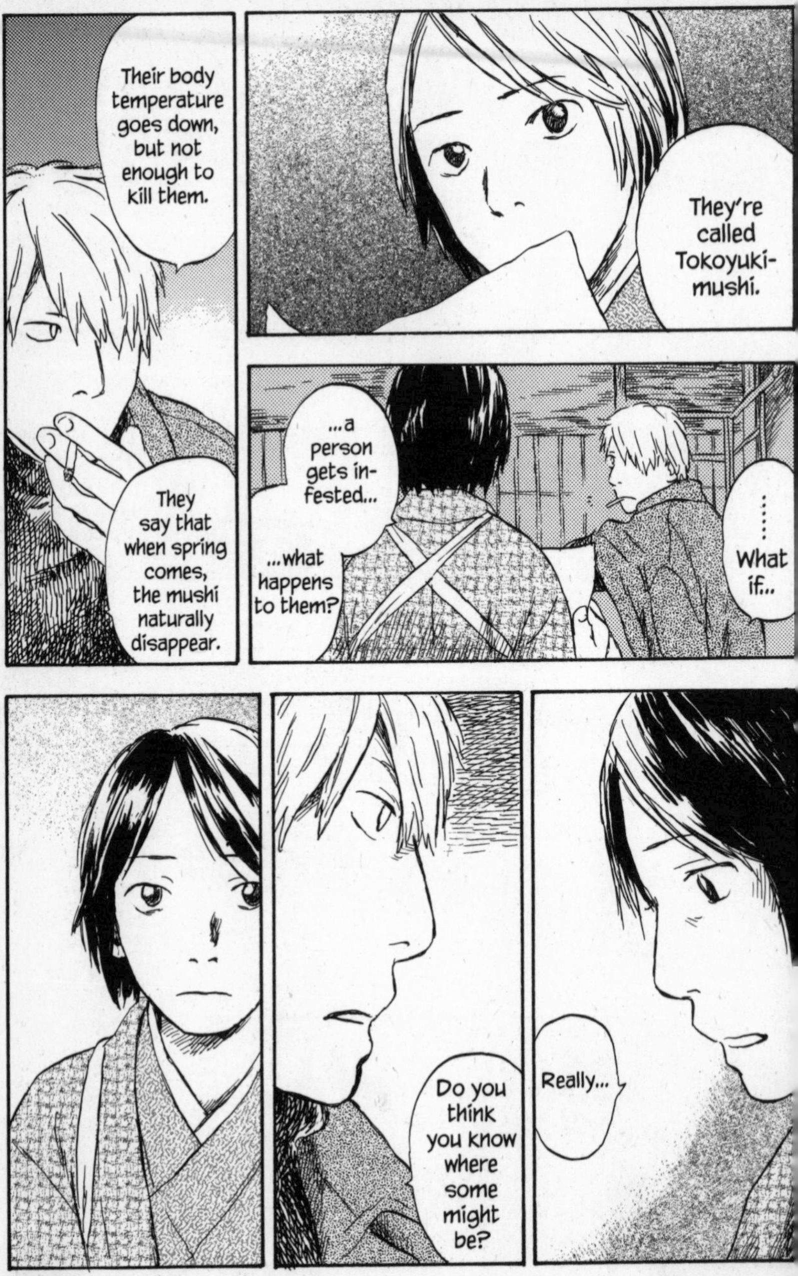
They're called Tokoyuki-mushi.
......
What if...
...a person gets infested...
...what happens to them?
Their body temperature goes down, but not enough to kill them.
They say that when spring comes, the mushi naturally disappear.
Really...
Do you think you know where some might be?

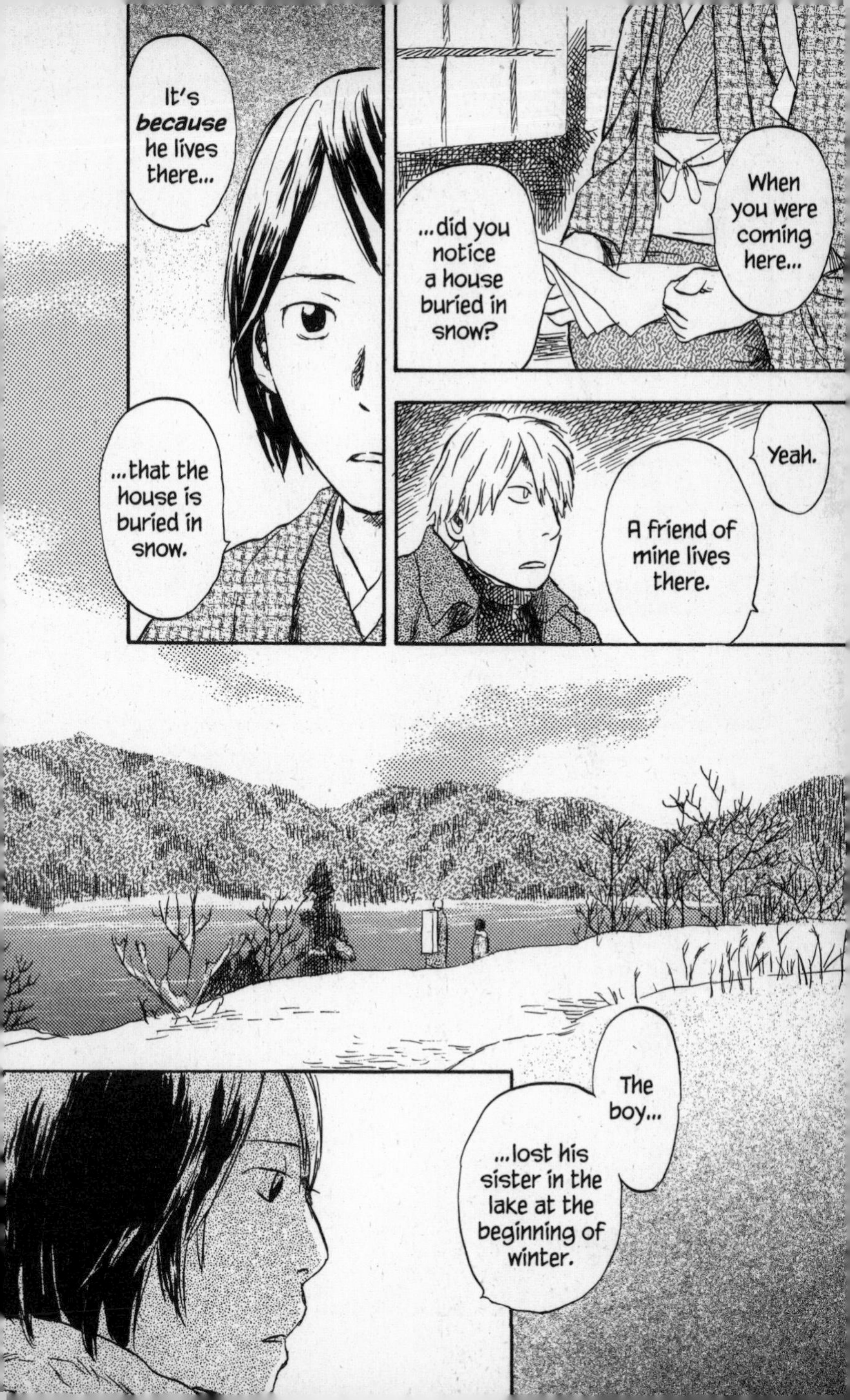
When you were coming here...
...did you notice a house buried in snow?
Yeah.
A friend of mine lives there.
It's *because* he lives there...
...that the house is buried in snow.
The boy...
...lost his sister in the lake at the beginning of winter.

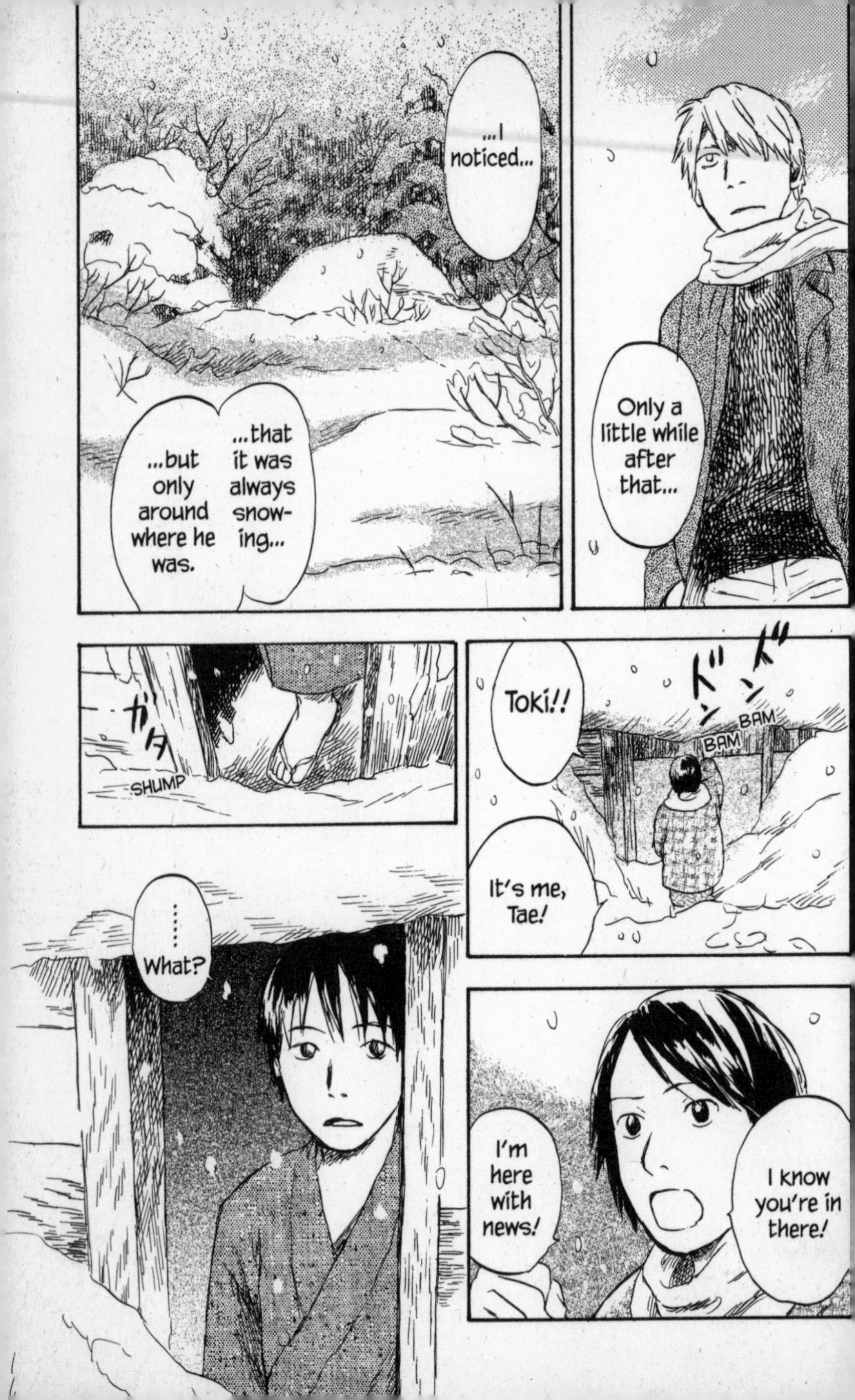
Only a little while after that...
...I noticed...
...that it was always snowing...
...but only around where he was.
Toki!!
ドンドン
BAM BAM
It's me, Tae!
I know you're in there!
I'm here with news!
ガタ
SHUMP
......
What?

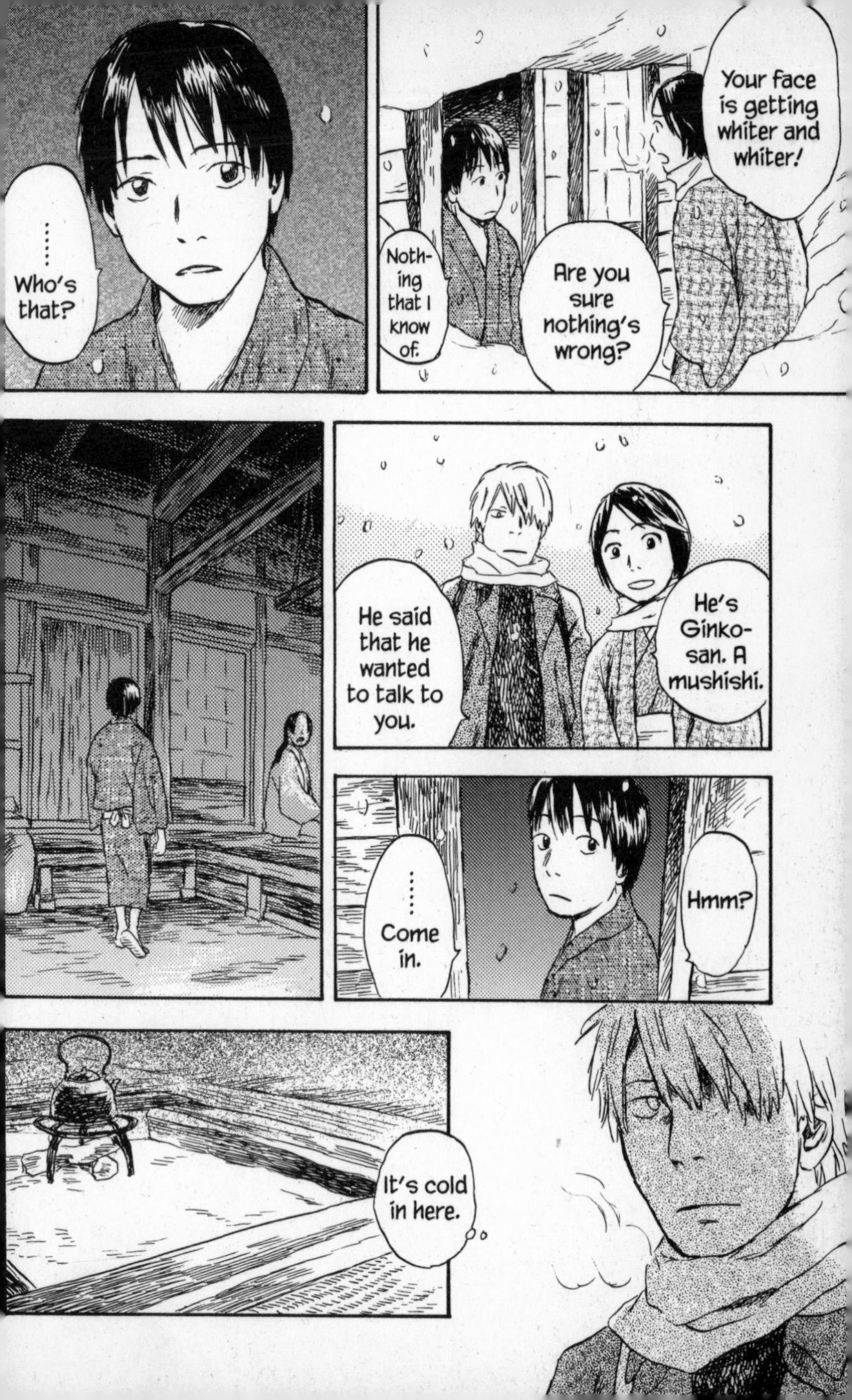
Your face is getting whiter and whiter!
Are you sure nothing's wrong?
Nothing that I know of.
...... Who's that?
He's Ginko-san. A mushishi.
He said that he wanted to talk to you.
Hmm?
...... Come in.
It's cold in here.

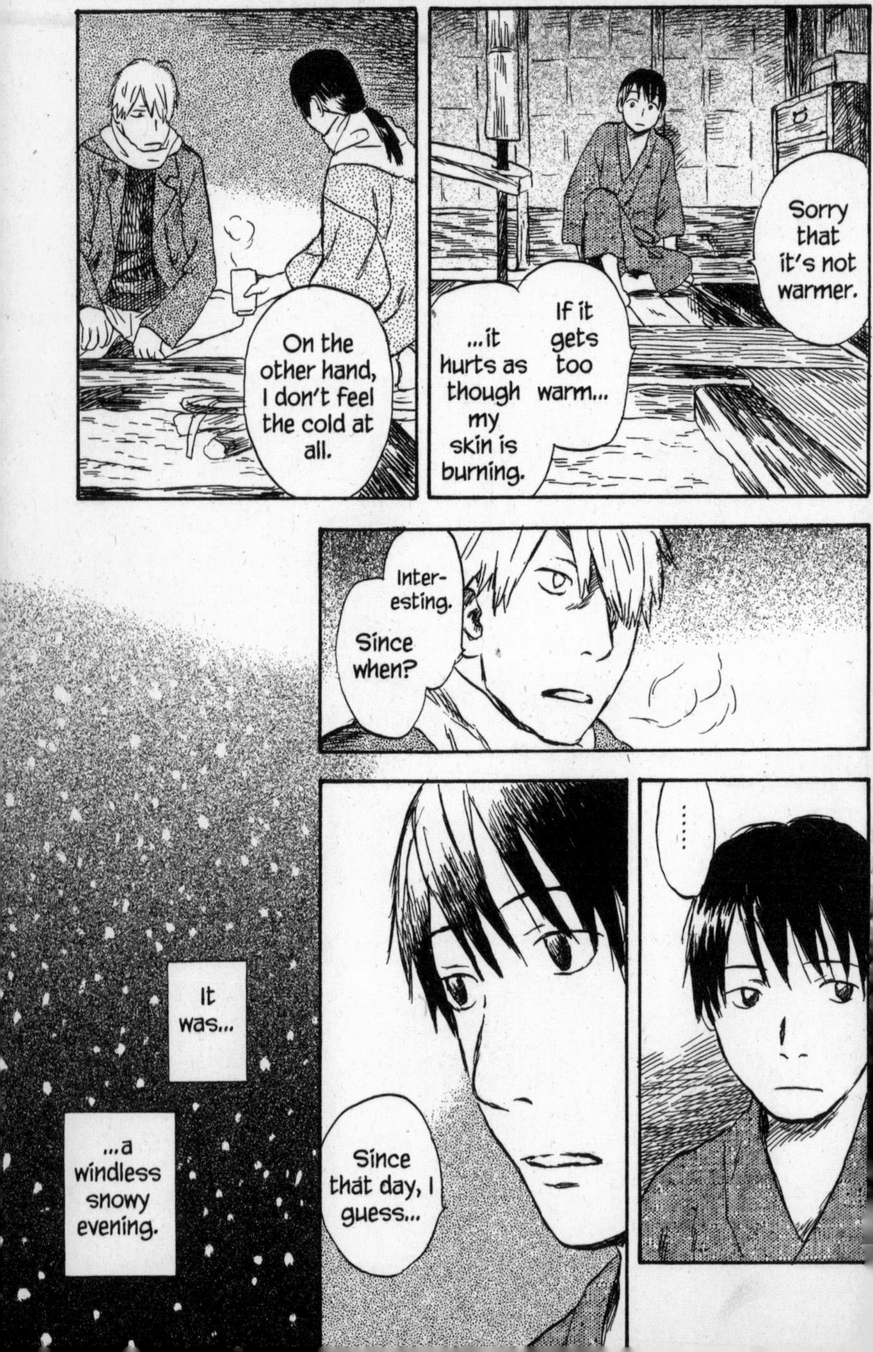
Sorry that it's not warmer.
If it gets too warm...
...it hurts as though my skin is burning.
On the other hand, I don't feel the cold at all.
Inter-esting.
Since when?
......
Since that day, I guess...
It was...
...a windless snowy evening.

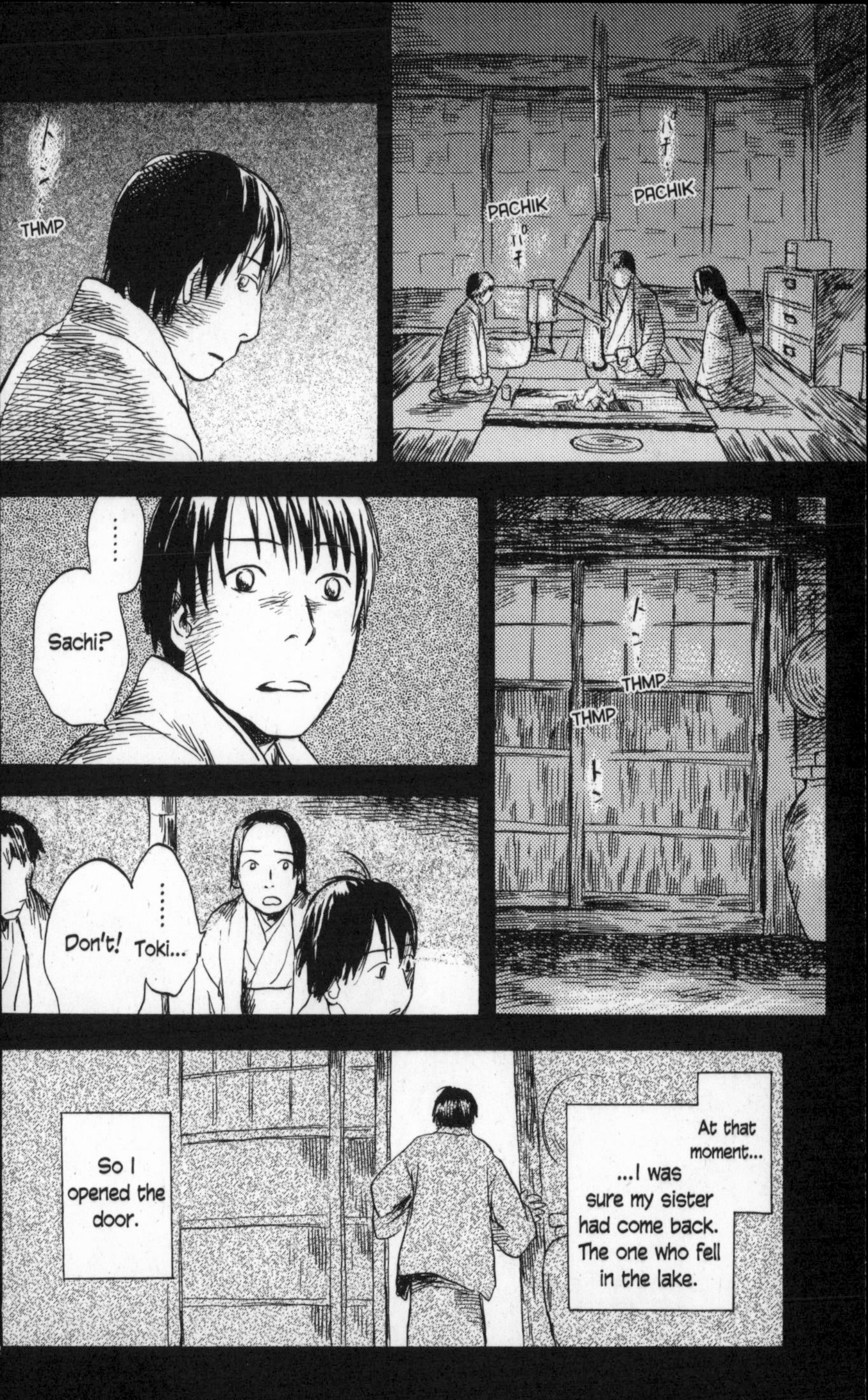
PACHIK
PACHIK
THMP
THMP
THMP
......
Sachi?
......
Toki...
Don't!
At that moment...
...I was sure my sister had come back. The one who fell in the lake.
So I opened the door.

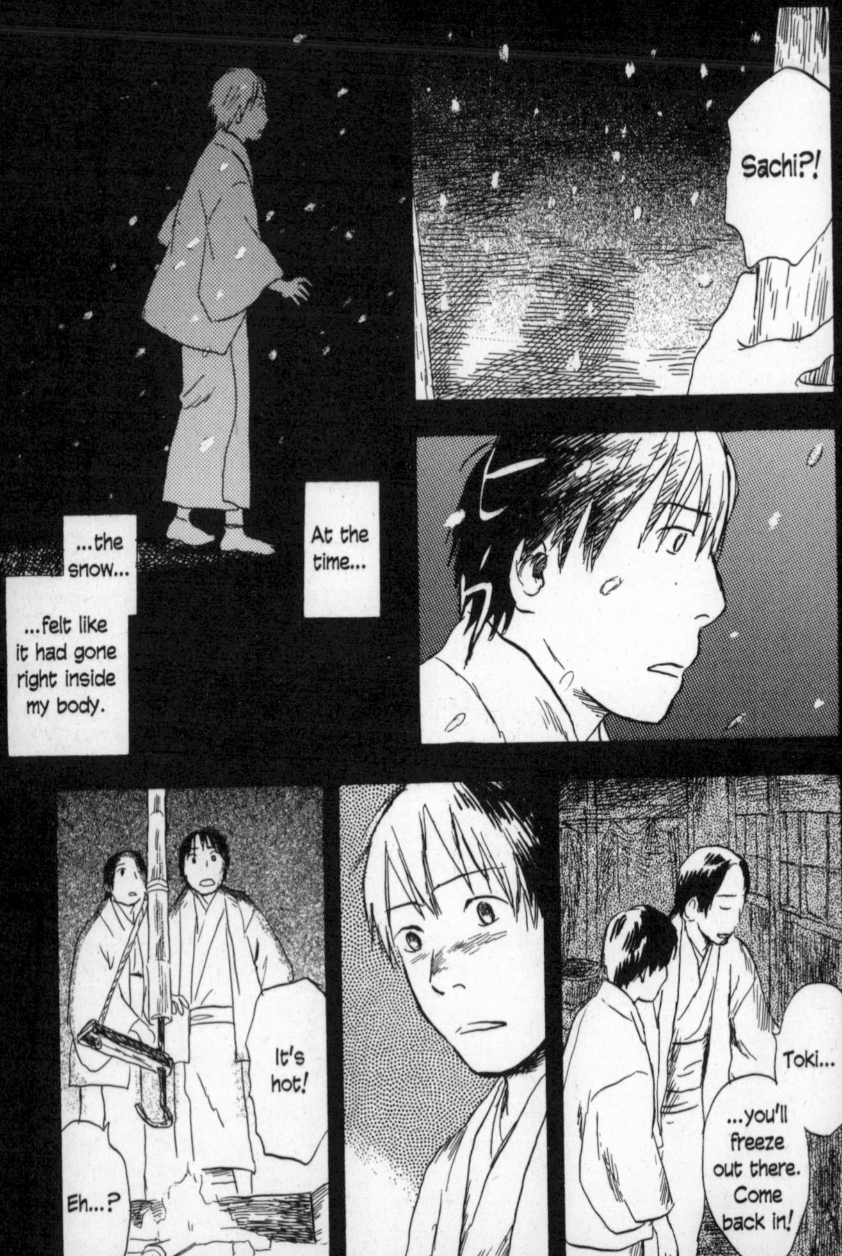
Sachi?!
At the time...
...the snow...
...felt like it had gone right inside my body.
Toki...
...you'll freeze out there. Come back in!
It's hot!
Eh...?

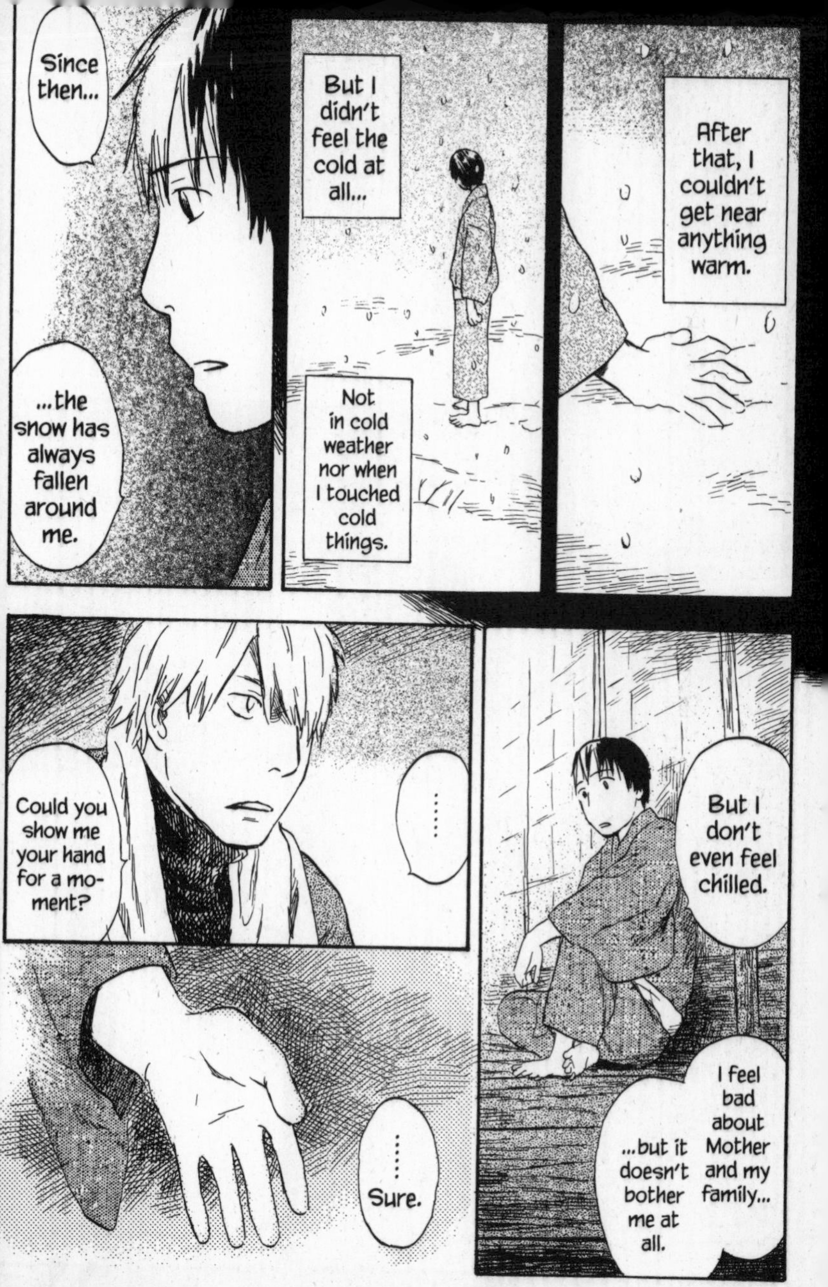
After that, I couldn't get near anything warm.
But I didn't feel the cold at all...
Not in cold weather nor when I touched cold things.
Since then...
...the snow has always fallen around me.
But I don't even feel chilled.
I feel bad about Mother and my family...
...but it doesn't bother me at all.
......
Could you show me your hand for a moment?
......
Sure.

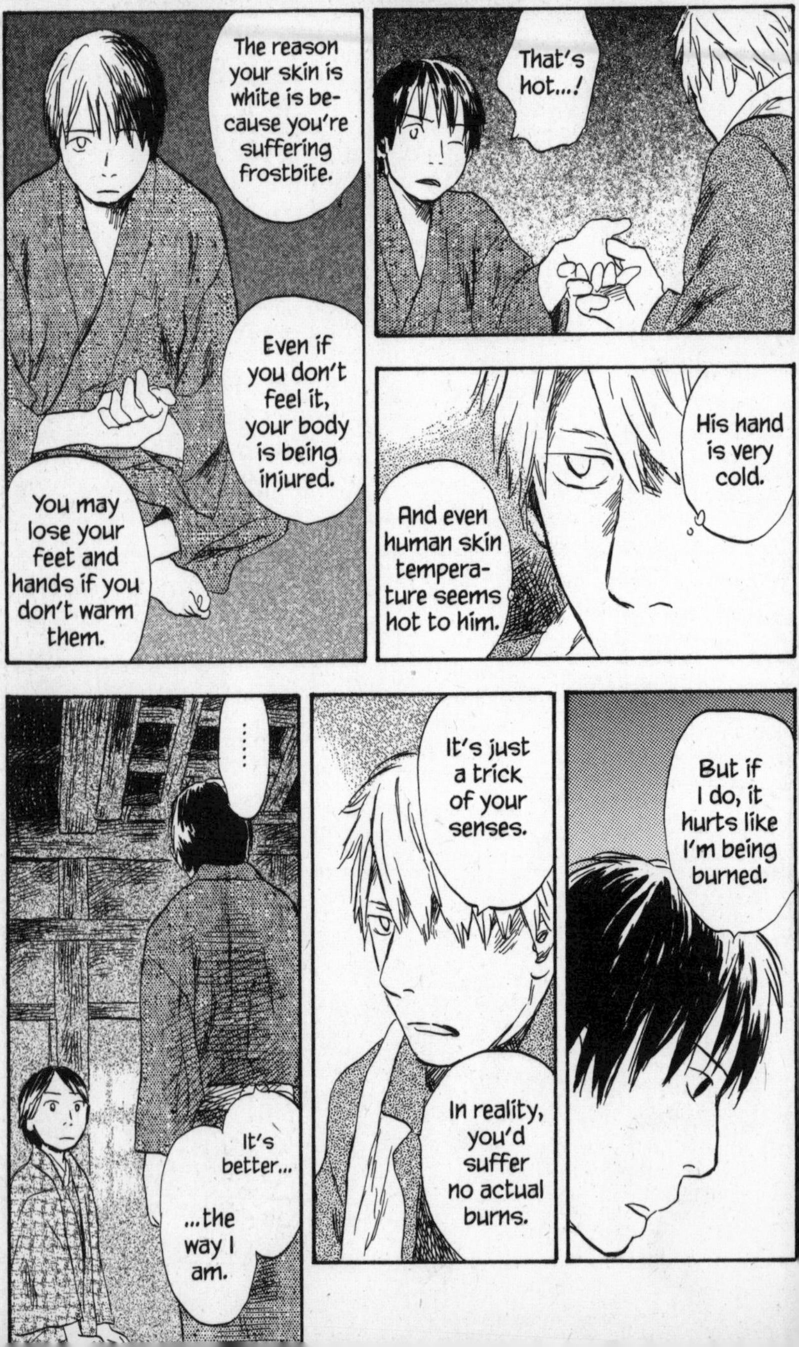
That's hot...!
His hand is very cold.
And even human skin temperature seems hot to him.
The reason your skin is white is because you're suffering frostbite.
Even if you don't feel it, your body is being injured.
You may lose your feet and hands if you don't warm them.
But if I do, it hurts like I'm being burned.
It's just a trick of your senses.
In reality, you'd suffer no actual burns.
......
It's better...
...the way I am.

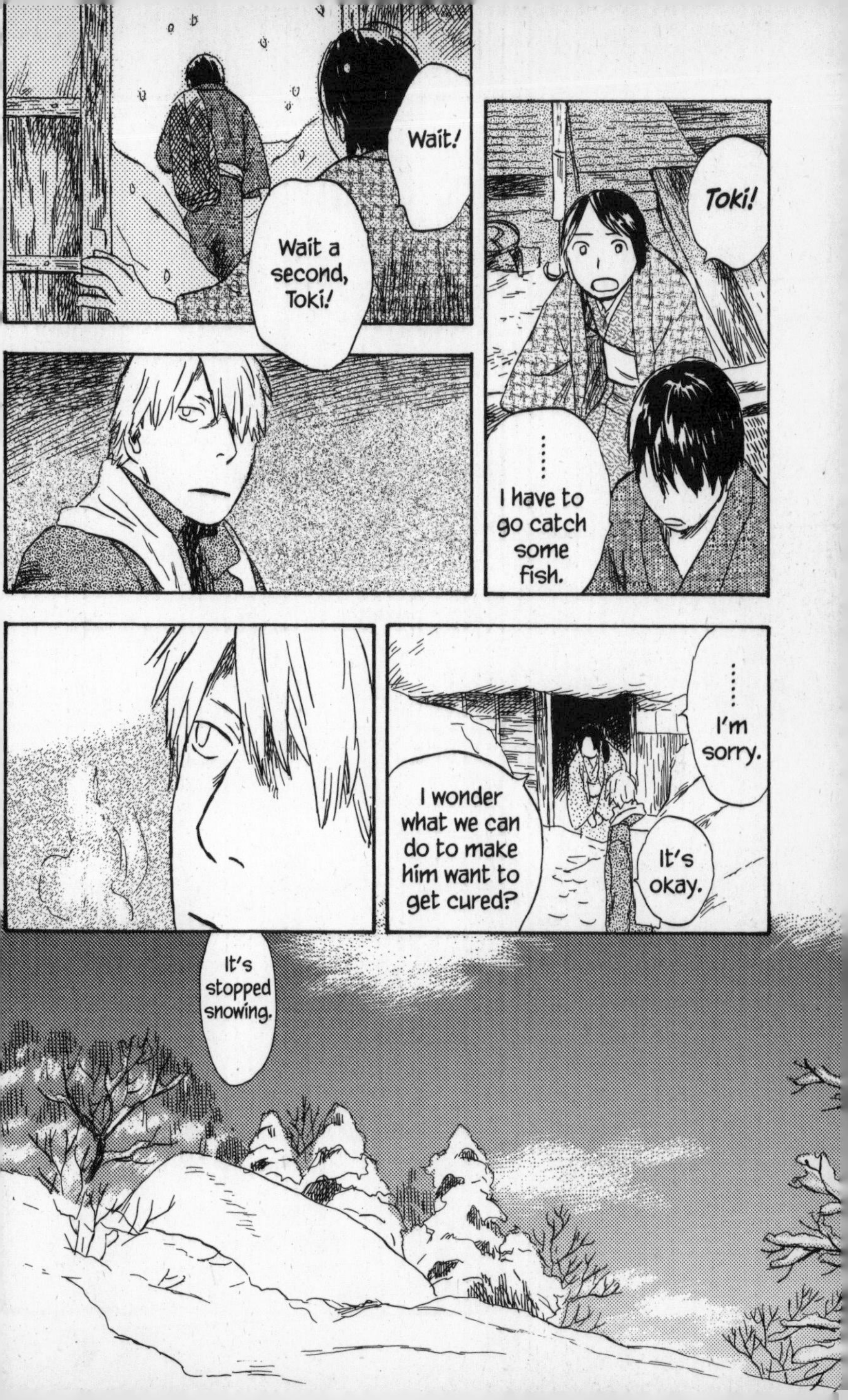
Toki!
...... I have to go catch some fish.
Wait!
Wait a second, Toki!
...... I'm sorry.
It's okay.
I wonder what we can do to make him want to get cured?
It's stopped snowing.

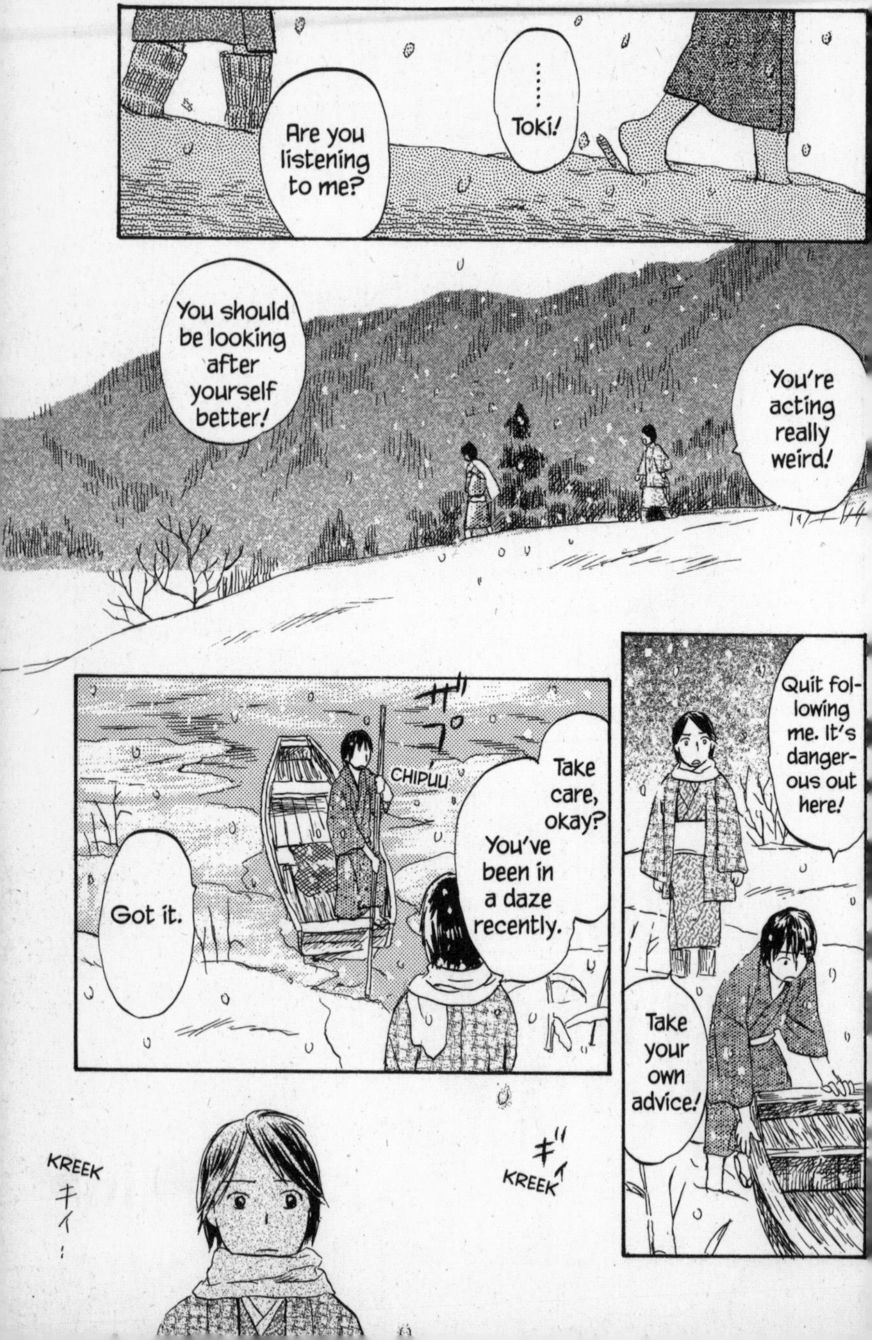
……
Toki!
Are you listening to me?
You're acting really weird!
You should be looking after yourself better!
Quit fol-lowing me. It's danger-ous out here!
Take your own advice!
ザブ
CHIPUU
Take care, okay? You've been in a daze recently.
Got it.
ギイ
KREEK
KREEK
キイ

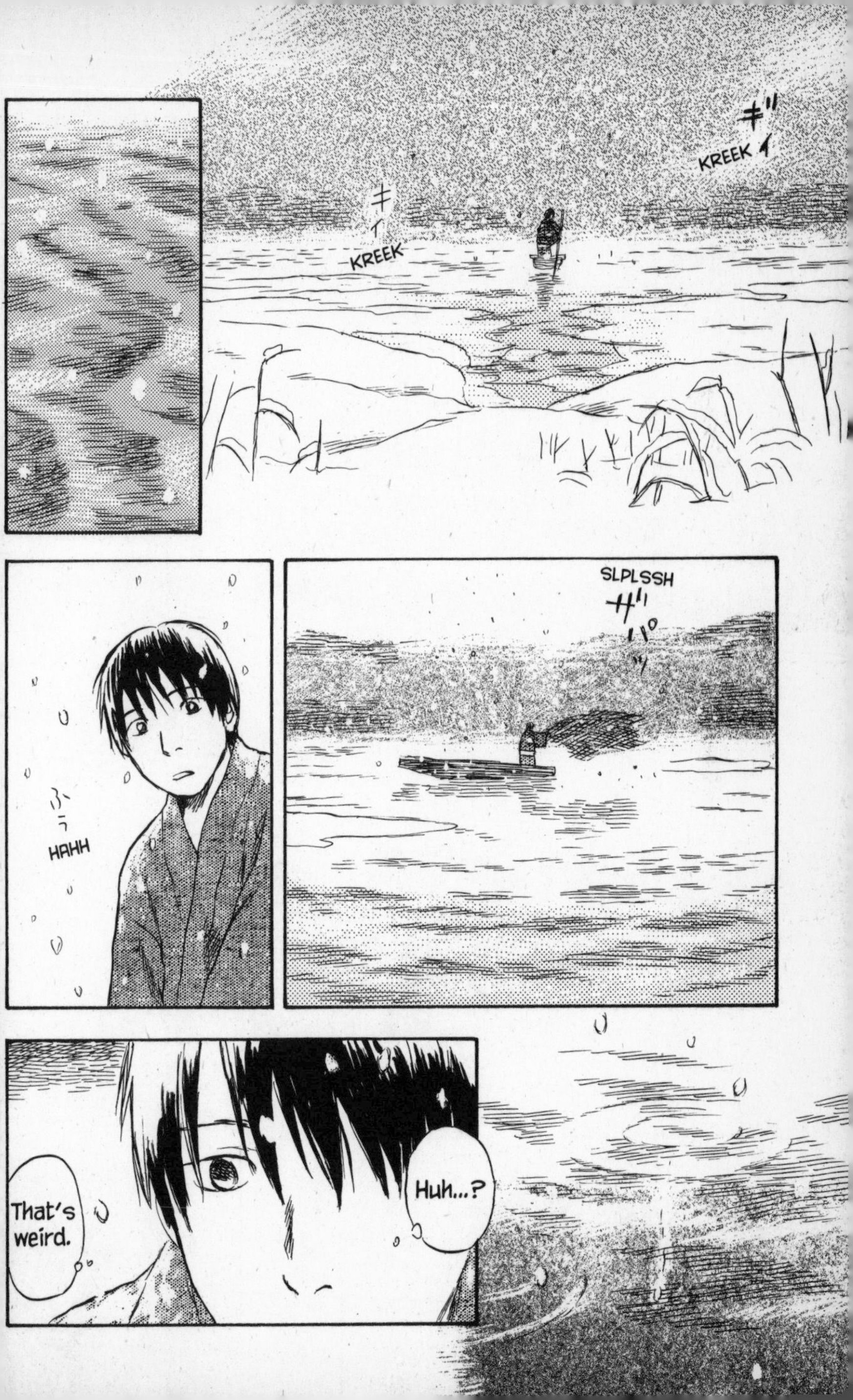
KREEK
KREEK
SLPLSSH
HAHH
Huh...?
That's weird.

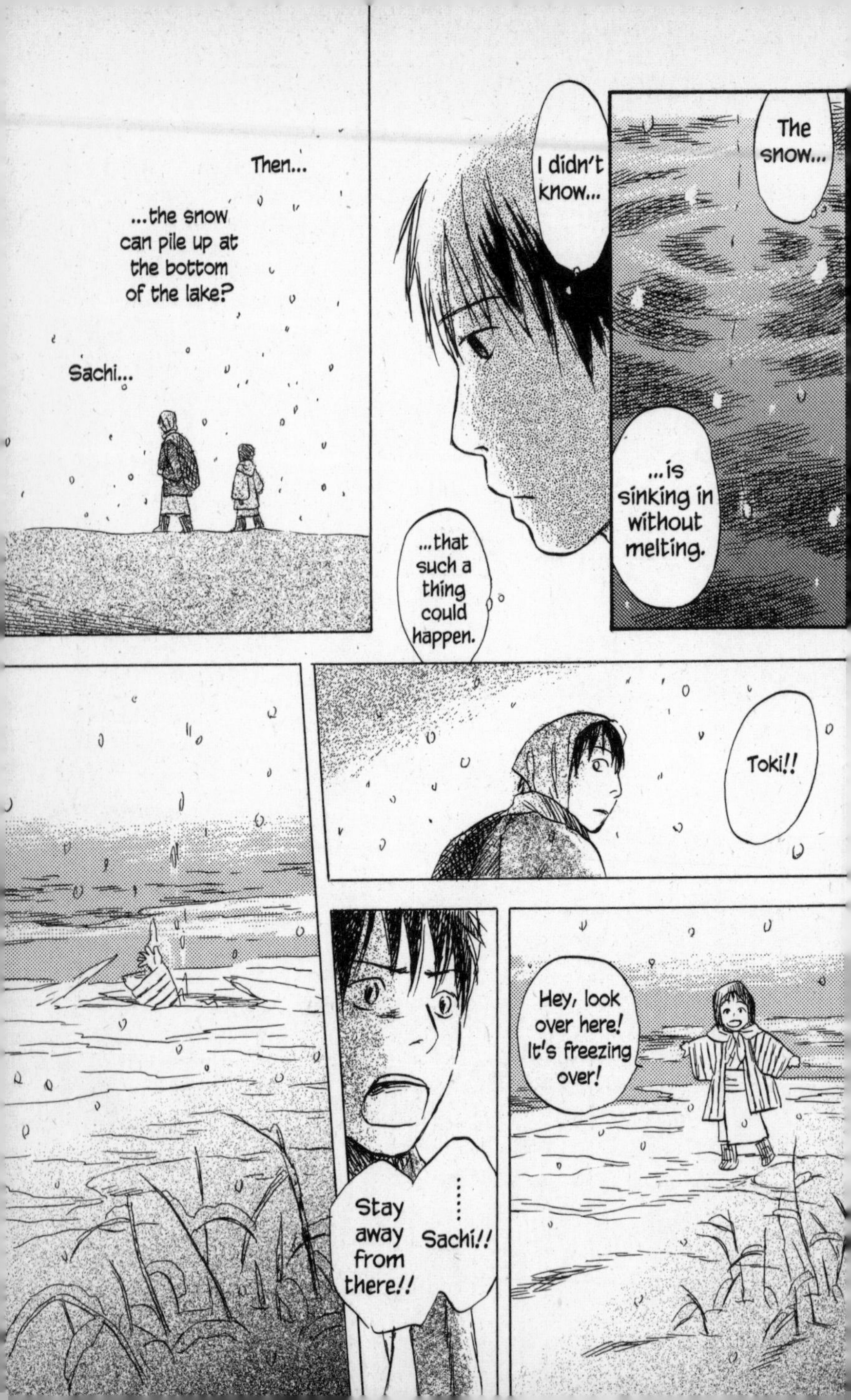
The snow...
...is sinking in without melting.
I didn't know...
...that such a thing could happen.
Then...
...the snow can pile up at the bottom of the lake?
Sachi...
Toki!!
Hey, look over here! It's freezing over!
...... Sachi!!
Stay away from there!!

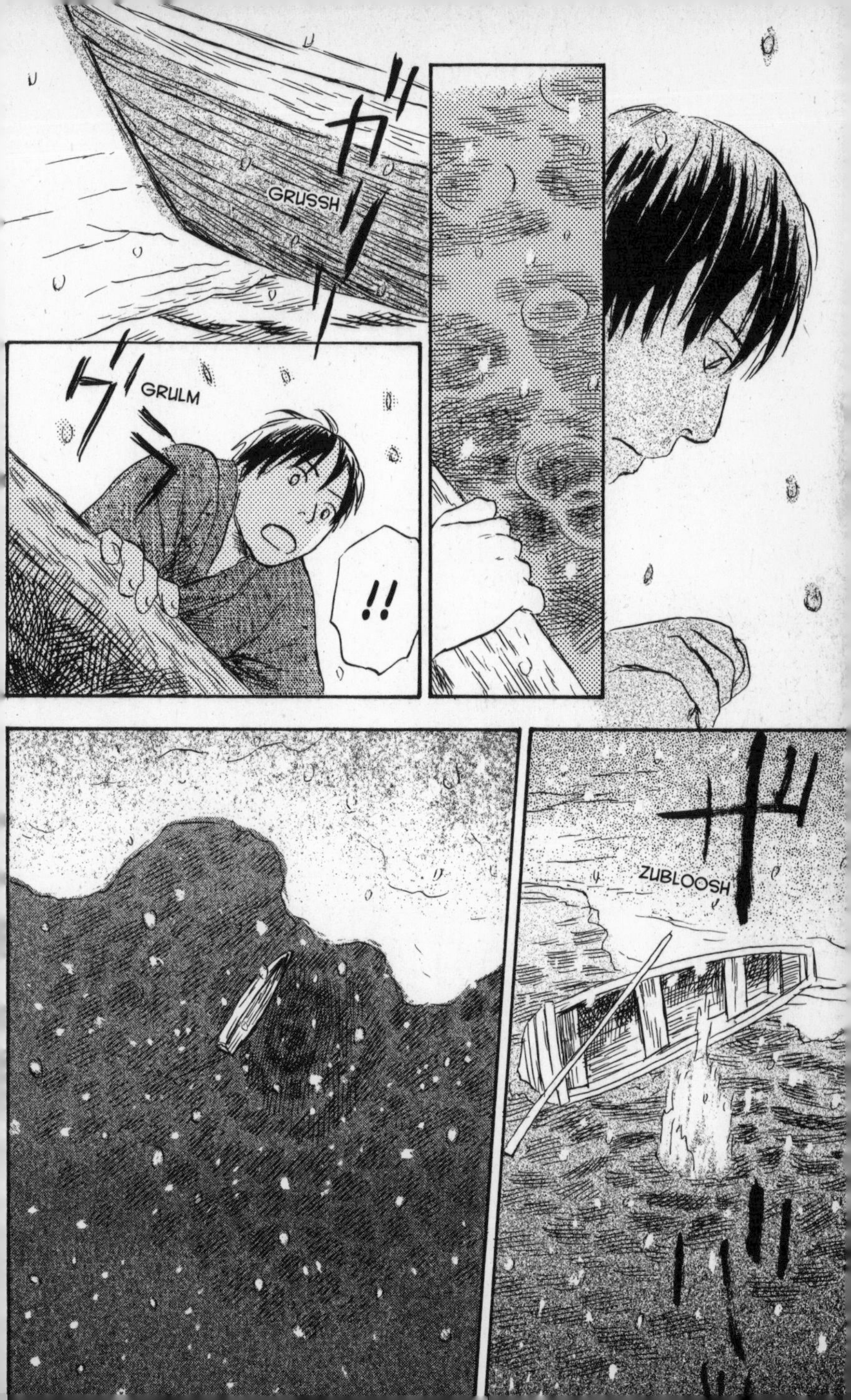
GRUSSH
GRULM
!!
ZUBLOOSH

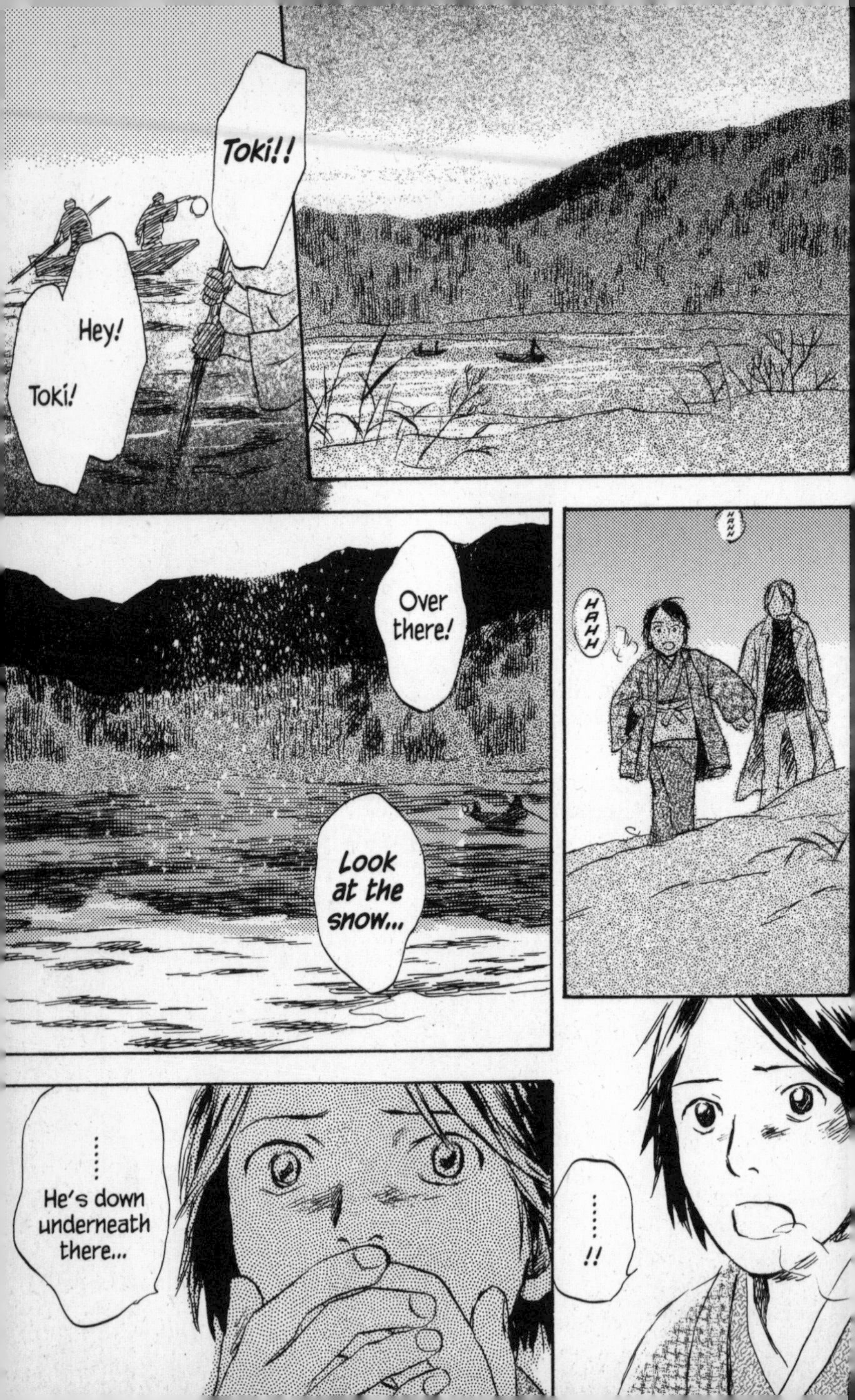
Toki!!
Hey! Toki!
HAHH
HAHH
Over there!
Look at the snow...
......!!
...... He's down underneath there...

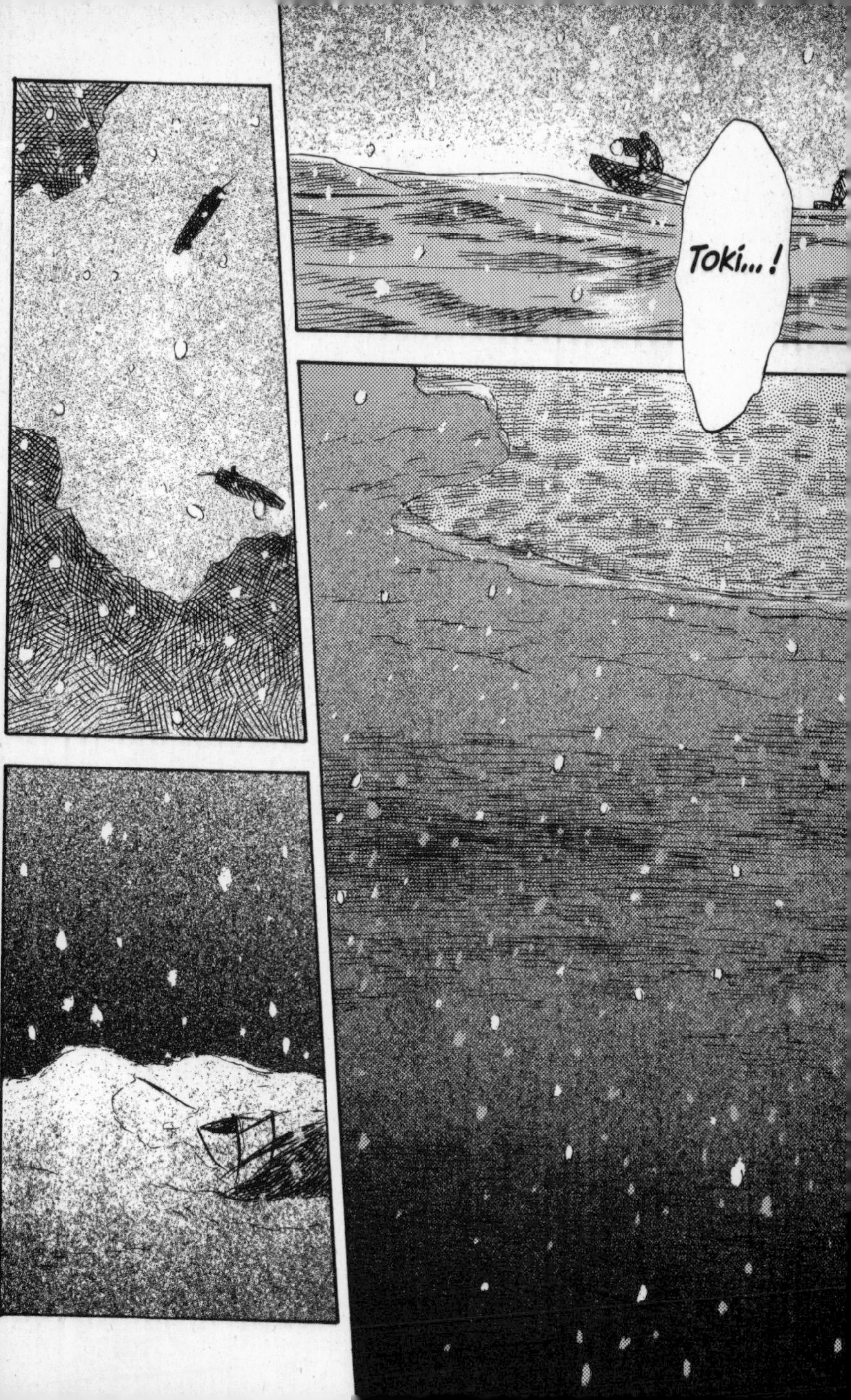
Toki...!

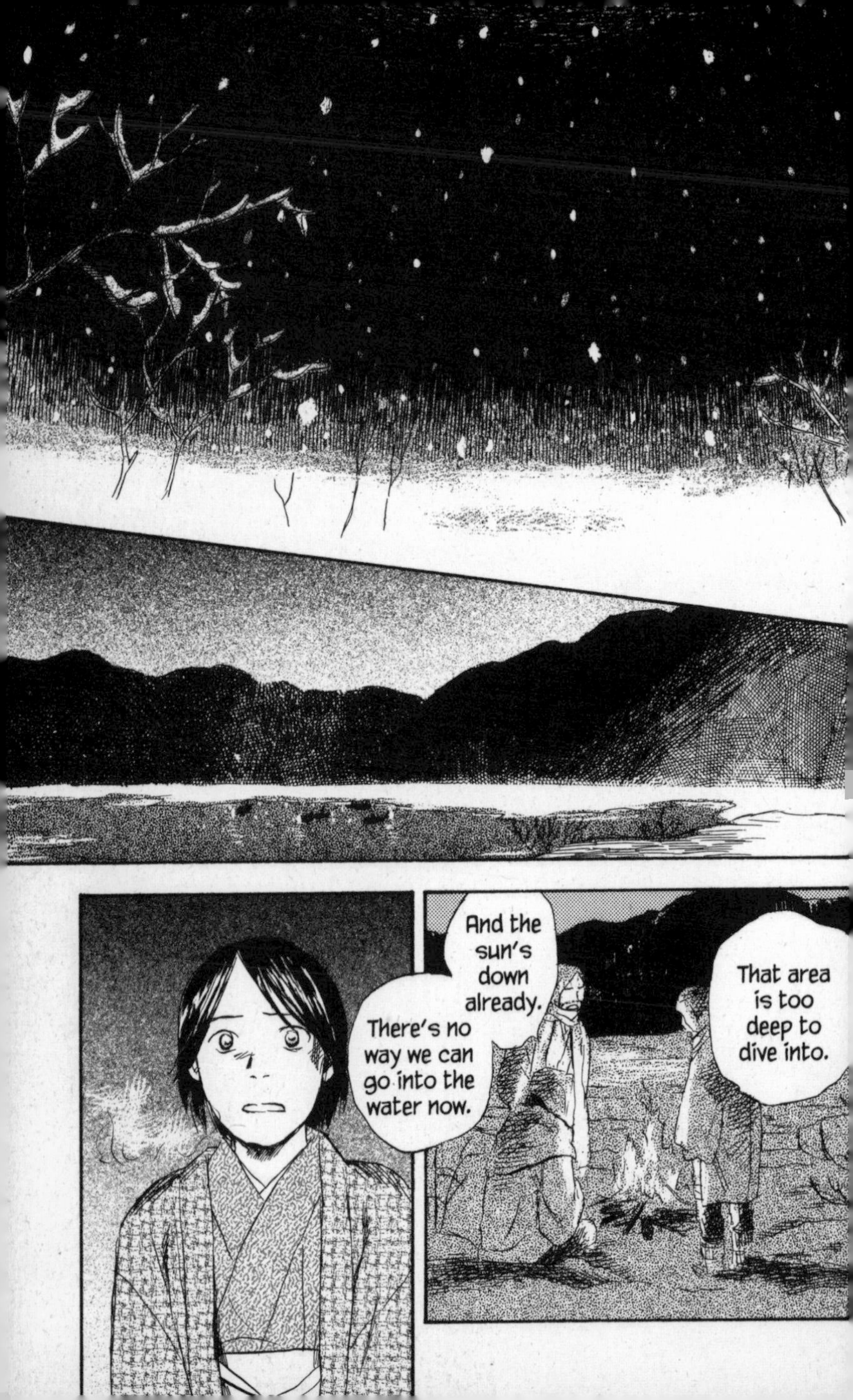
That area is too deep to dive into.
And the sun's down already.
There's no way we can go into the water now.

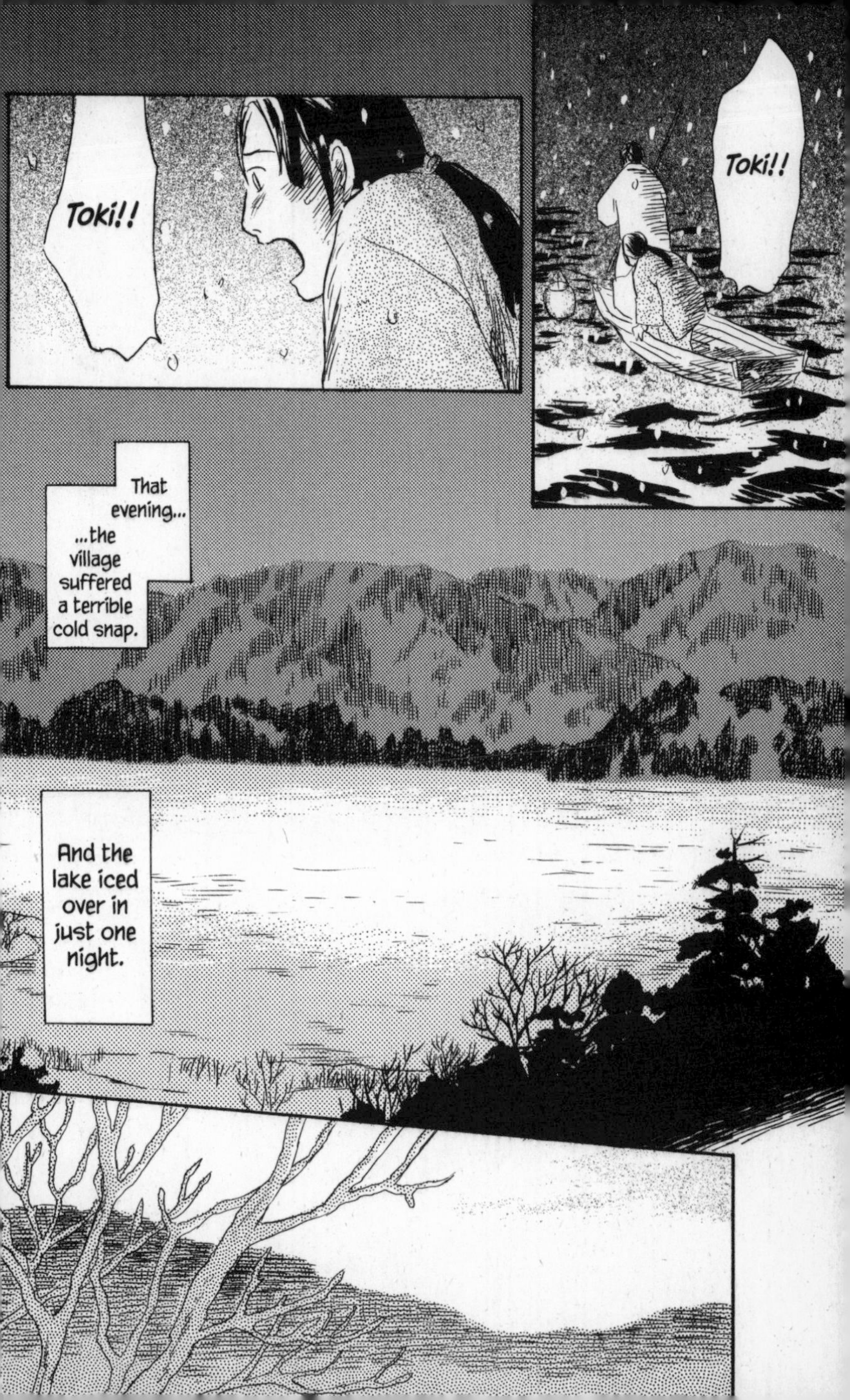
Toki!!
Toki!!
That evening... ...the village suffered a terrible cold snap.
And the lake iced over in just one night.

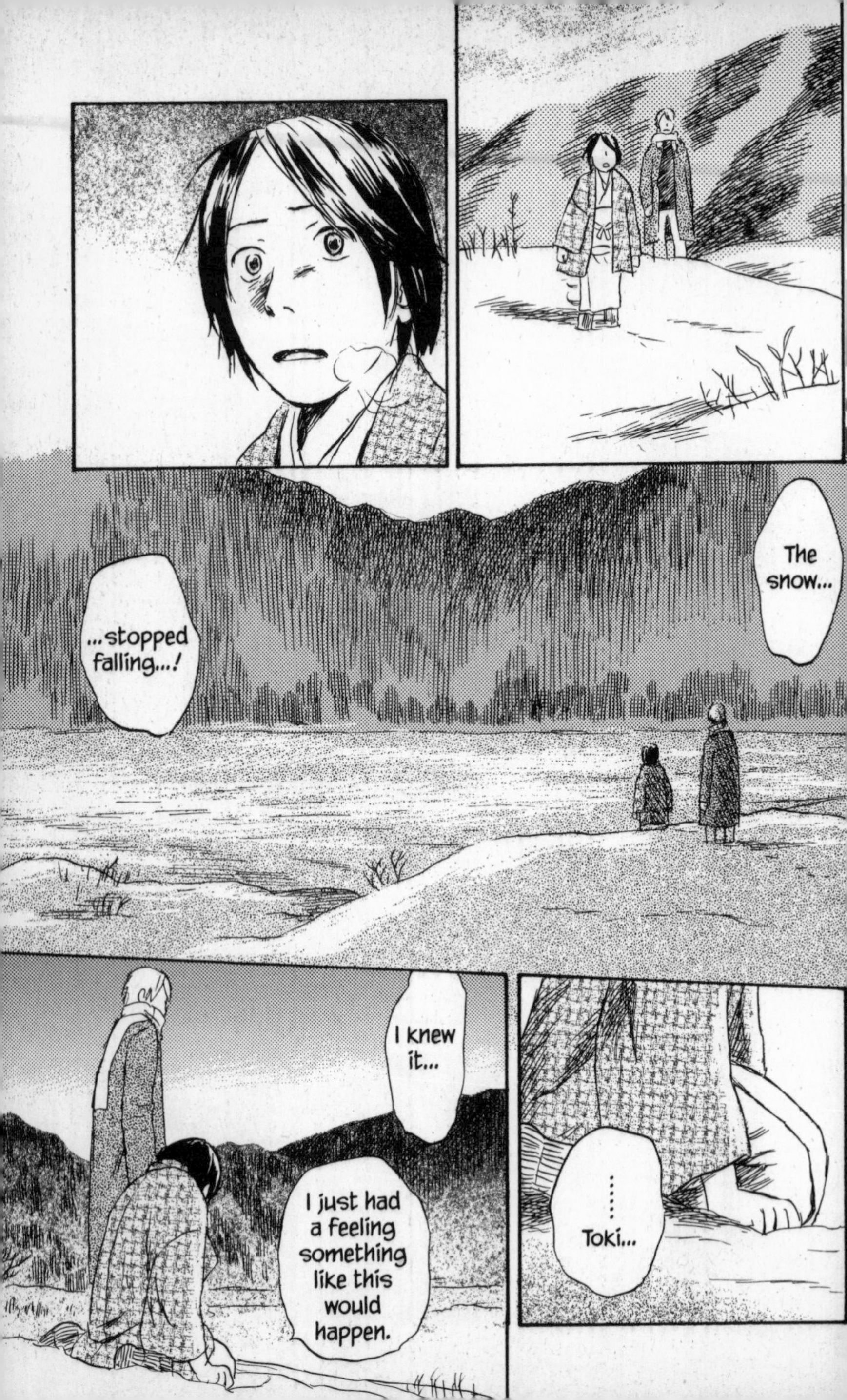
The snow...
...stopped falling...!
...... Toki...
I knew it...
I just had a feeling something like this would happen.

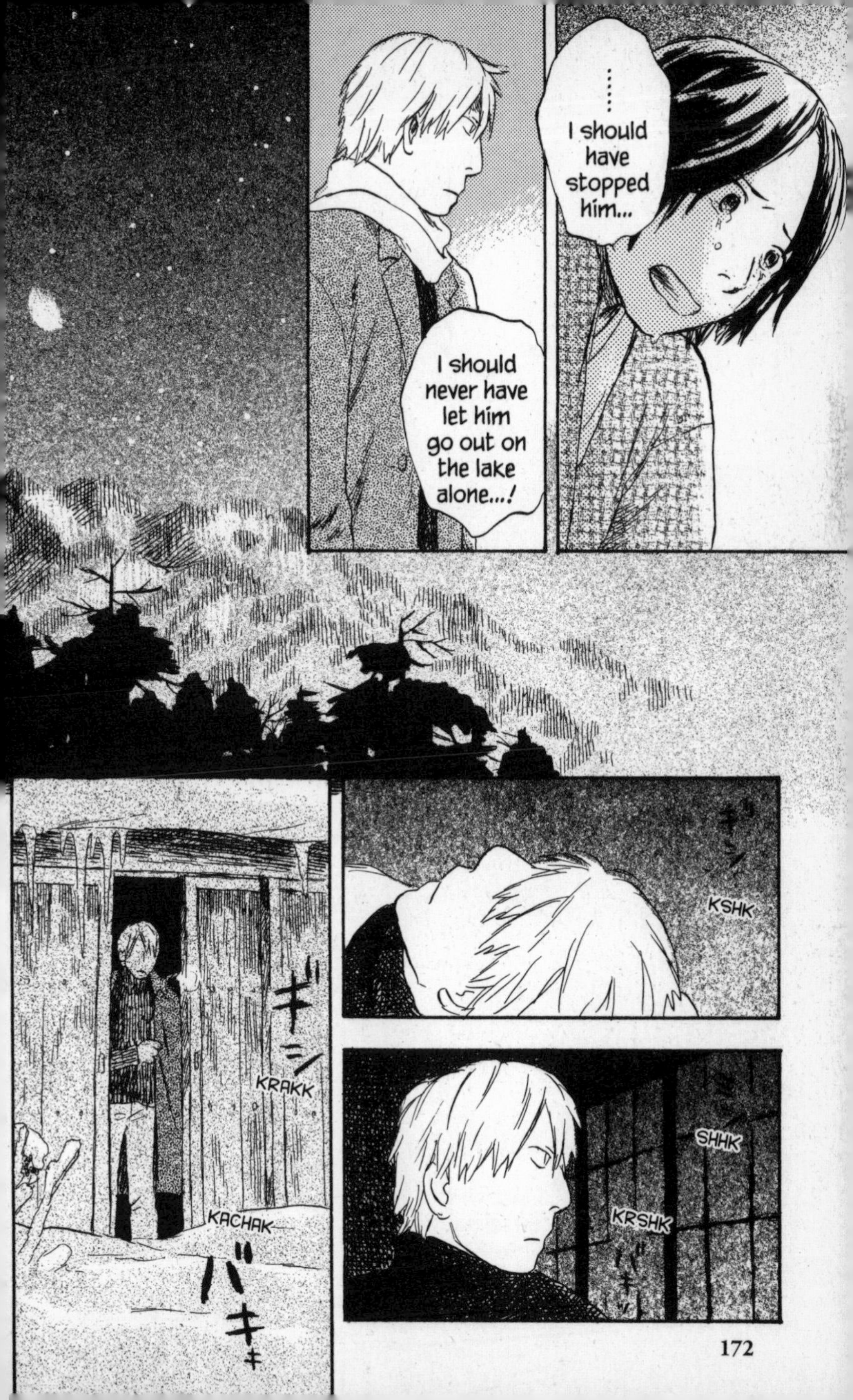

...... I should have stopped him...
I should never have let him go out on the lake alone...!
KSHK
SHHK
KRSHK
KRAKK
KACHAK

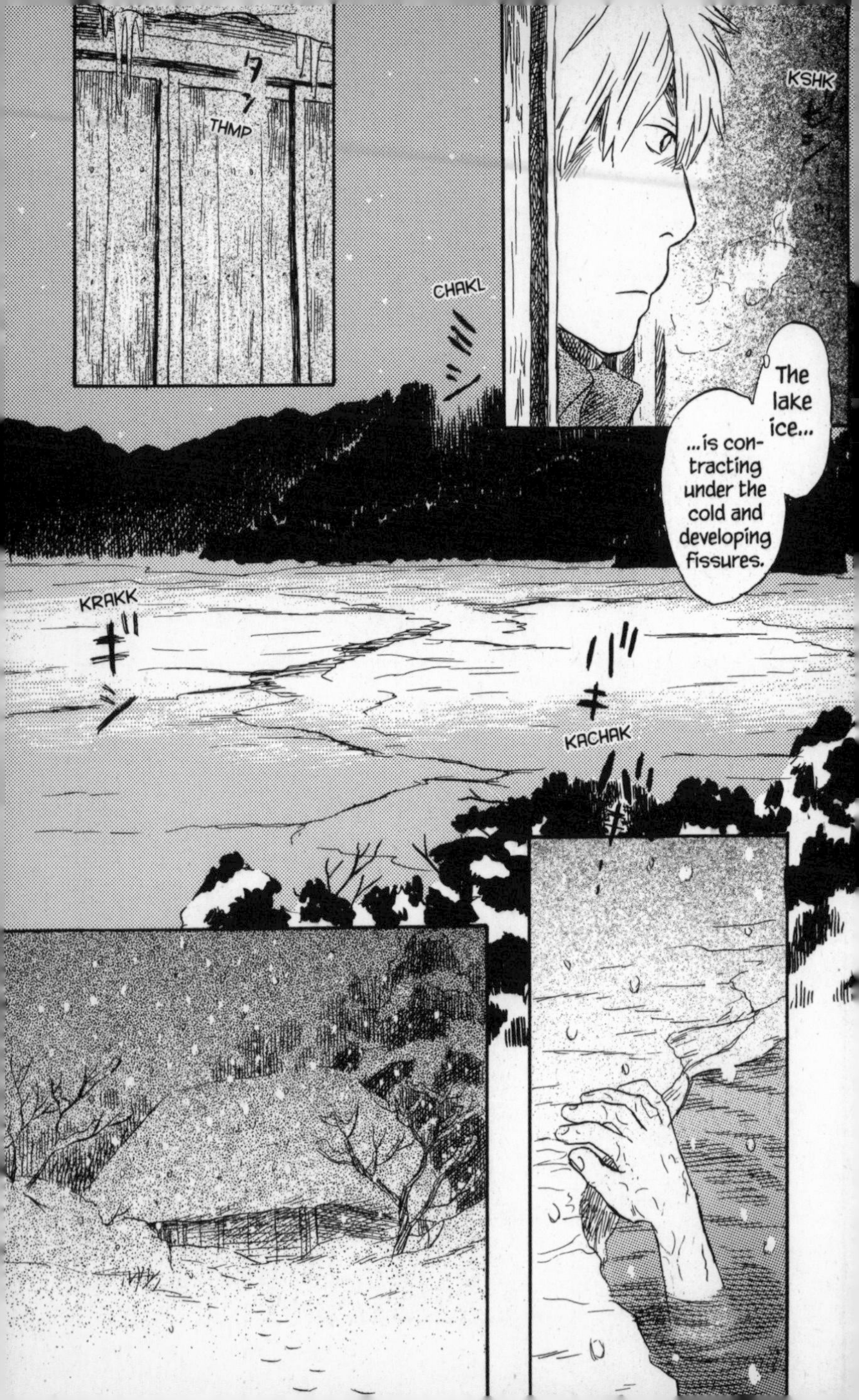
KSHK
The lake ice...
...is contracting under the cold and developing fissures.
THMP
CHAKL
KACHAK
KRAKK

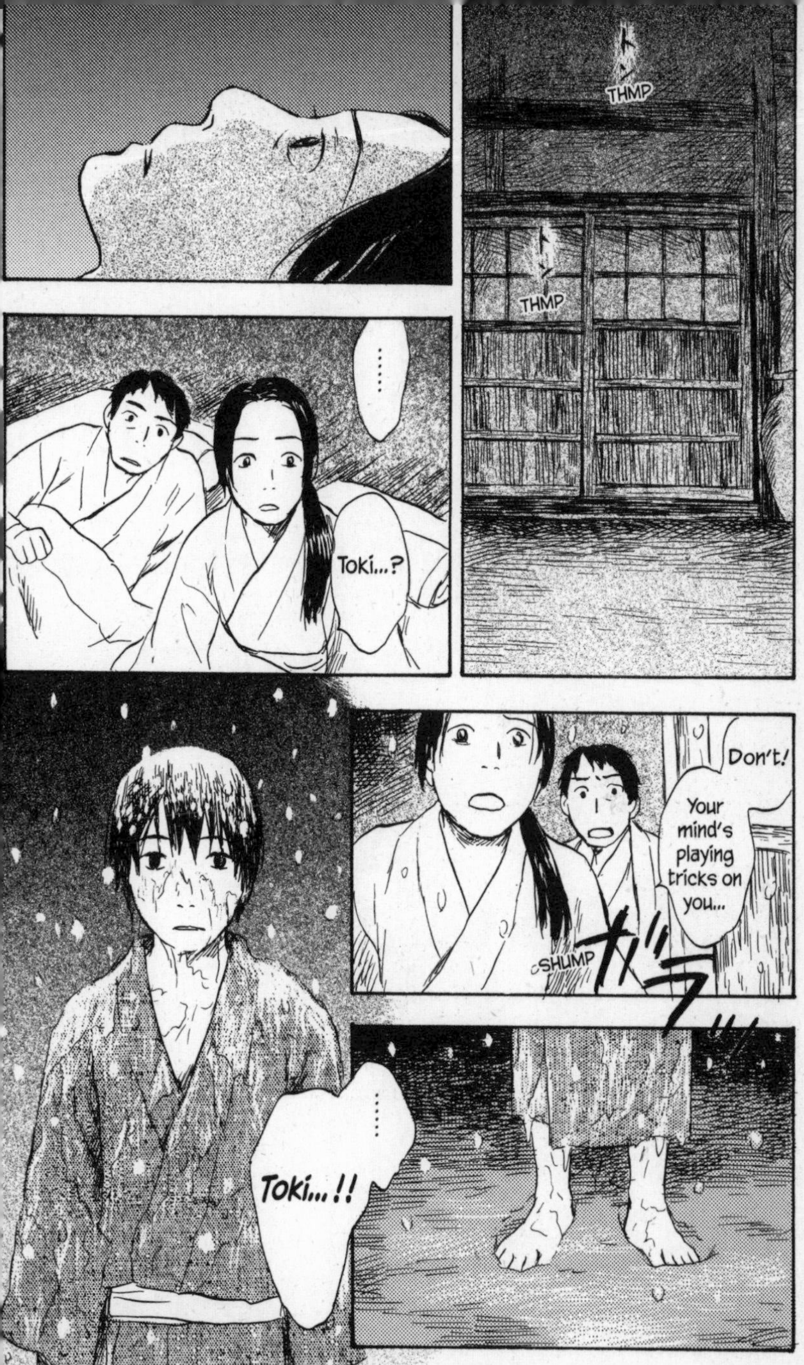
THMP
THMP
......
Toki...?
Don't!
Your mind's playing tricks on you...
SHUMP
......
Toki...!!

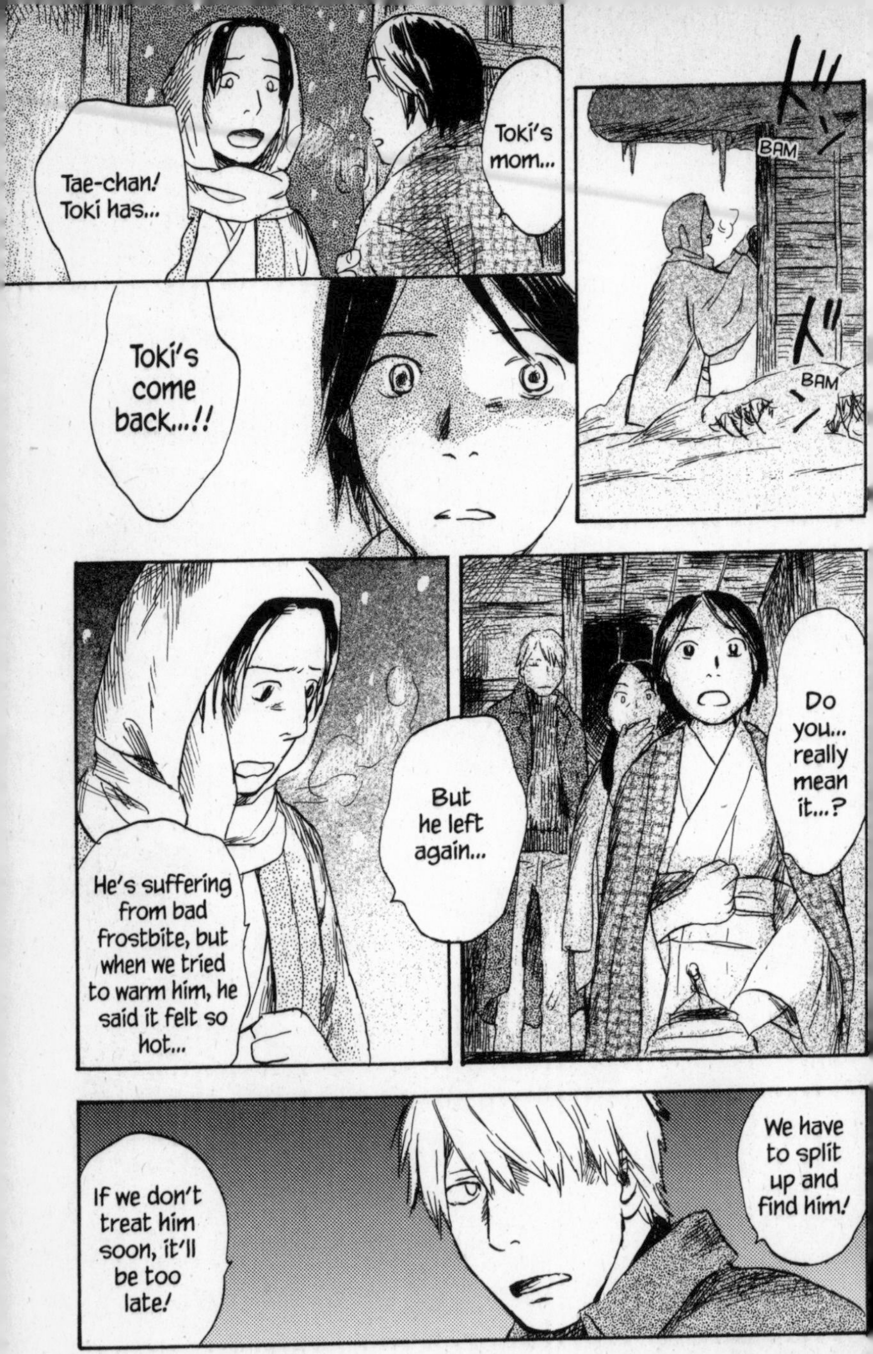
BAM
BAM
Toki's mom...
Tae-chan! Toki has...
Toki's come back...!!
Do you... really mean it...?
But he left again...
He's suffering from bad frostbite, but when we tried to warm him, he said it felt so hot...
We have to split up and find him!
If we don't treat him soon, it'll be too late!

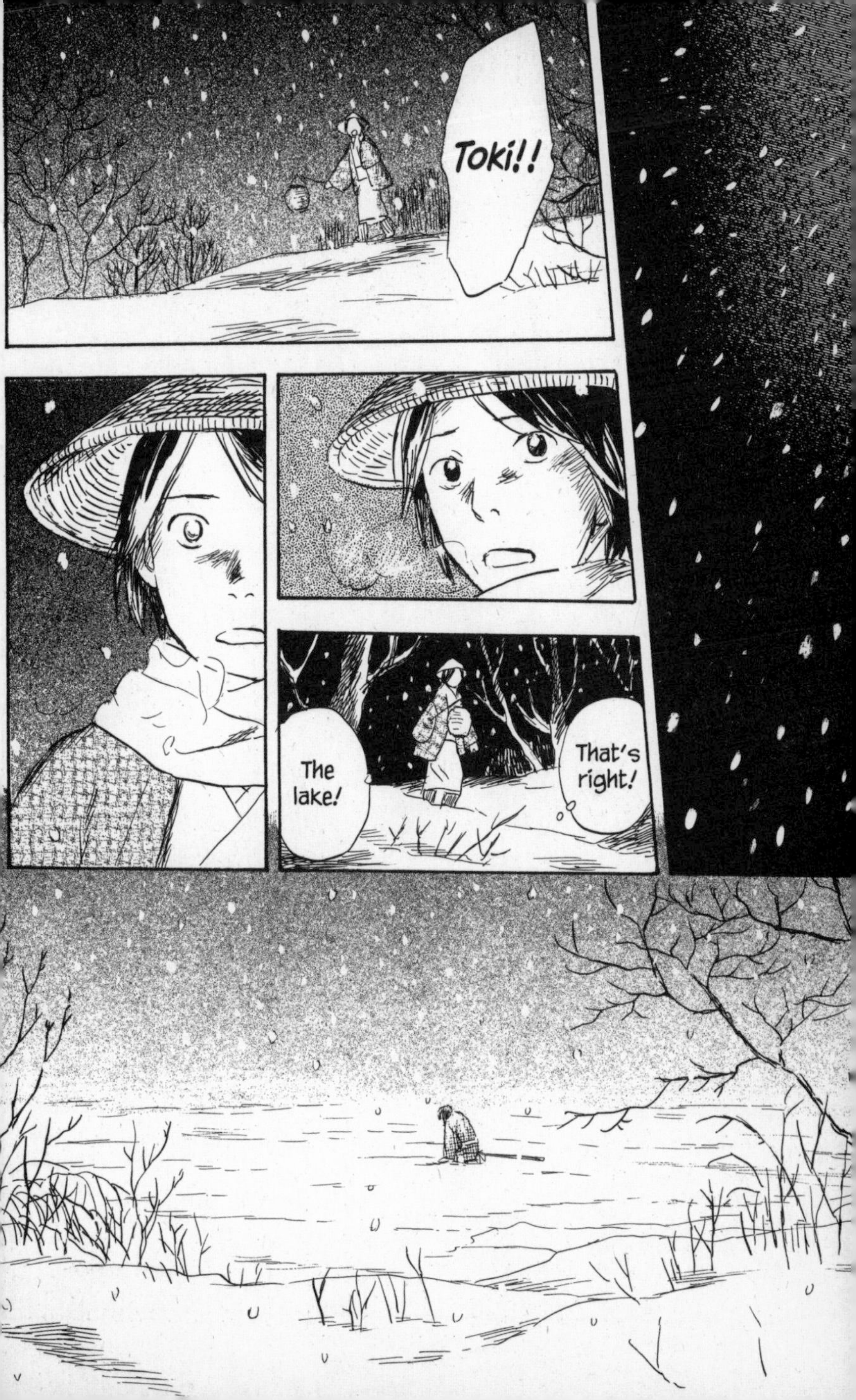
Toki!!
That's right!
The lake!

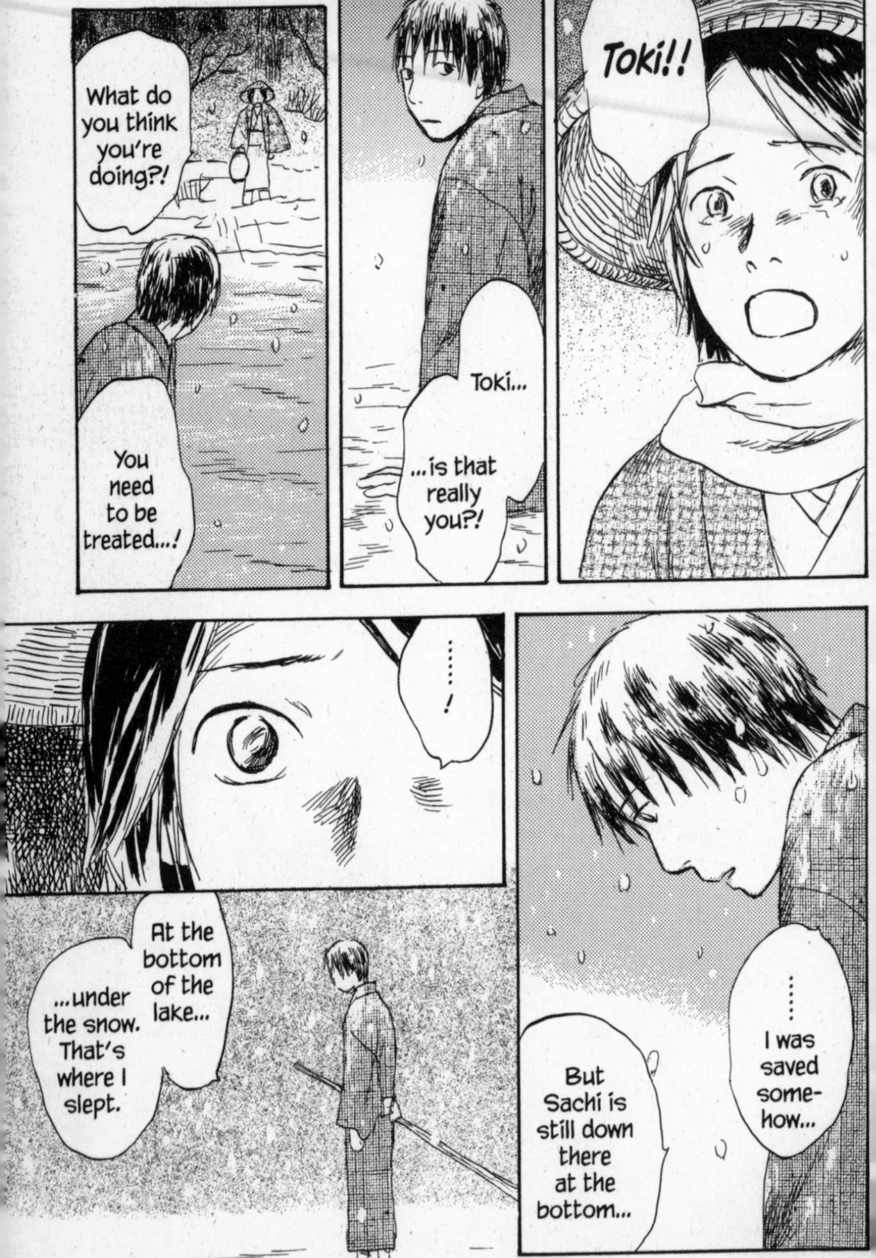

Toki!!
Toki...
...is that really you?!
What do you think you're doing?!
You need to be treated...!
......
I was saved some-how...
But Sachi is still down there at the bottom...
......!
At the bottom of the lake...
...under the snow. That's where I slept.

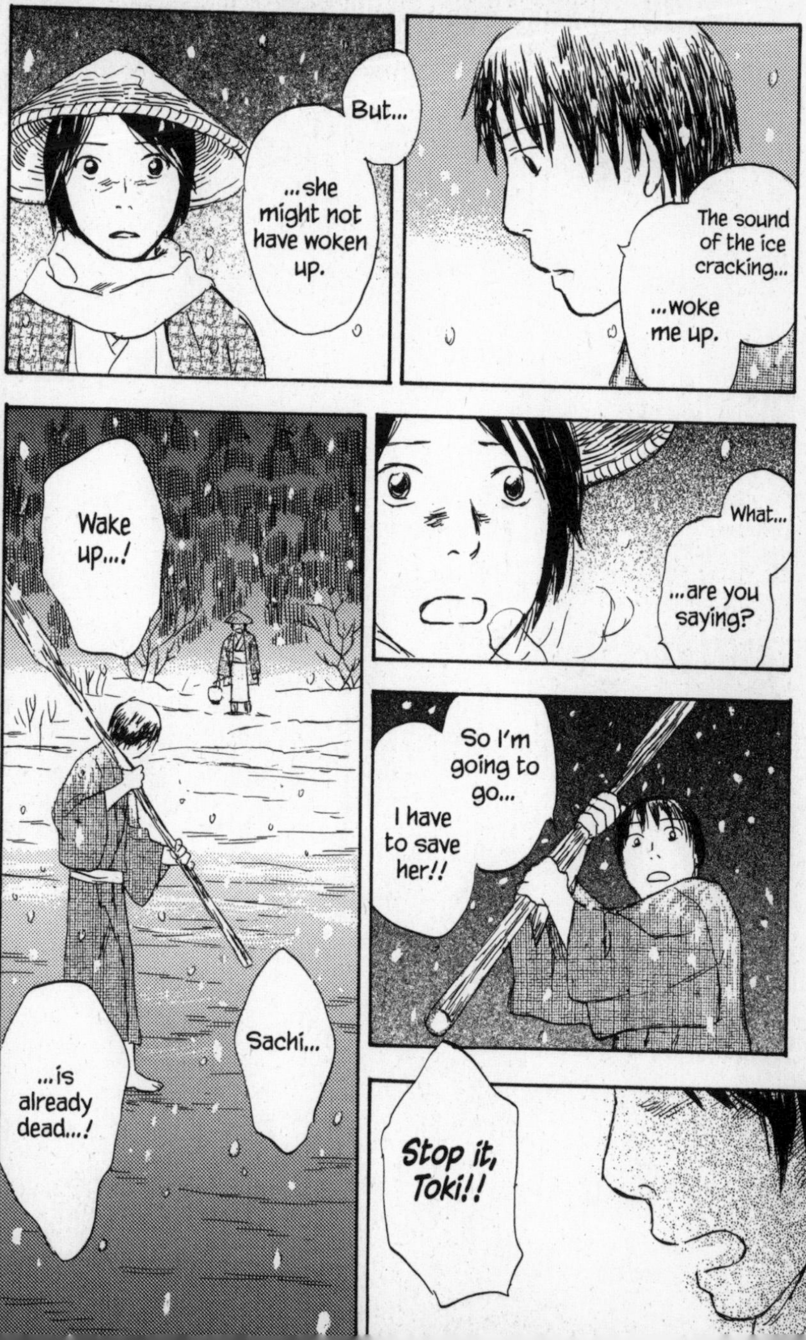
The sound of the ice cracking...
...woke me up.
But...
...she might not have woken up.
What...
...are you saying?
So I'm going to go...
I have to save her!!
Stop it, Toki!!
Wake up...!
Sachi...
...is already dead...!

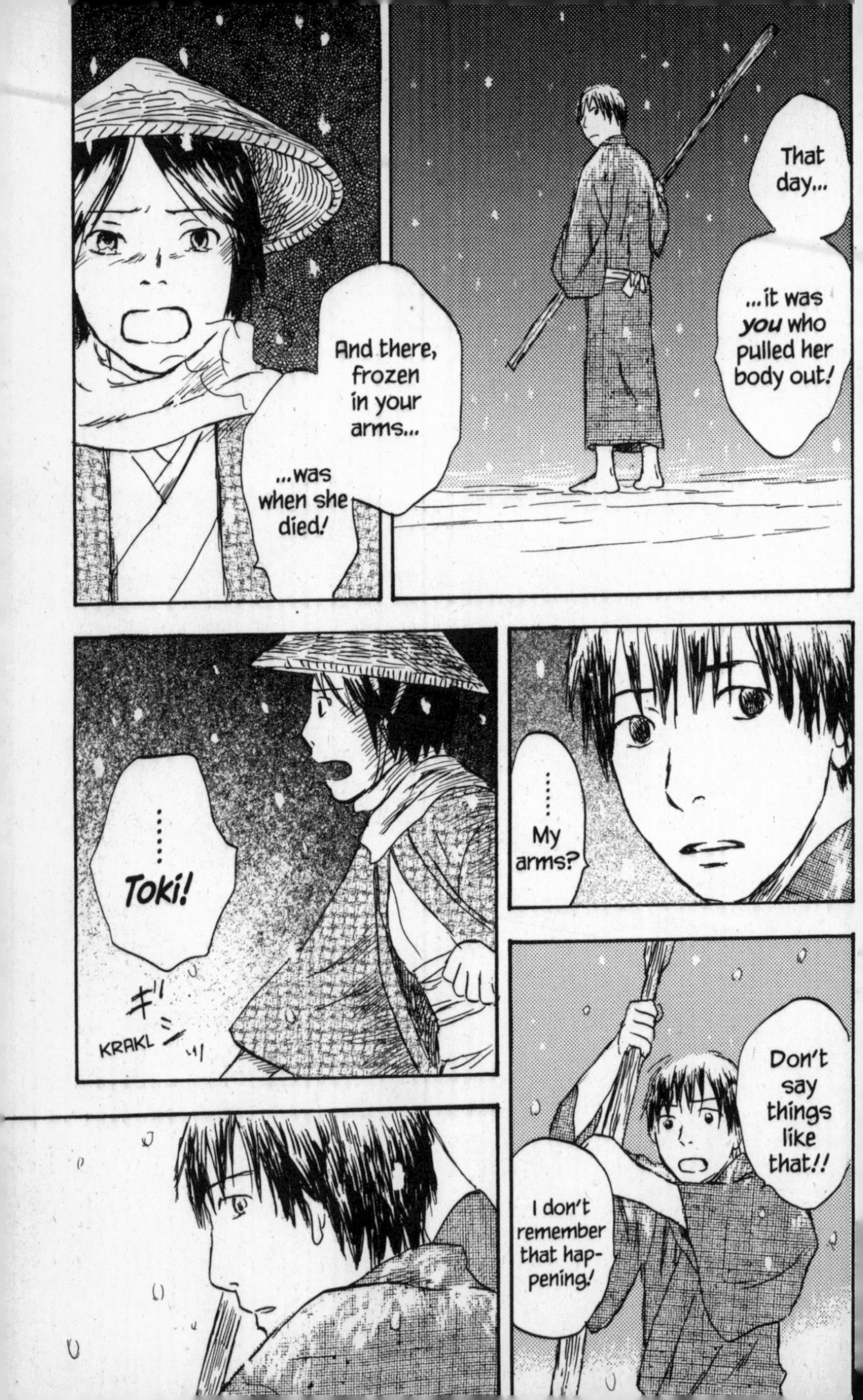
That day...
...it was *you* who pulled her body out!
And there, frozen in your arms...
...was when she died!
...... My arms?
...... Toki!
KRAKL
Don't say things like that!!
I don't remember that hap-pening!

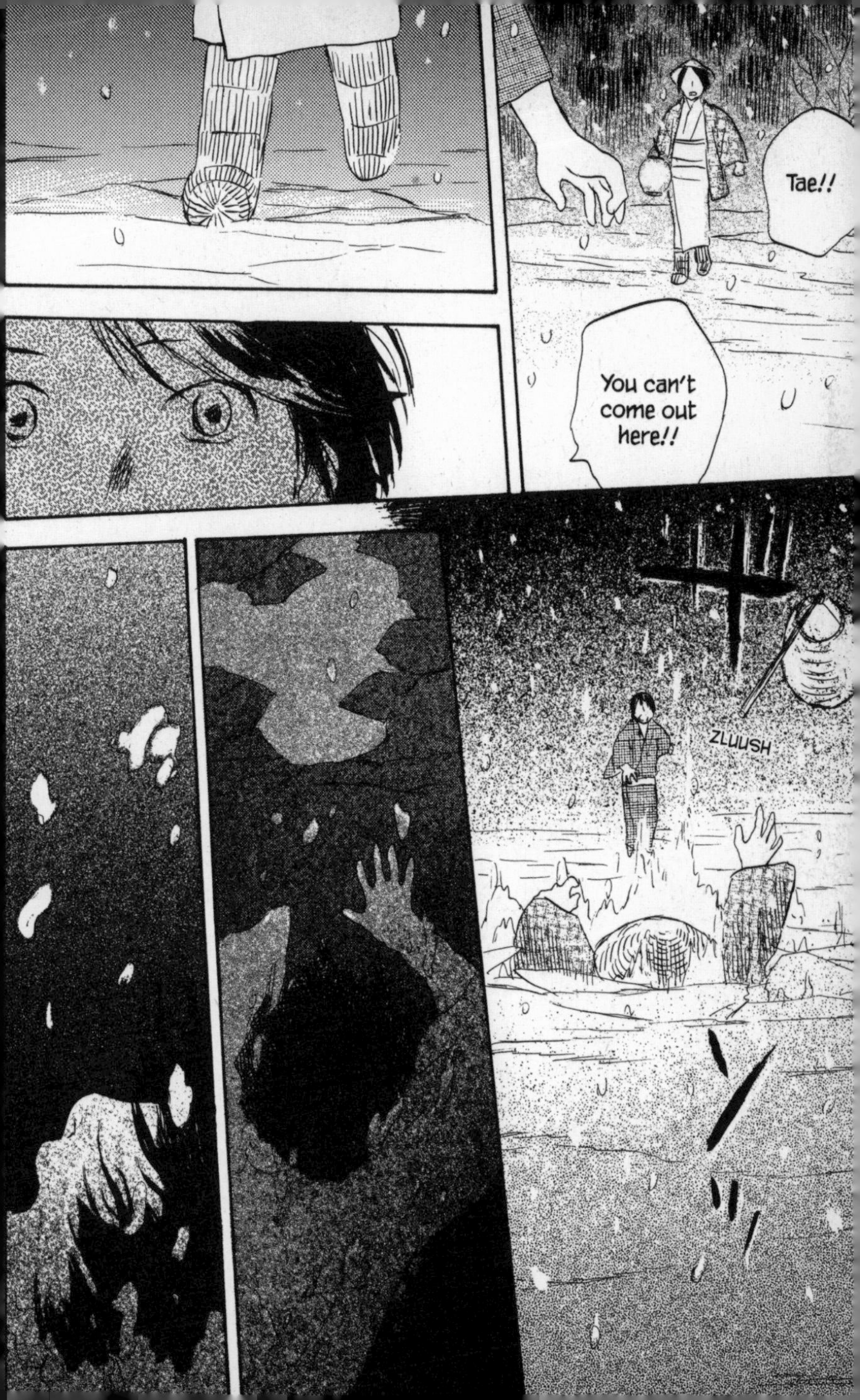
Tae!!
You can't come out here!!
ZLUUSH

ZUBLASSH

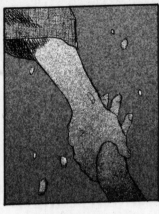

Can you stand?

....

Uh-huh...

Here...

...get on.

SHVR

SHVR

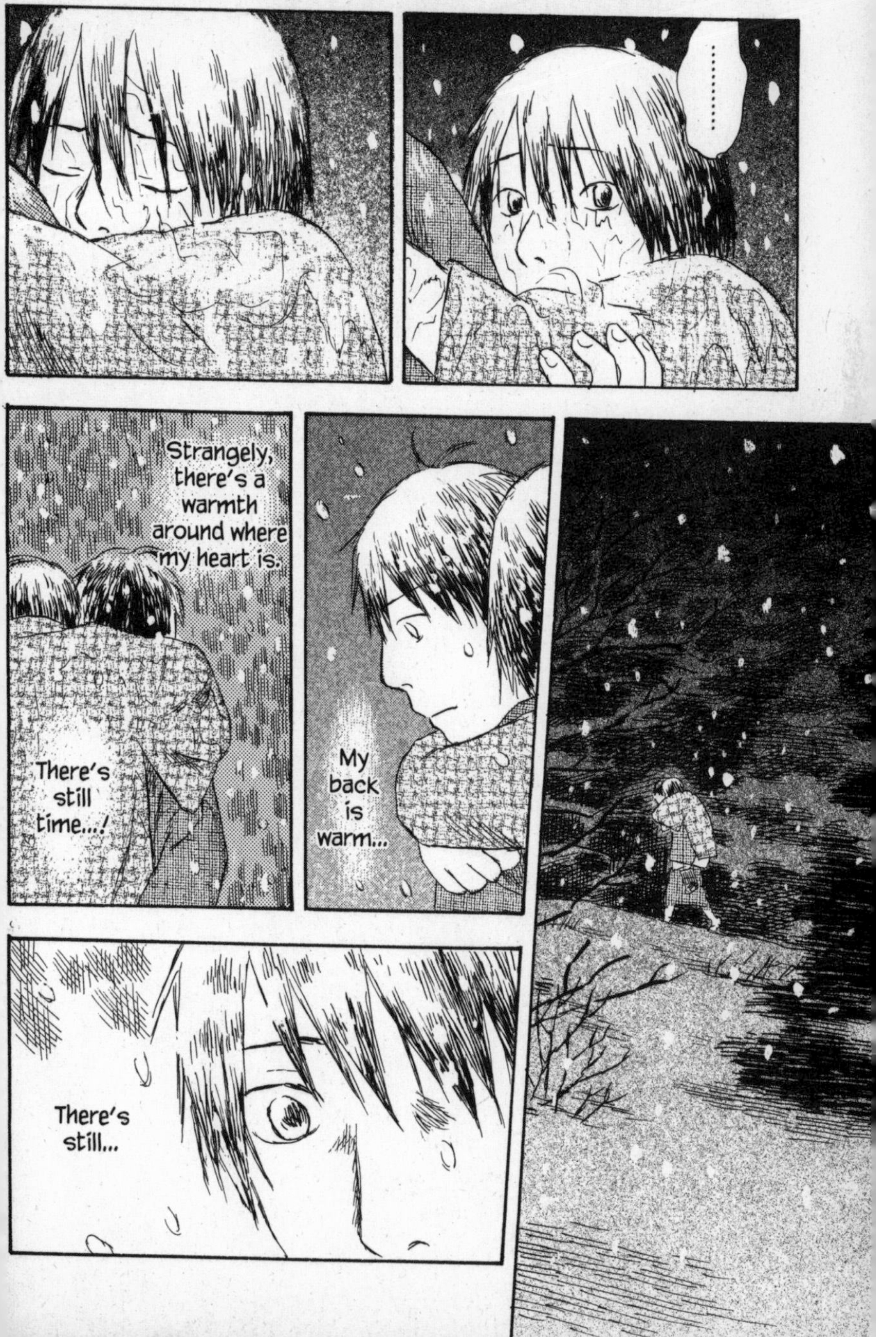
......
My back is warm...
Strangely, there's a warmth around where my heart is.
There's still time...!
There's still...

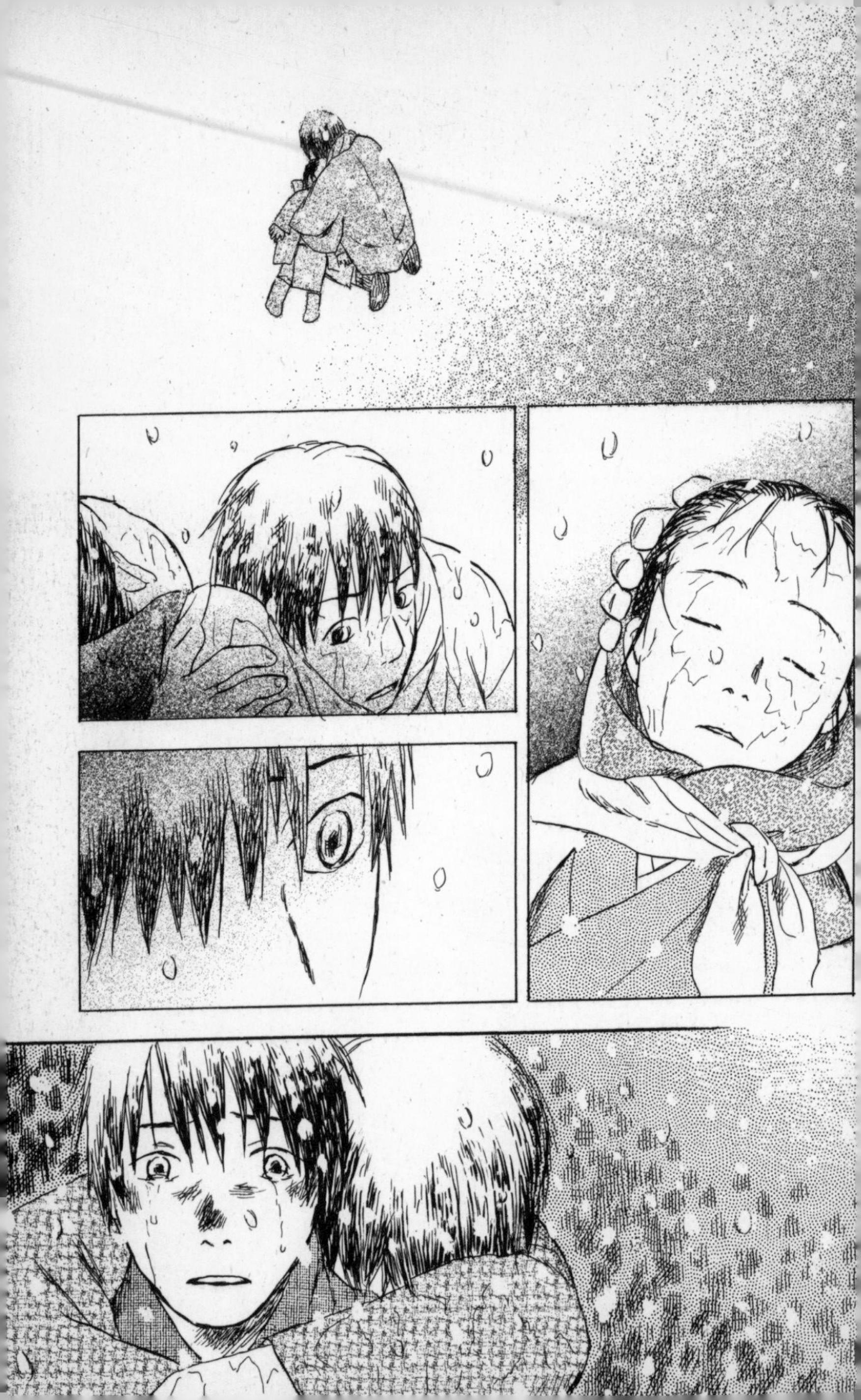

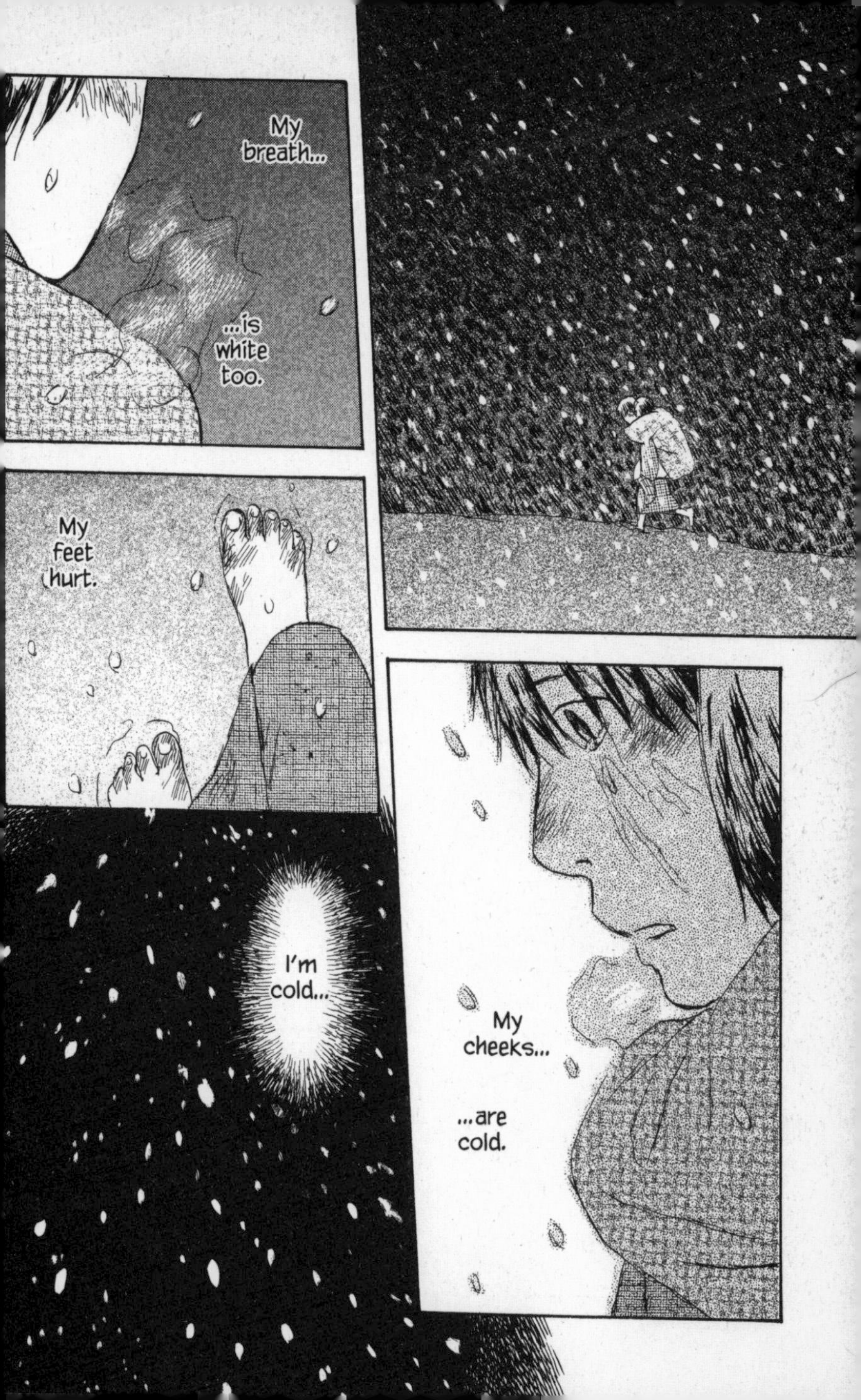
My breath...
...is white too.
My feet hurt.
My cheeks...
...are cold.
I'm cold...

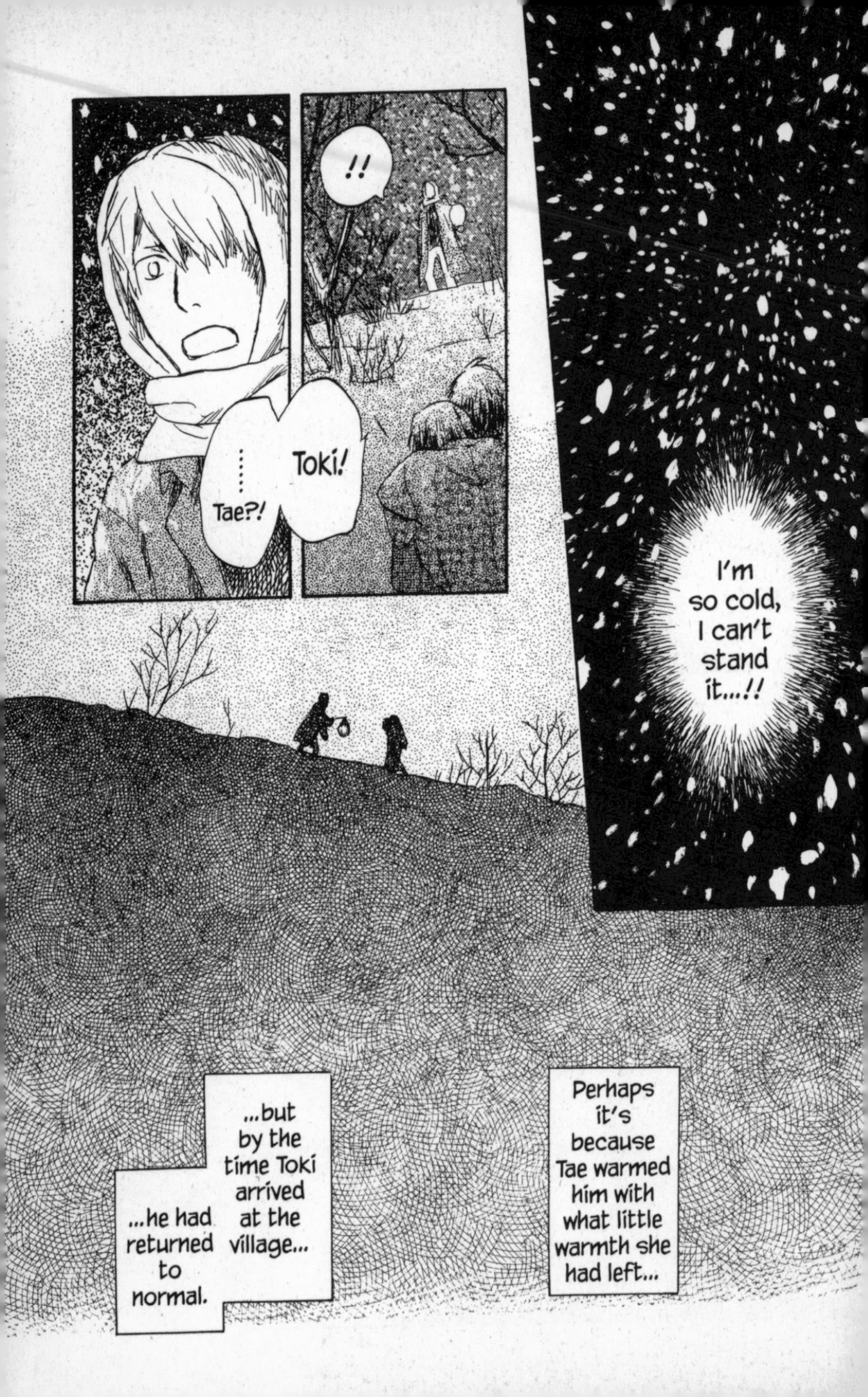
I'm so cold, I can't stand it...!!
!!
Toki!
...... Tae?!
Perhaps it's because Tae warmed him with what little warmth she had left...
...but by the time Toki arrived at the village...
...he had returned to normal.

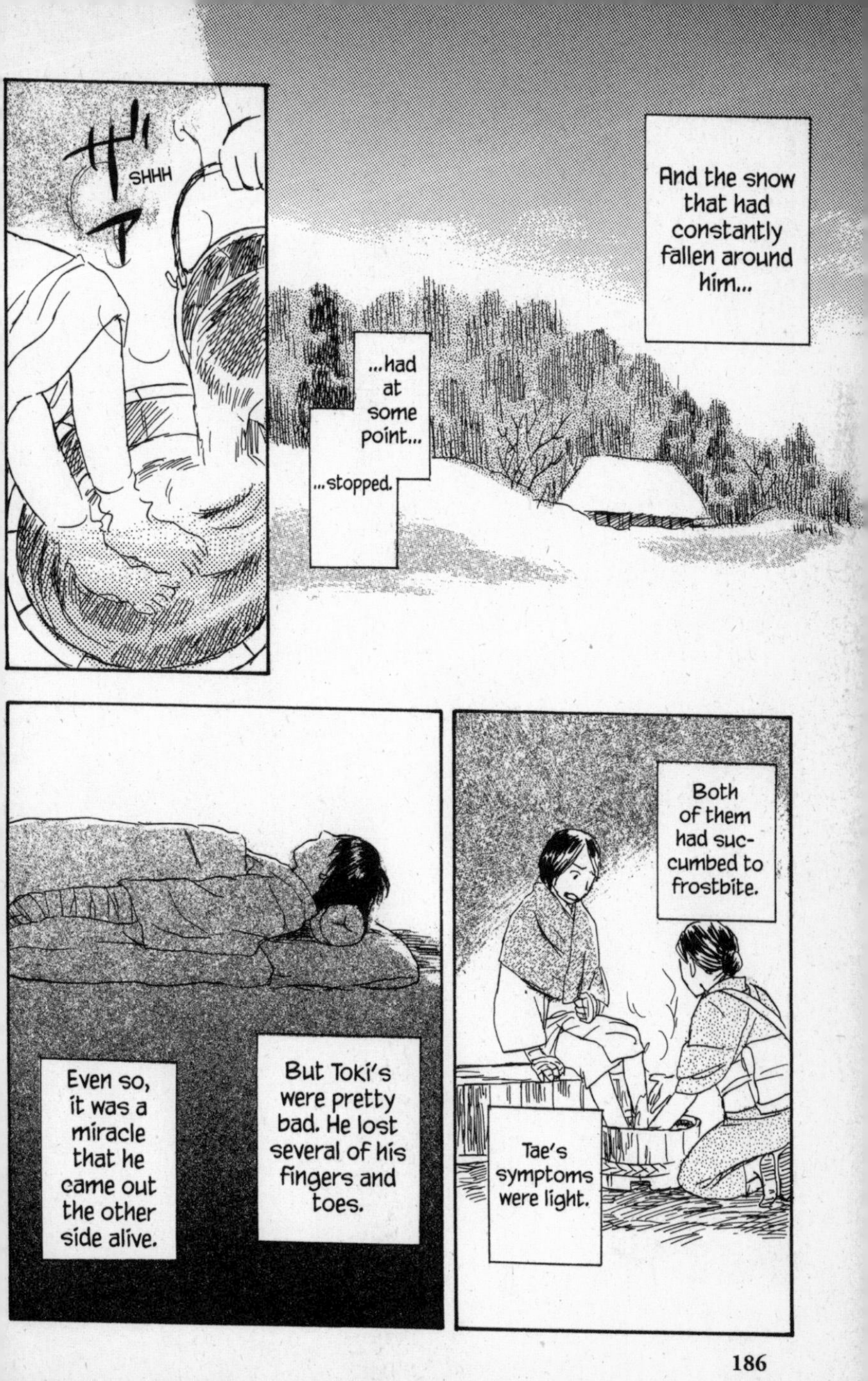
And the snow that had constantly fallen around him...
...had at some point...
...stopped.
SHHH
Both of them had succumbed to frostbite.
Tae's symptoms were light.
But Toki's were pretty bad. He lost several of his fingers and toes.
Even so, it was a miracle that he came out the other side alive.

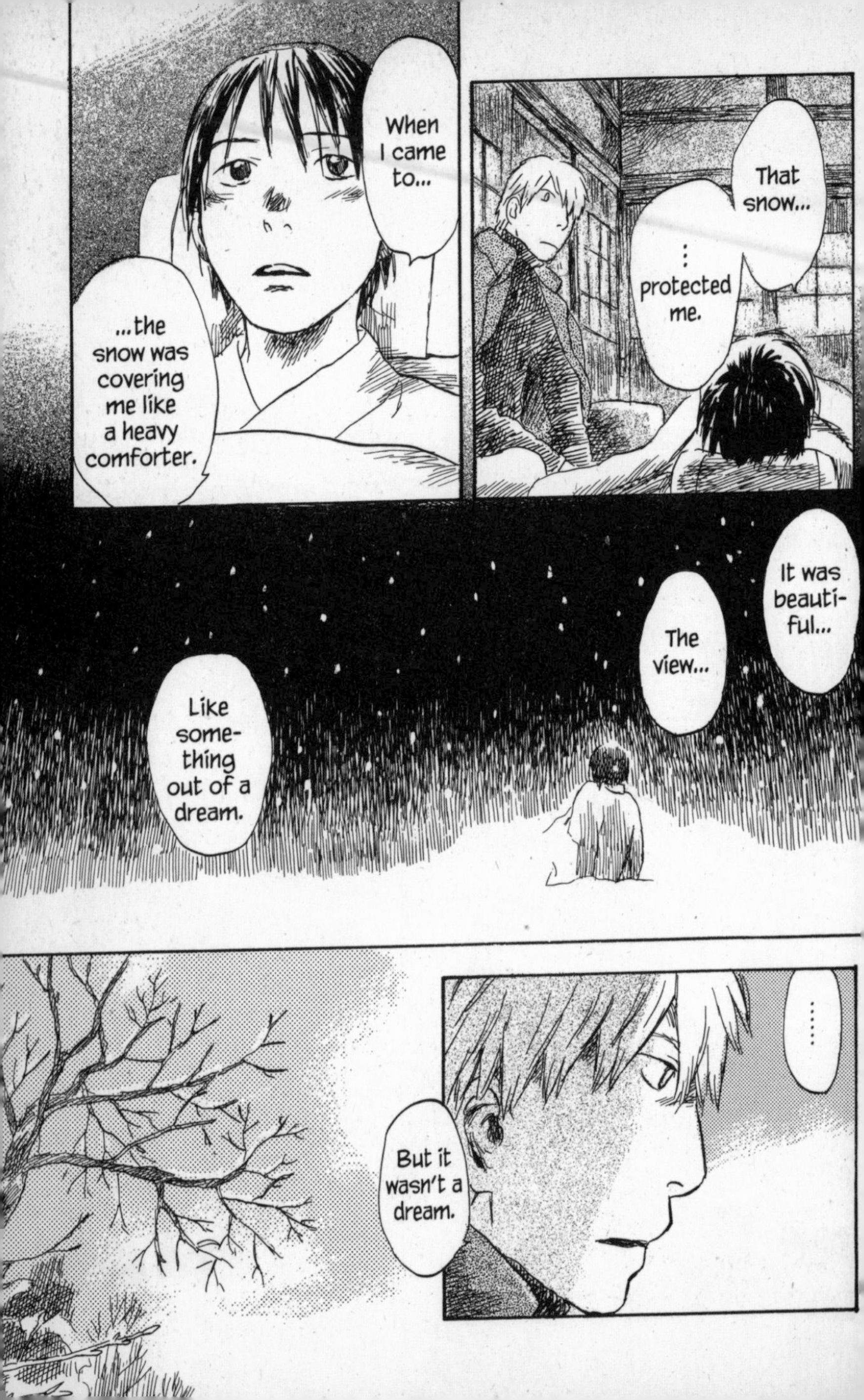
That snow...
...protected me.
When I came to...
...the snow was covering me like a heavy comforter.
It was beauti-ful...
The view...
Like some-thing out of a dream.
......
But it wasn't a dream.

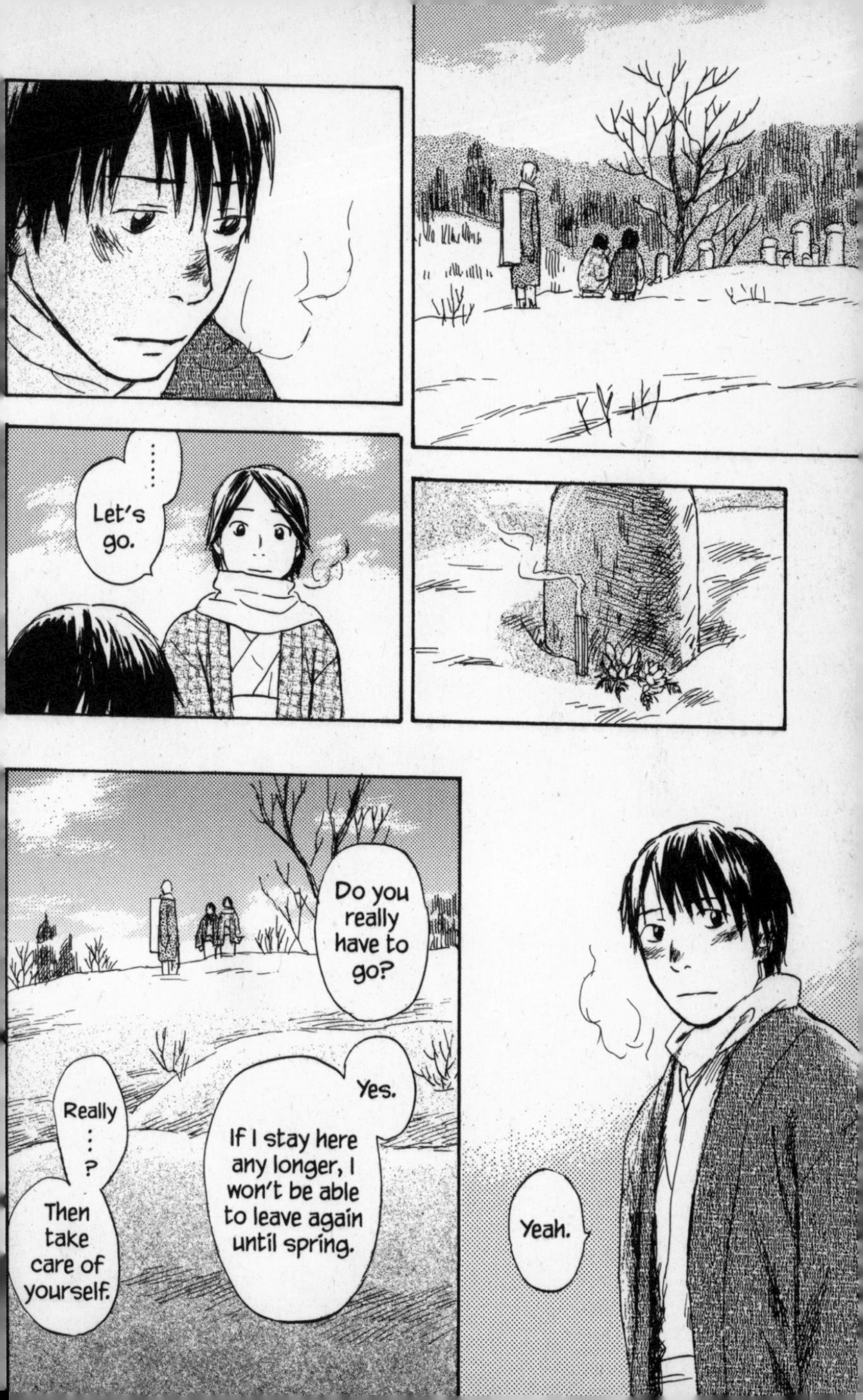
......
Let's go.
Do you really have to go?
Yes.
If I stay here any longer, I won't be able to leave again until spring.
Really...?
Then take care of yourself.
Yeah.

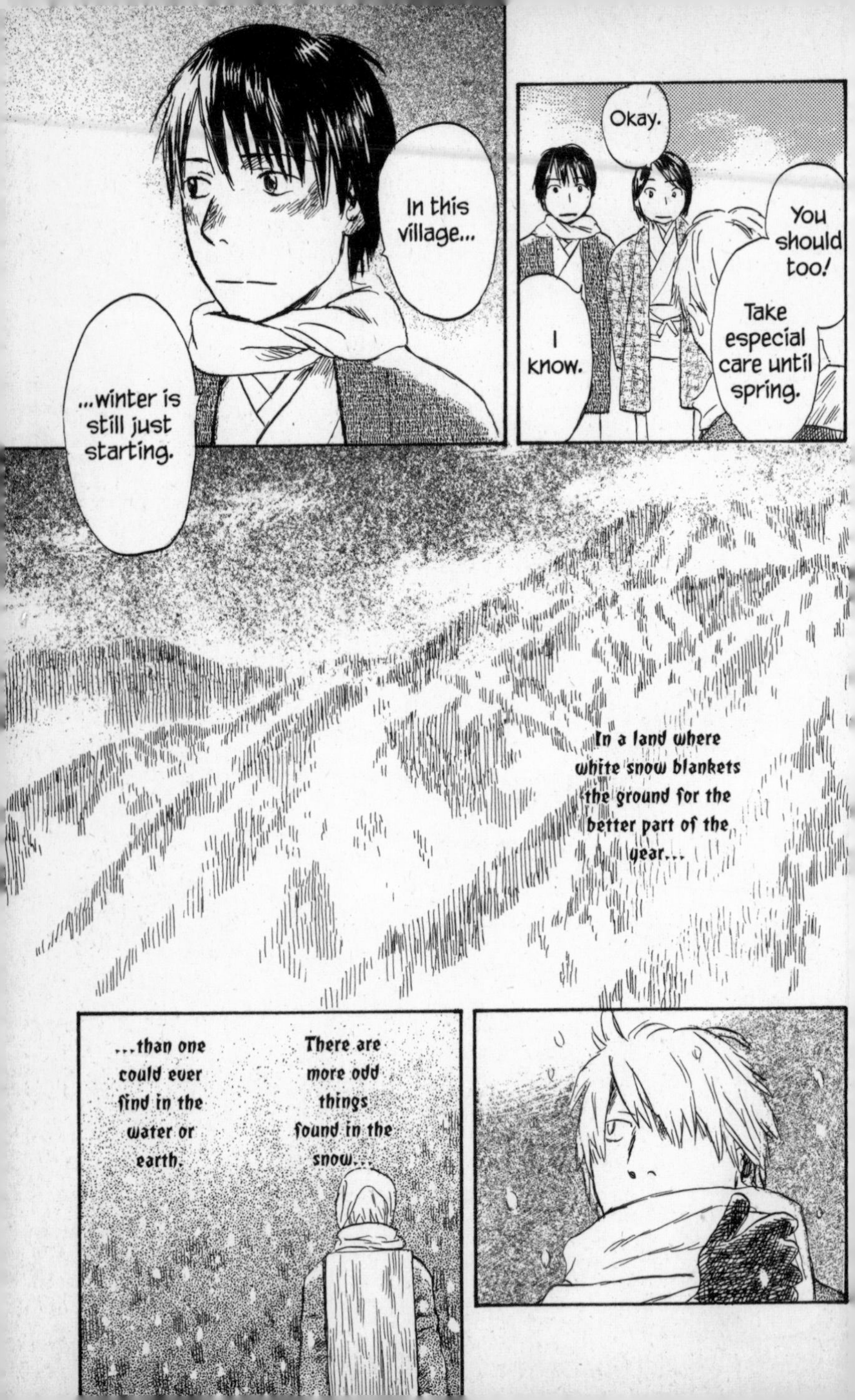
Okay.
You should too!
Take especial care until spring.
I know.
In this village...
...winter is still just starting.
In a land where white snow blankets the ground for the better part of the year...
There are more odd things found in the snow...
...than one could ever find in the water or earth.

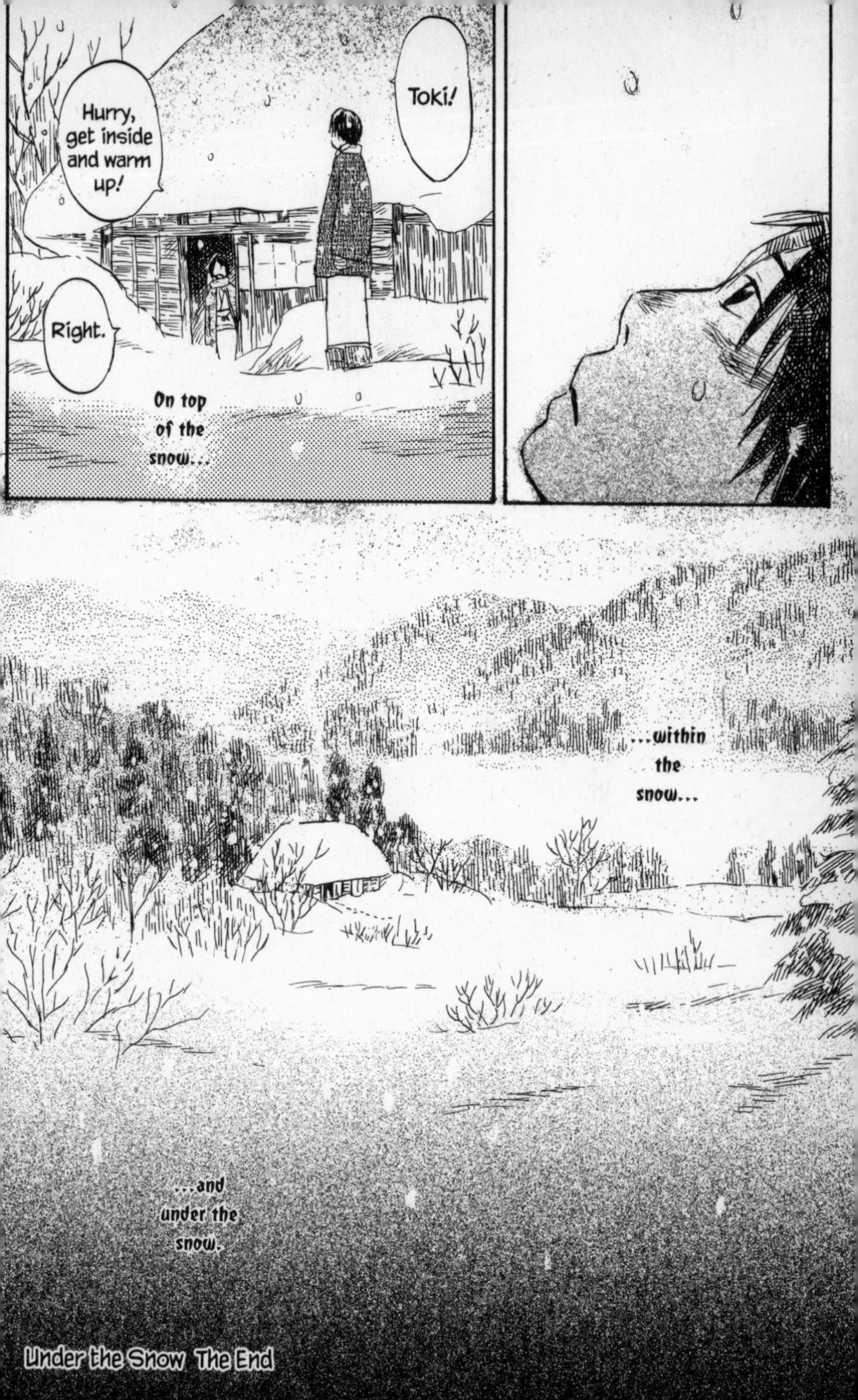
Toki!
Hurry, get inside and warm up!
Right.
On top of the snow...
...within the snow...
...and under the snow.
Under the Snow The End

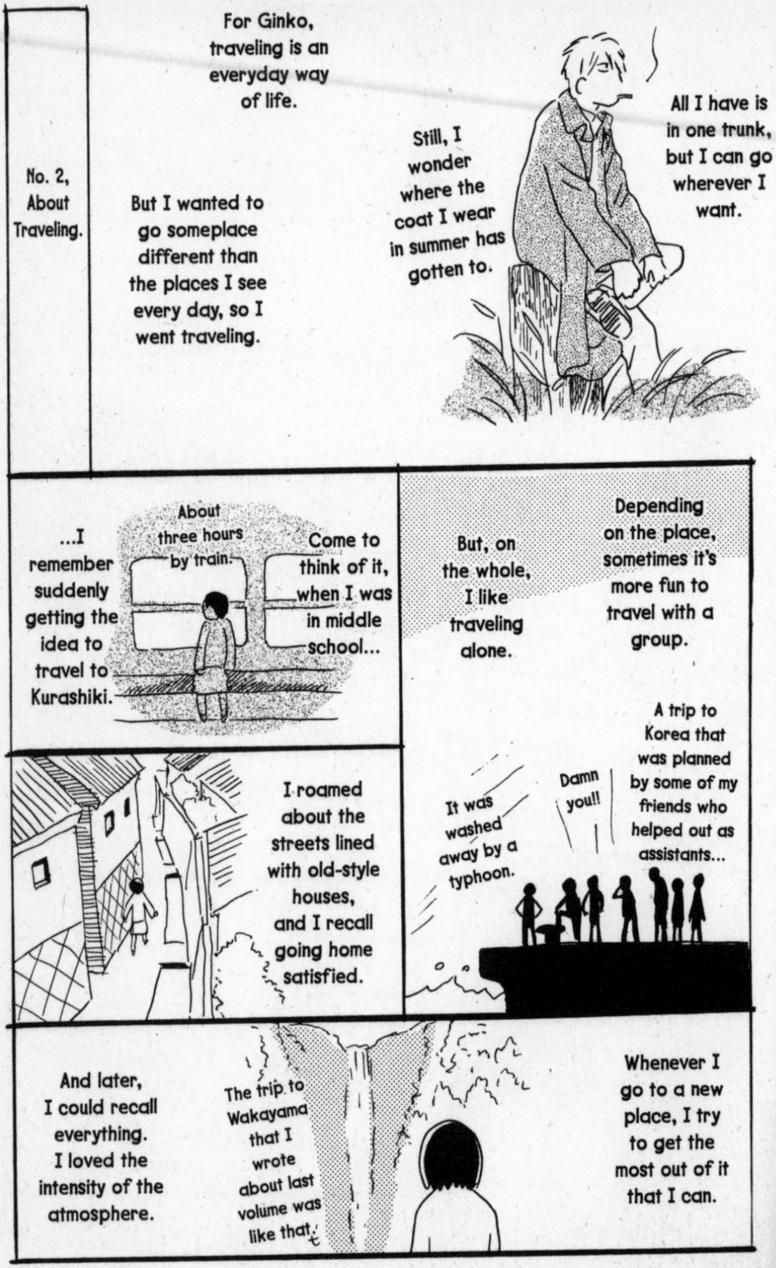
For Ginko, traveling is an everyday way of life.
All I have is in one trunk, but I can go wherever I want.
Still, I wonder where the coat I wear in summer has gotten to.
But I wanted to go someplace different than the places I see every day, so I went traveling.
No. 2, About Traveling.
Depending on the place, sometimes it's more fun to travel with a group.
But, on the whole, I like traveling alone.
Come to think of it, when I was in middle school...
About three hours by train.
...I remember suddenly getting the idea to travel to Kurashiki.
A trip to Korea that was planned by some of my friends who helped out as assistants...
Damn you!!
It was washed away by a typhoon.
I roamed about the streets lined with old-style houses, and I recall going home satisfied.
Whenever I go to a new place, I try to get the most out of it that I can.
The trip to Wakayama that I wrote about last volume was like that.
And later, I could recall everything. I loved the intensity of the atmosphere.

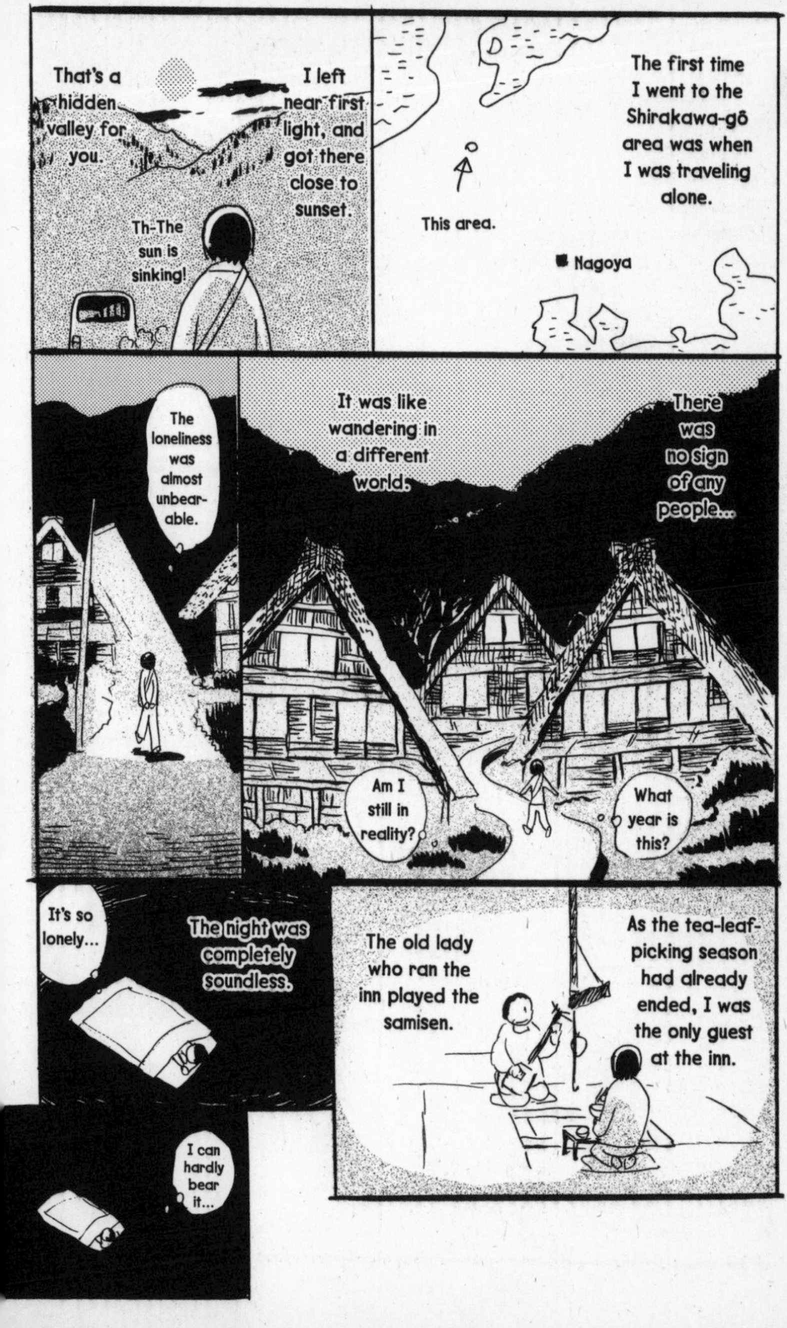
The first time I went to the Shirakawa-gō area was when I was traveling alone.
This area.
Nagoya
I left near first light, and got there close to sunset.
That's a hidden valley for you.
Th-The sun is sinking!
There was no sign of any people...
It was like wandering in a different world.
What year is this?
Am I still in reality?
The loneliness was almost unbearable.
As the tea-leaf-picking season had already ended, I was the only guest at the inn.
The old lady who ran the inn played the samisen.
The night was completely soundless.
It's so lonely...
I can hardly bear it...

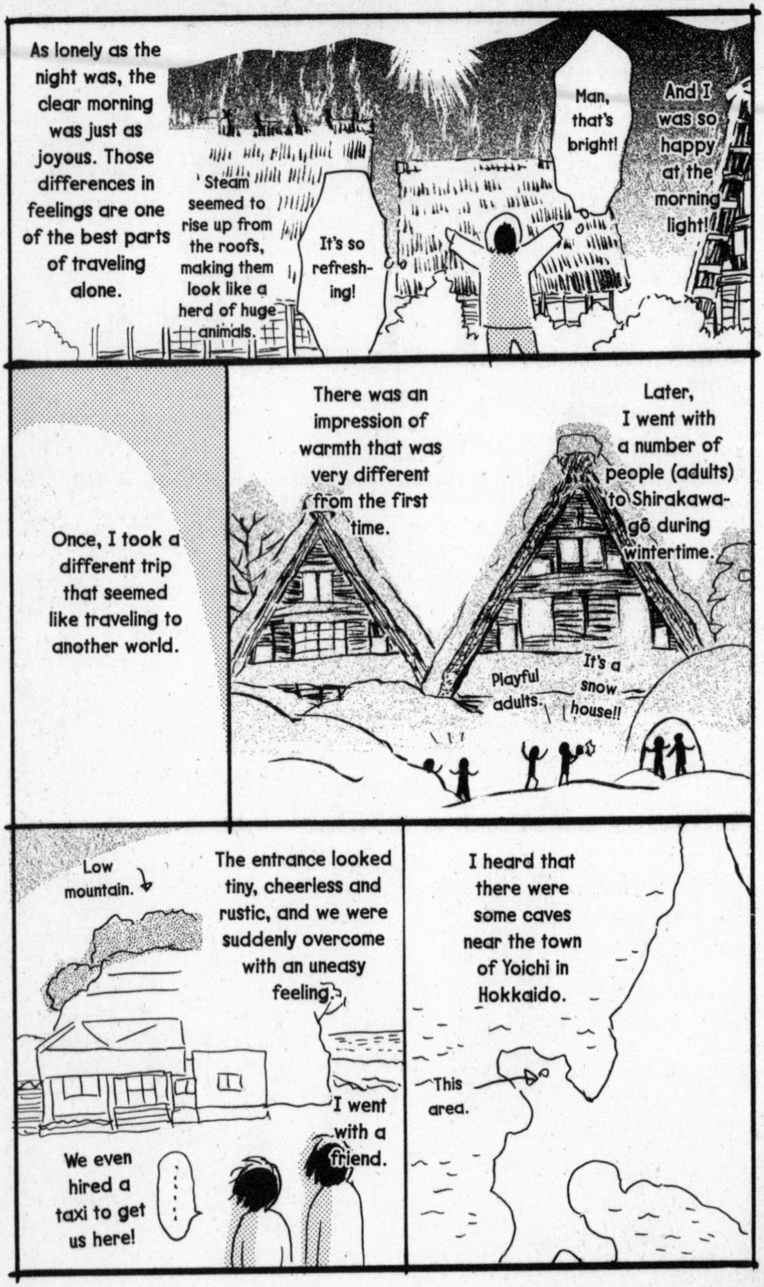
And I was so happy at the morning light!
Man, that's bright!
As lonely as the night was, the clear morning was just as joyous. Those differences in feelings are one of the best parts of traveling alone.
It's so refresh-ing!
Steam seemed to rise up from the roofs, making them look like a herd of huge animals.
Later, I went with a number of people (adults) to Shirakawa-gô during wintertime.
There was an impression of warmth that was very different from the first time.
It's a snow house!!
Playful adults.
Once, I took a different trip that seemed like traveling to another world.
I heard that there were some caves near the town of Yoichi in Hokkaido.
This area.
The entrance looked tiny, cheerless and rustic, and we were suddenly overcome with an uneasy feeling.
Low mountain.
I went with a friend.
We even hired a taxi to get us here!
......

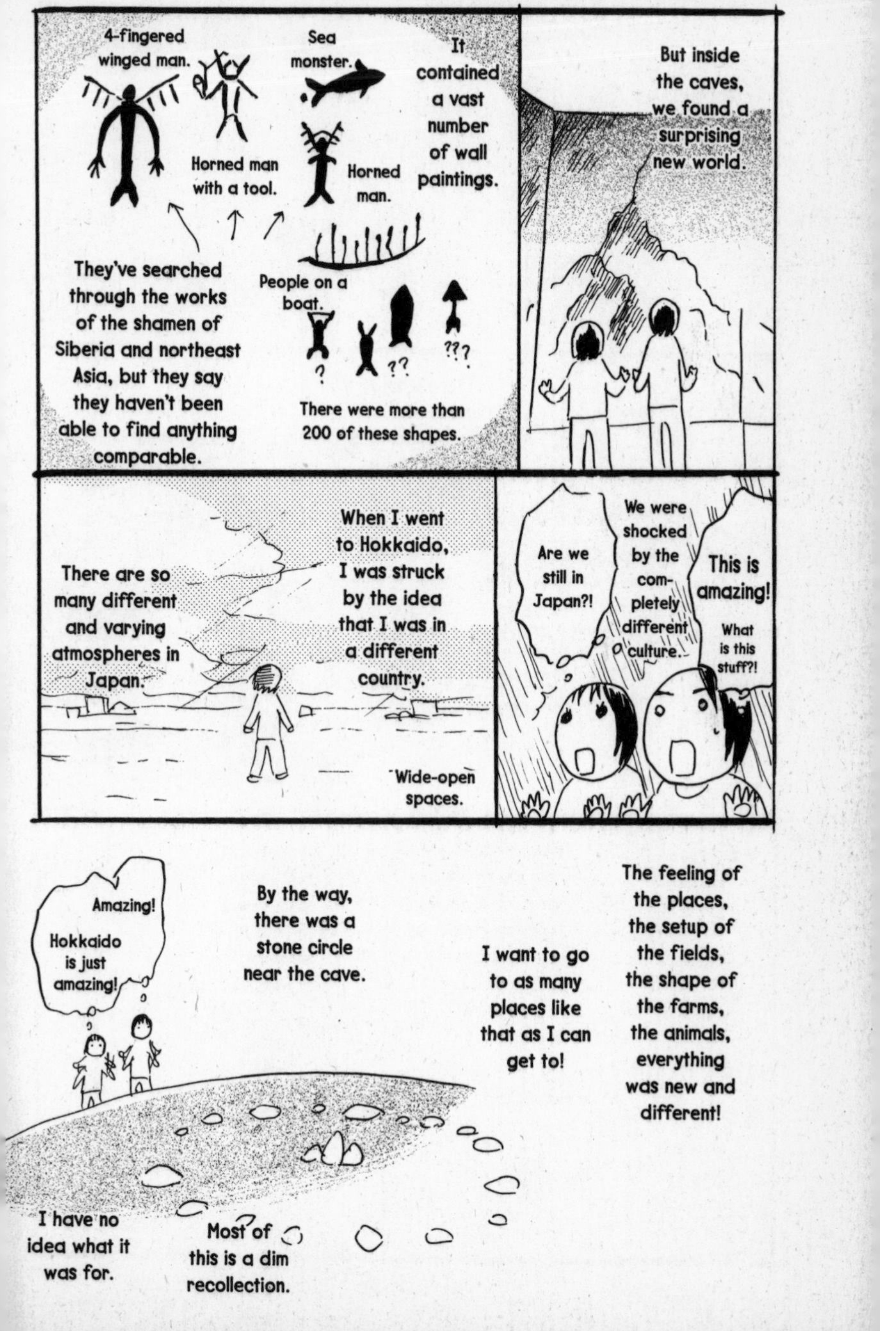
But inside the caves, we found a surprising new world.
It contained a vast number of wall paintings.
Sea monster.
4-fingered winged man.
Horned man.
Horned man with a tool.
People on a boat.
???
??
?
They've searched through the works of the shamen of Siberia and northeast Asia, but they say they haven't been able to find anything comparable.
There were more than 200 of these shapes.
This is amazing!
What is this stuff?!
We were shocked by the com-pletely different culture.
Are we still in Japan?!
When I went to Hokkaido, I was struck by the idea that I was in a different country.
There are so many different and varying atmospheres in Japan.
Wide-open spaces.
The feeling of the places, the setup of the fields, the shape of the farms, the animals, everything was new and different!
I want to go to as many places like that as I can get to!
By the way, there was a stone circle near the cave.
Amazing!
Hokkaido is just amazing!
Most of this is a dim recollection.
I have no idea what it was for.

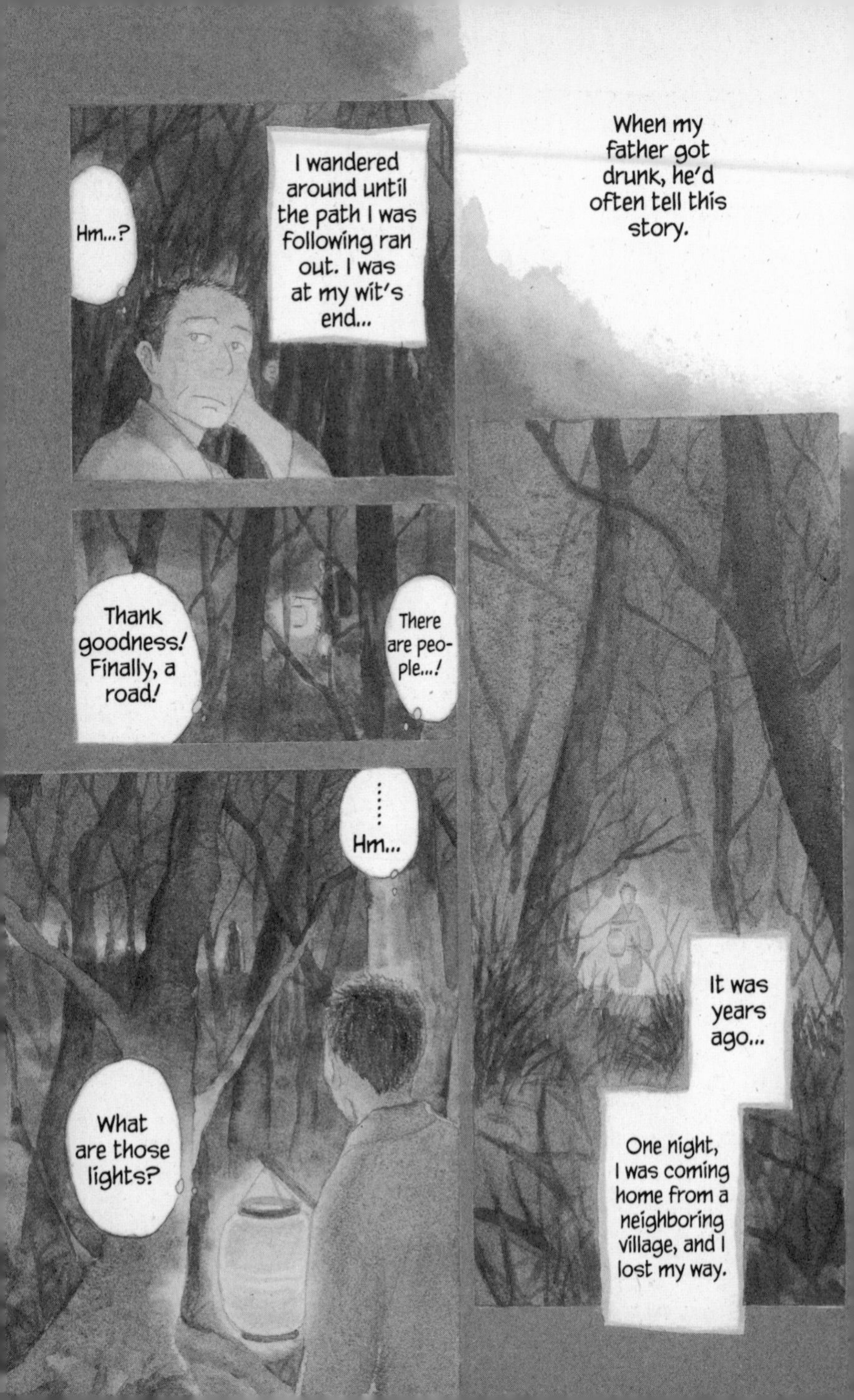
When my father got drunk, he'd often tell this story.
It was years ago...
One night, I was coming home from a neighboring village, and I lost my way.
I wandered around until the path I was following ran out. I was at my wit's end...
Hm...?
There are peo-ple...!
Thank goodness! Finally, a road!
...... Hm...
What are those lights?

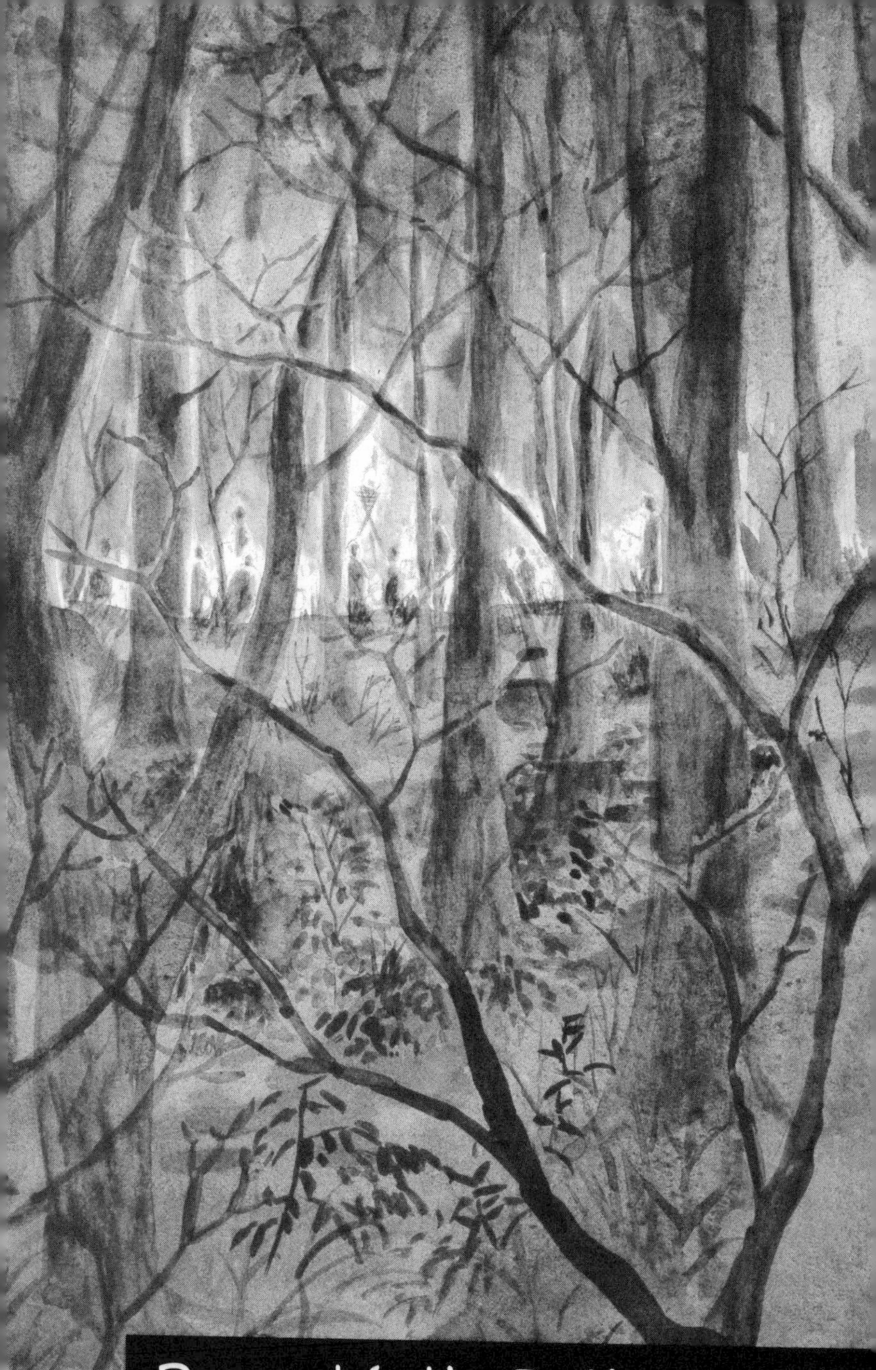

Banquet in the Farthest Field

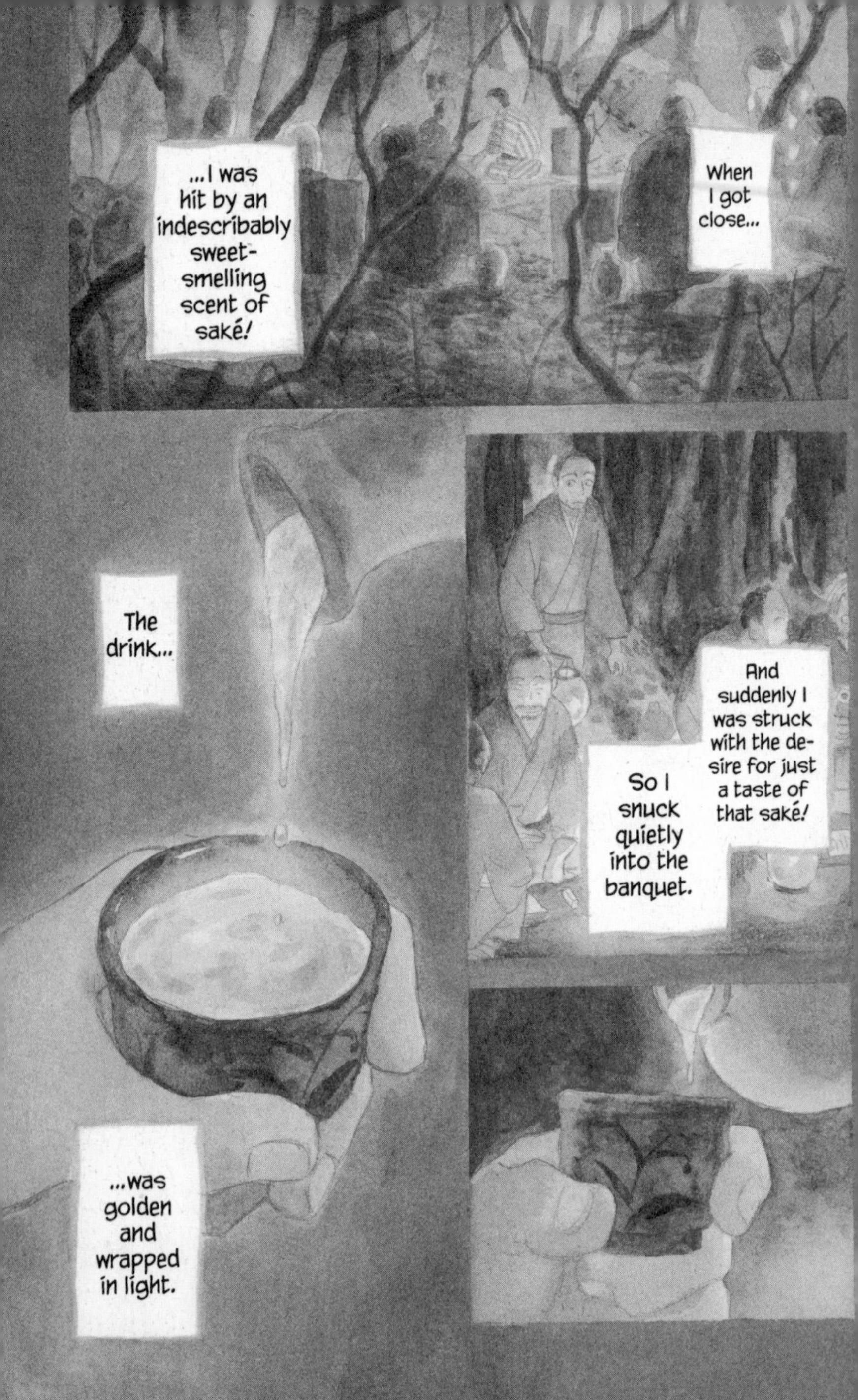
When I got close...
...I was hit by an indescribably sweet-smelling scent of saké!
And suddenly I was struck with the de-sire for just a taste of that saké!
So I snuck quietly into the banquet.
The drink...
...was golden and wrapped in light.

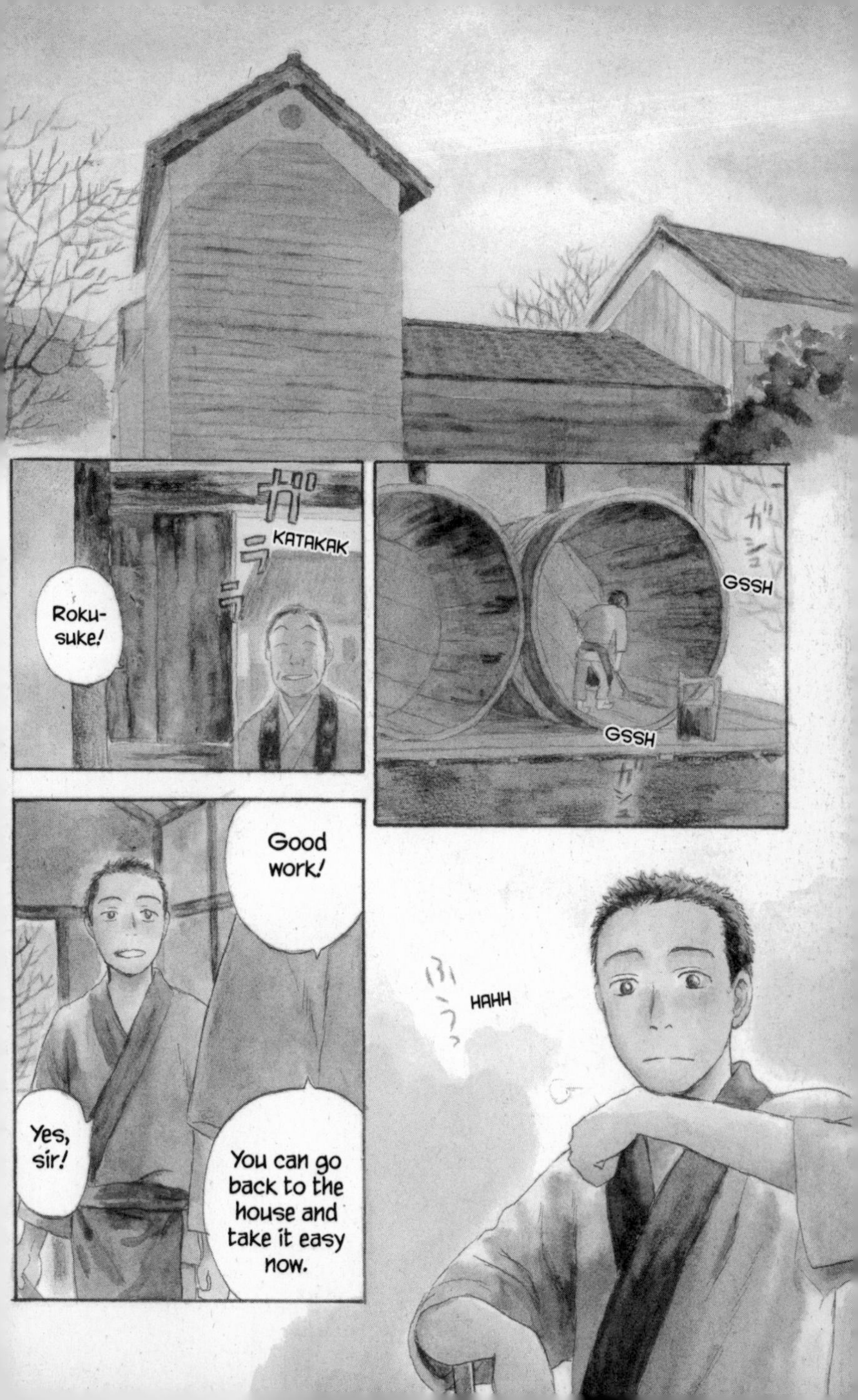

GSSH
GSSH
KATAKAK
Roku-suke!
HAHH
Good work!
You can go back to the house and take it easy now.
Yes, sir!

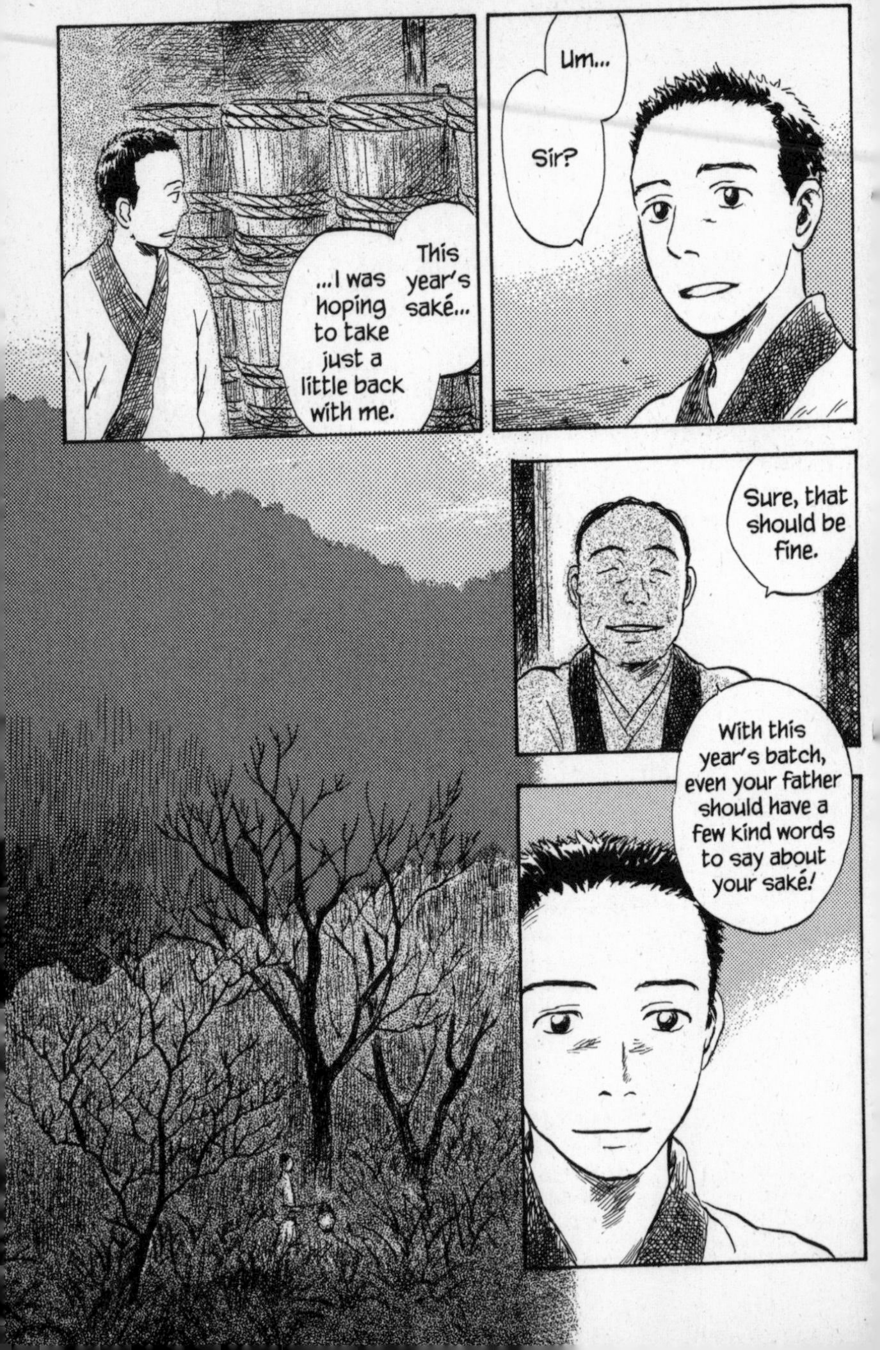
Um... Sir?
This year's saké... ...I was hoping to take just a little back with me.
Sure, that should be fine.
With this year's batch, even your father should have a few kind words to say about your saké!

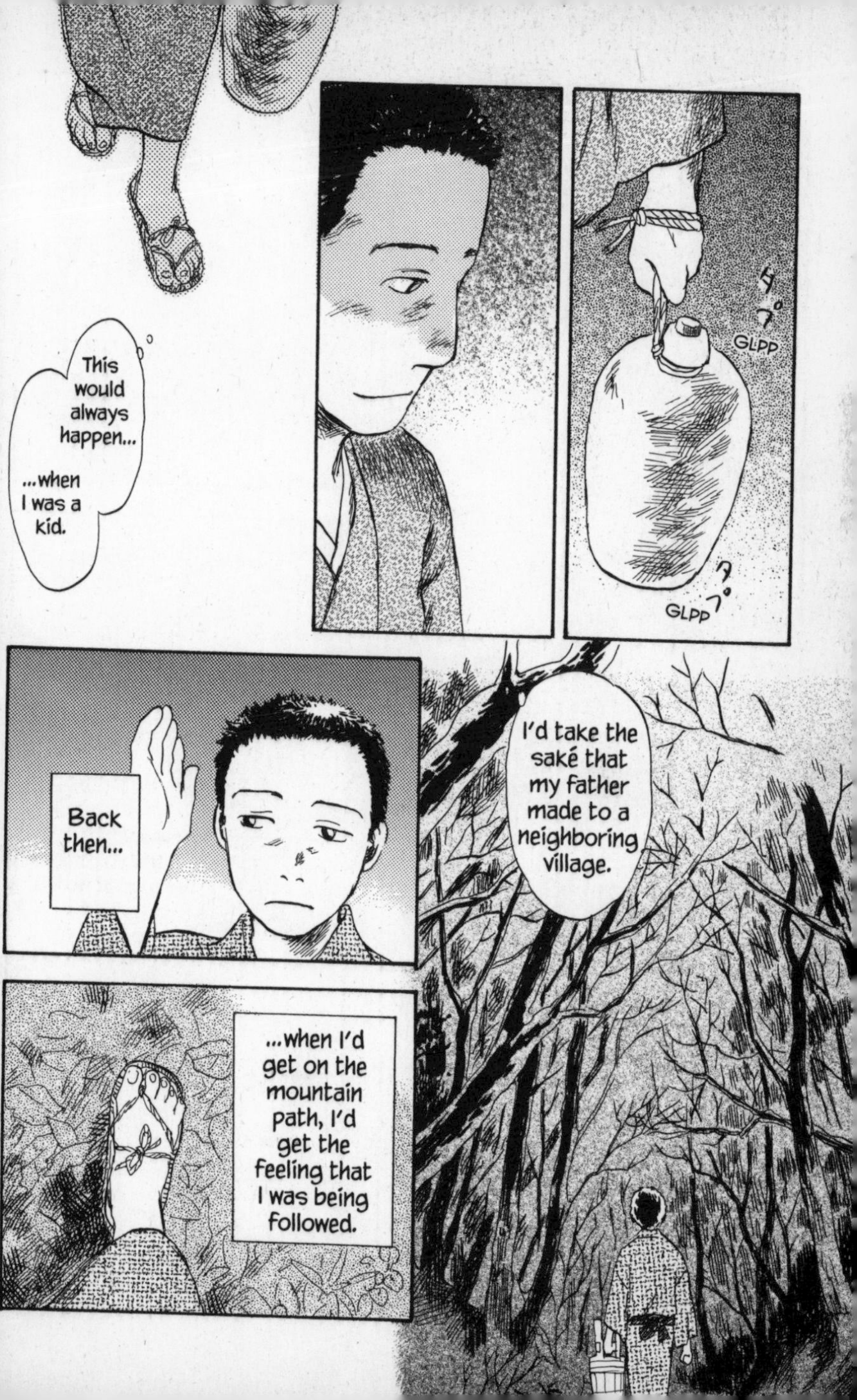
GLPP
GLPP
This would always happen...
...when I was a kid.
I'd take the saké that my father made to a neighboring village.
Back then...
...when I'd get on the mountain path, I'd get the feeling that I was being followed.

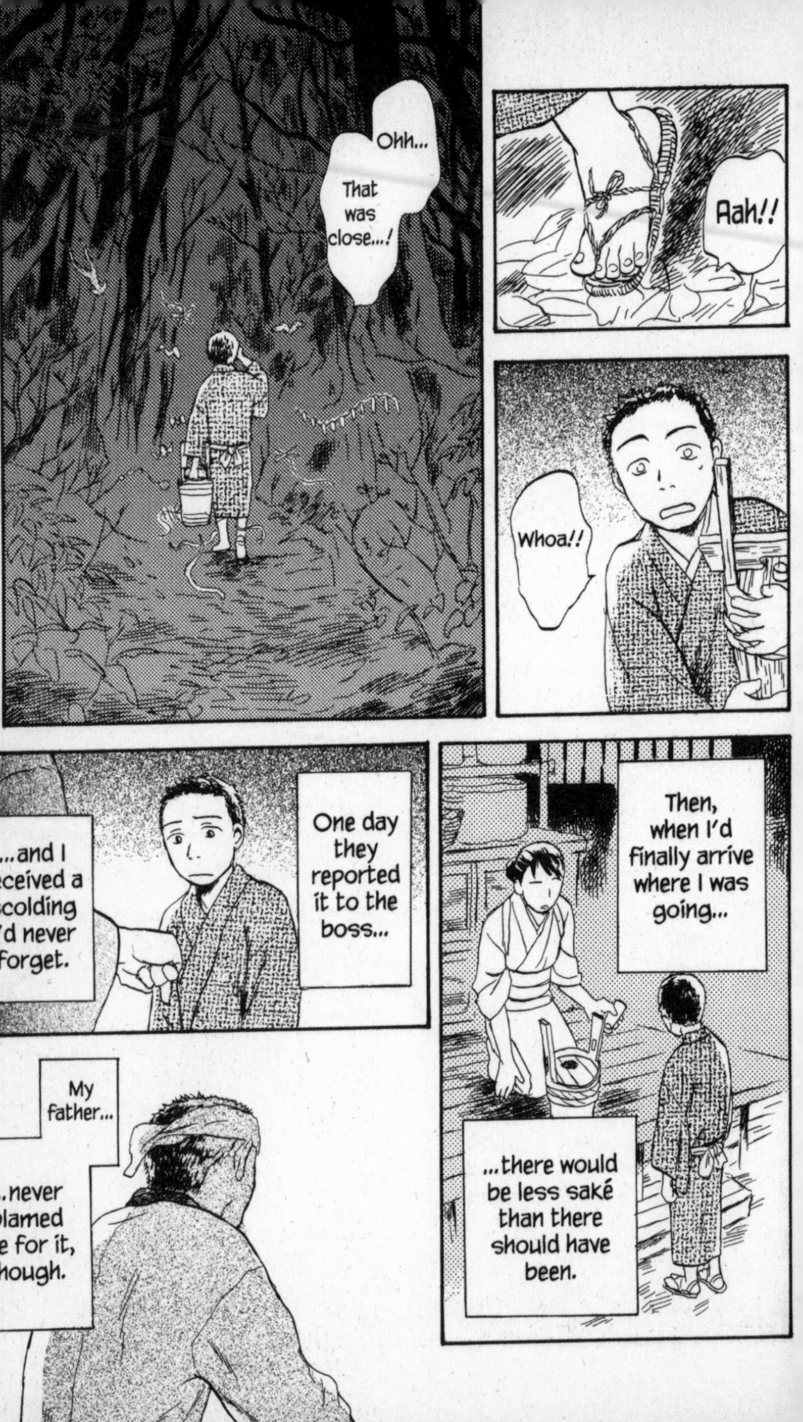
Aah!!
Whoa!!
Ohh...
That was close...!
Then, when I'd finally arrive where I was going...
...there would be less saké than there should have been.
One day they reported it to the boss...
...and I received a scolding I'd never forget.
My father...
...never blamed me for it, though.

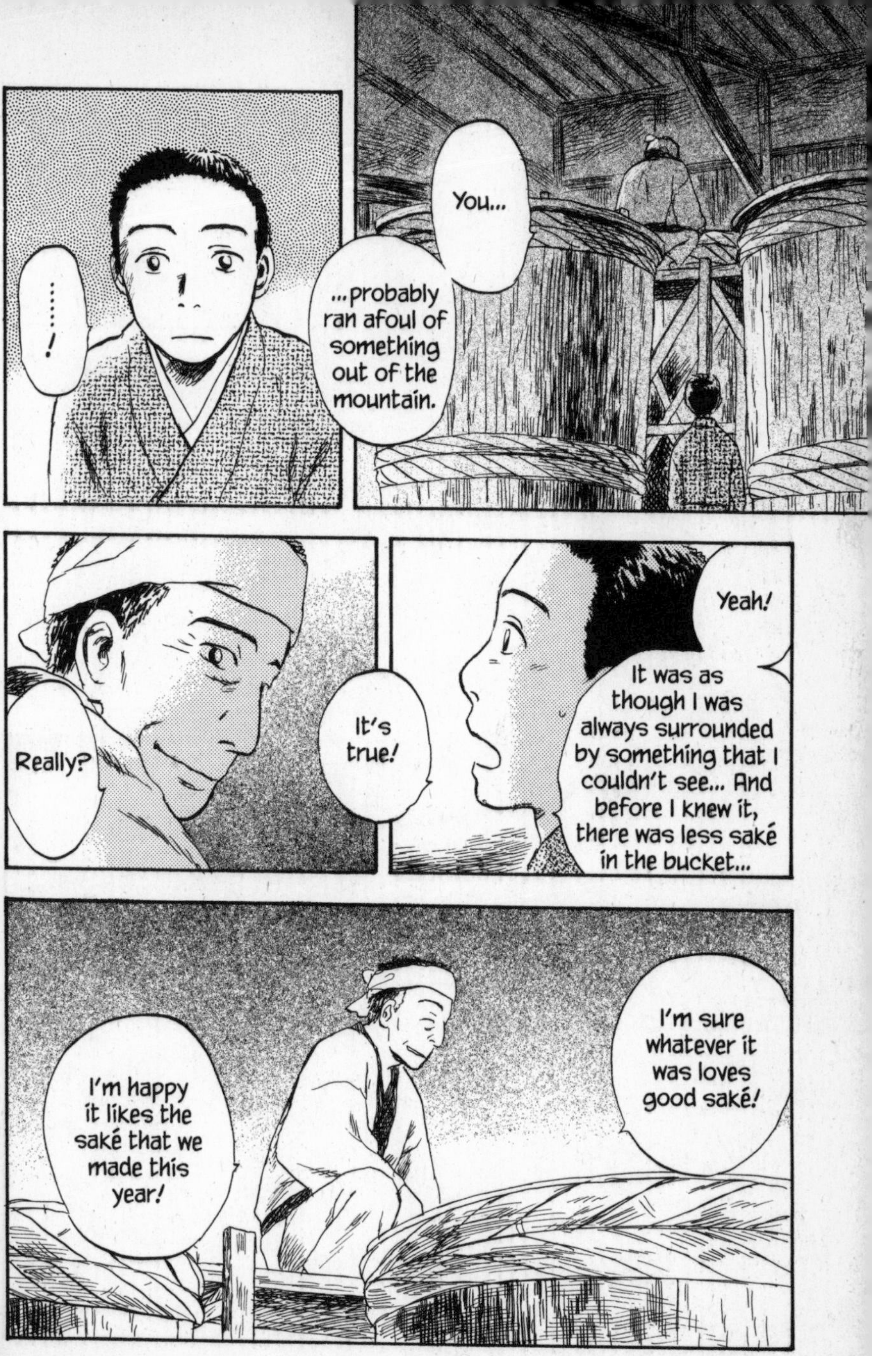
You...
...probably ran afoul of something out of the mountain.
......!
Yeah!
It was as though I was always surrounded by something that I couldn't see... And before I knew it, there was less saké in the bucket...
It's true!
Really?
I'm sure whatever it was loves good saké!
I'm happy it likes the saké that we made this year!

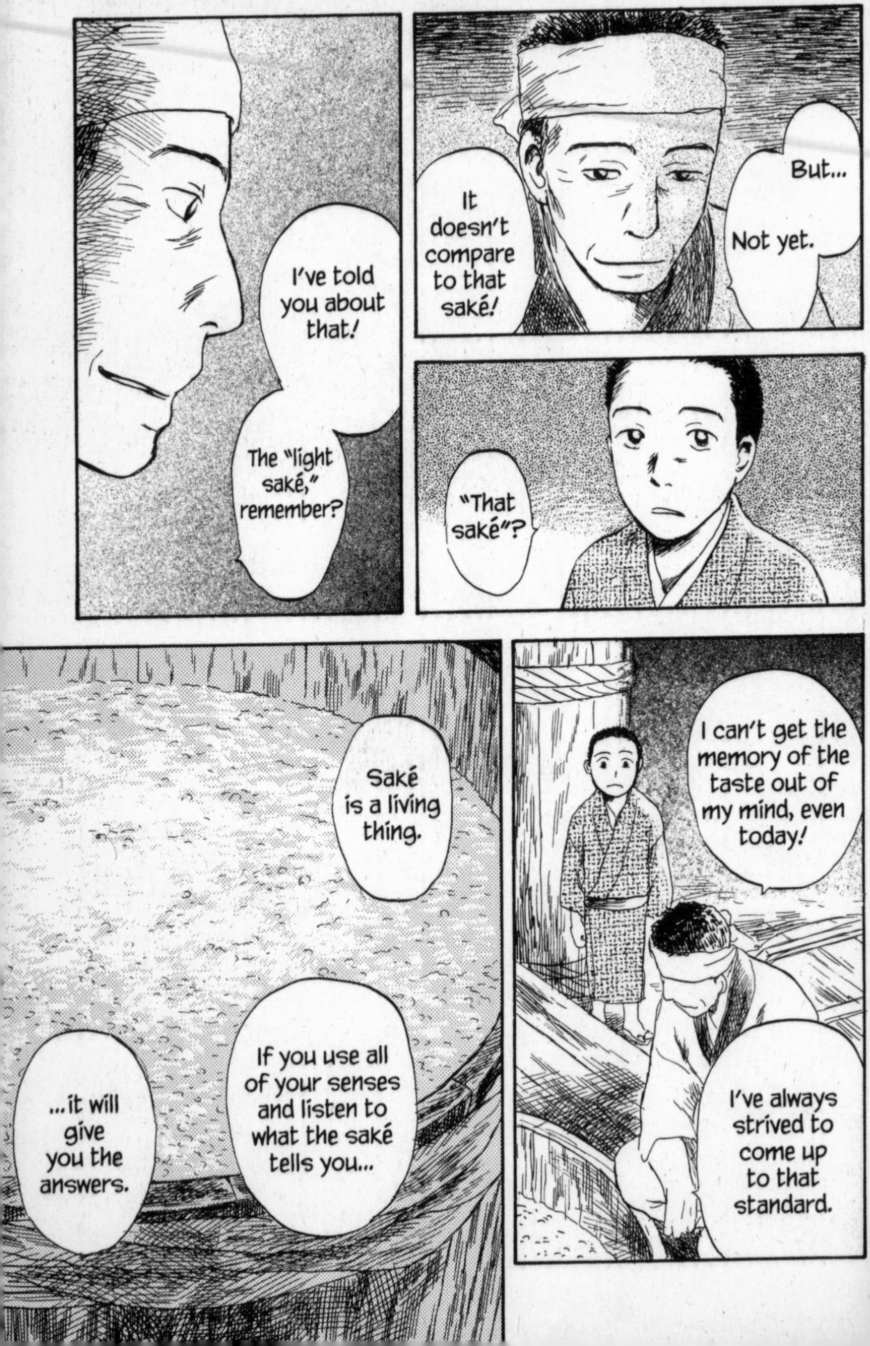
But...
Not yet.
It doesn't compare to that saké!
"That saké"?
I've told you about that!
The "light saké," remember?
I can't get the memory of the taste out of my mind, even today!
I've always strived to come up to that standard.
Saké is a living thing.
If you use all of your senses and listen to what the saké tells you...
...it will give you the answers.

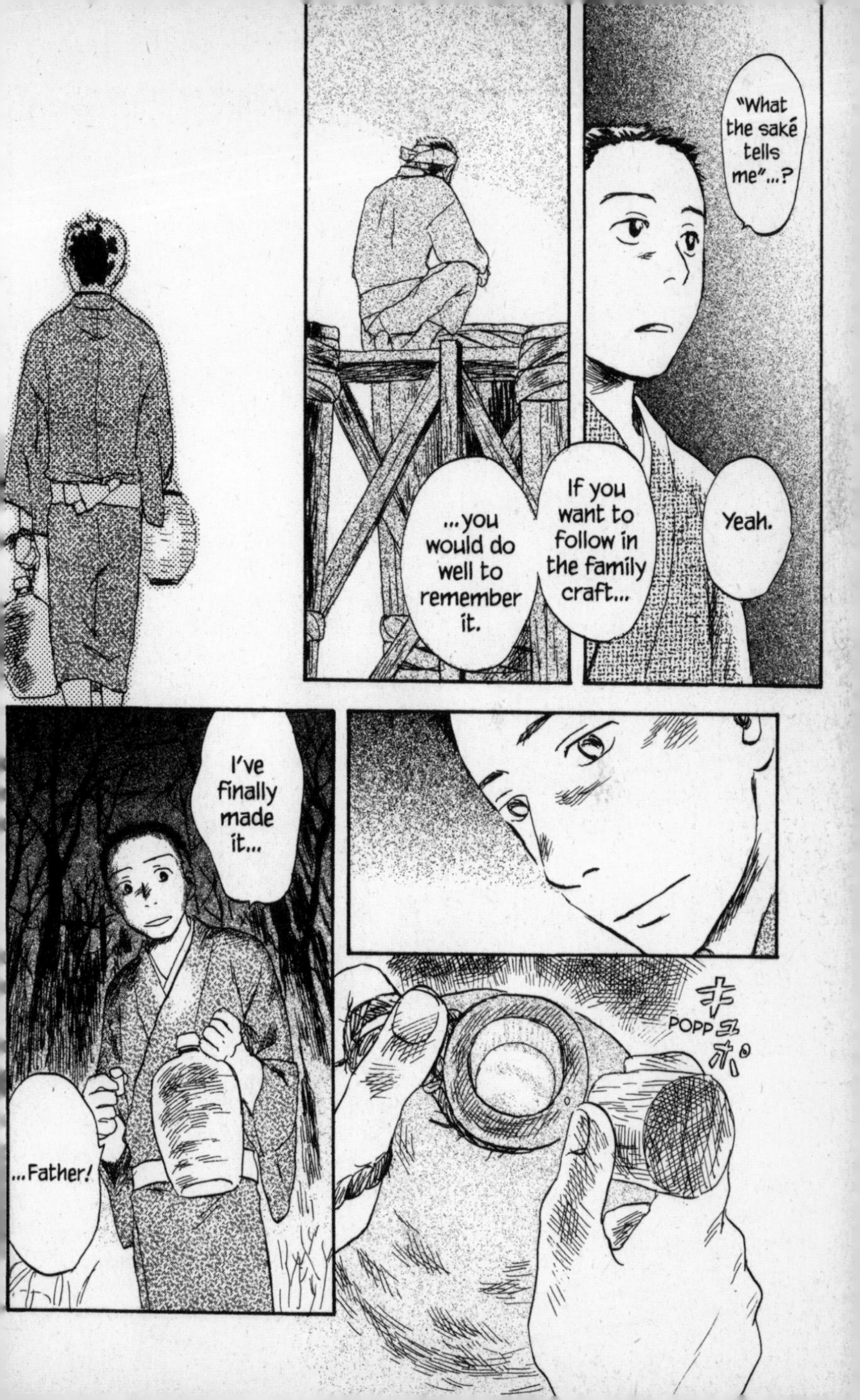
"What the saké tells me"...?
Yeah.
If you want to follow in the family craft...
...you would do well to remember it.
キュポ
POPP
I've finally made it...
...Father!

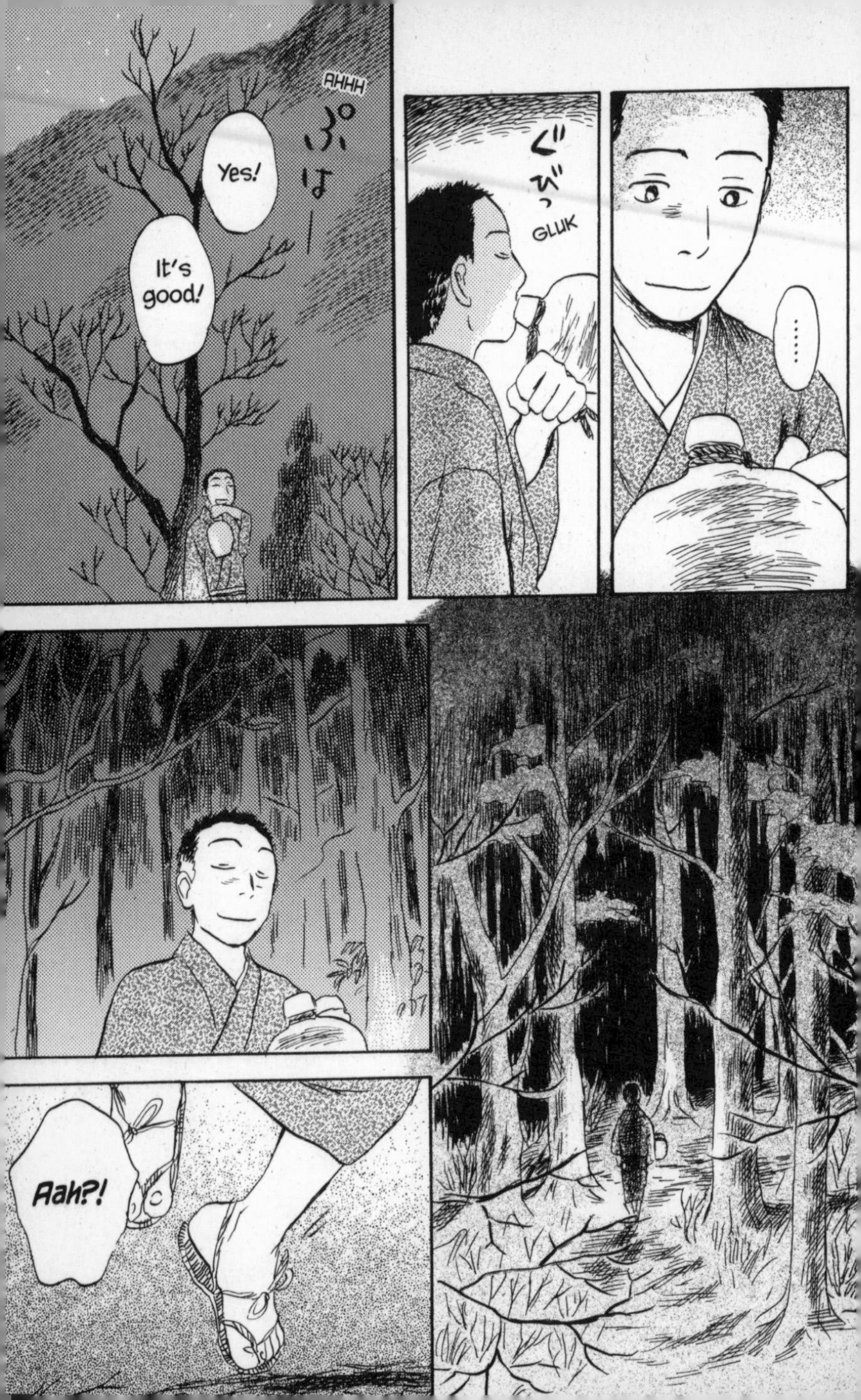
......
ぐびっ
GLUK
ぷはー
AHHH
Yes!
It's good!
Aah?!

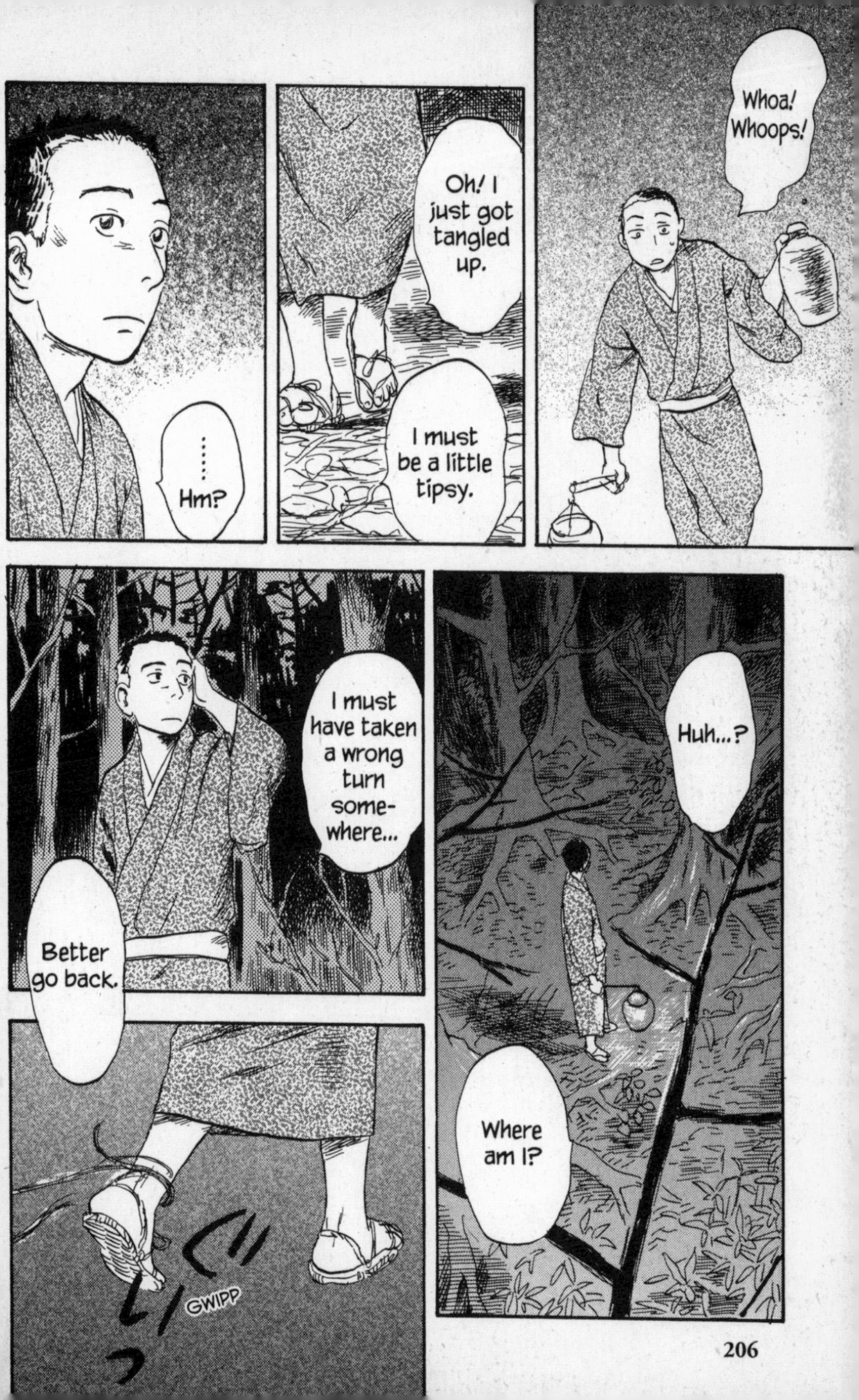
Whoa! Whoops!
Oh! I just got tangled up.
I must be a little tipsy.
...... Hm?
Huh...?
Where am I?
I must have taken a wrong turn somewhere...
Better go back.
GWIPP

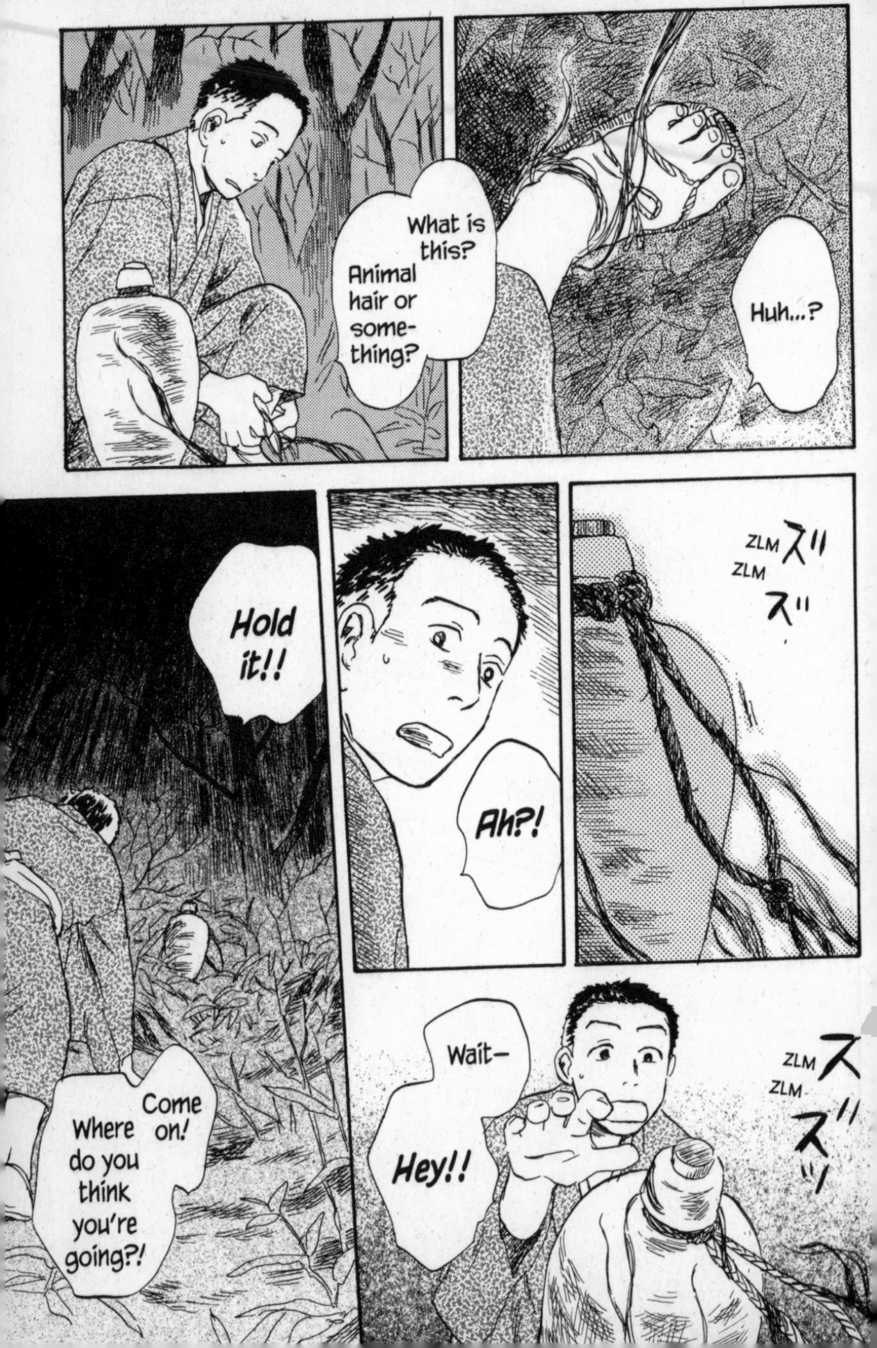
Huh...?
What is this? Animal hair or some-thing?
ZLM ズリ
ZLM ズ
Ah?!
Wait—
Hey!!
ZLM スリ
ZLM ズッ
Hold it!!
Come on!
Where do you think you're going?!

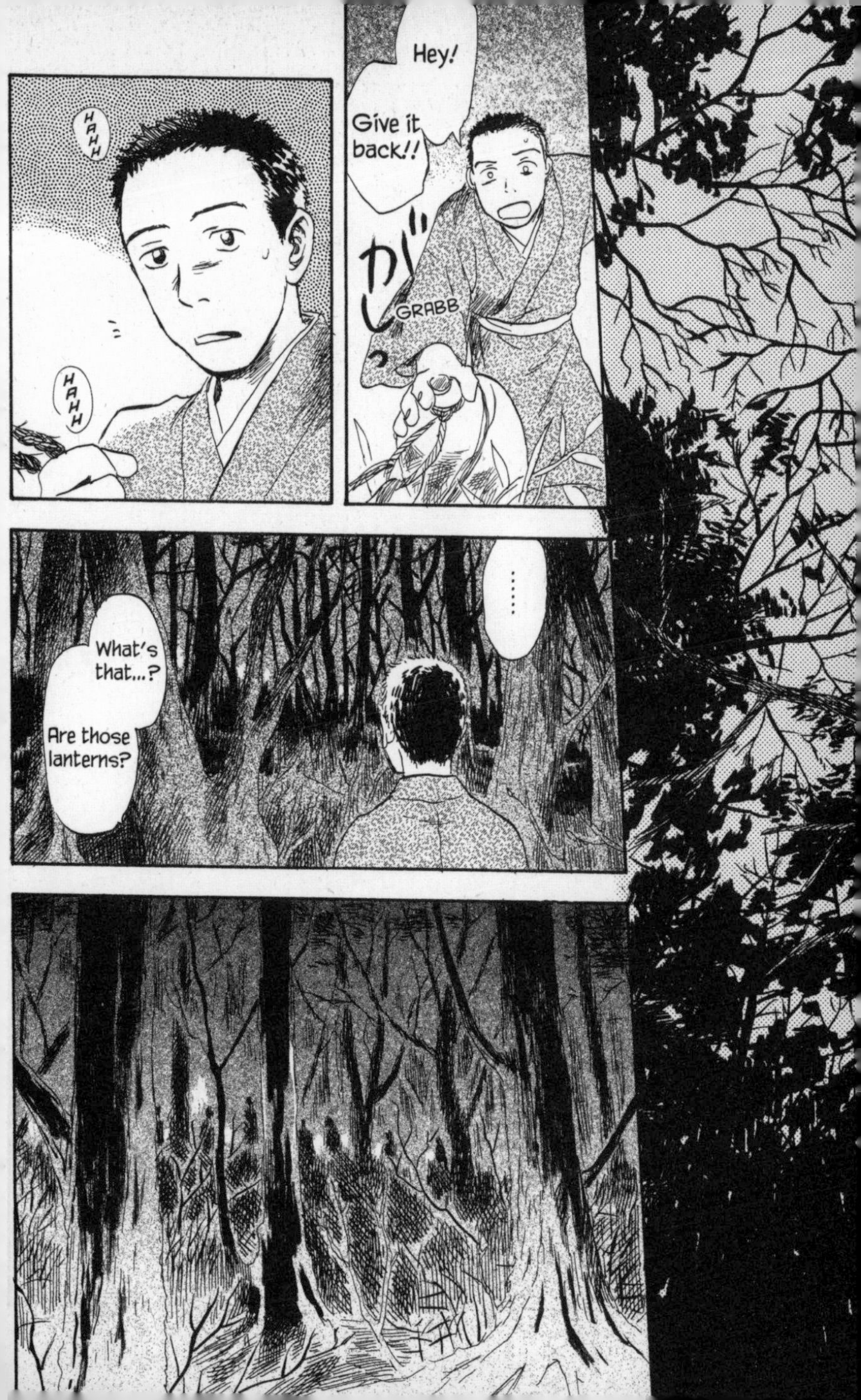

Hey!
Give it back!!
がしっ
GRABB
HAHH
HAHH
......
What's that...?
Are those lanterns?

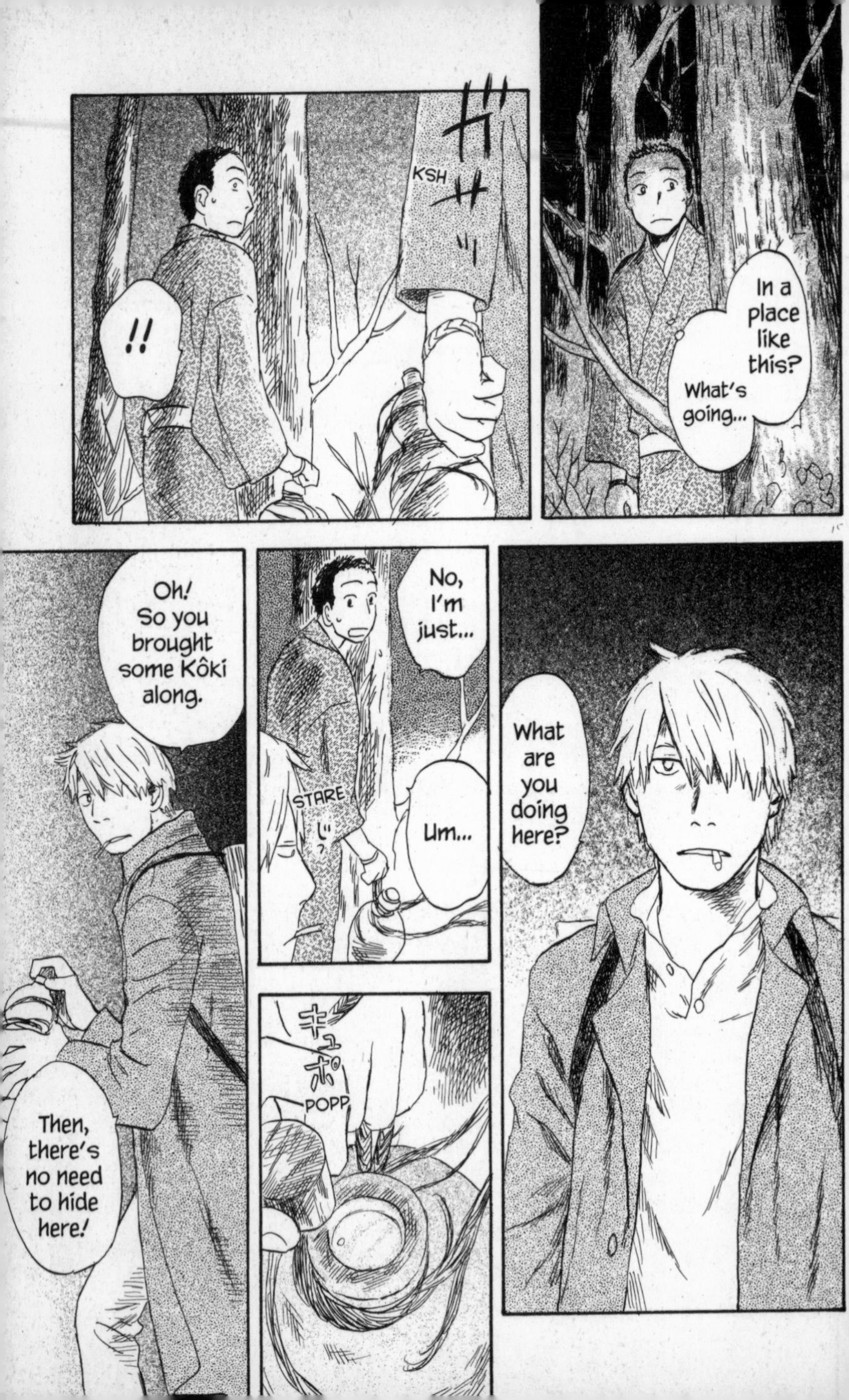
In a place like this?
What's going...
KSH
!!
What are you doing here?
No, I'm just...
STARE
Um...
キュポ
POPP
Oh! So you brought some Kôki along.
Then, there's no need to hide here!

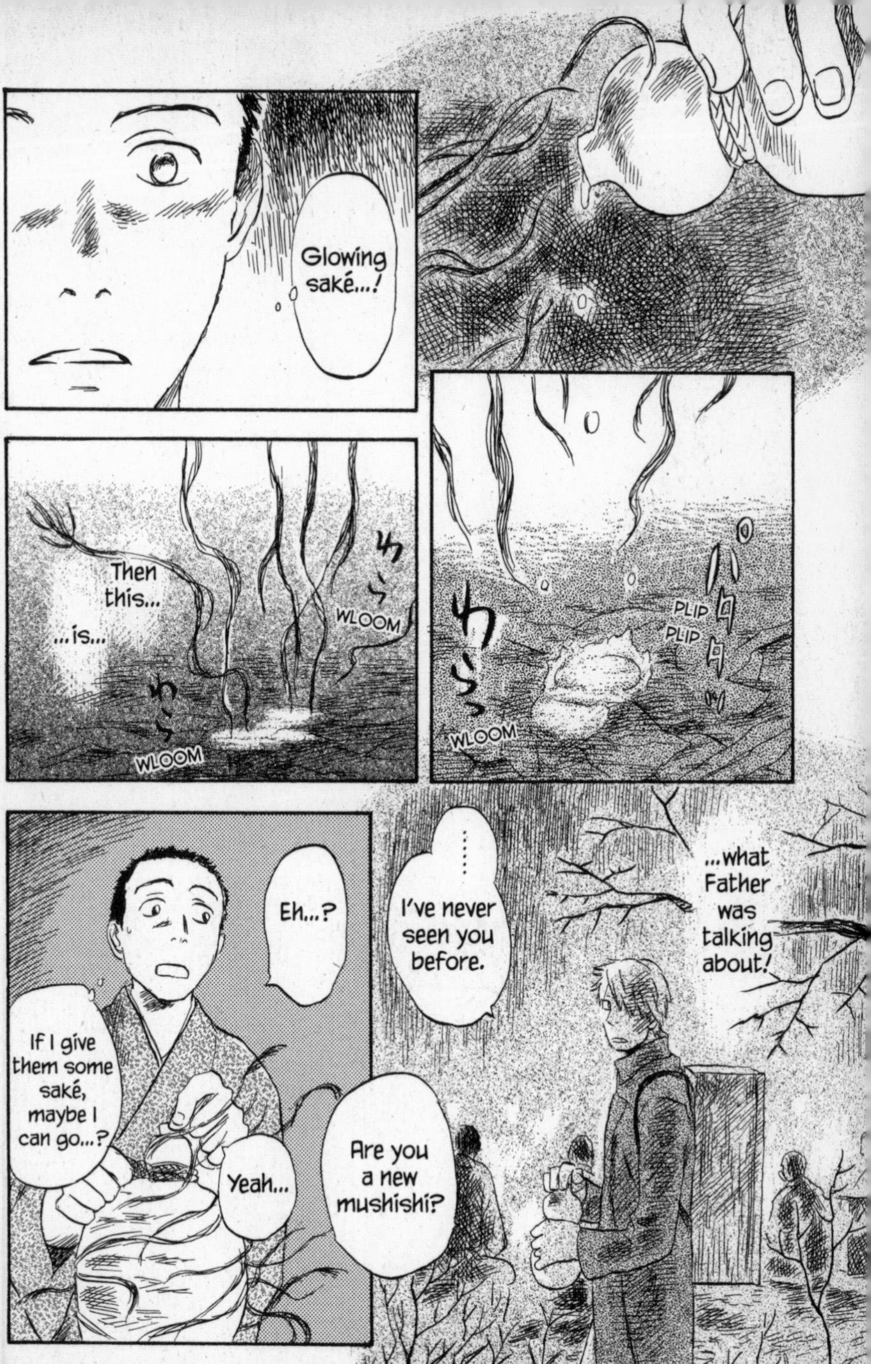
Glowing saké...!
PLIP
PLIP
WLOOM
Then this...
...is...
WLOOM
WLOOM
...what Father was talking about!
......
I've never seen you before.
Are you a new mushishi?
Eh...?
Yeah...
If I give them some saké, maybe I can go...?

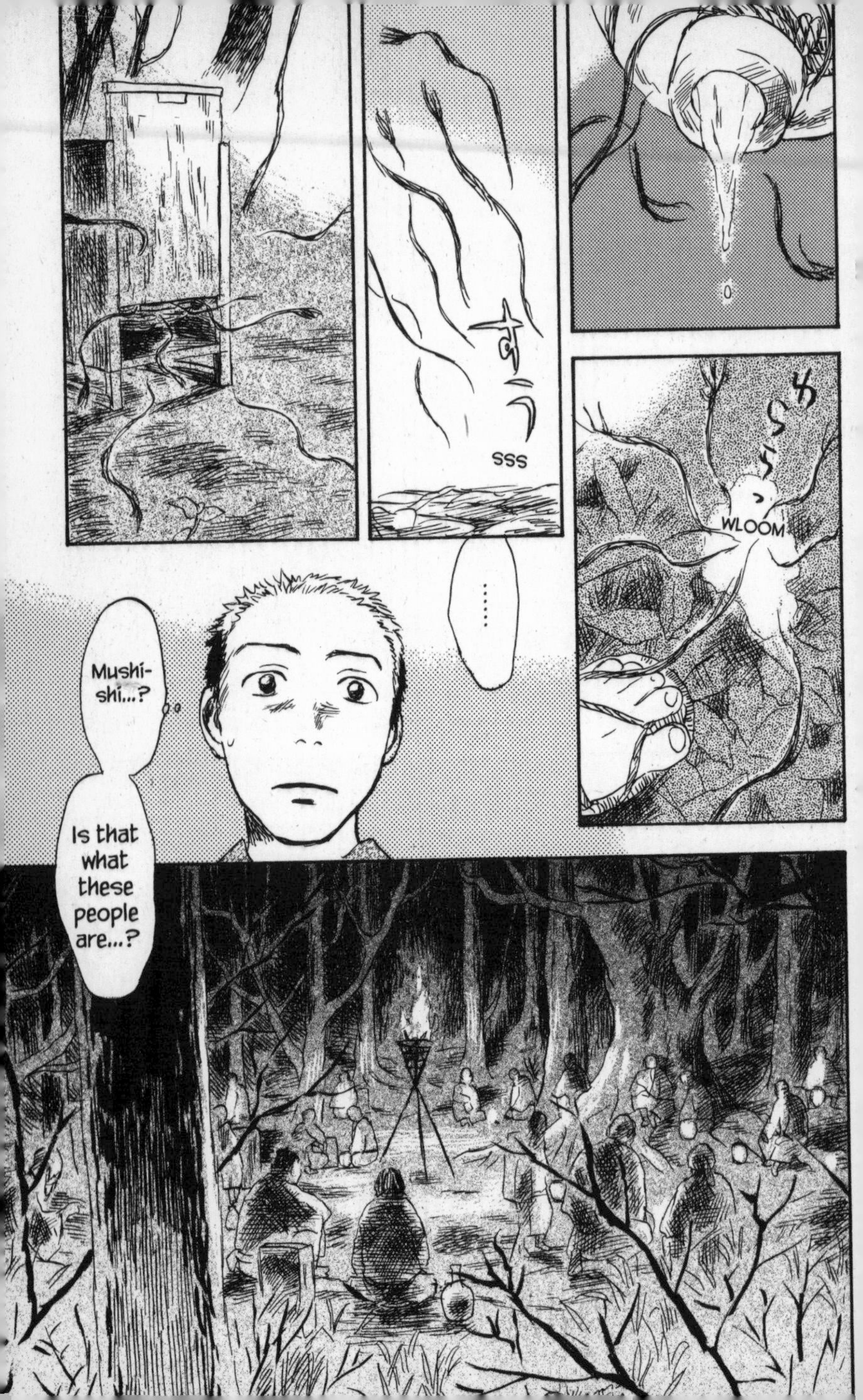
WLOOM
SSS
......
Mushi-shi...?
Is that what these people are...?

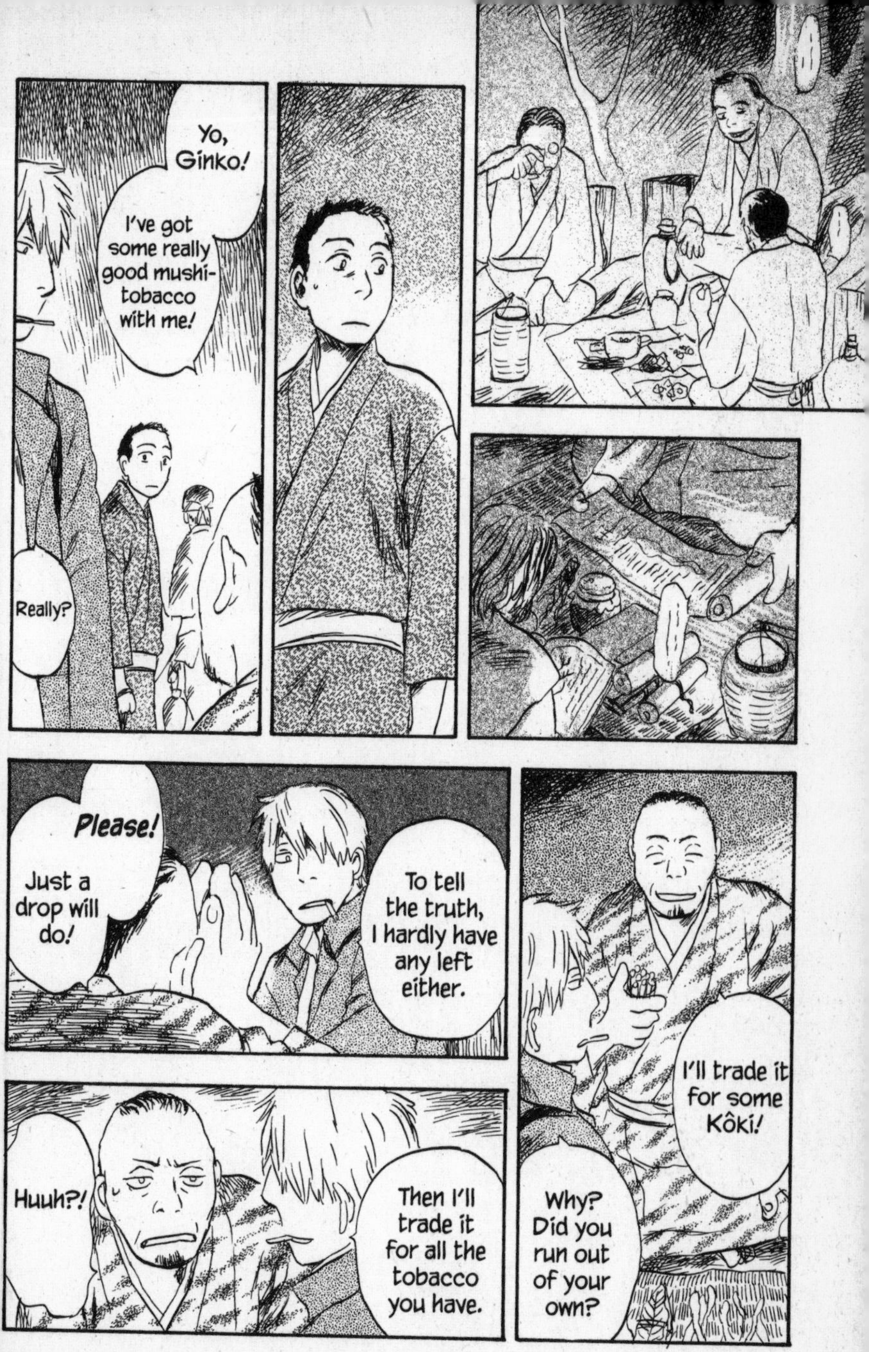
Yo, Ginko!
I've got some really good mushi-tobacco with me!
Really?
I'll trade it for some Kôki!
Why? Did you run out of your own?
To tell the truth, I hardly have any left either.
Please! Just a drop will do!
Then I'll trade it for all the tobacco you have.
Huuh?!

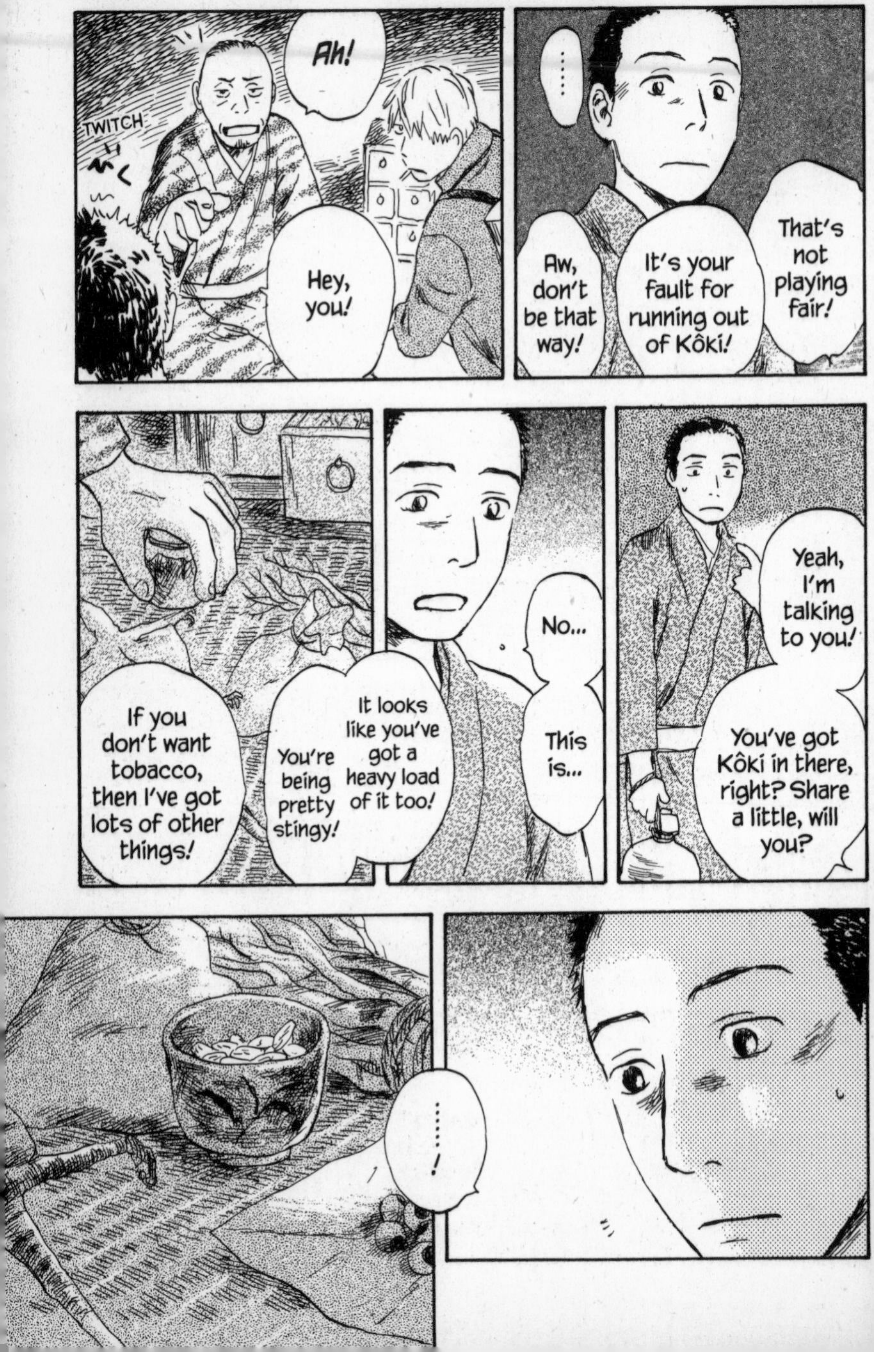
......
That's not playing fair!
It's your fault for running out of Kôki!
Aw, don't be that way!
Ah!
Hey, you!
TWITCH
Yeah, I'm talking to you!
You've got Kôki in there, right? Share a little, will you?
No...
This is...
It looks like you've got a heavy load of it too!
You're being pretty stingy!
If you don't want tobacco, then I've got lots of other things!
......!

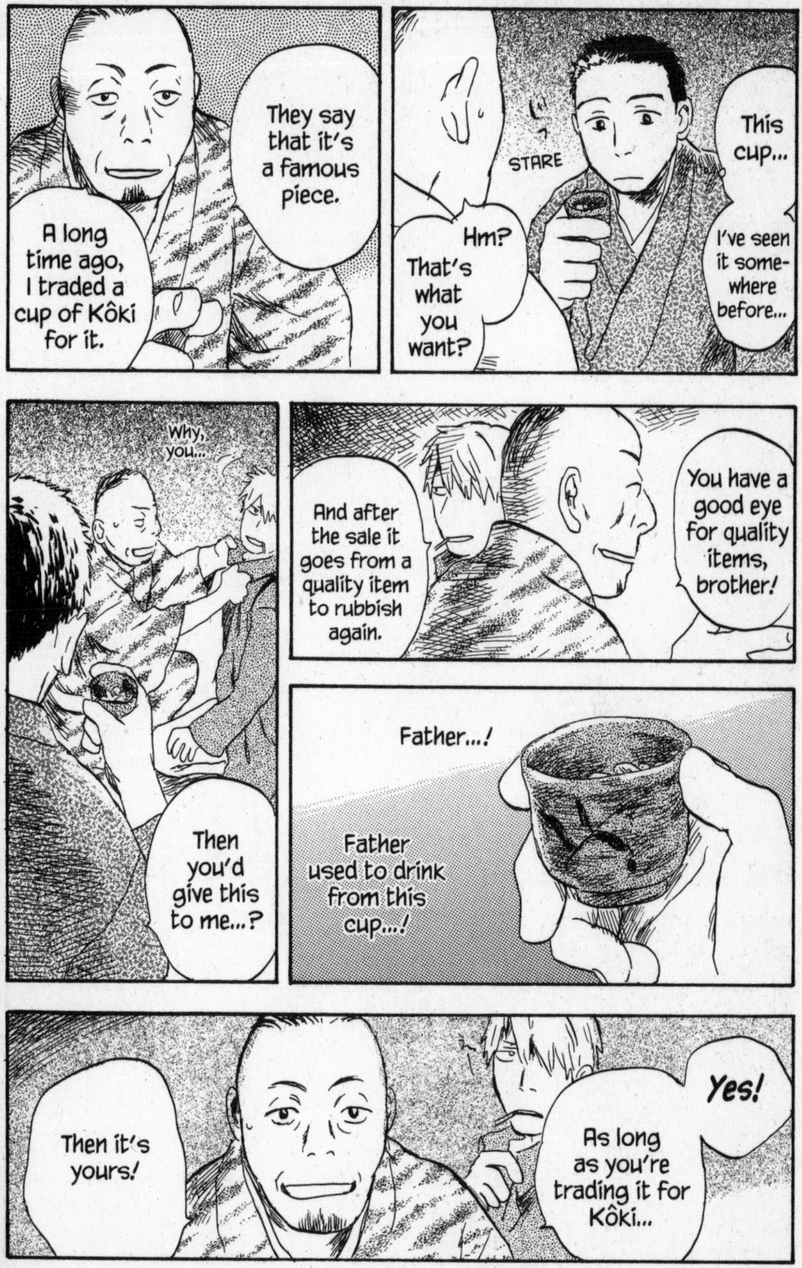
This cup...
I've seen it somewhere before...
STARE
Hm? That's what you want?
They say that it's a famous piece.
A long time ago, I traded a cup of Kôki for it.
You have a good eye for quality items, brother!
And after the sale it goes from a quality item to rubbish again.
Father...!
Father used to drink from this cup...!
Why, you...
Then you'd give this to me...?
Yes!
As long as you're trading it for Kôki...
Then it's yours!

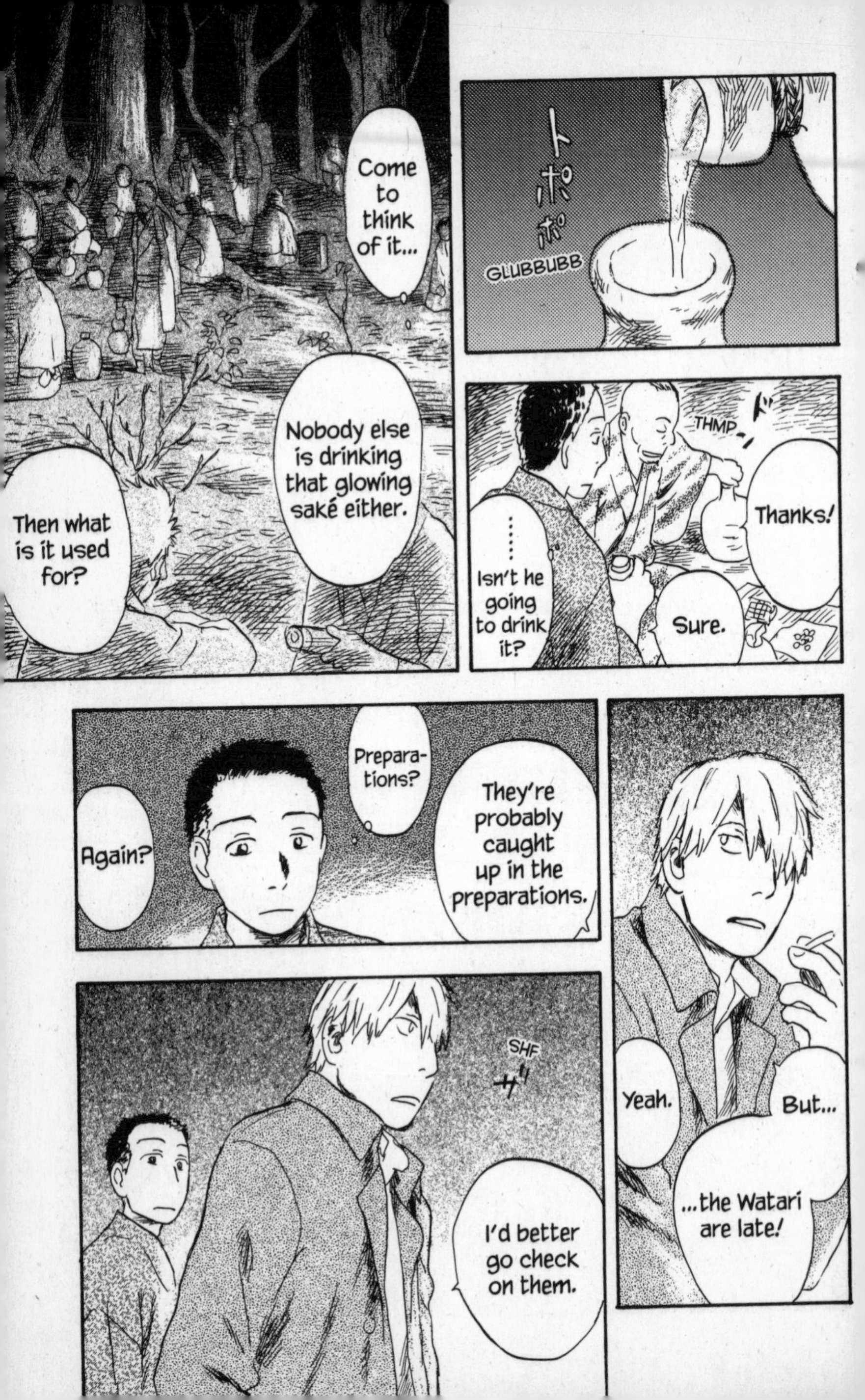
トポポ
GLUBBUBB
ド
THMP
Thanks!
Sure.
...... Isn't he going to drink it?
Come to think of it...
Nobody else is drinking that glowing saké either.
Then what is it used for?
Yeah.
But...
...the Watari are late!
They're probably caught up in the preparations.
Preparations?
Again?
サッ
SHF
I'd better go check on them.

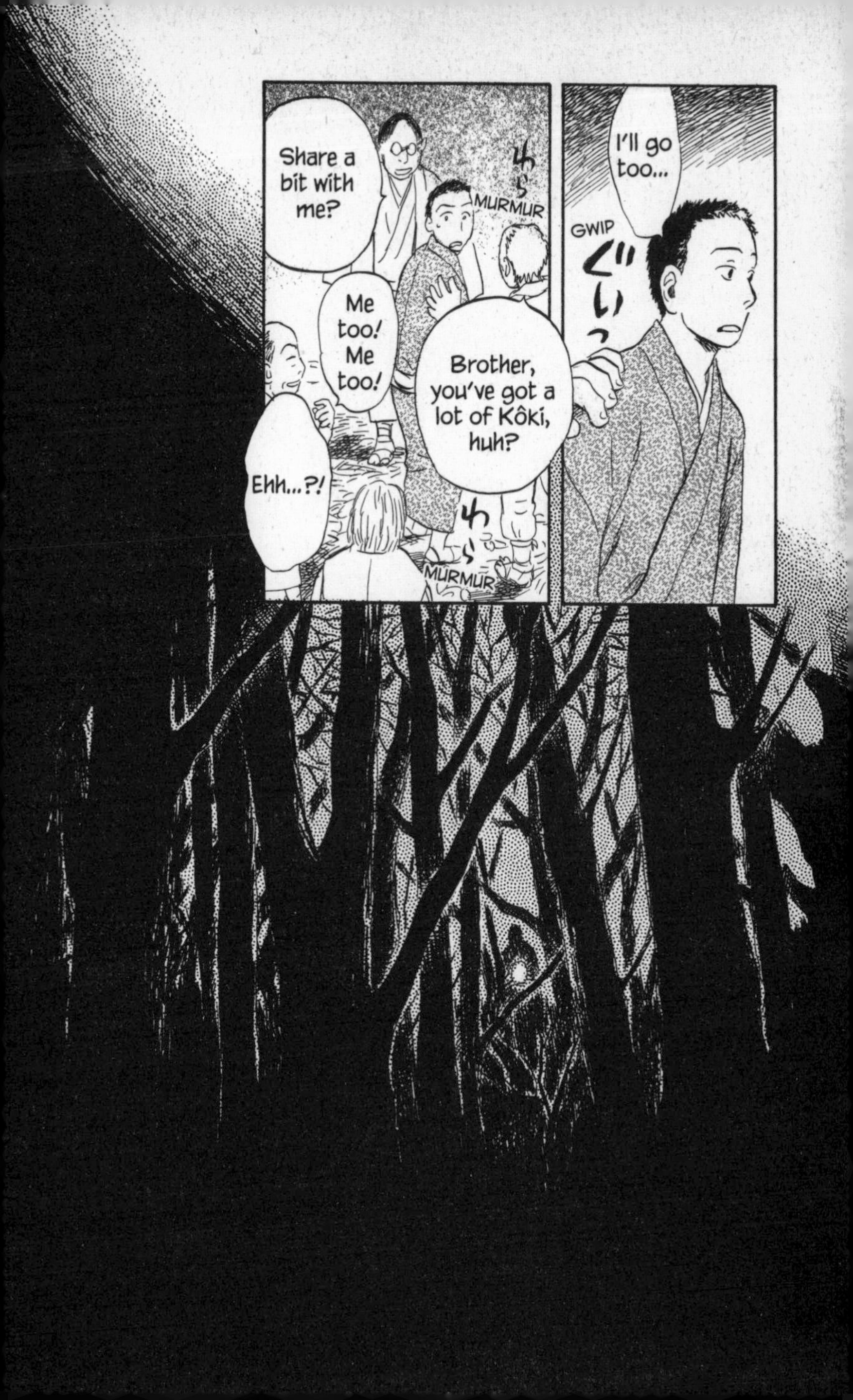
I'll go too...
GWIP
MURMUR
Share a bit with me?
Brother, you've got a lot of Kôki, huh?
Me too! Me too!
Ehh...?!
MURMUR

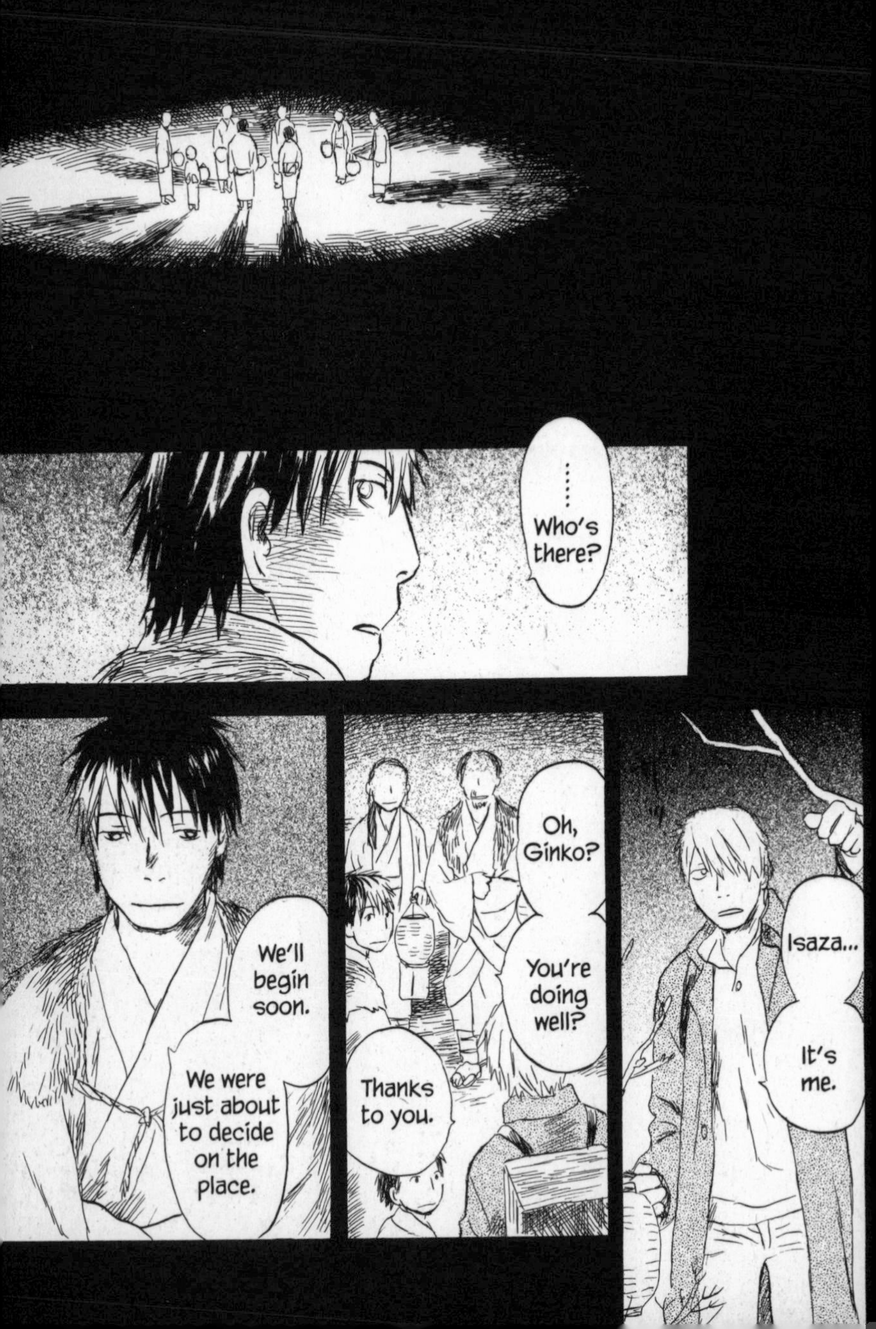
......
Who's there?
Isaza...
It's me.
Oh, Ginko?
You're doing well?
Thanks to you.
We'll begin soon.
We were just about to decide on the place.

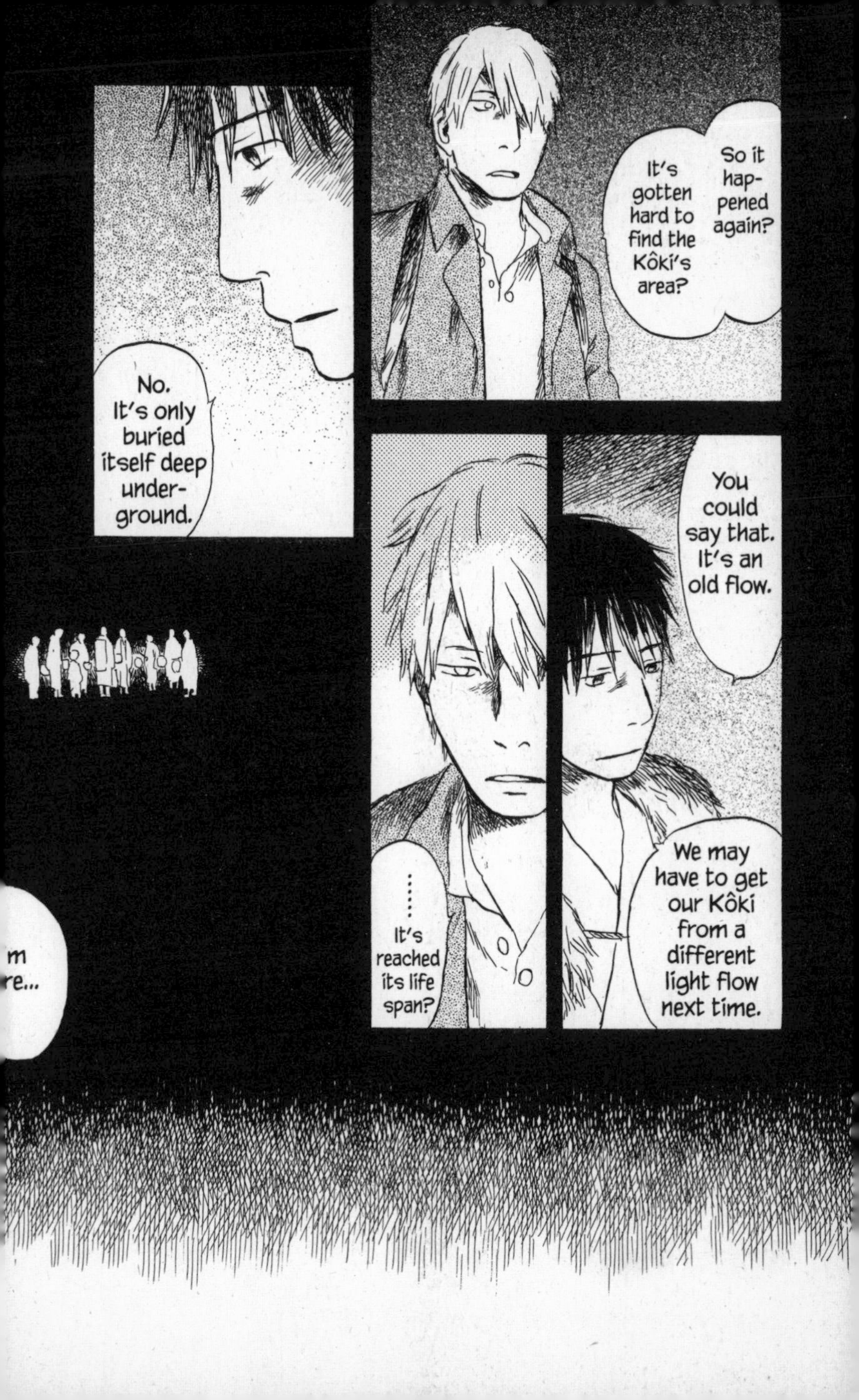
So it happened again?
It's gotten hard to find the Kôki's area?
No. It's only buried itself deep underground.
You could say that. It's an old flow.
We may have to get our Kôki from a different light flow next time.
...... It's reached its life span?

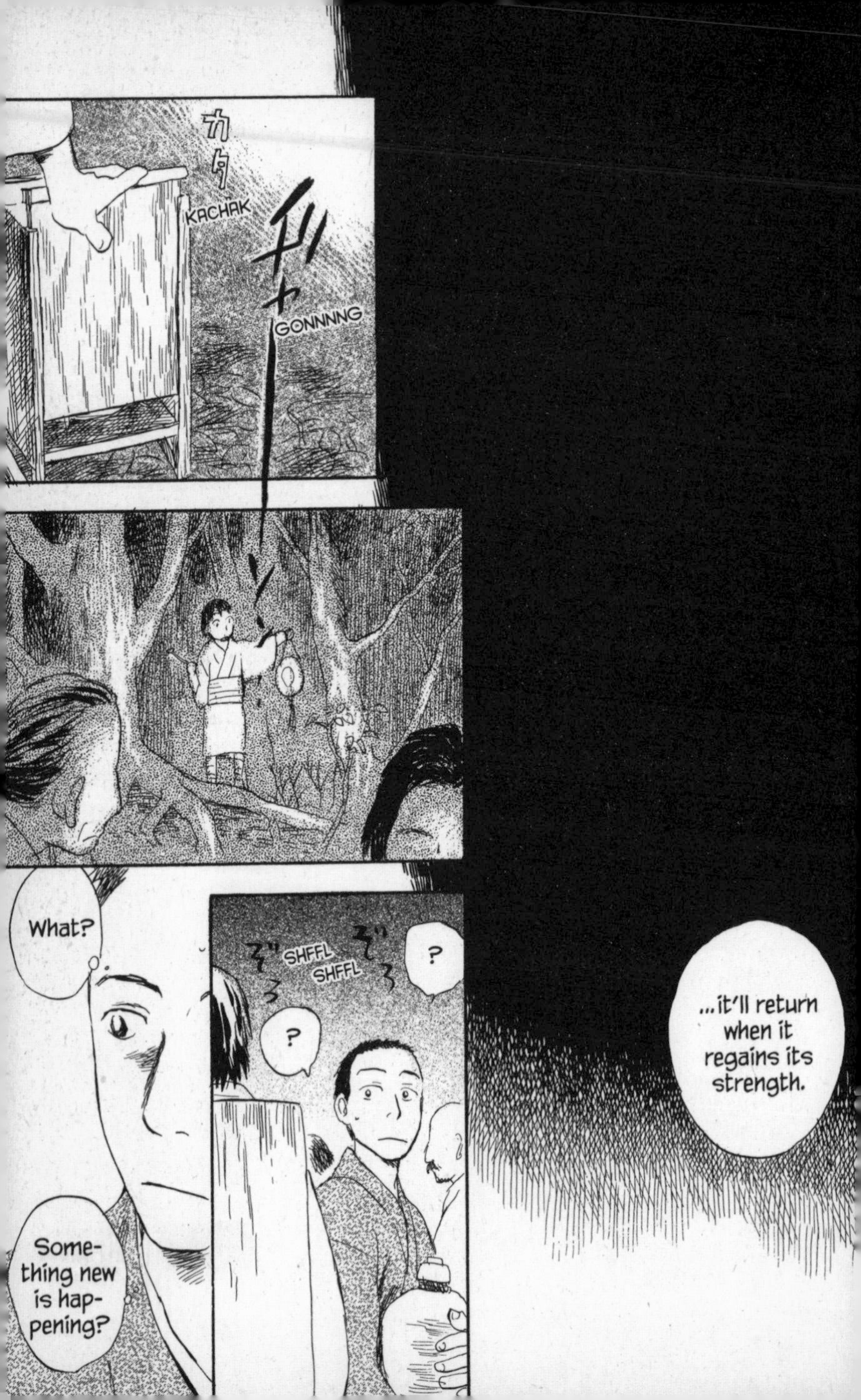
...it'll return when it regains its strength.
カタ
KACHAK
GONNNNG
?
SHFFL SHFFL
?
What?
Something new is happening?

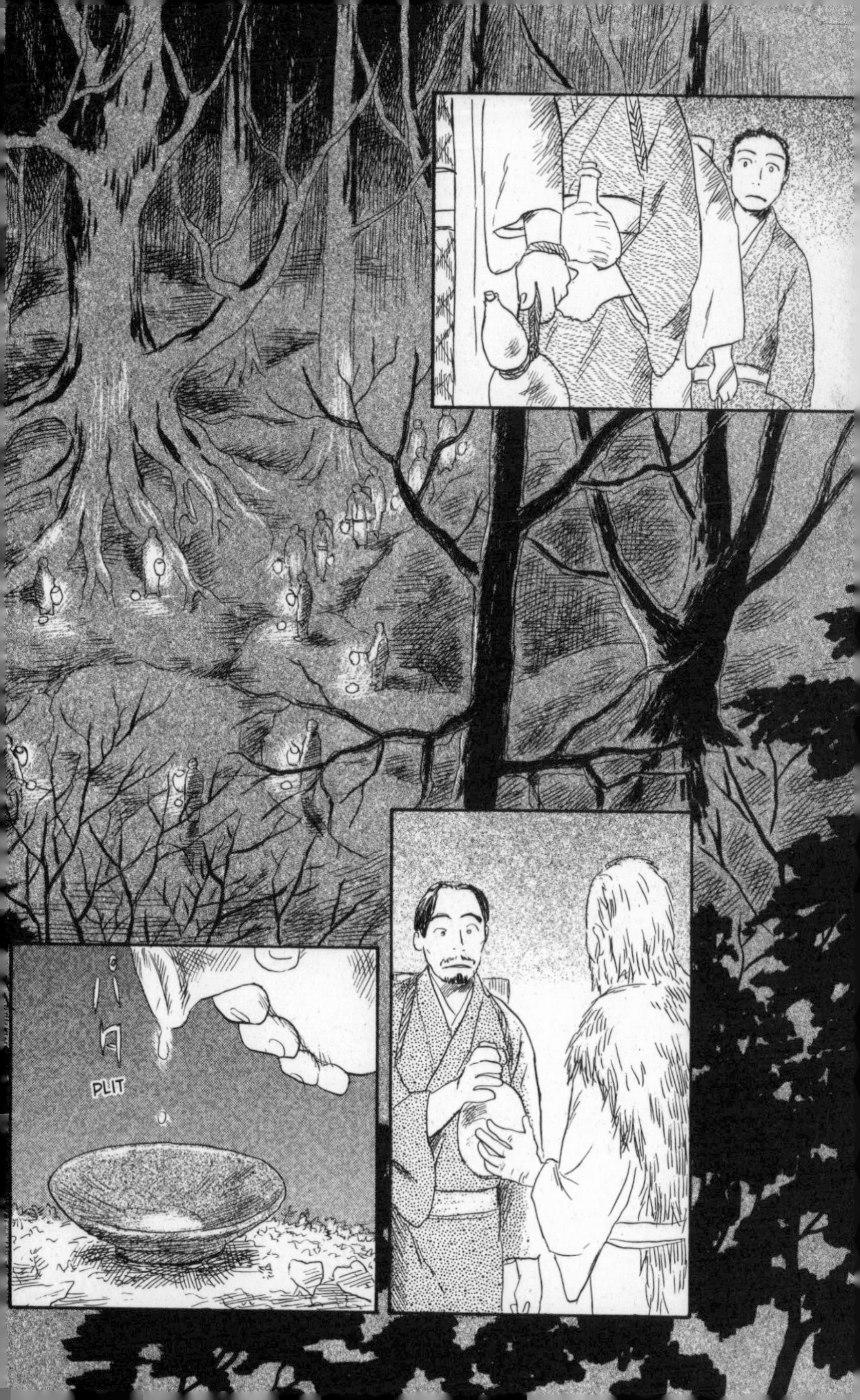
パク
PLIT

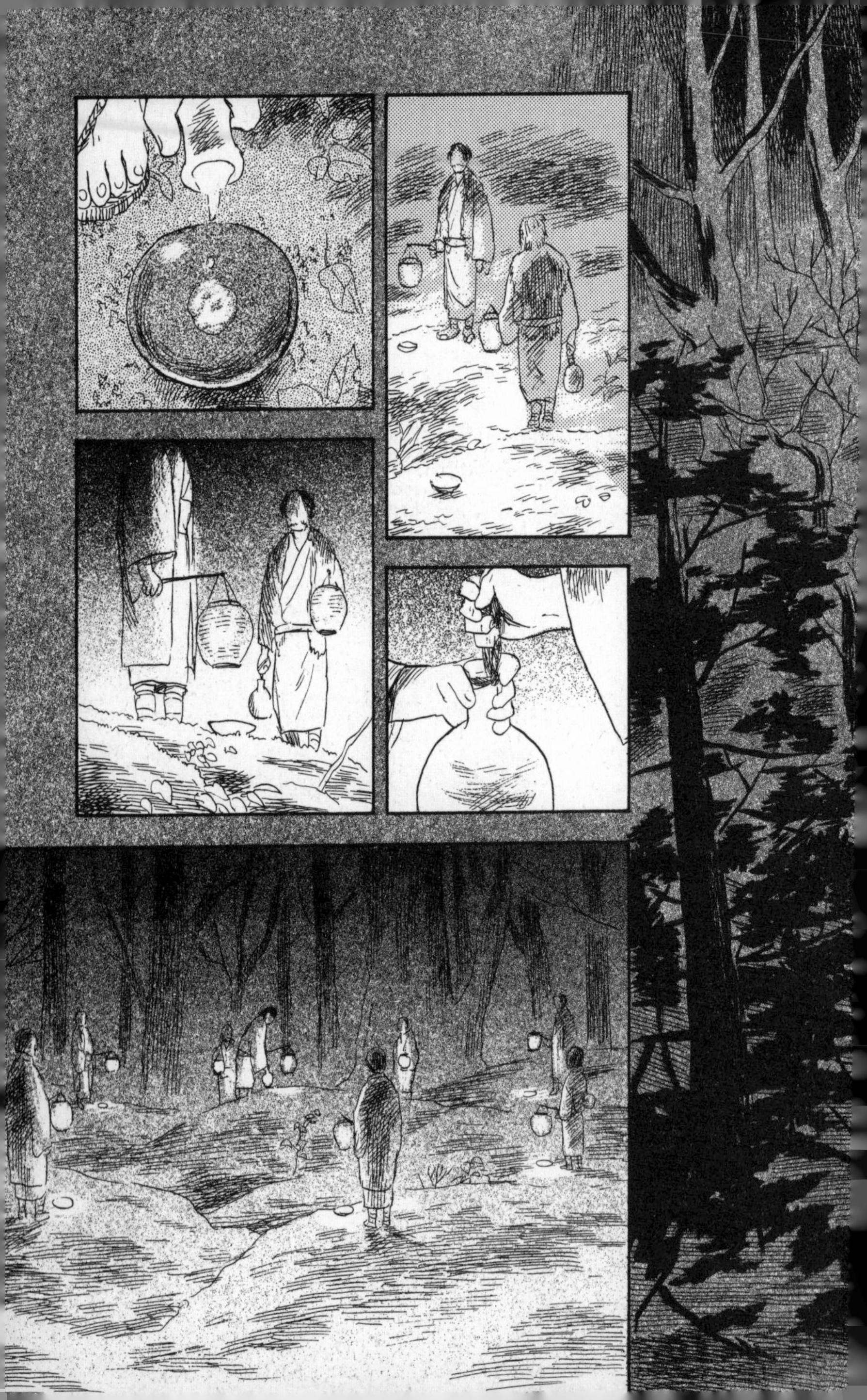

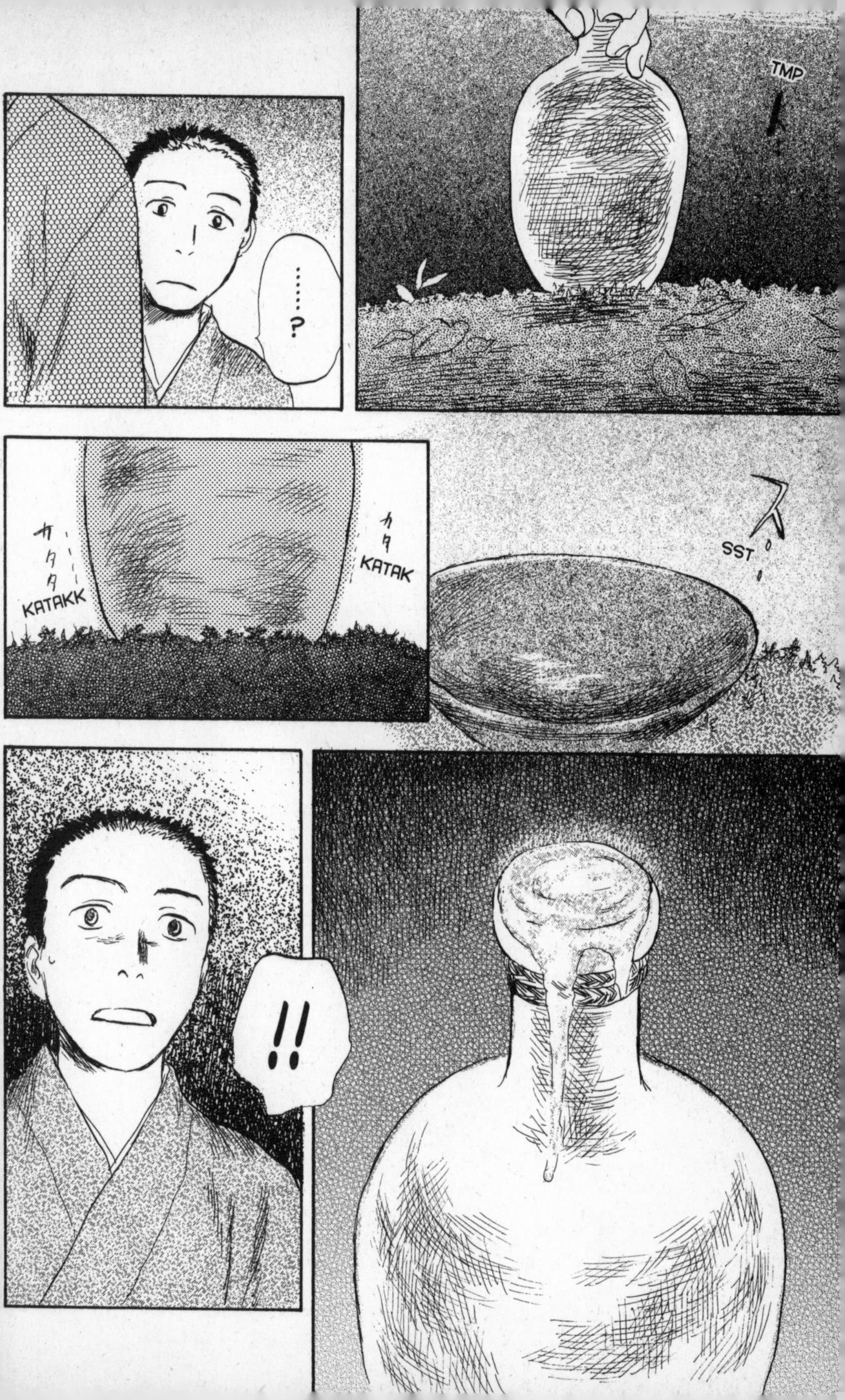

TMP
......?
ス
SST
カタ
KATAK
カタタ
KATAKK
!!

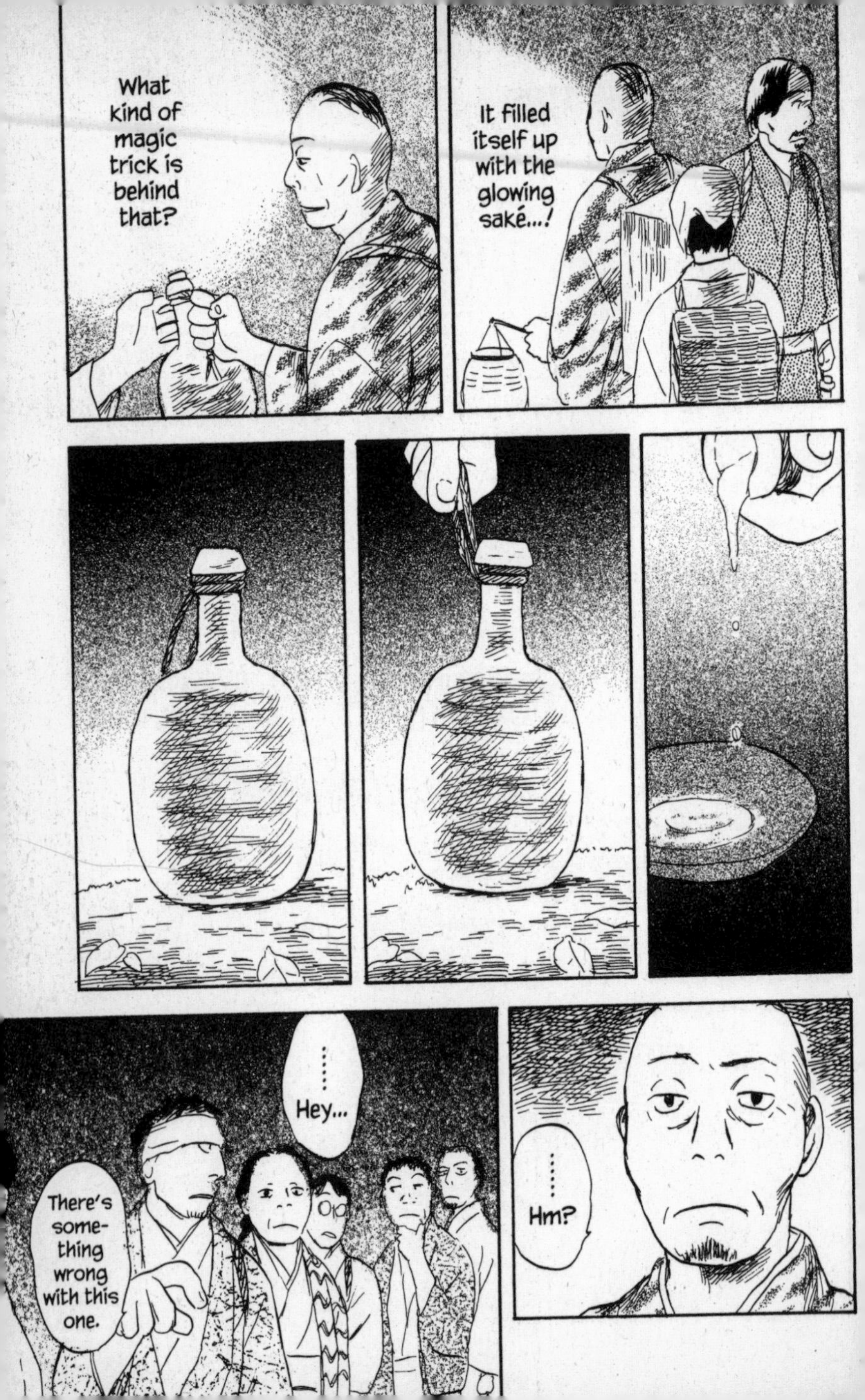
It filled itself up with the glowing saké...!
What kind of magic trick is behind that?
...... Hm?
...... Hey...
There's something wrong with this one.

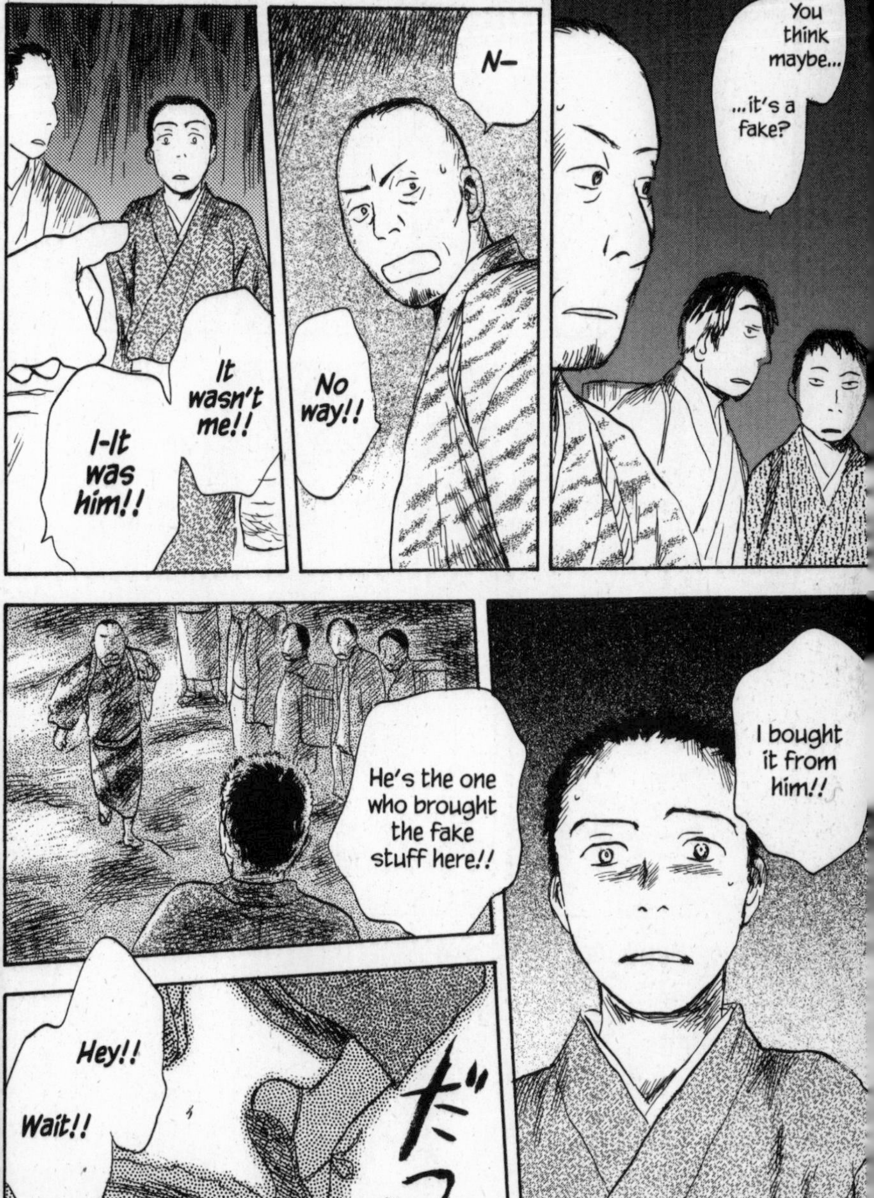
You think maybe...
...it's a fake?
N-
No way!!
It wasn't me!!
I-It was him!!
I bought it from him!!
He's the one who brought the fake stuff here!!
Hey!!
Wait!!
だっ
TMP

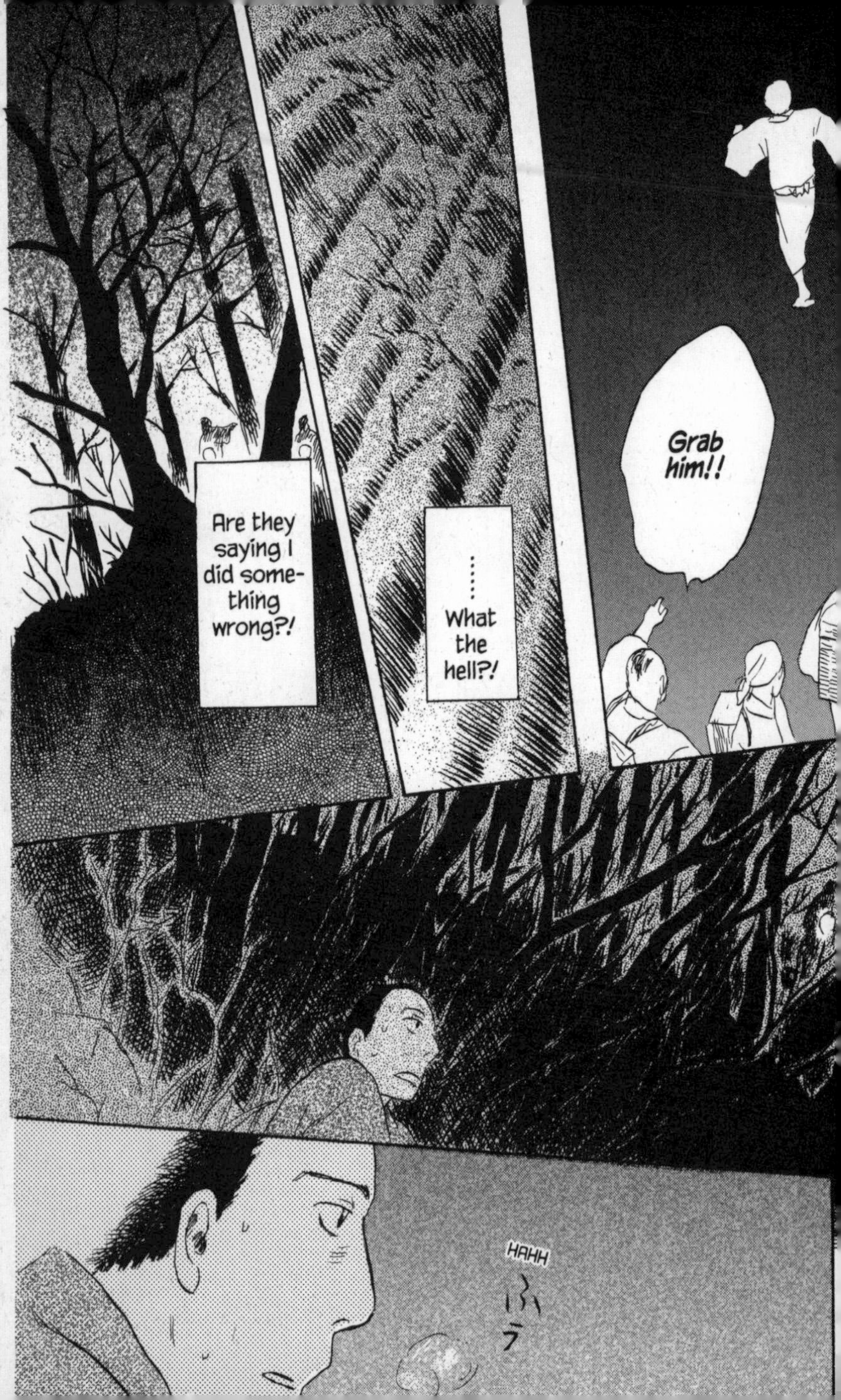
Grab him!!
..... What the hell?!
Are they saying I did some-thing wrong?!
HAHH
ふう

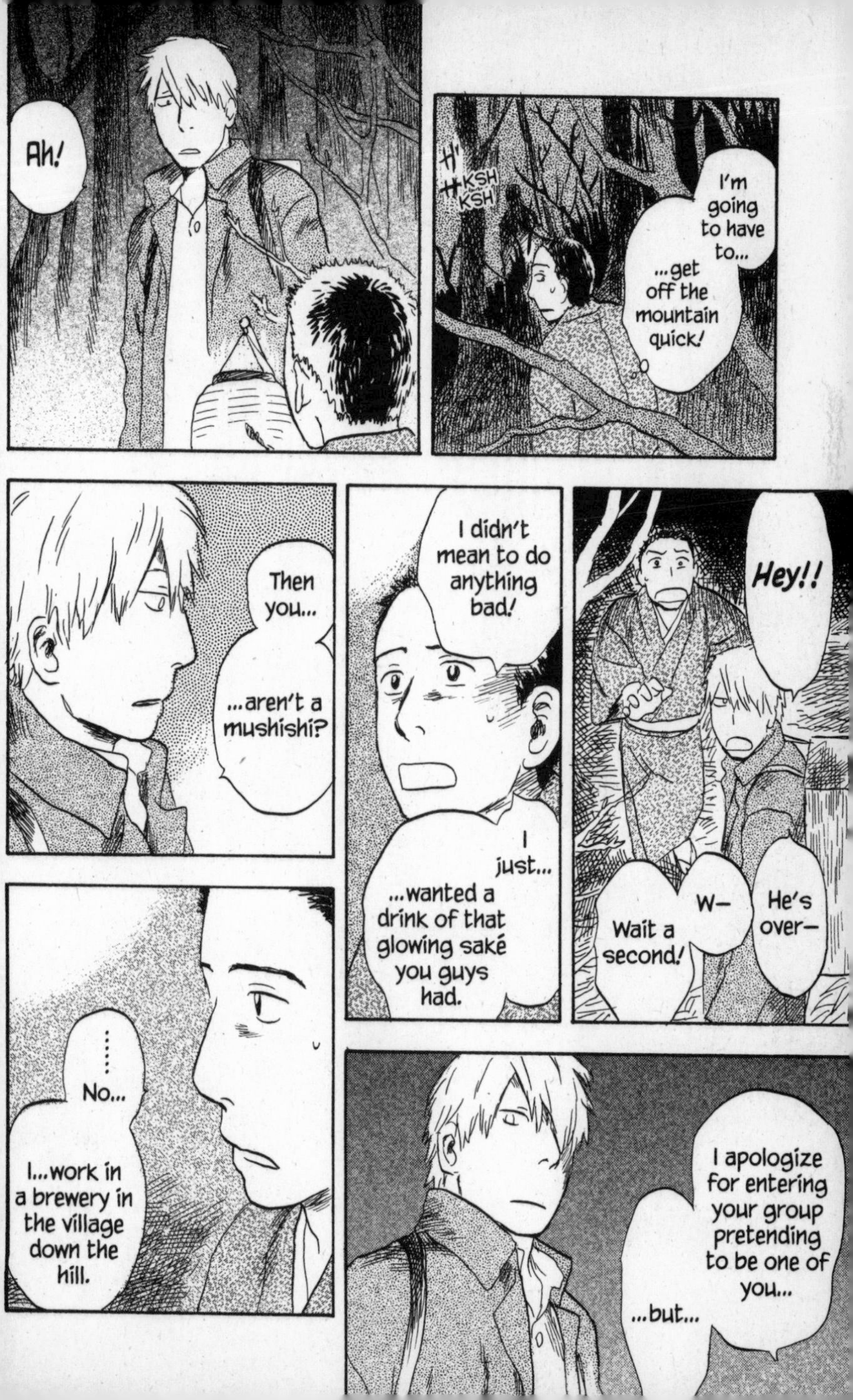
KSH KSH
I'm going to have to...
...get off the mountain quick!
Ah!
Hey!!
He's over—
W—
Wait a second!
I didn't mean to do anything bad!
I just...
...wanted a drink of that glowing saké you guys had.
I apologize for entering your group pretending to be one of you...
...but...
Then you...
...aren't a mushishi?
......
No...
I...work in a brewery in the village down the hill.

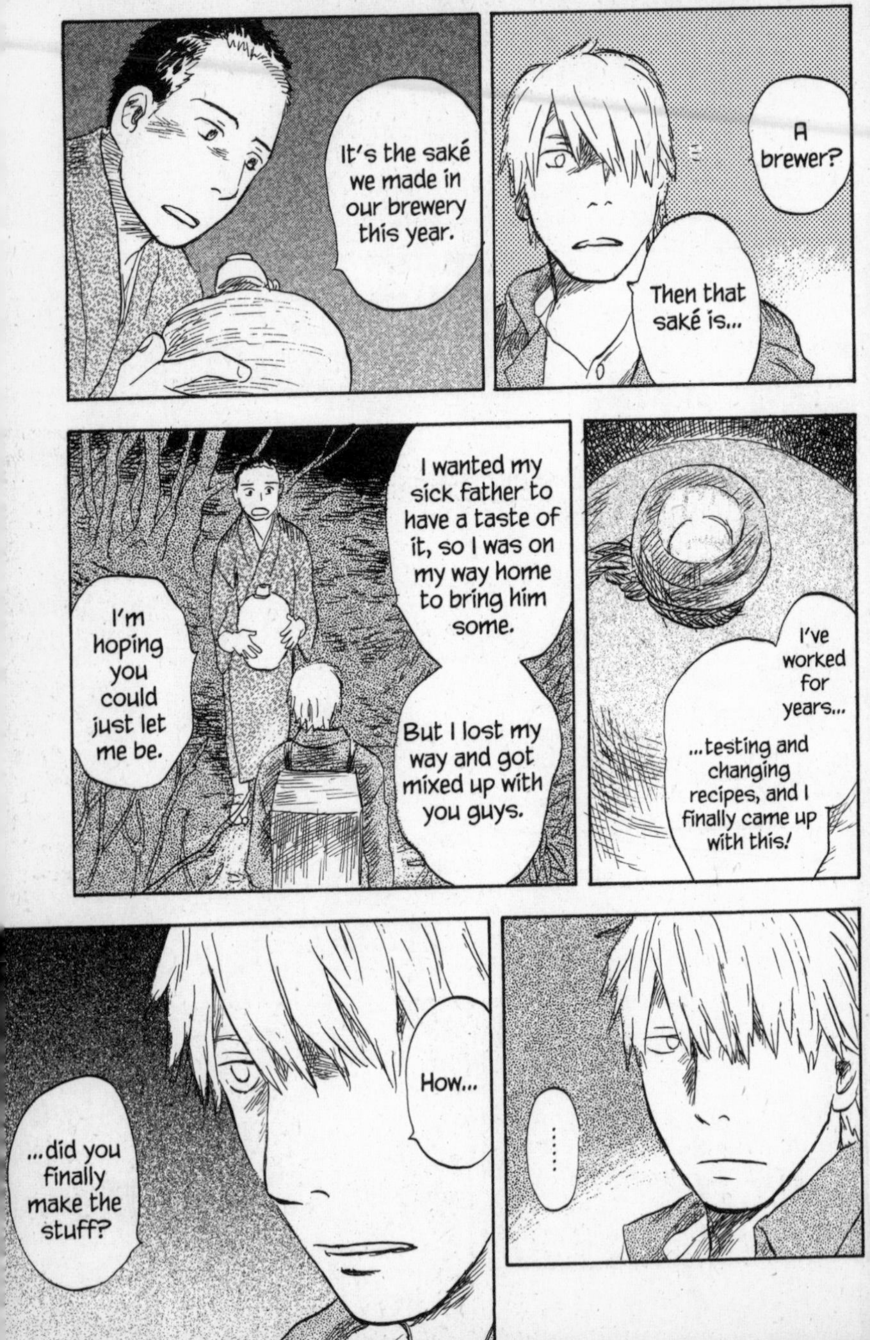
A brewer?
Then that saké is...
It's the saké we made in our brewery this year.
I've worked for years...
...testing and changing recipes, and I finally came up with this!
I wanted my sick father to have a taste of it, so I was on my way home to bring him some.
But I lost my way and got mixed up with you guys.
I'm hoping you could just let me be.
......
How...
...did you finally make the stuff?

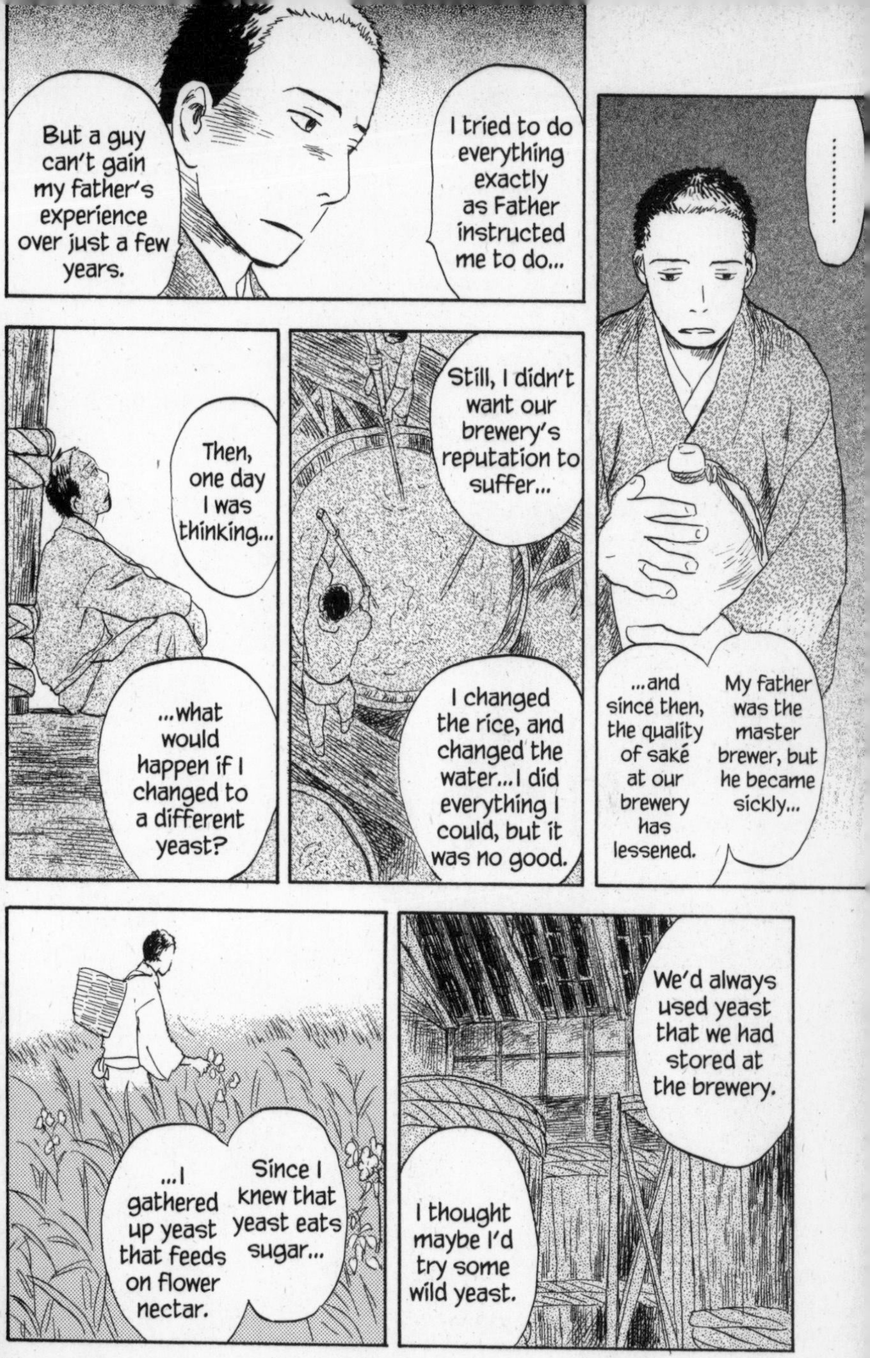
……
My father was the master brewer, but he became sickly...
...and since then, the quality of saké at our brewery has lessened.
I tried to do everything exactly as Father instructed me to do...
But a guy can't gain my father's experience over just a few years.
Still, I didn't want our brewery's reputation to suffer...
I changed the rice, and changed the water... I did everything I could, but it was no good.
Then, one day I was thinking...
...what would happen if I changed to a different yeast?
We'd always used yeast that we had stored at the brewery.
I thought maybe I'd try some wild yeast.
Since I knew that yeast eats sugar...
...I gathered up yeast that feeds on flower nectar.

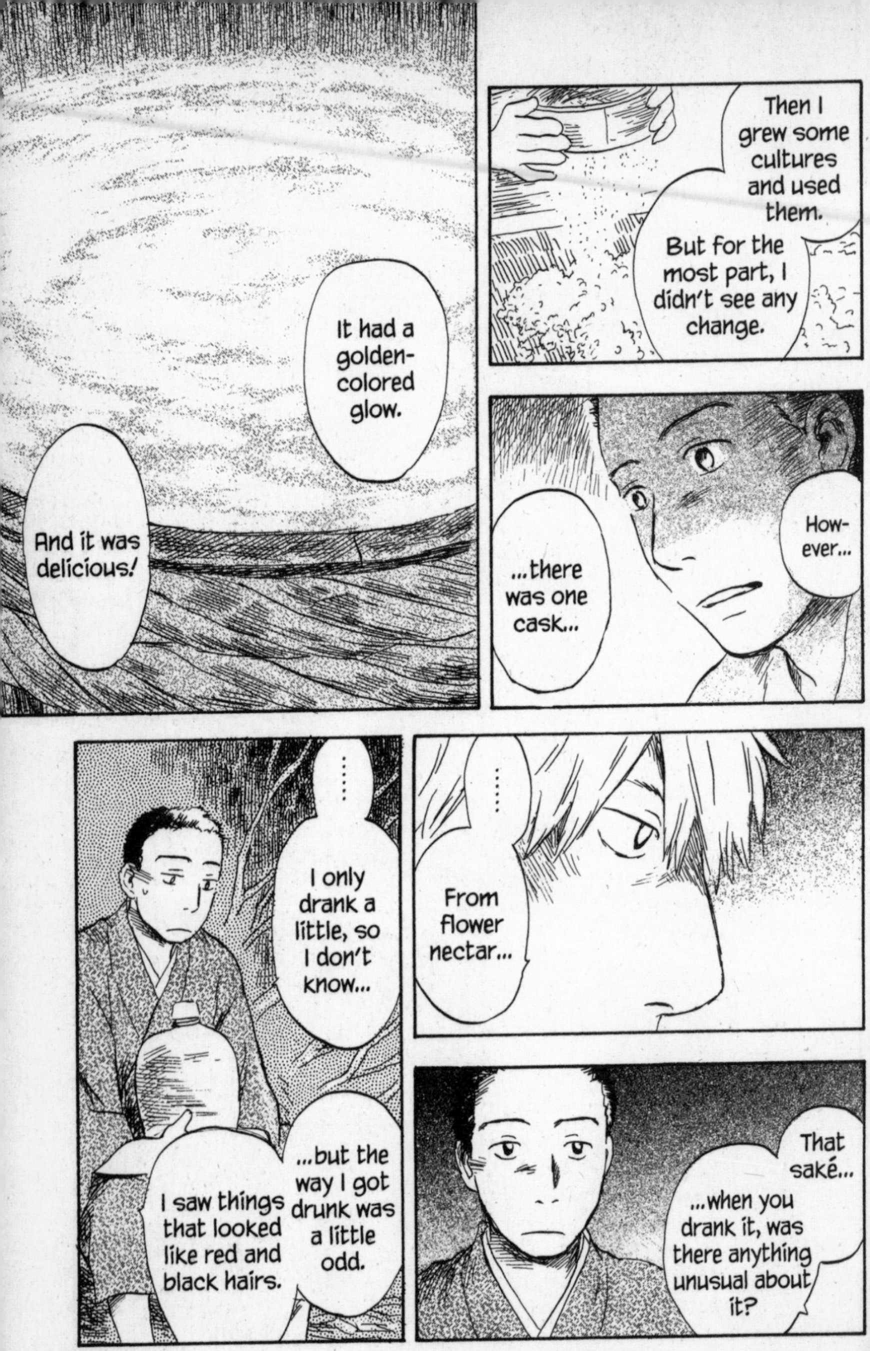

Then I grew some cultures and used them.
But for the most part, I didn't see any change.
How-ever...
...there was one cask...
It had a golden-colored glow.
And it was delicious!
......
From flower nectar...
That saké...
...when you drank it, was there anything unusual about it?
......
I only drank a little, so I don't know...
...but the way I got drunk was a little odd.
I saw things that looked like red and black hairs.

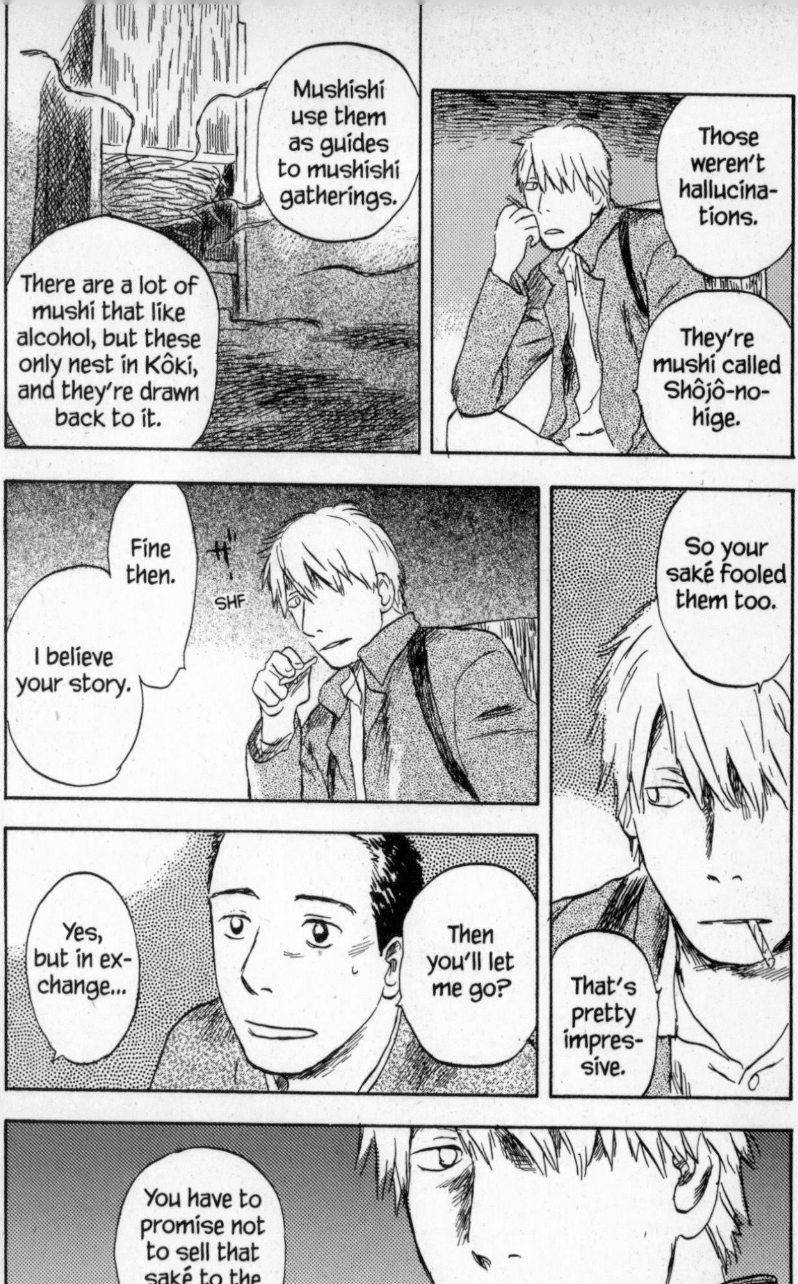
Those weren't hallucinations.
They're mushi called Shôjô-no-hige.
Mushishi use them as guides to mushishi gatherings.
There are a lot of mushi that like alcohol, but these only nest in Kôki, and they're drawn back to it.
So your saké fooled them too.
That's pretty impressive.
SHF
Fine then.
I believe your story.
Then you'll let me go?
Yes, but in exchange...
You have to promise not to sell that saké to the public.

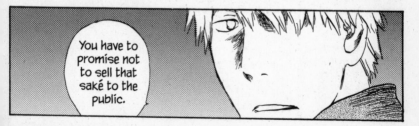

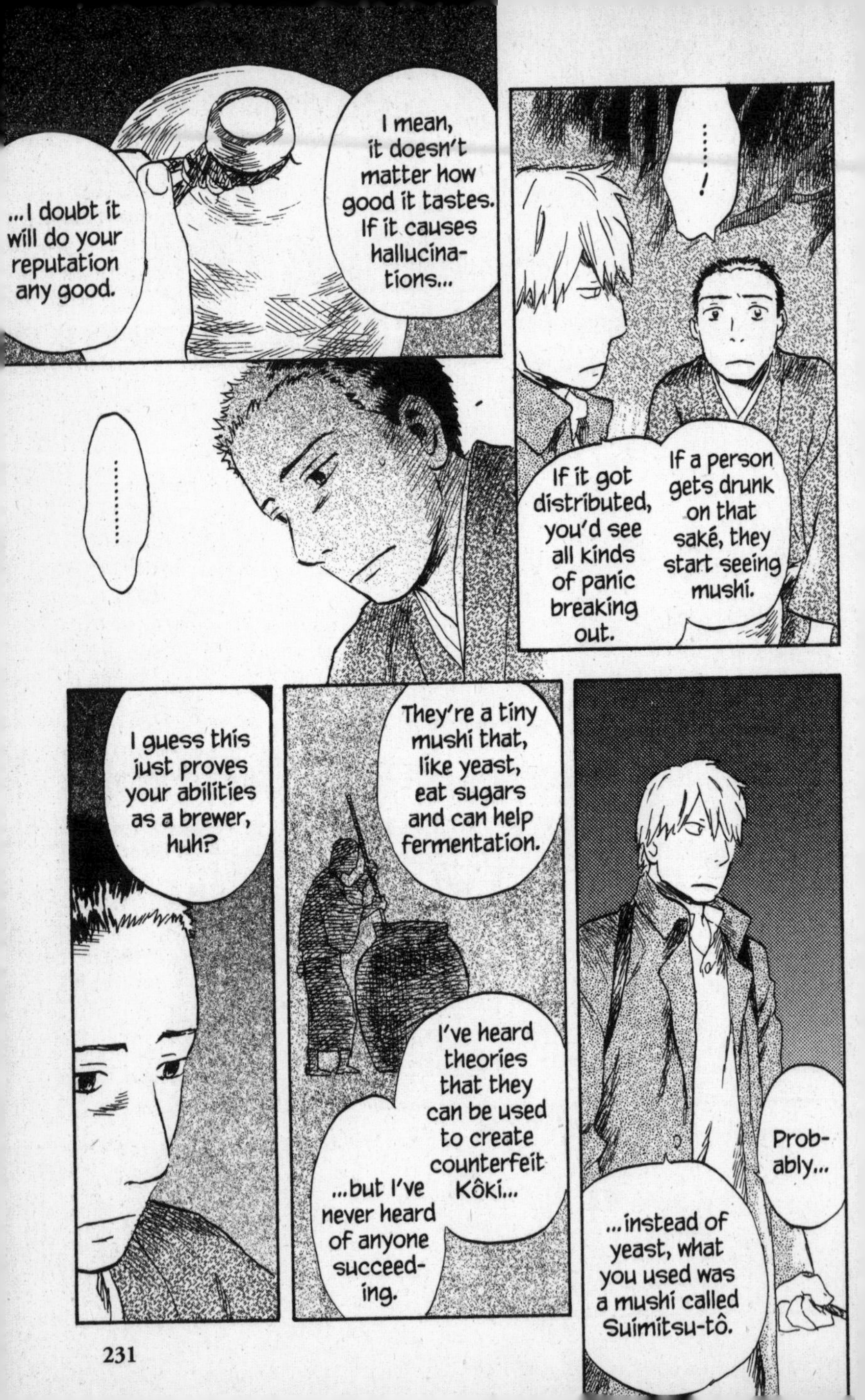
.....!
If a person gets drunk on that saké, they start seeing mushi.
If it got distributed, you'd see all kinds of panic breaking out.
I mean, it doesn't matter how good it tastes. If it causes hallucina-tions...
...I doubt it will do your reputation any good.
....
Prob-ably...
...instead of yeast, what you used was a mushi called Suimitsu-tô.
They're a tiny mushi that, like yeast, eat sugars and can help fermentation.
I've heard theories that they can be used to create counterfeit Kôki...
...but I've never heard of anyone succeed-ing.
I guess this just proves your abilities as a brewer, huh?

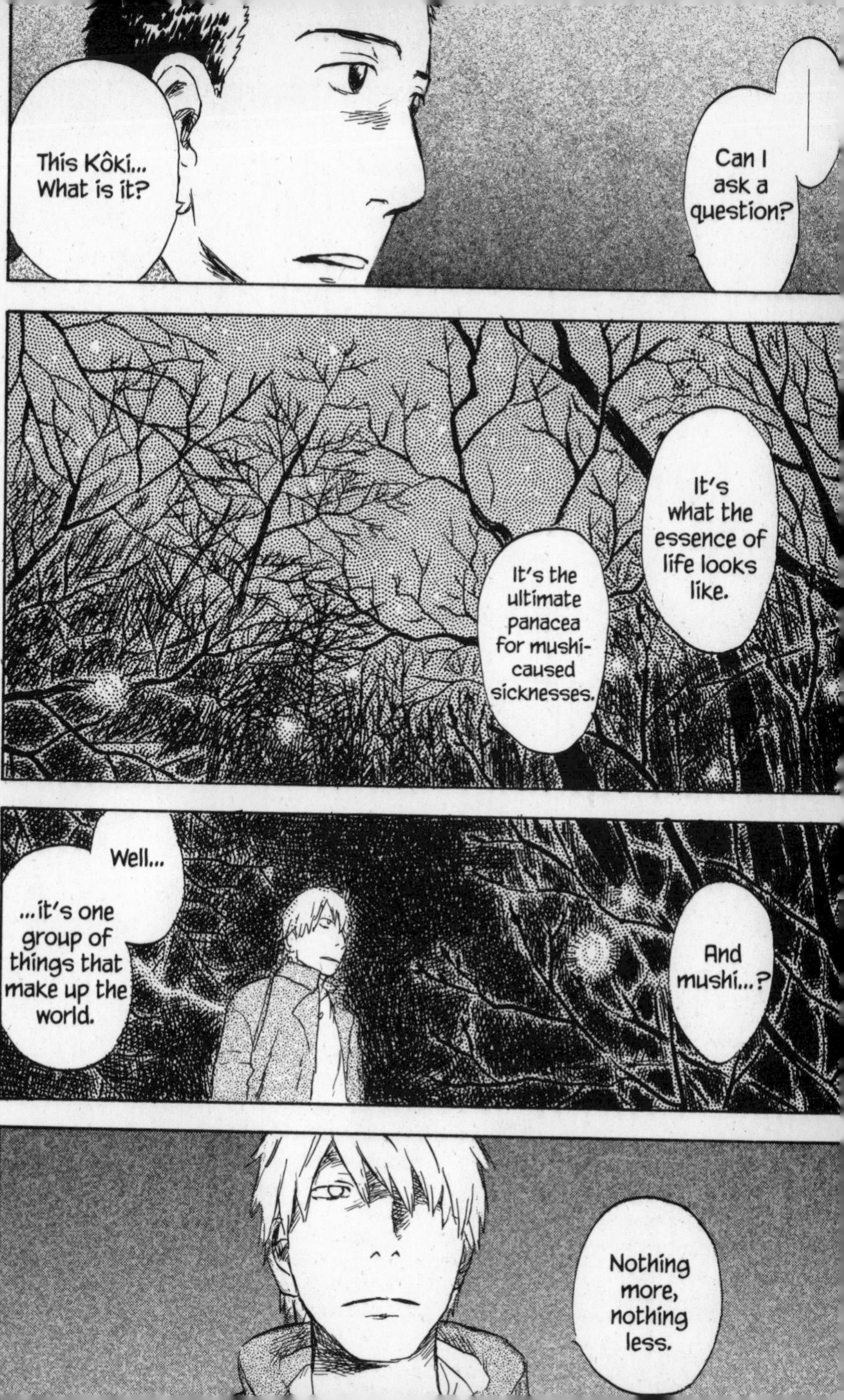
Can I ask a question?
This Kôki... What is it?
It's what the essence of life looks like.
It's the ultimate panacea for mushi-caused sicknesses.
And mushi...?
Well...
...it's one group of things that make up the world.
Nothing more, nothing less.

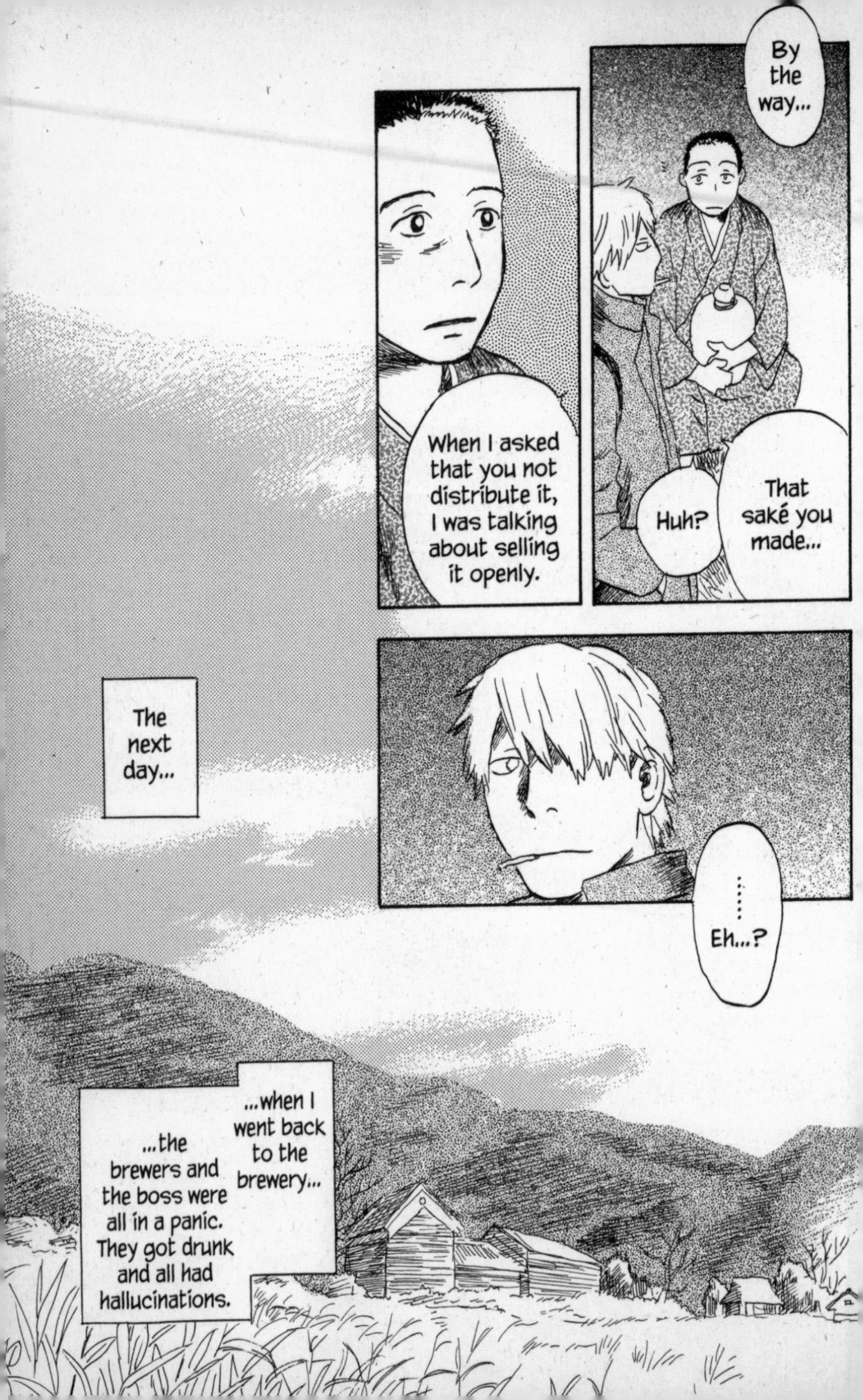
By the way...
That saké you made...
Huh?
When I asked that you not distribute it, I was talking about selling it openly.
......
Eh...?
The next day...
...when I went back to the brewery...
...the brewers and the boss were all in a panic. They got drunk and all had hallucinations.

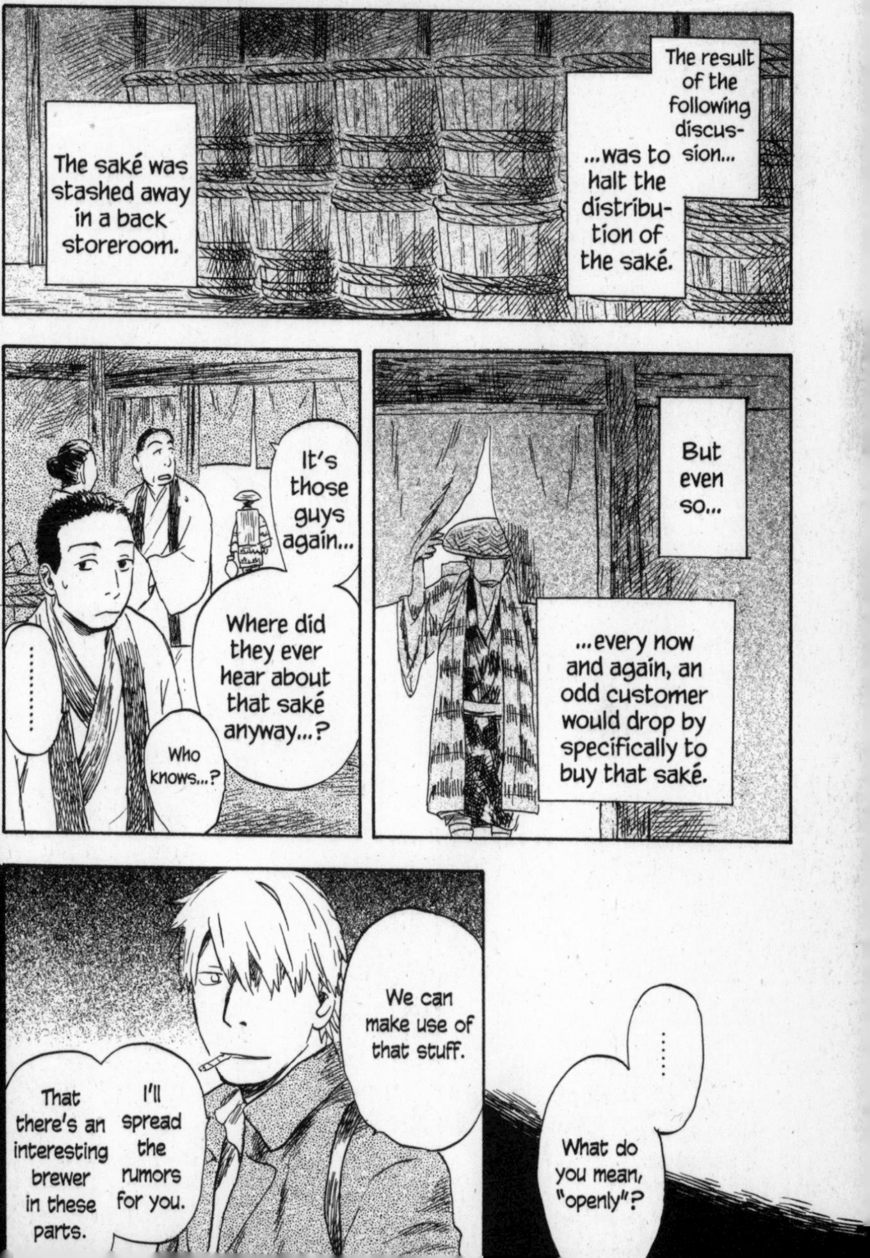
The result of the following discus-sion...
...was to halt the distribu-tion of the saké.
The saké was stashed away in a back storeroom.
But even so...
...every now and again, an odd customer would drop by specifically to buy that saké.
It's those guys again...
Where did they ever hear about that saké anyway...?
......
Who knows...?
......
What do you mean, "openly"?
We can make use of that stuff.
I'll spread the rumors for you.
That there's an interesting brewer in these parts.

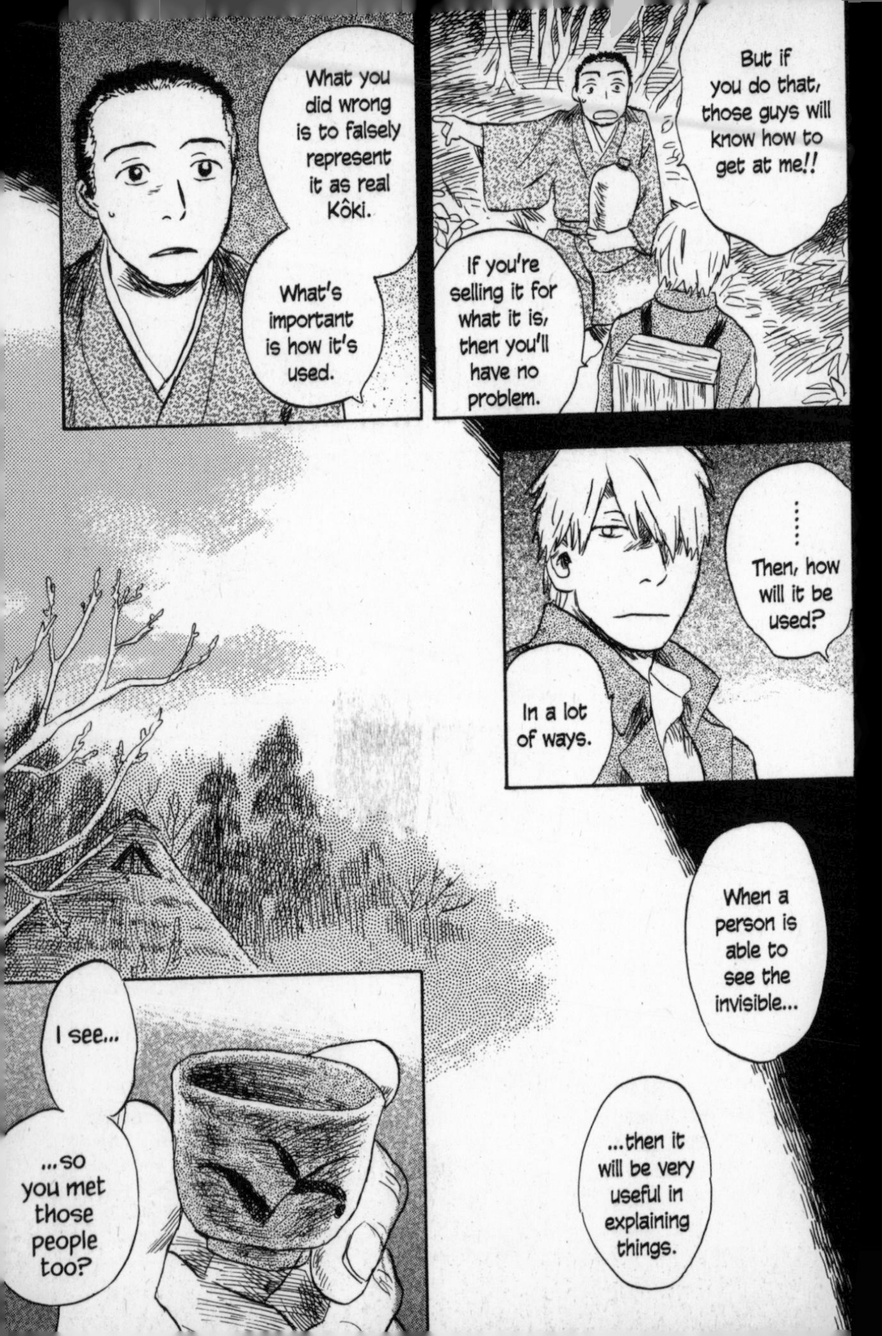
But if you do that, those guys will know how to get at me!!
If you're selling it for what it is, then you'll have no problem.
What you did wrong is to falsely represent it as real Kôki.
What's important is how it's used.
……
Then, how will it be used?
In a lot of ways.
When a person is able to see the invisible...
...then it will be very useful in explaining things.
I see...
...so you met those people too?

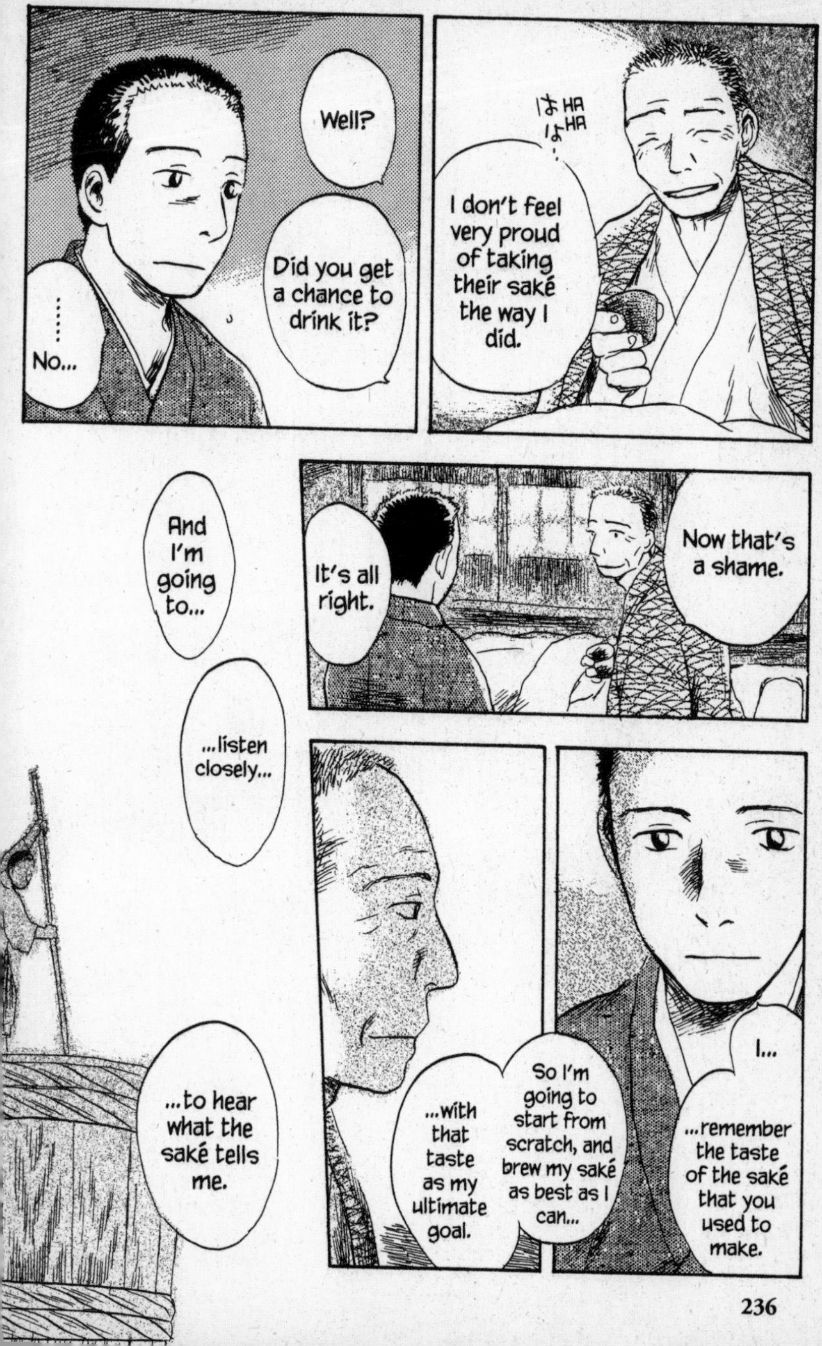
は HA
は HA
I don't feel very proud of taking their saké the way I did.
Well?
Did you get a chance to drink it?
......
No...
Now that's a shame.
It's all right.
I...
...remember the taste of the saké that you used to make.
So I'm going to start from scratch, and brew my saké as best as I can...
...with that taste as my ultimate goal.
And I'm going to...
...listen closely...
...to hear what the saké tells me.

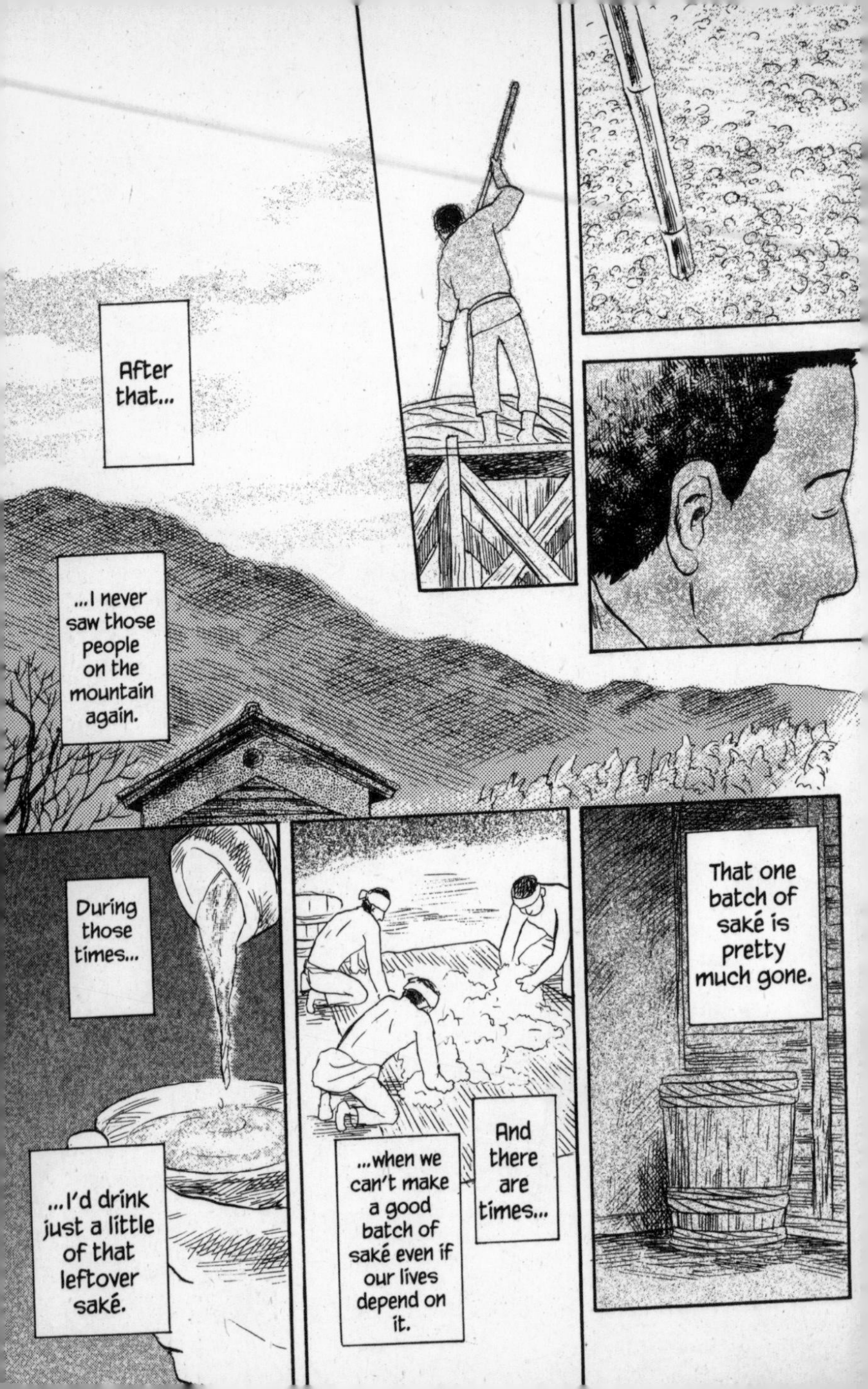
After that...
...I never saw those people on the mountain again.
That one batch of saké is pretty much gone.
And there are times...
...when we can't make a good batch of saké even if our lives depend on it.
During those times...
...I'd drink just a little of that leftover saké.

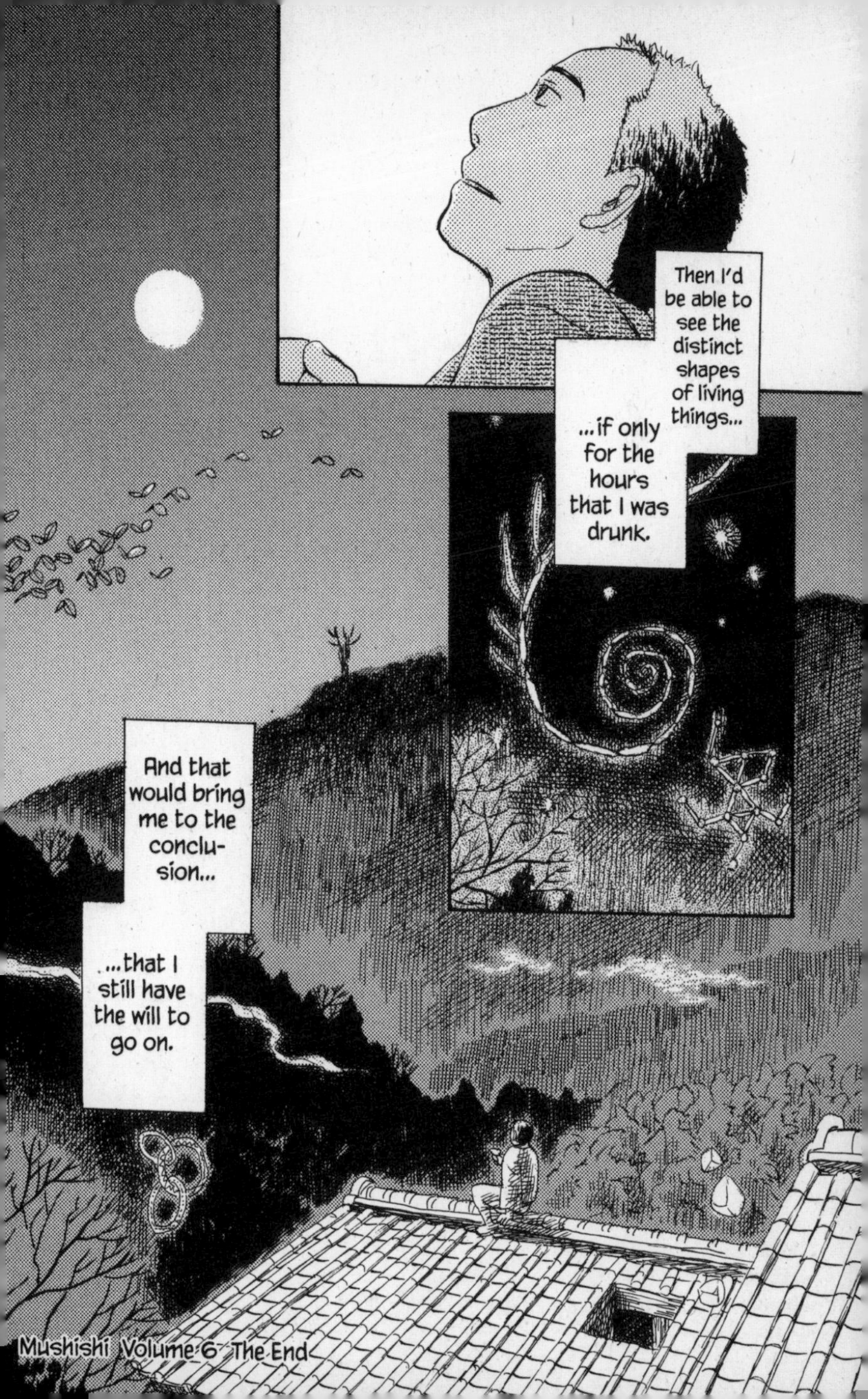
Then I'd be able to see the distinct shapes of living things...
...if only for the hours that I was drunk.
And that would bring me to the conclusion...
...that I still have the will to go on.
Mushishi Volume 6 The End

Afterword

Every previous volume of this manga appeared in the autumn, but this time it's coming out during the rainy season.

<Heaven's Thread> This is a story I thought of when reflecting on folk tales my grandmother told me. Tales about how missing people were left upon a huge rock. There are similar folk tales all over, but most of them involve finding people in trees or on rooftops. They were usually blamed on Tengu or other spirits who abduct people.

<The Chirping Shell> This story came from a time when I mused that it would be interesting if you didn't hear the ocean in a shell but rather a different sound. But I'd hate it if that sound was a human voice.

<The Hand That Pets the Night> A long time ago, I saw a snake hunt down a frog. The frog should have easily seen the snake coming, but it didn't run away. I thought it over several ways: "Maybe the idea that snakes hypnotize frogs isn't just a old wives' tale...Maybe the frog is so scared, it can't move..." Or maybe the frog realized that running away was useless.

<Under the Snow> A bedtime story I really loved as a child was "The Snow Queen." Maybe that was an influence. Even today I love stories about children and snow. I reread it recently. The boy main character was such a loser, it's possible that my love of hopeless-case characters stems from there.

<Banquet in the Farthest Field> I lived in an apartment which looked out on a brewery, and that became the model for this story. It had a nice atmosphere, but I had to move away, so now whenever I taste saké that's been strained through cloth, I get a very nostalgic feeling.

It's nice to read during the long rainy days, isn't it? If one of the books you're carrying is mine, it'll make me very happy.

Until next time.

<Thank yous for this volume>
Tnaka, Mami-chin, Yōko-chan, Yone, Hiro, Yayoi-chan!!

Translation Notes

Japanese is a tricky language for most Westerners, and translation is often more an art than a science. For your edification and reading pleasure, here are notes on some of the places where we could have gone in a different direction, or where a Japanese cultural difference is used.

General notes on *mushi* and *mushishi*

The kanji for *mushi* is made up of three kanji meaning bug (also called *mushi*) put together. The kanji can be used interchangeably to mean insect, but they can easily take on other meanings. In CLAMP's *xxxHolic*, the kanji was introduced as the name for a type of magical vermin.

Mushishi can be translated as "mushi master." Ginko is a man who made a study of *mushi* and seems to have learned to control some through his own senses and others through medicines, remedies, or just a knowledge of their nature. Ginko probably learned his craft from other older *mushishi* who wander Japan.

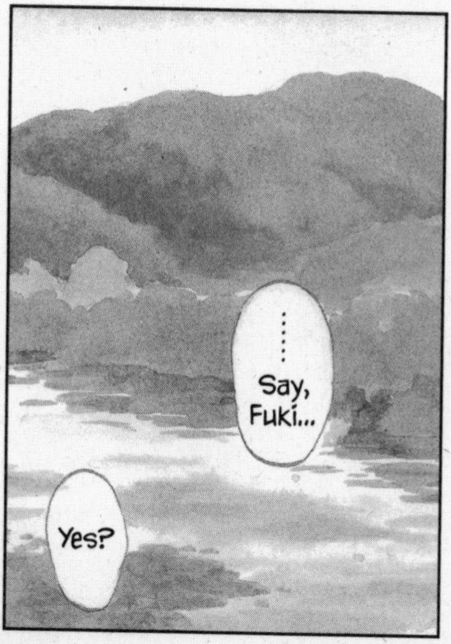
......
Say, Fuki...
Yes?

Fuki, page 3

The name Fuki is represented by the kanji meaning to blow, as in the wind. An apt name, considering the events of the story.

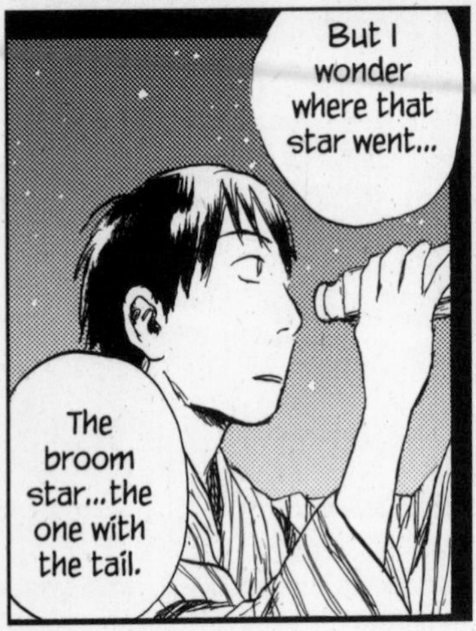
But I wonder where that star went...
The broom star...the one with the tail.

Broom star, page 8

One of the words for comet in Japanese is *hôkiboshi*, or "broom star." It is probably an older word and describes the long tail, which looks a little like a Japanese-style broom. Since Fuki obviously didn't know much about astronomy, it seemed more appropriate for her character and the time period to use the literal translation of *hôkiboshi* rather than the more scientific-sounding equivalent.

Tenpengusa, page 28

As in previous volumes, the names for the *mushi* in this volume come either from the look of the *mushi* or the effect it has on humans and the world. The name for this *mushi* comes from the Japanese word *tenpen*, which means heaven, and *kusa*, which means grass.

Nami and Shima, page 60

The names of the two little girls are both maritime related. *Nami* means waves, and *Shima* means island.

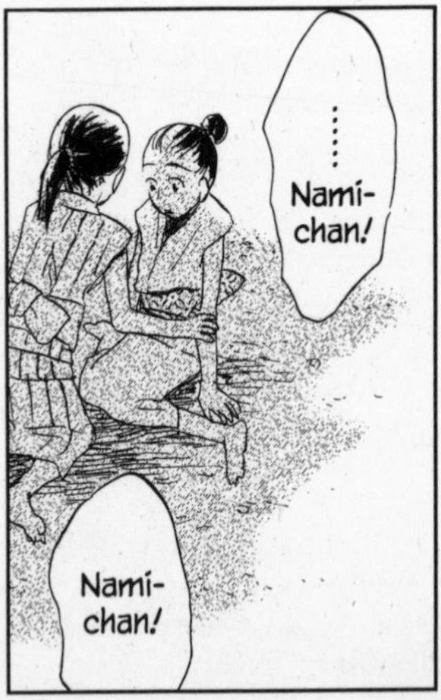
...... Nami-chan!
Nami-chan!

Song in the shell, page 62

One of the kanji used for the English word song has two parts that can be read as kanji in themselves. One part is the kanji for mouth and the other for shell. Oddly appropriate for this story.

Yado-karidori and Sezuri-kai, page 62

The name *Yado-karidori* is a pun. The hermit crab is called *yadokari* in Japanese, but *karidori* means to reap. So the name would translate out to "hermit reaper." *Sezuri-kai* would simply mean "chirping shell."

Red tide, page 83

The red tide is a sudden upsurge in poisonous algae such that the clumps of algae (also called a bloom) can be seen by the human eye. The poison kills lower animals in the food chain, and eating the poisoned fish and other seafood can kill animals higher in the food chain such as larger fish, aquatic mammals, seabirds, and humans. "Red tide" is a misnomer, since only a few of the poisonous algae are red and the tide really has nothing to do with the occurrence. Red tides may recede within days, but some have been reported to stay in one area for up to eighteen months.

Fuki, page 107

Unlike the heroine's name from the first story in this volume, this Fuki is made up of two characters: *fu*, which means to rot, and *ki*, which means liquor. *Ki* is the same final kanji character in the "light liquor" from the first *Mushishi* story, Kôki.

Guns, page 128

What were you shooting at?!

Many romantic movies involving Japanese feudal times—such as the film *The Last Samurai*—tend to avoid showing guns, preferring swordfights. By watching such films, one may get the idea that guns were scarce and shunned in feudal Japan, but that is not historically accurate. Histories record that a Chinese sloop carrying Portuguese nationals shipwrecked on the island of Tanegashima in 1543. Two of their rifles were purchased by the local lord, Tanegashima Tokitaka, and he soon had a blacksmith replicate them. Thereafter, rifles were called *tanegashima* in Japan, and they became very popular. Prior to 1600, there were even several martial arts schools for gunmanship: the Yasumi School and the Inatomi School, among others. Guns played a large role in all of the major battles from the end of the warring states period on. The Japanese made full use of guns on both sides of the historical conflict depicted in *The Last Samurai*.

Tanada, page 139

According to reports, about 70 percent of Japan's landmass can be described as hilly or mountainous. So it is only natural that as much of that land as possible has been converted to producing crops. *Tanada* (the terraced farms) account for nearly 8 percent of Japanese farmland. The Japanese government, realizing the cultural significance of *tanada*, has enacted some programs (such as a top-100 best *tanada* list to promote tourism) to help protect them, but only time will tell how effective these programs can be.

Ah!

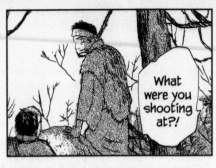

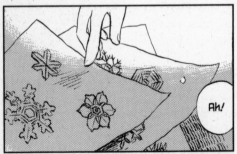

Yukimushi, page 150

This is the class of *mushi* that are found in and around snow. The word *yuki* means snow, so the word is rather straightforward.

Yuki-narashi, page 151

As said in the note above, *yuki* means snow, and the verb *narasu* (from which one may get the noun *narashi*) means to even out—as in leveling bumps and pits to form a smooth surface.

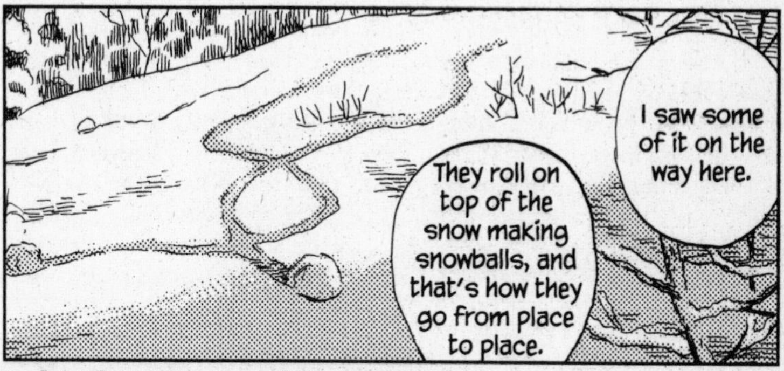
I saw some of it on the way here.
They roll on top of the snow making snowballs, and that's how they go from place to place.

Yuki-dango-mushi, page 151

As noted above, *yuki* means snow, and *dango*, aside from being a tasty snack, is also a word used for different kind of balls (such as *niku-dango*, which means meatballs). Although a different word is used for the type of snowballs that children play with, Yuki-dango-mushi could be translated to "snowball mushi."

Tokoyuki-mushi, page 153

The first part of this *mushi*'s name, *toko*, means endless. As mentioned previously, *yuki* means snow, so this *mushi*'s name would mean "never-ending snow mushi."

Shôjô-no-hige, page 230

Shôjô-no-hige comes from the words *shôjô*, one meaning of which is drunk (note that this is a different word from the popular manga term meaning young girl), and *hige*, which refers to human whiskers such as a beard or mustache. The name would translate out to a phrase meaning "drunk's beard."

Suimitsu-tô, page 231

Mitsu means nectar, *tô* means sugar, and *sui* means to inhale or suck. So this *mushi* would have a name something like "nectar sugar sucker."

Rainy season, page 239

Although the actual dates vary year by year, the rainy season generally starts in June and runs through early July. During this period it is likely to rain every day, and one should not be out without one's umbrella.

Tengu, page 239

Tengu are traditional Japanese spirits. There are several *Tengu* types: *Daitengu* are the red-faced, long-nosed goblins that one may see in prints and wooden sculptures. *Kurama Tengu* are master swordsmen and tricksters associated with Kurama Yama (Horse-saddle Mountain) and the Buddhist temple there. And *Karasu Tengu* (Crow *Tengu*) are servants to magical masters.

Please check our website
(www.delreymanga.com) to see
when volume 7 of Mushishi will
be available in English.

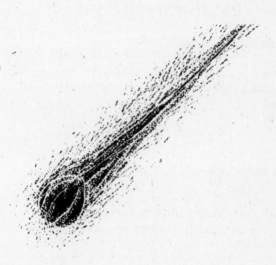

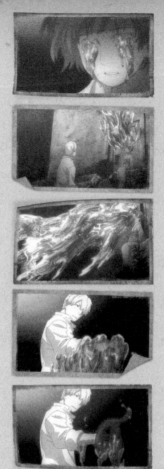

THE CURE LIES IN THE CURSE

MUSHI-SHI蟲師

OWN VOLUMES 1-6 ON DVD TODAY

TOMARE!
[STOP!]

You are going the wrong way!

Manga is a completely different
type of reading experience.

To start at the *beginning*, go to the *end*!

That's right! Authentic manga is read the traditional Japanese
way—from right to left, exactly the *opposite* of how American
books are read. It's easy to follow: Just go to the other end of
the book, and read each page—and each panel—from right side
to left side, starting at the top right. Now you're experiencing
manga as it was meant to be.